BUILDING THE COMPENSATORY STATE

Contemporary public administration research has marginalized the importance of "taking history seriously." With few exceptions, little recent scholarship in the field has looked longitudinally (rather than cross-sectionally), contextually, and theoretically over extended time periods at "big questions" in public administration. One such "big question" involves the evolution of American administrative reform and its link since the nation's founding to American state building. This book addresses this gap by analyzing administrative reform in unprecedented empirical and theoretical ways. In taking a multidisciplinary approach, it incorporates recent developments in cognate research fields in the humanities and social sciences that have been mostly ignored in public administration. It thus challenges existing notions of the nature, scope, and power of the American state and, with these, important aspects of today's conventional wisdom in public administration.

Author Robert F. Durant explores the administrative state in a new light as part of a "compensatory state"—driven, shaped, and amplified since the nation's founding by a corporate–social science nexus of interests. Arguing that this nexus of interests has contributed to citizen estrangement in the United States, he offers a broad empirical and theoretical understanding of the political economy of administrative reform, its role in state building, and its often paradoxical results. Offering a reconsideration of conventional wisdom in public administration, this book is required reading for all students, scholars, or practitioners of public administration, public policy, and politics.

Robert F. Durant is Professor Emeritus, American University. He is the recipient of several lifetime achievement awards for his research, teaching, and service to the field.

PUBLIC ADMINISTRATION AND PUBLIC POLICY
A Comprehensive Publication Program

EDITOR-IN-CHIEF

DAVID H. ROSENBLOOM
Distinguished Professor of Public Administration
American University, Washington, DC

RECENTLY PUBLISHED BOOKS

BUILDING THE COMPENSATORY STATE

AN INTELLECTUAL HISTORY AND THEORY OF AMERICAN ADMINISTRATIVE REFORM

ROBERT F. DURANT

Routledge
Taylor & Francis Group

LONDON AND NEW YORK

First published 2020 by Routledge

2 Park Square, Milton Park, Abingdon, Oxon, OX14 4RN
605 Third Avenue, New York, NY 10017

Routledge is an imprint of the Taylor & Francis Group, an informa business

First issued in paperback 2020

Library of Congress Cataloging-in-Publication Data
A catalog record for this book has been requested

ISBN: 978-0-367-34844-1 (hbk)
ISBN: 978-0-367-77777-7 (pbk)

Typeset in Garamond
by Apex CoVantage, LLC

In memory of Bruce K. Birch and Thomas R. Heafey, early friends who always saw things with new eyes.

Contents

Biography

Robert F. Durant is Professor Emeritus, American University. He is the recipient of several lifetime achievement awards, including the 2014 John Gaus Award for a lifetime of exemplary scholarship in the joint tradition of political science and public administration from the American Political Science Association and the 2013 Dwight Waldo Award for distinguished contributions to the literature of public administration from the American Society for Public Administration. He is a fellow in the National Academy of Public Administration.

Acknowledgements

The author wishes to thank David Rosenbloom and Laura Stearns for their encouragement of this project, and Jennifer Durant for her technical assistance and support.

Epigram

The real voyage of discovery consists not in seeking new landscapes, but in having new eyes.

—Marcel Proust

Chapter 1

Fuzzy Pictures in Our Heads?

Contemporary public administration scholarship has made significant strides in advancing our understanding of the topical areas that it has emphasized since the 1980s. However, it has largely marginalized the field's traditional appreciation of the importance of "taking history seriously" in public administration research. With few notable exceptions (e.g., Cook, 2014; Peters, 2001; Raadschelders, 2017; Stillman, 1990, 2017), little scholarship has emerged in the field that looks longitudinally (rather than cross-sectionally), contextually, and theoretically over extended time periods at "big questions" in public administration (Durant, 2014a, 2014b; Durant & Rosenbloom, 2017; Milward et al., 2016; Peters & Pierre, 2017; Pollitt, 2017; Roberts, 2013).

One such question in the field of public administration involves the evolution of American administrative reform[1] and its link since the nation's founding to American state building (for notable and insightful exceptions, see Cook, 2014; Raadschelders, 2017; Stillman, 1990, 2017). This, despite the major contributions of empirically grounded, cross-sectional, and historically informed scholarship (e.g., Adams, 1992; Box, 2018; Carpenter, 2001, 2010; Lee, 2008, 2013, 2016; Roberts, 1994, 2012; Schachter, 2010; Stivers, 2000; Van Riper, 1958; and others in the Public Administration Theory Network). As such, the public administration literature on this topic is largely atheoretical, metaphorical, and decontextualized (for partial exceptions in public administration, see Raadschelders, 2017; in political science, see Skowronek, 1982, and much of the American political development literature). Even Leonard D. White's (1948, 1951, 1954, 1958) contextually rich, multi-volume study of public administrative reform focused on singular reform eras (and concluded its analysis in 1901). Moreover,

1

although Dwight Waldo's 1948 classic, *The Administrative State* (1984), was historically and philosophically grounded, reexamination of its arguments in light of developments since then has been rare (e.g., Rosenbloom & McCurdy, 2006). Indeed, more recent trends in the public management literature show a narrowing of the analytical lens of the field that rhymes in some ways with the early 20th-century scientific management focus. This, by failing to integrate analytically such traditionally important contextual factors as politics, power, and the law, and to marginalize comparative research over extended time periods.

This book addresses these gaps in subject, scope, and methodology by analyzing in empirical and theoretical ways the evolution of American administrative reform and its links to state building since the nation's founding. In taking a multidisciplinary approach stressing intellectual history, it incorporates recent developments in cognate research fields in the humanities, the law, and the social sciences that have been mostly ignored in public administration. Consequently, the book also takes seriously Marcel Proust's advice to pursue the voyage of discovery by seeing familiar landscapes with new eyes. It thus challenges existing images in public administration of the nature, scope, and power of the American state and its reciprocal relationship to the evolution of American administrative reform. It also challenges other important aspects of today's conventional wisdom in public administration and finds paradoxes in the field's development. Demonstrated in doing so is the wisdom of the novelist, William Faulkner (2011), who wrote that the "past isn't dead. It's not even past" (p. 73).

The book argues, first, that the image of a *compensatory state* comprised of networks of public, private, and voluntary actors (now called nonprofits) has always best captured the link between the evolution of American administrative reform and state building. Elected officials have repeatedly relied on the private and nonprofit sectors to compensate institutionally for a conscious effort to hide the visible size of government (especially the federal government) from Americans. Thus, the reigning image that contemporary networking trends are new is false: instead, they must be seen as amplifications of historic trends. Moreover, although the contemporary image of increasing administrative complexity differentiates it from earlier instances of this networking approach, the roles of Americans' self-image and of administrative reformers in amplifying this complexity are typically overlooked.

Discerned from the analysis is a "legitimacy theory" of American administrative reform and its reciprocal relationship to state building that captures and explains these dynamics. The book also shows that deterministic views of the evolution of each must give way in public administration to a more structured agency approach featuring choices among conflicting alternatives. Specifically, the compensatory state has been repeatedly driven, shaped, and amplified since the nation's founding by various elements of a corporate–social science nexus of actors. This nexus has repeatedly sought to gain, retain, regain, or enhance members' legitimacy (and the expressive, material, and authority gains it brings) by promoting reforms based on instrumental rather than substantive (e.g., democratic administration and the law) rationality. In offering a "pulse model" of administrative reform derived from the analysis, the book shows how this nexus' relative power has triumphed over proponents of alternate models of administrative reform and state building—despite uneven impacts and recurring disappointments with their results. This, because of "inefficient" path dependency (Mahoney & Thelen, 2010; Stinchcombe, 1968), a "pentimento effect" (Adams, 1992), and better resonance with Americans' "self-conception," exceptionalist values, and millenarian vision. It also shows how and why conflict and power disparities linked to legitimacy within the nexus itself have privileged larger over small businesses, urban over rural concerns, and economics over other social science disciplines in the minds of reformers.

The book also shows that, despite reform proponents' consistent promises of enhancing democracy, their *instrumental rationality project* (IRP) has ironically contributed to citizen marginalization, and even estrangement, from government in the United States. Political theorist Harvey Mansfield's (2001) critique of the social sciences applies to American administrative reformers as well: a misguided faith exists that a focus on "facts" and "reason" will eventually bring agreement (which is good), while a focus on values breeds political conflicts (which are bad, but reduceable by reason). But debate—or disputation—over basic assumptions, facts, and values is inherent in politics, administration, and a democratic republic. And without free and open disputation, incorrect, extreme, and heinous views and values cannot be countered democratically (see, e.g., Berlin, 1992; Pinker, 2002).

The remainder of this chapter elaborates on these points and sets the conceptual, methodological, and theoretical premises discerned from analysis in the remaining chapters of the book. It begins the process of seeing with new eyes and with a broader scope by reviewing the challenges from other fields to the foundational basis—viz., the peculiar stateless origins of the American state (Skowronek, 1982; Stillman, 1990, 2017)—of much conventional wisdom in public administration, including the evolution of American administrative reform and its relationship to American state building. After making this case for the compensatory state as a more useful image and accurate basis for understanding these dynamics, the chapter reviews how and why our current images in public administration of the evolution of American administrative reform are metaphorical, misleading, and atheoretical. This is followed by a discussion of why this gap in our understanding is important—specifically, because it distorts this and other key aspects of our conventional wisdom in public administration. After reviewing what is lost by not taking history seriously (and, especially, the constraining effects of American exceptionalist values), the chapter then reviews how and why a legitimacy theory of American administrative reform and state building is useful for understanding its evolution since the nation's founding. Specifically, a nexus of business and social science interests has resulted in administrative reformers persistently opting since the nation's founding for business and market-based solutions (i.e., the IRP) rather than alternative reform approaches, and how this political economy of interests has inadvertently helped create self-defeating and paradoxical results in our democratic republic and in public administration.

*****

In his classic book, *Public Opinion*, Walter Lippmann (1922) wrote that the "pictures inside people's heads do not automatically correspond with the world outside" (p. 19). Nonetheless, these pictures go unquestioned and, thus, distort people's perceptions of "realities" deduced from them. This book argues that such is the case when it comes to contemporary discussions about the evolution of what Dwight Waldo (1984) famously called the "administrative state" in America (p. 90). Moreover, these fuzzy pictures have led to other misinterpretations of the evolution of American administrative reform since the nation's founding. The essence of the administrative state is expert unelected bureaucrats in public agencies "tasked with important governing functions through loosely drawn statutes" that permit them to make policy decisions for society (Rohr, 1986, p. xi). And because of its European roots, the term "state" evokes the image that the source, scope, and power of the state resides in federal government agencies.

Conventional wisdom in public administration sees the creation and expansion of a modern, specialized, and expertise-based administrative state occurring in the 20th century as the inevitable consequence of the societal complexities of the modern era.[2] As the 20th century dawned, a major mismatch occurred between existing institutional structures of the state—typically called a "state of courts and parties"—and the socioeconomic, commercial, and military challenges facing the nation (Skowronek, 1982; Stillman, 1990, 2017; but see, e.g., Carpenter, 2001). Thus, the United States had no choice. It had to discard the nation's "peculiar stateless origins" and create a modern administrative state in Washington comprised of hierarchically structured, expertise-based, and scientifically informed and managed agencies in the federal government.

Moreover, the narrative continues, the development of expertise-informed bureaucracies in the administrative state happened because no alternative was available and has not arisen since. Bureaucracy—in all its various formats (see du Gay, 2005)—was the "best way of getting work done [efficiently and with economy] because it is the only form of organization that deals [successfully] with [organizational] size, complexity, and the need for accountability"—what governing in modernity requires of its institutions (Thompson & Alvesson, 2005, p. 91; also see du Gay, 2005; Jaques, 1990; Meier & Hill, 2005; Perrow, 1979; Raadschelders, 2017).

Proponents of this element of the IRP claimed that the administrative state would do all this logically and objectively by (re)aligning administrative structures and processes to gain policy, program, and state-building goals. Reduced, if not alleviated, would be politics, demagoguery, corruption, and emotionalism from policymaking, administration, and state building—all dysfunctional characteristics of pre-20th-century American governance. Proponents saw the IRP as necessary for bringing "order" (meaning the ability to guide society) out of political, social, and economic chaos. They also argued that the IRP was necessary to advance the cause of democracy.

This deterministic narrative then continues that the administrative state apparatus based in Washington reigned until the late 20th century. From its Progressive Era origins, subsequent expansions of federal administrative capacities and power occurred through the 1970s, but especially during the New Deal in the 1930s and the Great Society in the 1960s. Yet, there began in the 1980s a largely Republican Party effort to undermine existing administrative agencies by reducing the size, scope, and power of the administrative state apparatus in Washington. They were joined by other, more positive-state critics who again stressed a mismatch between contemporary problems and expertise-based public agencies. Together, these led to calls by administrative reformers for "post-bureaucratic organizations" gaining efficiencies and responsiveness through another form of the IRP—the business-inspired rationality of markets (e.g., contracting), quasi-markets (e.g., enterprise management in agencies), and networks consisting of public, private, and nonprofit organizations. Wrought was a *new* kind of state: a disarticulated state (Frederickson, 1999) where state power was shared or coordinated within and among members of public–private–nonprofit networks (Durant, 2000; Kettl, 1993; Light, 2019; Milward & Provan, 1998; O'Toole, 1997; Salamon, 1989, 2001).

In embracing this narrative, public administration scholars joined those in other academic fields by using continental European notions of what constituted the state, its scope, and its power. The characteristics of the state were "unification, centralization, rationalization, organization, administration, and bureaucratization" in nations' capitals (Novak, 2008, p. 761; Stillman, 1990, 2017). Scholars thus saw a laggard and relatively powerless US state in comparison to European nations prior to the 20th century, because it lacked a visibly strong national administrative apparatus (e.g., Boorstin, 1953; de Tocqueville, 2012; Hartz, 1955; Lipset, 1996; Lipset & Marks, 2000; Schlesinger, Sr., 1949).

This narrative is accurate to the extent one works within the continental European paradigm of the state. However, since the 1980s, a robust body of scholarship outside of public administration has grown and challenged this narrative and its accompanying imagery. So powerful has the impact of this research been that a "burgeoning historical revision" of the stateless origins thesis has occurred (see Novak [2008] for a comprehensive summary of this robust literature).[3]

Spearheading this revisionism is a multidisciplinary group of political scientists and sociologists in the American political development (APD) movement (e.g., Skocpol, 1992); proponents of the "organizational synthesis" in business history (e.g., Galambos, 1970); legal historians (e.g., Storrs, 2013); scholars in policy history (e.g., Balogh, 1991); religious historians (e.g., McLoughlin, 1978); economic historians (e.g., Chandler, 1993); students of political culture (e.g., Appleby, 2001; Bailyn, 1992); gender historians (e.g., Storrs, 2013); diplomatic historians (e.g., Herring, 2008); social historians (e.g., Katz, 1986); and researchers in political and administrative history (e.g., Carpenter, 2001; Zelizer, 2012). Thus, "historians can no longer depict the 19th century as a wasteland for federal governance . . . and . . . the roots of the twentieth century can be traced from these [earlier] decades" (Zelizer, 2012, p. 97). Even within public administration, Leonard White's classic four-volume administrative history offered its own examples of the direct power of the federal government in the 19th century.

Grounded firmly in the pragmatist tradition of such American theorists as John Dewey, Henry James, and Charles Peirce, these researchers came to this conclusion by abandoning continental European definitions of the state in favor of examining governance in "practice" and in "consequence" (Dewey, 1935; James, 1907).[4] They argue that, although the continental European paradigm of the state and its concentrated power fit the historical development of these nations, it is inappropriate to apply it to America. This, because of the United States' very different historical, constitutional, and institutional experience of separate institutions sharing power, checks and balances, bicameralism, and federalism (what de Tocqueville called an "incomplete national government").

Thus, the state should not be measured in the United States merely by the amount and scope of federal legislation, the number and power of federal agencies, the size of federal budgets, and the number of federal bureaucrats in agencies. Rather, the "reach of public authority" is the real basis for discerning the contours of the state and its power, not merely the constitutional and bureaucratic "organization of officialdom" in Washington (Novak, 2008, p. 762). As Michael Mann (1986) puts it, the breadth of the state and its power is comprised of those actors able "to 'penetrate civil society' and implement their policies throughout a given territory" on behalf of society (Novak, 2008, p. 763).[5] Taking this "infrastructural" perspective on the state means focusing on the "institutionalized relations between the government and societal actors" who wield public policy authority—regardless of level of government or sector (public, private, or nonprofit) (Sparrow, 1996, p. 15).

Consequently, the federal administrative apparatus and the power it wields is one important part of the compensatory state, but it is only one part.[6] The state that emerges from an infrastructural perspective is also comprised of bureaucratically structured subnational governments, as well as similarly administered private and nonprofit actors delegated authority to act on behalf of society. They

compensate for conscious decisions since the nation's founding to limit the visible size and administrative capacity of the federal government (Eisner, 2000a). Relatedly, what economist Mariana Mazzucato (2015) identifies as state entrepreneurialism (viz., providing research and development [R&D] funding for existing and new products and markets) has been characteristic of the compensatory state since the nation's founding. Moreover, nongovernmental actors do these things without altering their status as private or voluntary organizations. This, because not all aspects of their operations are involved in wielding what is normally government authority and enterprise on behalf of society (e.g., certifying eligibility for welfare applicants and affording R&D money for projects leading to the Internet, Tesla, and iPhones).

This is *not* to say that national and subnational actors agree on policy or that the federal government always gets its way. They do not, and this is not a bad thing. Learning from the fall of ancient Rome and Athens, respectively, that both extreme centralization and decentralization produced regime failure, the Founders[7] saw federalism as a check and balance on the power of the federal government and reserved certain powers for the states alone. Much as constitutional scholar Edwin Corwin (1952) wrote of the relationship between Congress and the president in foreign policy, the "Constitution is an invitation to struggle" between the federal government and the states as well—a struggle influenced, if not resolved, by the courts (p. 470).

As scholars studying intergovernmental relations and networked government have long known, bargaining is the essence of both governance approaches, and the relative influence of actors is dynamic, shifting, contextually driven, and dependent on policy area (e.g., Conlan, Posner, & Beam, 2014; Derthick, 2010; Ingram, 1977; Posner, 2010; Radin & Posner, 2010; Salamon, 2001).[8] Moreover, actors frequently shift responsibilities from states and localities to the federal government, and vice versa, either to narrow or expand the scope of the conflict to advantage their policy preferences (Schattschneider, 1960). In addition, the courts often settle disputes among them. Nor is it to say that compensation only comes from subnational actors in all sectors filling in the gaps for federal lack of capacity (although this is a primary focus of this book). At times (e.g., the 1930s and 1960s), the federal government compensates for a lack of will, resources, or skills on the part of subnational actors in all sectors. And when it comes to the evolution of administrative reform in the United States, innovations in the states and localities often are adopted later at the federal level. It *is* to say that the image of a compensatory state comprised of the federal apparatus and state and local public, private, and nonprofit actors compensating for each other's shortcomings best captures the nature of the state in America since the nation's founding.

Historians explain why this diffusion, rather than concentration, of state power occurred in America. Since the nation's founding, those pursuing an activist federal government have been split, with some such as Alexander Hamilton arguing that Americans needed to see how the national government (referred to as the General Government) was helping and protecting them if they were ever to identify with it. But others argued that "hiding" the national government's presence in Americans' lives was more prudent due to the nation's anti-statist culture (Balogh, 2009).

The latter position has persistently prevailed, except in times of crisis. In the 18th and 19th centuries, for example, rather than rely on a direct income tax, the national government relied on tariffs and land sales, making tax collectors less visible by placing them, in effect, only at the nation's borders and coastlines. Moreover, local governments collected most taxes, and local control "was reinforced by covenants that joined family to church, church to town, and town to commonwealth" (Balogh, 2009, p. 33). Such an environment "fostered capitalist economic development bounded by strong communal and religious ties" (pp. 33–34).

Likewise, instead of the federal government directly delivering goods and services to citizens, it often used grants, subsidies, mandates, tax breaks, and pressures for conformance to coax subnational governments, private companies, and volunteer groups to do its will. Nor can one overstate the formative powers of American tax, fiscal, and monetary policies—and their interaction with the same at the subnational government levels. Certainly, the policy tools used by the federal government have expanded over the years to include income transfers, direct loans, vouchers, tax expenditures, loan guarantees, deposit insurance, and regulation (Salamon, 2001). But the logic of the compensatory state still underlies this amplification of the nation's preference for hiding the visible size of the federal apparatus.

Similarly, as Elizabeth Clemens and Doug Guthrie (2010) write of the development of the nonprofit and philanthropic sectors since the nation's founding, "what has been described as a domain of voluntary activity has been grounded in a pervasive legal framework, supported [and encouraged] by the coercive powers of the state" (p. 18). For example, several states in New England granted tax support for churches providing moral instruction through the mid-1830s, while the mid-Atlantic and New England states chartered hundreds of corporations during the 1820s and 1830s to provide charity and education services (Hartz, 1955; Novak, 2008). Wrought was a belief that "uncoerced cooperation and voluntary efforts could do the work of central government" (Appleby, 2001, p. 22).

Laura Jensen (2003) also shows that, contrary to conventional images regarding the stateless origins thesis, American social policy had its roots in the Pension Act of 1818 to help revolutionary soldiers deal with poverty. This was essentially the first "entitlement" program in the United States, because it singled out a subset of Americans—as well as a subset of war veterans—who deserved government assistance because of their contributions to American independence. Moreover, this program was layered atop a variety of direct payments to disabled veterans, who had earlier qualified for free land grants because of their service. Likewise, Kimberley Johnson (2007) has demonstrated the existence of a formidable system of intergovernmental grants to states and localities that occurred between 1877 and 1929 in what she calls the "first new federalism" in America. She later identified how progressives in southern states were the architects of the odious Jim Crow "state" in that region, partly with the encouragement of federal progressives and northern philanthropies such as the Rockefeller Foundation (Johnson, 2010).

Relatedly, Williamjames Hull Hoffer (2007) has argued, based on analyses of congressional debates between 1858 and 1891, that a "second American state" developed to alter gradually the first American state of Jeffersonianism–Jacksonianism (but see Raadschelders, 2008). This state was one wherein citizens began looking to the federal government for assistance. They were granted programs shaped and implemented by subnational governments, the private sector, and nonprofit providers (with the courts arbiters of disputes). Moreover, the second American state also had "elements of the regulatory administrative model of the Progressive Era" (p. 199)—most notably, the creation of the Interstate Commerce Commission and the elevation of the Bureau of Labor to departmental status. Likewise, Jason Scott Smith (2006) has shown how important public works (or infrastructure) grants from the Public Works Administration and the Works Progress Administration funneled through states and localities helped advance both political support for New Deal liberalism and compensatory state building between 1933 and 1956.

Nor was this reliance on third-party (or proxy) actors to compensate for the relative weakness of federal administrative capacity limited to domestic policy. In the first decades of the 20th century, for example, public–private partnerships between American state officials and American financiers were integral to the expansion and management of American imperialism (through "Dollar Diplomacy"). This happened with the encouragement of government but with minimal political, financial, and logistical support from the US Congress. Moreover, this propensity to hide the visible size and power of the federal government has continued ever since, even in periods of federal activism during World War I, the New Deal, the Great Society, and the 2007–2009 Great Recession (Durant, 2014a, 2014b; Hart, 1994; Hawley, 1997).

As Novak (2008) summarizes, the "most significant and lasting tenet of this [infrastructural] revisionism is that the American state is and always has been larger and more powerful, capacious, tenacious, interventionist, and redistributive than was recognized in earlier accounts of US history" (p. 758). He continues that the

> work of a generation [of scholarship] makes clear [that such things as]
> Indian removal, slavery, immigration restriction, and racial, ethnic,

religious, and gender-based forms of segregation and discrimination were not the products of laissez-faire or a hesitancy to draw on the powers of the state or a public preference for leaving people alone. *The trail of the state is over all.*

(p. 758; emphasis added)

As such, the "idea of American state weakness, statelessness, or anti-statism is quickly being abandoned . . . because they no longer explain the past, and they certainly cannot account for the present" (p. 759).

Importantly, taking an infrastructural perspective creates profound differences in the "pictures" we carry in our heads of both state building and administrative reforms' role in helping craft it. For example, and contrary to conventional wisdom, it shows that America's "divided welfare state" often affords greater social service benefits (on a per capita basis) than does Europe. The United States merely provides those goods, services, opportunities, and regulations differently from continental European states through the participation of public, private, and nonprofit actors rather than solely through the federal government (see, e.g., Hacker, 2002). For instance, the Centers for Medicare and Medicaid Services technically oversaw 20 percent of the US gross domestic product in 2016 and reviewed programs comprising 45 percent of the federal budget each year. Yet, its workforce comprised only .02 percent of all federal employees (Kettl, 2009, p. 10), relying instead on contractors for program implementation (and even design).

The infrastructural perspective on the state and its power has also caused a rethinking of such things as the origins of the administrative state itself, the beginnings of agency-centered bureaucratic politics, and the nature of the political economy of administrative reform that accompanied APD. For instance, historians such as Richard Bensel (1990) identify the origins of central state authority in America long before the New Deal. In Bensel's classic, *Yankee Leviathan*, he finds its origins occurring between 1859 and 1877. Similarly, Richard Harris and Daniel Tichenor (2002–2003) have challenged the conventional wisdom that the expansion of interest groups and their interaction with agencies came after the expansion in government during the New Deal in the 1930s and the Great Society in the 1960s. Instead, they find it came at least as early as the Progressive Era. Moreover, as this book will show, these sinewy relationships were integral to the development of the compensatory state in America since its founding, as well as to the evolution of administrative reform within it.

Likewise, a multidisciplinary set of scholars such as Max Edling, Richard John, Barry Karl, Morton Keller, Jerry Mashaw, Thomas McCraw, and Richard White have used the infrastructural approach to challenge conventional wisdom. Collectively, they have shown that the Founders created a "strong 'fiscal-military' state," that a "powerful and centralizing national administrative law" can be traced to the earliest days of the republic, and that strong federal government centralization of the promotion and regulation of communication occurred prior to the New Deal (Novak, 2008, p. 758, passim).

An infrastructural approach also suggests that deterministic views of the evolution of American administrative reform and state building are misguided. Changes in historical circumstances (political, social, economic, demographic, philosophical, and technological; see Gaus, 1947) create opportunities for reform, but they do not determine the specific administrative reforms, or the shape and power of the state, that will be adopted. Nor does the inherent superiority of the IRP explain its persistence in reformers' toolkits. Reform alternatives to the IRP exist throughout American history and have been contested by coalitions of actors both within and across different schools of thought regarding state building. Granted, the IRP approach to American administrative reform overwhelmingly has been taken in the compensatory state since the nation's founding. Nonetheless, these have been political choices, not foregone conclusions.

Thus, the rise of the national administrative state—as important as it is in hiking the visible size, presence, and impact of the federal government—is only a part of the amplification of the IRP, the compensatory state, and state power. As historian Max Edling (2009) argues:

> liberal progressives now have to . . . learn that the twentieth-century state they celebrate as a new beginning in [the exercise of federal power was] in fact built on the 19th-century associational state—a polity where the federal government acted in partnership with local and state governments, voluntary organizations, the professions, interest groups, and even private corporations. The conservatives [are] learn[ing] that the American associational state did not spring out of the progressive movement but was present from the nation's founding. No matter how much they would like to, conservatives cannot return their nation to a "stateless" laissez-faire society for the simple reason that no such society ever existed in America.
>
> (p. 462)

****

The salience of these observations for understanding the nature of the American state and the evolution of administrative reform in the United States seems obvious. Yet insights from the research supporting these claims have been largely ignored in American public administration circles. This distorts images of the evolution of the state and administrative reforms. Taking an infrastructural approach offers a first step toward what Marcel Proust saw as the "real voyage of discovery": seeing old landscapes with new eyes and reassessing their implications for what we think we know about the evolution of American administrative reform, its role in compensatory state building, and what the implications of reform choices have been for government legitimacy.

Whether based on continental European or infrastructural perspectives, understanding in public administration of the evolution of American administrative reform and its links to state building is not as empirically well grounded nor theory-based as it should be (but, for partial exceptions, again see Raadschelders, 2017; Skowronek, 1982).[9] Indeed, public administration studies of these dynamics since the nation's founding are nonexistent since White's aforementioned classic series that concluded in the year 1901 (again, see Cook, 2014, for an important exception). Consequently, the field has been left to reason from analogy. Paraphrasing the novelist E. M. Forster about this reasoning process, "everything is like something, so what is this like?" Thus, the field is left today with three prominent metaphors based on "old landscapes" that try to characterize the evolution of American administrative reform and, implicitly, state building: cycles, tides, and tectonics.

Herbert Kaufman's (1981) cyclical view of the evolution of administrative reform sees reforms coming and going, with transitions premised on the excesses of any one iteration of reform. This pendulum swings periodically among three "core values" of administrative reform: representativeness, neutral competence, and executive leadership. For example, a focus on reforms for increasing citizen participation (representativeness) develops once citizens perceive that executive-centered management or neutral competence has marginalized their interests.

Meanwhile, Paul Light's (1997) metaphor of "tides of reform" portrays reform movements as the sedimentary layering of one movement upon the other without finding out if reforms work at all or how they interact with each other. Thus, "layering without learning" occurs. Analyzing reforms since the mid-20th century, Light describes how combinations of political, economic, and social factors influence their rise at different points in time. He also notes how reform efforts appear in recycled guises—e.g., the Planning, Programming, and Budgeting System in the 1960s begets strategic planning in the Government Performance and Results Act in the 1990s and the Program Assessment Rating Tool in the 2000s.

In contrast, Jonathan Koppell's (2010a) tectonic perspective uses the geological metaphor of plate tectonics to argue (in contrast to Light) that tectonic shifts have slowly and persistently reshaped the nature of administration and the state apparatus in Washington. Individually, the tides that Light cogently describes are merely the visible earthquakes, tornados, and mountain peaks—i.e., the surface phenomena—of administrative reform. They mask the cumulative ascent over time of subterranean shifts since the 1980s toward indirect, quasigovernmental, and nongovernmental administrative solutions to public problems and alter the nature of the state.

Koppell (2010a) later refines the tectonic metaphor by arguing that both the tidal *and* tectonic metaphors for administrative reform movements are incomplete. Instead, these two metaphors are complementary and together offer a more coherent account of the impacts of administrative reforms and state building than either does alone. Even then, however, both metaphors are flawed, because they blur the importance of human actors in shaping the development of American bureaucracy and the state and how they do so. This can be remedied, Koppell argues, by going down another metaphorical path: borrowing concepts from physics (viz., relativity) and sociology (viz., reflexivity) to inform his theoretical framework.

Relativity reinforces negative perceptions of agencies, because even improved bureaucratic operations appear to citizens to lag relative to the pace and nature of the world around them. Even as agencies try to reform themselves administratively, citizens' expectations heighten given advancements in the private sector. Perceiving public agencies as laggards, they see them as inefficient and ineffective relative to the private sector. Citizens do not make a link between laggardness and congressional appropriations (e.g., in not funding state-of-the-art information technology). Meanwhile, the concept of reflexivity means that negative citizen perceptions of bureaucracy (and, thus, the state) get magnified and perpetuated once elected officials and the media (justly or undeservedly) vilify agencies for ineffectiveness.

As suggestive and important as they are, each of these metaphors leaves much to be desired for theory building and practice. The cycles metaphor implies that tipping points arise in the implementation of administrative reforms, generating calls for administrative reforms that advance neglected values. It thus portrays an almost self-regulatory or "thermostatic" system dynamic that is not helpful for theory building and that misses the point that each swing leaves behind institutional changes that constrain newer swings. It also offers little prospective guidance as to when tipping points for change are likely to arrive, for when the ebb and flow of supporting political coalitions occur (Rosenbloom & Ross, 1994), and for knowing when excess has occurred. Also lost is a sense of the internal dynamics causing change or continuity. Opaque, too, is the political economy of actors—and changes therein over time—who contest and propel the trajectory of reform. Thus, the cycles metaphor leaves unspecified the struggles underlying the maintenance, erosion, or replacement of administrative reforms and related changes in the nature and power of the state. Additionally, by grouping administrative reforms into three categories of values, the cycles thesis examines only the surface features of reform movements. Ignored are the continuities and discontinuities in their "deep structure" over time (e.g., philosophical consistency resulting in advantages to certain values and interests rather than others).

Similarly, the tides of reform metaphor incorporates the existence of periodic pressures for reform at any point in time. However, it does not clarify why they occur, whether the timing and ordering of factors or events make a difference in prompting reform and state building, whether prior reform efforts limit future options for reform, or why the recurring selection in recycled guises of tools of reform occurs. Nor, given the relatively short time period involved, does this metaphor deal with the cumulative effects of factors or events that produce either consistency or qualitative changes in the nature of the state itself.

The tectonic metaphor is more focused than the tides metaphor on the longer-term secular trends driving these dynamics, such as demographic shifts, technological innovations, and economic globalization. However, like the tides metaphor, its thesis is discerned from the study of a relatively short period of American history. Also, it does not offer a theoretical framework for understanding these dynamics, their causal mechanisms and relationships, or the recurring propensity of reforms to turn to the same recycled guises. Likewise, the amendment to the original tectonic metaphor begs more systematic analysis within and across longer periods of time in American history.

****

As mentioned, the aim of this book is to improve our empirical and theoretical understanding of the evolution of American administrative reform and its relationship to building the compensatory state. As Waldo (1984) expressed it so well, administrative reform and political philosophy are interrelated. Taking this view, this book applies an infrastructural approach to explore the dynamics of their interacting evolution from the nation's founding to the end of the Obama presidency. However, it is not simply a historical account of these dynamics or merely an intellectual history of the ideas informing them. Traditionally, historians tend to see events as unique and, thus, unamenable to theorizing. But history need not be interpreted in this way. Historical institutionalists and APD scholars in political science, for example, have discerned "theoretical models" to explain the "trajectory of policy in different domains" (Zelizer, 2012). Ira Katznelson puts it best: "American political development scholars produce *model-like stories* that shadow actual history at a higher level of abstraction and with more portability goals [generalization] than can be found in most writing by historians" (Zelizer, 2012, pp. 97–98, emphasis added).

To afford "model-like stories," this book applies Arthur Stinchcombe's (1968) idea of "historical causation" to the evolution of American administrative reform and its role in building a compensatory state in America. Evolution is seen as a series of events and political choices at different points in time. Earlier events and choices affect later events and choices that amplify over time to limit choices or create opportunities. Importantly, the

> sequence of events [and choices] is not a strictly necessary one, predictable from the conditions of the starting point according to general

laws. . . [But] there is nonetheless an explicable pattern which relates one point [event or choice] to another, especially in the early part of the sequence [of events] . . . . [Produced is a] . . . contingent sequence [of events in which] each turning point renders the occurrence of the next point more likely until, finally, lock-in occurs and a general causal mechanism, such as increasing returns, takes over the work of explanation.

(Howlett & Rayner, 2006, p. 5)

Moreover, instead of examining this evolution during so-called eras of reform movements as typically done by historians and public administrationists (e.g., the Jacksonian Era or the Progressive Era), this book explores its dynamics across historical time periods. This allows a comparative analysis of reform efforts and the compensatory state across time to determine continuities and discontinuities in approach and nature. Focusing on historical periods rather than movements also allows a more nuanced view of American administrative reform and state building than is typically given by studies of specific eras. It also affords a broader conceptualization of these dynamics, as well as a tracing of the evolution of the political, policy, and philosophical environments (both domestic and international) that are so closely linked to them in reciprocal ways. Relatedly, reform movements and compensatory state building "are not as coherent or homogeneous as many have assumed and . . . attending to the internal fissures within them allow[s] us to rethink agency [i.e., actor choices] and change" (Hattam & Lowndes, 2007, p. 199; also see Sheingate, 2003, 2007).

This book also takes the coevolution of institutions (domestic and international) and alternative social movements seriously and applies them to the study of American administrative reform and compensatory state building. As Katznelson (2002) points out, much has been lost until recently by the tendency of even APD scholarship to marginalize the linkages between domestic and international politics. The same can be said of American public administration when it comes to the evolution of American administrative reform and its link to state building.

Likewise, this book ignores convention by treating administrative reforms as public policies in their own right rather than merely administrative tools (as Barzelay, 2001, advocates). Moreover, since the 1980s, studies of administrative reform movements in public administration tend mostly to focus on them as independent variables and assess their impacts on efficiency, economy, effectiveness, employee motivation, and social equity (e.g., did contracting reduce costs or did structural reforms negatively impact perceptions of agency goal attainment?). Meanwhile, historians tend to focus on administrative reform movements as dependent variables and, thus, place them within the context of larger political, economic, institutional, religious, and social forces related to state building. As historian Jacob Kramer (2015) illustrates, for example, countering radical anarchist, syndicalist, and socialist attacks on the political and business communities in the early 20th century both animated President Woodrow Wilson's (D-VA) New Freedom agenda and accelerated the pace and substance of the Progressive reform movement more generally. However, not only do historians tend to eschew the study of the evolution of these dynamics since the nation's founding, but they also fail to place them within the ongoing coevolution of the executive, legislative, and judicial branches of government as each reacts to the reform initiatives of the others as policies in themselves.

Finally, and relatedly, this book also departs from convention by reviewing the efforts of both positive- and minimal-state proponents to use administrative reform to advance their philosophical, policy, and state-building goals since the nation's founding. Both groups have used the IRP of administrative reform to advance their goals and to undermine, if not thwart, those of their opponents.[10] Ignoring this reality masks a great deal of the evolution of American administrative reform and its links to state building (both positive and negative).

****

Discerned from taking this approach to studying the evolution of American administrative reform and its relationship to compensatory state building are several other important challenges to current pictures in our heads in public administration. Identified, first, is the path dependency of that evolution and, thus, continuities within that path. As typically conceived and alluded to earlier, path dependency occurs as early decisions in a sequence of events shape, amplify, and constrain the path taken by subsequent reforms. Moreover, the earliest events in a time series have the most impact, even more than seemingly more momentous events that occur later. Once a choice among alternatives is made, the "probability of further steps along the same path increases with each step down the path. . . [and] the costs of switching to some previously possible alternative rises" (Pierson, 2004, p. 21).

Importantly, the path dependency discerned from the analysis in this book is *not* the path dependency that sees frictionless determinacy. Rather, the path dependency identified is more akin to what James March and Johan Olsen (1989) call "inefficient history." This is a path dependency involving what James Mahoney and Kathleen Thelen (2010) call "structured agency," whereby, within those paths, "frictions" and "abrasions" over different policies or strategies occur within and across existing authority structures and interests. Power balances remain or shift over time to produce stability or change. This type of path dependency also shows how actors' perceptions of their interests can change over time. The analysis reveals "institutional and ideological divisions within periods and regimes, as well as changes across reform eras" (Hattam & Lowndes, 2007, p. 199).

Second, and related to path dependency, the approach taken in this book reveals the amplifying importance of what historical institutionalists call "initial conditions" for understanding the evolution of American administrative reform and the compensatory state. More precisely, interpretations regarding this evolution have too heavily discounted the enduring importance of America exceptionalist values as an initial condition guiding the practice of reform and the nature of the state across time. Even Dwight Waldo (1984; also see Rosenbloom & McCurdy, 2006) portrayed the administrative state as comprised exclusively of public agencies and described administrative reform prescriptions as changing to suit the material and ideological background of different eras. Thus, he, too, underreported the cumulative effects of Americans' rhetorical embrace of American exceptionalist values as the IRP-informed predicates for realizing the nation's millenarian vision of escaping the failure of earlier republics.

Among other values, American exceptionalism rhetorically touts limited government, individualism, free markets, equal opportunity (rather than equality of outcomes), volunteerism, and localism (Kingdon, 1999; Lipset, 1996; Schuck & Wilson, 2008; Shafer, 1991).[11] Following these precepts, no European-like hereditary, aristocratic, or clerical barriers to social mobility would exist, thus avoiding the religious and class-based struggles that destroyed earlier republics. The aim of American exceptionalism was to do something that neither ancient Rome nor Athens had accomplished: to reconcile authority with liberty. Others have collapsed these values into two competing traditions in American political life: economic liberalism and civic responsibility (e.g., Hartz, 1955; Schlesinger, Sr., 1949). Still others have added a third, more odious tradition that has affected American political development, the state and its power, and the evolution of administrative reform: an "ascriptive" tradition of racial, ethnic, Native American, and gender discrimination (Smith, 1993).

Regardless, their better resonance with American exceptionalist views has consistently privileged IRP-based administrative reforms and state building stressing bureaucratic techniques, markets, quasi-markets, and cross-sectoral partnerships over alternative approaches. This is partly because the enduring power of American exceptionalism makes these reforms easier "sells" politically to elected officials and in terms of "sunk costs" than reforms emphasizing the building of public agencies' administrative capacity to match their ever-expanding responsibilities. Because of American exceptionalist values, it is also the path-dependent result of choices made in the founding period to focus on the building of private-sector rather than public-sector administrative capacity. This created a persistent tendency to turn, first, to military, business, and market-based models of organizations in the early 19th century and, ever since, to corporate images of how best to build and run the American state.

As Peter Schuck (2014) argues,

> what is incontrovertible is that American society, more than perhaps any other nation on earth, favors markets as the strong default condition

[for public action]. The United States defers entirely or partly to market actors to perform many of the functions that in other advanced societies are reserved almost exclusively for government—for example, in health-care, pensions, low-income housing, education, social services, and jail bonding.

(p. 28)

In the process, notes Skowronek, so far "American exceptionalism has not been transcended by twentieth-century state-building, it has only taken on a new form" (Novak, 2008, p. 756).

Also easier to sell to elected officials because of American exceptionalist values are administrative reforms that are premised on instrumental rather than constitutive perspectives of the relationship among elected officials, their political appointees, and the career bureaucracy. Brian Cook (2014) frames the issue compellingly in terms of a choice to view public agencies as "instruments" or "tools" of elected officials rather than portraying them "constitutively" as legitimately sharing with elected officials and the courts the governance of the nation. The notion of a need to contain government and its agencies in order to protect civil liberties has persevered across time, making instrumental perspectives on reform dominant. This, despite the reality that public agencies at all levels of government cannot be "instrument[s] because [they] belong [simultaneously] to everyone and to no one" (Rohr, 1986).

Third, the approach taken in this book also reveals that inaccurate images of the evolution of American administrative reform and its relationship to compensatory state building stem as well from an under-emphasis in public administration on the impacts of war, religion, and discrimination (ascriptive hierarchy). The impact of wars on the visible growth of the federal government has been documented by public administration scholars. So, too, has the role of wars in fostering corporate capitalism and amplifying protean subsystem politics. Scholarship has also shown how the end of "hot" wars typically results in a rollback of the visible size of the federal government, with the major exceptions being the end of World War II because of the Cold War and the global fight against terrorism (what McFaul, 2018, calls "hot peace"). However, their persistent link throughout American history to corporate and social science interests[12] seeking to retain, gain, or regain legitimacy through compensatory state building has been underappreciated (see more below), as have their roles in advancing the estrangement of citizens from government. Also underappreciated are the direct and indirect roles (positive and negative) that religion (especially evangelicalism, plus the Judeo–Christian ethic), its detractors, and spiritualism have played in the evolution of American administrative reform and the compensatory state (see Stillman, 1998, for an important exception). And, although values (ascriptive and otherwise) have always been a concern of public administration scholarship, discrimination—both pursuing it and trying to remedy it—has played a vastly understated role in the evolution of administrative reform.

Fourth, the approach taken in this book also shows the disingenuousness of reformers selling administrative reforms as apolitical in nature, as they have done since the nation's founding. Reformers of all persuasions and historical periods offer competing prescriptions that redefine citizens' relationships to the state (also see Clarke & Newman, 1997; Durant, 2000; Raadschelders, 2017). For example, various actors throughout American history have offered reforms premised on IRP-based (i.e., bureaucratic and market) rationality and instrumental views of the bureaucracy that marginalize citizens. Others have stressed reforms based heavily on producing substantive rationality and constitutive views of the bureaucracy. This *substantive rationality project* (SRP) denotes reforms promoting and protecting positive values, ethics, and processes (e.g., citizen participation) that can compromise economy and efficiency and, thus, are otherwise marginalized by the IRP (Thompson & Alvesson, 2005).[13] They contend that the "value of the bureau . . . lies not simply in its efficiency and effectiveness but in its capacity to support and develop responsible governance" (du Gay, 2005, p. 6). To achieve responsible governance, they offer reforms designed to advance democratic constitutional values in administration (e.g., constitutional integrity, transparency, the rule of law, civic involvement, and individual rights) (Rosenbloom, 2007). The pursuit of "democratic administration" also involves agencies working with employees and citizens to coproduce policy decisions, program designs, and results—what Cheng (2018) calls "cogovernance" and others call "co-creation" (Torfing, Sorensen, & Roiseland, 2016) and "co-delivery" (see Nabatchi, Sancino, & Sicilia, 2017, for a review of the variety of coproduction types existing primarily at the local government level of the compensatory state).

Fifth, as noted, the approach taken in this book also disabuses "deterministic" images in our heads of the evolution of American administrative reform and its link to state building. Administrative reforms are not selected by elective officials based on their objective merits, because no alternatives exist, or as the necessary consequences of changing events or challenges. They are the product of choices (or actor "agency") among various reform alternatives by actors with different and varying degrees of power (see more below).

Despite contenders such as the SRP, the dominant paradigm for administrative reform adopted by elected officials that has helped shape and amplify the compensatory state since the nation's founding has been IRP-based. This, in IRP reformers' quests to take politics, "emotionalism," and demagoguery out of policymaking, is a fatal conceit of all reformers (Oakeshott, 1962). This does not mean that SRP reforms cannot be pursued at the same time or subsequently. They have been. Rather, the issue is the relative balance and perdurability of the two in administrative reformers' emphases over time. Guy Adams (1992) analogizes what typically happens to administrative reforms to what the art world calls "pentimento." Like the original images that "bleed" through when artists paint over earlier canvases to save money, IRP initiatives that disconnect or marginalize citizens from agency deliberations bleed through each "new" iteration of SRP-based administrative reform. Moreover, this happens regardless of the repeated deficiencies of earlier bureaucratic, market-based, and networked IRP reforms when it comes to efficiency, control, or effectiveness across different implementation situations. It also does so despite the tensions among the ends of the administrative, political, legal, and market traditions of public administration (Lan & Rosenbloom, 1992; Rosenbloom, 1983, 2013).

Sixth, the approach taken in this book also shows how asymmetries of power among proponents of competing reforms contribute to these dynamics. More precisely, it illustrates how the relative power of IRP proponents over proponents of alternative administrative reform approaches has repeatedly meant the ascendancy of the IRP. What is more, this ascendancy has been repeatedly shaped, propelled, and amplified over time by an enduring nexus of corporate (including private business interests and nonprofit foundations) and social science interests.[14]

This corporate–social science nexus is not a conspiracy—although actors in both communities have sometimes worked together. Rather, the nexus represents a largely uncoordinated effort by intendedly rational corporate and social scientific actors to create or seize opportunities to advance their respective interests. As such, their interests sometimes diverge, with one dominant, but cumulatively the results are the same: the ascendancy of the IRP over rival reforms. Thus, no "hand"—visible or invisible—has guided or coordinated the building of America's compensatory state. Nor are either the business or social science elements of this nexus working within or outside the governmental components of the compensatory state homogeneous in composition. Divisions within the business community are well and widely known (e.g., between small and big or corporate businesses), and the inherent nature of the social science enterprise produces conflicting perspectives. These divisions and conflicts are documented in this book and play central roles in the development of its arguments. Still, because of the privileged position of business in any system with a market economy such as the United States (Lindblom, 1977),[15] the social sciences have typically been the "junior partner" in this nexus of interests. In turn, and for the same reason, the salience of the economics profession enjoys the same privileged position within the social sciences in the minds of most elected officials. All this, in turn, helps perpetuate an instrumental rather than a constitutive perspective on public agencies in the compensatory state, one pursued through the IRP and including the latest versions of "best business practices," "market-based" administrative reforms, and/or civic republican approaches (e.g., volunteer organizations).

Propelling this nexus of actors is the interaction of three interest-based motives designed to gain, retain, or revive their legitimacy in society: (1) a sincere belief that the IRP offers greater collective benefits for society than other administrative reform and state-building alternatives (an expressive motive); (2) a wish for the financial gains they will acquire to implement their expressive goals (a material motive); and (3) a desire to gain, enhance, or regain status as an authority structure in society defining and interpreting how the world works and can be improved (an authority motive). The compensatory state has not been built by the corporate–social science nexus' pursuit of legitimacy alone; others with the same aims have contributed (e.g., nonprofits, engineers, and lawyers). Although they are identified in this book, its focus remains on the corporate–social science nexus.

In this quest for legitimacy, the corporate–social science nexus of interests has pushed consistently, and seized opportunities, to associate itself with government, bring the scientific methods of the natural (i.e., physical) sciences to government, and expand the proxy components of the compensatory state. These efforts embed them in governance, state building, and policymaking and implementation. Elements of the nexus also have both helped to initiate and shape narratives about existing historical–structural gaps (i.e., existing institutions are not able to deal effectively with current or emerging threats to the nation) and/or taken advantage of them to press their arguments. And, despite differences in political philosophy and aims, those embedded have subsequently pressed for greater government activism, thus creating more policy, administrative, and state-building complexity.

Seventh, the approach taken in this book also shows how pursuit of the IRP has sometimes produced paradoxical results for administrative capacity, compensatory state building, and government legitimacy. For starters, and consistent with numbers 68 through 77 of *The Federalist Papers*, IRP proponents have assumed that good administration is a means for reaching higher political ends and gaining public support for government (and the federal government, in particular). They have also posited that a focus on the IRP's embrace of economy and efficiency will improve citizen perceptions of government agencies. As James Madison wrote in Federalist 46, citizen attachment to the federal government would occur only because of better administration than the states provided.

However, this book reveals flaws in the causal theory linking good administration and the IRP to gains in public trust, support, and legitimacy. Akin to the logic of Frederick Herzberg's (1964) motivation–hygiene theory, citizens *expect* instrumental rationality and do not reward agencies for attaining it. They *will* punish reputationally the absence of instrumental rationality (Carpenter, 2001, 2010). But only improvements in *substantive rationality* can boost their views of agency legitimacy (i.e., perceptions that agencies provide positive values, ethics, and practices that improve governance).

Also paradoxically, the IRP's unwavering quest for technical or instrumental rationality has repeatedly fallen prey to *political rationality*. Indeed, it has often been "weaponized" to advance policy agendas unrelated to administrative improvements per se (Durant, 2008). But, beyond this, the quest for instrumental over substantive rationality—and the focus of many reformers on making public agencies as insulated as possible from political influence—has only furthered politicization of administration. Consonant with coevolution theory, this happens as the understandable aim by agencies for gaining relative bureaucratic autonomy prompts further efforts by political actors and institutions in the Madisonian system to (re)gain control over them (Durant, 2015).

Furthermore, the pursuit of legitimacy (including funding support from public and private foundations) by means of the IRP has not only propelled the social sciences (and many in public administration) toward the "scientific" study of administrative topics and away from other methodological approaches (e.g., critical emancipatory approaches). It also has come to fruition in the late 20th and early 21st centuries amid a questioning of the scientific method and expertise generally among vocal segments of the American citizenry. The conscious pursuit of scientific rationality was definitely profound in gaining legitimacy within the social sciences, as well as among citizens and their elected representatives through the 1960s. But, since then, and despite the insights social science research has provided for governance, a questioning of scientific rationality has helped to erode the very legitimacy the social sciences have sought (Orren & Skowronek, 2017).

In yet another paradoxical development, a reversal of fortunes has resulted from the IRP over the years to diminish the legitimacy of government and the social sciences as voices of authority in American governance. Government agencies originally strived for legitimacy by adopting administrative approaches from the military and business spheres. Likewise, the corporate–social science nexus of interests historically sought legitimacy by association with government and business. Beginning in the late 20th century, however, government has reverted to pursuing legitimacy by associating itself with the latest private management innovations. These are mostly developed and marketed with enormous profit by national and international consulting firms (often with ties to business schools) without sufficient reference to public administration scholarship. And, in perhaps the ultimate irony for public administration, the field's defining of itself in the early 20th century as a field of business rather than law (Moe & Gilmour, 1995) lost a primary basis of differentiation from private management. This was a recurring choice that would come home to roost by the 1980s as many citizens hitched their views of government legitimacy partly on SRP-based notions of legality, ethics, and justice.

Also contributing to this development, the IRP has consistently marginalized nonexperts from policy deliberative processes. This, although sold historically as a means for enhancing democracy. Rather, the IRP further contributes to citizen cynicism of, and even estrangement from, government in America. This has happened as a sense among vocal segments of working-class and lower-middle-class

Americans has arisen that experts touting IRP-based solutions to public policy and administration problems are a cultural elite untethered to the concerns and preferences of average citizens (Bachner & Ginsberg, 2016). This perception contributed to the populism in America that helped elect Donald J. Trump (R-NY) president in 2016. So, too, did the negative impacts of the IRP-based globalization and deregulation promoted by Democrats and Republicans since the 1980s revive illiberal and ethnic nationalism in the United States (and abroad). Indeed, as this book documents, throughout history, important intellectual leaders in business and the social sciences have implied, and sometimes explicitly claimed, that they *should be* elites leading society. Fairly or unfairly, these claims or impressions have often been used by opponents of activist government to delegitimize policy and administrative activism, as well as positive-state building.

Finally, the approach taken in this book challenges several aspects of the conventional wisdom in contemporary public administration. First, the networked state that public administration scholars first emphasized in the late 1980s and early 1990s is not new or novel—despite repeated claims that it is. Admittedly, most public administration scholarship readily acknowledges that governments have used contracting and voluntary organizations (today's nonprofits) since the nation's founding. What scholars see as different is the greater scale of these efforts since the mid-1980s, their expanded scope, and the spiraling complexity of collaborative networks in the compensatory state. More precisely, public administration scholarship now portrays agency partnering, networking, and collaborative government as a novel and complex deconstruction or "disarticulation" of the administrative state (Frederickson, 1999; Frederickson, Smith, Larimer, & Licari, 2012).

In some ways, these arguments are unassailable. But, as noted earlier, this book illustrates how these network and contracting developments are actually only the latest manifestations and amplifications of the compensatory state. They *are* more multifaceted in type (e.g., information sharing versus resource sharing), source (e.g., both mandated and emergent), and degree of hierarchy than networks in the 18th and 19th centuries. But, like their predecessors, they all involve bargaining, negotiation, carrots, and sticks. Moreover, cogovernance and co-creation have been present in different types of networks and contracting since the nation's founding.

Proponents of this view also fail to convey that the *proportion* of what the federal government does through networked, third-party, or proxy actors has always been substantial and potent in advancing national goals. For example, in arguing that the national government had switched from being a direct provider of goods, services, and opportunities to an indirect provider through third parties, Lester Salamon (2001) observes that direct service provision by federal agencies comprised only approximately 30 percent of its activities on the eve of the 21st century. Likewise, Donald Kettl (1993) points out that "every major policy initiative launched by the federal government since World War II . . . has been managed through public–private partnerships" (p. 4). But with the absence of visible federal agency capacity to meet their legislated responsibilities throughout the nation's history, similar, if not greater, percentages of proxy involvement certainly applied in the 18th and 19th centuries, as well. Moreover, scholarship has yet to acknowledge the major contributions that administrative reformers, corporations, and the social sciences have made—individually and collectively, directly and indirectly, advertently and inadvertently—to the complexity of governance many now lament.

This book also challenges contemporary public administration images that the state is now "hollow" due to the scope of contracting and proxy government since the 1980s and that hollowness means less state authority or power (Milward & Provan, 2000; relatedly, see Jessop, 1993). Hollowing implies that "third-party" or proxy government (see, e.g., Kettl, 1993) has not played an integral role in American governance since the nation's founding. Again, public administration scholarship and media commentators may not have explicitly recognized or emphasized this fact until the last quarter of the 20th century. However, the history of American administrative reform chronicled in this book shows that the compensatory state is not a recent or hollow aberration from a strong state. If proxy government makes the American state "hollow" (which is debatable), then it has always been hollow relative to the responsibilities that government has assumed and proxies implement. Moreover, it is an open question whether the federal government is made more or less powerful by its use of proxies in the compensatory state given the mutual resource dependency relationship created.

Questionable, too, are images that the "blurring" of the sectors or the "publicness" of organizations (Bozeman, 1987, 2004)[16] may not have been an equally integral part of public administration since the nation's founding. The harnessing of the two sectors for public and private purposes has been a feature of the compensatory state since America's founding. Brian Balogh (2009) calls this the "national integration of public and private" (p. 352). Questionable, too, are unicausal explanations of administrative reforms adopted in any given time period because of what citizens and some elected officials perceive as the major administrative problem they face (e.g., corruption in the early 20th century) (Moynihan, 2014). This perspective ignores the contests over which type of reform should prevail in any historical period, the role of radical political elements in increasing the pace and nature of administrative reform choices (Kramer, 2015), and the path-dependent role of the corporate–social science nexus in pressing for and shaping the dominance of the IRP throughout American history.

****

Although these findings are important in themselves, they also offer the broad contours of a "legitimacy theory" of the evolution of American administrative reform and compensatory state building. Sociologist Mark Suchman (1995) defines legitimacy as a "generalized perception or assumption [on the part of society] that the actions of an entity are desirable, proper, or appropriate within some socially constructed system of norms, values, beliefs, and definitions" (p. 574). He argues that actors employ a variety of strategic and institutional approaches to try to manage perceptions of their legitimacy in order to gain, increase, or regain authority status in society.[17]

In the case of American administrative reform and its association with the building of a compensatory state, legitimacy theory envisions reformers with alternative perspectives and political philosophies competing in pursuit of expressive, material, and authority gains (see earlier). In the process, legitimacy theory affords a model-like narrative describing how this process unfolds in ways akin to what Andrew McFarland (2004) calls a "pulse model." In a pure cyclical process model, the "arrows" of the fundamentals of reform travel "through some pattern but eventually go back to point A, or perhaps just swing back and forth between points A and B" after excesses occur between reforms (p. 79). In a pulse model, however, the deep structure of reform reinforces and amplifies over time as a secular, slow-moving, hardly visible phenomenon.

Applied to the consistent adoption of the IRP in American administrative reform and the building of a compensatory state since the nation's founding, the pulse model works as follows:

1. Calls for administrative reform arise from elected officials and administrative reformers arguing that (a) existing institutions are not able to deal effectively with current or emerging threats to the nation (i.e., a historical–structural mismatch exists),[18] and (b) Americans' exceptionalist values and millenarian vision cannot escape the fate of other republics and are threatened unless reform occurs.

2. Various sets of reformers with different perspectives and political goals (e.g., government activists and minimalists) take advantage of this window of opportunity to pursue expressive, material, and authority benefits and to link their arguments to American exceptionalist values (especially limited government, economic liberalism, and civic republicanism) in pursuit of (re)legitimacy gains. In the process, the original political coalition supporting the last round of reform (typically the IRP) must contend with alternative visions of administrative reform. In this battle, the combatants pursue their aims in whatever forums—public, private, or nonprofit—hold potential in the compensatory state to advance their visions and legitimacy.

3. The IRP repeatedly trumps other reform alternatives (often based on the SRP) because of the relative power of elements in the corporate–social science nexus of actors promoting and benefiting from it from within and outside public agencies. Elected proponents of activist government turn to the IRP either to bring "order" to its operations or to maintain influence

when the executive branch is in the hands of political opponents (Moe, 1985). Elected opponents of activist government turn to the IRP to add complexity to its operations when the executive branch is controlled by proponents of activist government. Cumulatively, both camps add complexity to governance by amplifying the compensatory state—and, especially, its proxy components—in order to hide the government's visible size. This also happens because of the scramble of coevolving branches of government to rachet up overhead accountability mechanisms.

4. The IRP, coevolution, and the amplifying of the compensatory state not only diminish citizen support for improving the administrative capacity of public agencies as citizens perceive themselves marginalized by expertise-based administrative processes. These processes also disappoint operationally and in terms of the SRP. As such, they contribute to citizen confusion, estrangement, and distrust of government; reinforce the idea of a government of elite experts out of touch with average Americans; and, thus, paradoxically help undermine government legitimacy. Consequently, the initial advantage of adopting the IRP that has been amplified over the centuries produces collective irrationality in its negative effects on legitimacy.

5. All this leads to calls for the next round of administrative reform and state building based on yet another set of claims of historical–structural mismatch. But triumphant again for the reasons noted is the IRP over other reform alternatives, including the SRP. And even when other reform alternatives are taken, the IRP tends to "seep through the canvas" of these initiatives to complicate seriously, and even dominate, agency and network operations in pentimento fashion.

****

The remainder of this book offers the empirical evidence undergirding the arguments and theory outlined in this chapter. Chapters 2 through 7 explore seven different periods wherein administrative reform initiatives ebbed and flowed and restarted again. Analysis begins with the Founding Era in Chapter 2 to set up the importance of initial conditions in America that have since informed and constrained the evolution of administrative reform. Analysis ends with the Obama administration in Chapter 7; it is too early, if not dangerous given its unpredictability, to assess anything but the broad contours of the Trump administration.

A highly granular and comprehensive review of all events, dynamics, methodological or philosophic conflicts, scholarship, and thought leaders relevant to American administrative reform and compensatory state building is impossible in a book covering so much historical ground. However, those ideas, actors, and controversies recounted in this book offer a sense for the general parameters of political, economic, philosophical, and social debates over the evolution of American administrative reform and state building since the nation's founding.

For analytical purposes, administrative reforms are comprised of major efforts to change structures, processes (e.g., budgeting and personnel processes), and cultures at work in the compensatory state. Because administrative reforms are policy, they are affected by politics, and politics are affected by context, the reforms discussed are linked in each chapter to seven contextual factors that have affected administrative reform. These are changes in people, place, physical technology, social technology, wishes and ideas, catastrophes, and personality (Gaus, 1947, pp. 9–10). These affect, and are affected by, administrative reforms. At the same time, political and policy initiatives are included in the analysis of administrative reforms, because reforms are often predicated on them. They also afford the general context of administrative reform efforts and their influence on compensatory state building, help create perceived needs for change, and trace the ebb and flow of political power that determine the aims of reforms and their durability.

Chapter 8 then revisits the evidence given in earlier chapters to assess the validity of the arguments made. It also distills the implications of these arguments for future research and theory building on the evolution of American administrative reform. Reviewed is how seeing existing "landscapes" of the state and American administrative reform with "new eyes" offers new pictures and interpretations, new practical and theoretical grounding, and new venues for future research and theory building on this and other "big questions" in public administration. Revising the thinking of American administrative reformers would be a welcome bonus.

Notes

1. The use of the term "administrative reformers" in this book applies to elected officials adopting the reform recommendations of numerous executive and legislative branch studies and commissions (e.g., the Brownlow, Grace, and Hoover commissions). Informing their recommendations were private consulting groups, persons popularizing business techniques (e.g., reinventing government), and ideas offered or ascribed to by some members of the academic community (e.g., the Civil Service Reform Act of 1978 and the New Public Management).
2. Historically, the terms administration and management were used interchangeably (Lynn, 2006). Dwight Waldo (1984) made a classic differentiation in *The Administrative State*. He defined management as focusing on the nuts and bolts of administrative decisions after policy or program aims were established. This book does not address whether public management is a separate field from public administration or a subfield of it. For simplicity, it uses the more inclusive term "public administration," referring to public management when solely discussing scholarship in today's self-identified public management school.
3. Also see Baldwin (2005); Balogh (2009); Bensel (1990, 2000); Edling (2003); Hawley (1966); Hays (1980); John (1995, 2006); Karl (1983); Keller (1977); King

and Lieberman (2009); Lieberman (2002); Mashaw (2006); Orren and Skowronek (2004); Pierson (2004); and Skocpol (1992).

4. Pragmatism's animating premise was that abstract arguments about what constituted such things as the state had to give way to "actual social investigation of an idea's real-world [processes and] consequences for living human beings" (Novak, 2008, p. 764).

5. Mann contrasts this with a "despotic power" of a state. By this, he means the "organizational capacity of state elites to rule unchecked by other centers of power or by civil society" (Novak, 2008, p. 763).

6. The idea of a "compensatory state" builds on the insightful scholarship of Marc Allen Eisner (2000a), who identified compensatory state building in his book, *From Warfare State to Welfare State*. Eisner's term, however, refers to events from World War I to World War II, while this book makes the case that compensatory state building has been present since the Founding Era.

7. This book takes the "Founders in argument" perspective that portrays both the Federalists and Anti-Federalists as Founders of the American republic (Rohr, 1986). It differentiates, however, when the arguments of the Federalists and Anti-Federalists were, on balance, supported.

8. Research making this point is robust, especially in the policy implementation literature. A seminal use of the bargaining image of intergovernmental relations was employed by Helen Ingram (1977). Scholarship demonstrating how the nature of intergovernmental relations morphed over the years includes: Conlan et al. (2014); Derthick (2010); McGuire and Agranoff (2010); Posner (2010); Wright (1990). Ample, as well, is the literature on bargaining in networks. As Salamon (2001) contends, "network theory argues [that] the standard relationship among actors is one of interdependence. As a consequence, no single actor . . . can enforce its will" (p. 1631).

9. Metaphors are useful when they can help scholars and lay publics understand complex phenomena. But, when they are inaccurate, they can adversely affect understandings.

10. The notion of the IRP is adapted from Deborah Stone's (2011) characterization of policy analysts, who she sees as fundamentally averse to politics. It is equally applicable to how administrative reformers in America portray their initiatives.

11. For a comprehensive and social science-based review of how American exceptionalism pervades various policy fields today, see Schuck and Wilson (2008). For an excellent debate on this topic, see Shafer (1991). As leading historians (e.g., Thomas Bender) have noted, all nations need a national story to produce a common national identity and future. As Jill Lepore (2019) argues, "very often, histories of nation-states are little more than myths that hide the seams that stitch the nation to the state" (p. 12). Moreover, they can vary over time, as they have in America. And although unrealized at various points in time, the ideas contained in them serve as ideals or aspirations against which to hold the nation accountable. One such national story is that of American exceptionalism.

12. In one sense, the terms "social science" and "social sciences" had their origins in the late 18th century and initially were called the political and moral sciences. In the 19th century, they became associated with academic disciplines (e.g., economics, political science, and sociology) and their professional associations (e.g., the American Economic Association). In another sense, however, the origins of many of their ideas and objectives go back to the ancient Greeks with their rationalist approaches to understanding the state and morality.

13. It is also possible that the preference for bureaucracy and hierarchy in America is instinctual in humankind because of its evolutionary journey, as moral foundations theory contends (Haidt, 2012). This may be the case, but how one structures authority (e.g., inclusive or exclusive) is a choice with power implications (Waldo, 1984). The question, of course, is not whether elites will lead but *which* elites will lead, how, and with what legitimacy.

14. In defining the social sciences broadly, this book follows precedents established by historian Arnold J. Toynbee and others to include scholarship from a variety of research areas addressing human, social, and administrative problems.

15. Lindblom argues that because the economic prosperity of America is fundamental to the survival of government and the support of its citizens, business has a heavily disproportional influence on politics and policy. This book explicitly extends this thesis to administrative reform as a critical part of governance and American state building. Lindblom's book remains a classic in the political science literature.

16. Moreover, as Karl Polanyi (1944) argued, "economic history reveals that the emergence of national markets was in no way the result of the gradual and spontaneous emancipation of the economic sphere from government control. On the contrary, the market has been the outcome of a conscious and often violent intervention on the part of government" (p. 258). (But see Hayek, 1944, 1989.)

17. In the present case, business and the social sciences have been engaged in a persistent effort to be viewed as capable of speaking authoritatively on the major issues of their day.

18. These threats include such things as immigration, industrialization, technological advances, religious awakenings, and/or short-term immediate threats to American exceptionalist values (e.g., wars).

Chapter 2

The Founding Era, the Corporate–Social Science Nexus, and American Administrative Reform, Circa 1730–1824

President Lyndon Johnson (D-TX) once observed, "power is where power goes" (Caro, 2012). Politicians and administrative reformers throughout American history have understood this and sought to replace, reconfigure, or buttress existing authority structures to advance their state-building interests. They have also learned that the best way to advance their state-building and administrative reform proposals, or to curb opposition to them, is to frame them rhetorically in terms of American exceptionalist values. This said, and with these initial philosophical foundations so central to the path-dependency and structured-agency arguments in this book, this chapter discusses the origins of American exceptionalism's values from the colonial era through approximately the first two decades of the 19th century.

Reviewed also among these "initial conditions" is the shift from the founding generation's animating spirit of civic virtue (i.e., the dedication of citizens to promoting societal welfare rather than parochial interests) to the second generation's shift to an "interest-based" commercial republic (see, e.g., Elkin, 2006; Schocket, 2007). This shift placed the United States on a path inextricably linking capitalism and democracy in citizens' minds, a path that would repeatedly amplify throughout American history to the present day. This was a commercial republic in which democracy, religion, faculty psychology, migration, technology, and capitalism helped forge Americans' enduring self-conception of the virtues of economic liberalism and civic responsibility, along with a dysfunctional ascriptive hierarchy.

The congruence of these factors led Americans to what historian Daniel Walker Howe (2009) calls a passion for "self-construction" and "self-culture" that, in turn, fostered visions of the proper size, role, and scope of American political institutions. As Aaron Friedberg (2002) argues, the American

> founders succeeded . . . in encoding a strong strain of antistatism into the new nation's political DNA, one that would reproduce itself and continue to fulfill its protective function in future generations . . . [as well as institutionalize a fear of] the dangers of excessive concentrations of governmental power.
>
> (p. 240)

Adds historian Gordon Wood (2009a), the "emergence of the liberal, individualistic, commercial, and interest-ridden world of early 19th-century America" remains today "part of the nation's understanding of itself" (p. 255).

The chapter begins by reviewing how the 17th-century wave of Scottish and Scotch–Irish immigration, British parliamentary and administrative misfeasance and malfeasance, geometric population growth, a breakdown of community ties, military machinations, and evangelical fervor led to perceptions of a historical–structural mismatch of administration with social developments and problems. Identified also is how a nexus of nascent corporate–social science interests propelled these results, a nexus animated over the years by a quest for legitimacy that would bring expressive, material, and authority gains to them. In the process, the scaffolding was laid for seeing American administrative reform as best informed by the instrumental rationality project (IRP), limited government, and, hence, the building of a compensatory state.

Discussed as part of this dynamic is the search for "order" and "control" through "Republican Arithmetik" in response to tumultuous times, most prominently the challenges to traditional authority that ensued as the second generation of Americans came to power (Cohen, 1999, p. 81). This is followed by a discussion of how these dynamics led, first, to conflicts over instrumental versus constitutive visions of government bureaucracies and, then, to a deliberate marginalization of citizens in administrative processes by both Federalists and Jeffersonian Republicans (e.g., Caldwell, 1988). This, in turn, produced calls for the next wave of administrative reform—the Jacksonian revolution—discussed later in Chapter 3.

****

Any discussion of the foundations for Americans' enduring embrace of such American exceptionalist values as anti-authoritarianism, limited government, individualism, civic republicanism, and market forces must begin with the colonists' changing demographics, enhanced financial standing, and improved communication systems. Demographic change produced what Gordon Wood (2002) calls the "fragmentation of households, churches, and communities" between 1760 and 1776 and played a central role in diminishing respect for authority generally (p. 9).

First came population and migration increases that challenged the legitimacy of existing colonial governments. Reflecting high fertility rates, the population doubled in the colonies (from one to two million) alone. Most notable was a heavy increase of Scottish and Scotch–Irish immigration after the Seven Years' War in Europe (1756–1763; played out in America as the French and Indian War). Among these immigrants were indentured servants from Britain, slaves from Africa (about one-fifth of the American population), and convicts sent from England to Georgia. The Scottish and Scotch–Irish who came to America were organized by profit-minded proprietors (e.g., the Virginia Company) and were mostly trying to escape poverty and religious wars and persecution. These included Puritans in New England, Quakers in Pennsylvania, and Catholics in Maryland. Independent-minded, "undeferential," and bureaucratically hostile (except for Catholics) (Baron, 2013, p. 16), they spread into Philadelphia and then into the southeastern states and Missouri territories over the next 50 years (Baron, 2013; Woodard, 2011).

This in-migration also made the several-hundred-mile strip of the Atlantic coast extremely overcrowded in already developed small towns and made less land available for sons to settle as their fathers had before them. Consequently, younger men—especially those who were not first-born sons and Presbyterians who bought into the values of enterprise and frugality—moved further West and left established family and community ties behind them. From the perspective of these far-off and isolated frontier settlers, British colonial governors had little relevance or legitimacy and were constrained by the American equivalent of Britain's privy councils.

Western migration also pressured the British to establish Native American reservations. For some, reservations were to protect Native Americans from land speculators, but for others, they were designed to make colonial settlement and land speculation possible on Native American lands. Not surprisingly, these actions prompted rebellions by the Cherokees, Shawnees, and coalitions of tribes under the Ottawa chief, Pontiac, which, in turn, made the British commit to a standing Crown army in the colonies that would only infuriate many Americans. The British first sent 10,000 troops to the colonies and then issued the Royal Proclamation of 1763 forbidding further settlement of the West by colonists. But this only resulted in these Native American tribes joining with the French to drive out the British and colonists from these lands during the Seven Years' War noted earlier. In 1765, and much to the chagrin of many colonists, the Quartering Act required the colonies to give lodging to British soldiers in their communities.

The British decision to maintain a standing army in the colonies was also prompted by disorders in the "backcountry" lands between the Appalachians and the Mississippi River. There, violent vigilante justice took root in the absence of established colonial governments (e.g., the "Regulators" in South Carolina and elsewhere). Also, as the number of settlements grew from immigration both within the Atlantic seaboard and in the western backcountry, deference to authority deteriorated and rebellions had to be put down by colonial authorities. Pennsylvania and North Carolina, for example, witnessed armed uprisings by settlers against what they claimed was "exploitation by remote eastern governments" (Wood, 2002, p. 11). County courts were seized, petitions for greater representation in legislatures arose, and calls for local control of governance mounted.

The delegitimating of British colonial political and administrative authority was also fanned by the colonies' rising economic influence in the British Empire. By 1760, Americans—especially merchants—were prospering financially because of increasing exports of grain, tobacco, and foodstuffs to Great Britain. This, in the wake of the British Industrial Revolution and growing populations whose food and material needs could not be met domestically. Manufacturing also gained a small but important toehold in America (especially in the textile and shoe industries in the North), which, along with rising prices for colonial products, sparked a "consumer revolution," further stimulating economic growth. Initiated, too, were a miscellany of small, artisan-based urban and rural businesses targeted for profit-making in local, regional, and interstate markets. Increasing commerce also prompted infrastructure building—including roads, port facilities, and post offices—to get products to more distant markets.

Meanwhile, a corrupt, administratively flawed, and disorderly British government (the Crown and Parliament) saw in this prosperity the bases for tax revenues to help pay for the standing army in America and England's battles with the French. Previously, the colonies paid nothing for British defense, enjoyed great independence in their general domestic affairs from Britain under what Edmund

Burke termed a policy of "salutary neglect," created their own representative assemblies and governance sensibilities, and set their own taxes. But facing massive debt from its European wars and rising military costs in North America, the British Parliament first enacted the Molasses Act of 1733 and imposed higher duties affecting a wide range of goods (e.g., sugar) vital to the livelihood of many Americans. Next came the Stamp Act of 1765, the first direct tax ever imposed on the colonists. Lawyers and the emerging printing and newspaper businesses in the colonies were hard hit by the Stamp Act (due to taxes on paper). Combined with general outrage by the colonists for the Quartering and Molasses Acts, this led all but four colonies to meet in New York in 1765. The result was the issuance of a "Declaration of Rights and Grievances" that led Parliament to end the Stamp Act in 1766.

But victory proved pyrrhic with Charles Townshend's appointment in 1766 as British Chancellor of the Exchequer, an appointment from which the colonies would not get minimal relief until Lord North assumed this position in a new government and eliminated all but Townshend's duty on tea. Until then, Townshend's pressure on Parliament resulted in a series of external taxes on items such as tea, paper, and glass imported from England. Adding insult to injury, these taxes were administered by, and paid the salaries of, British colonial governors. This ended the major lever of influence the colonists had over their governors: appropriation of salaries by colonial legislatures.

Also propelling the assault on existing authority structures in America for the founding generation were improvements in the communication of grievances (Burns, 2006), including newspapers; the development of the US postal system; and the Committees of Correspondence opposing the Crown.[1] As Bernard Bailyn (1992) points out, printing presses issued pamphlets replete with references to classical history. But these were often superficial and "dragged in" to increase the "weight of an argument" (p. 24). However, in these jeremiads, ample references were also made to 18th-century Continental Enlightenment thinkers such as Montesquieu and Voltaire, as well as philosophically disparate Scottish and British Enlightenment (circa 1630–1830) thinkers such as Jeremy Bentham, David Hume, Francis Hutchinson, John Locke, Thomas Reid, David Ricardo, and Adam Smith.

As Bailyn (1992) writes,

> in pamphlet after pamphlet, the American writers cited Locke on natural rights . . . and the social and government contract, Montesquieu . . . on the character of British liberty and . . . the institutional requirements for its attainment, [and] Voltaire on the evils of clerical oppression.
>
> (p. 27)

Also figuring prominently was their belief in the English common law tradition (derived largely from William Blackstone's *Commentaries on the Laws of*

England), the Magna Carta's (1215) emphasis on the primacy of law over kings, and the writings of "country politicians" with their prolific and radical denunciations of the monarchial power embraced by the Tories.

Nurtured on such writings and sentiments, the question for the first generation of Americans remained what to do about it in terms of governance. Samuel Huntington (1968) argued that the roots of America's system of diffused responsibility, separation of powers, checks and balances, bicameralism, and federalism lay in the colonists' embrace of Tudor values of the 17th century rather than those of the new 18th-century British constitution of parliamentary sovereignty. Contrasting political development in America, on the European continent, and in Great Britain, Huntington argued that the first American colonists left England about a century before a "rationalization of authority" on the European continent revoked the complexity of feudal authority structures with a unified monarchial structure and, in Great Britain, with parliamentary supremacy. Put more simply, a "single authority replaced the many which had previously existed" (p. 98).

Leaders of the 18th-century revolutions in Europe and Great Britain believed in reason, "reject[ed] external restraints on men," and minimized notions of "natural law" (Huntington, 1968, p. 99).[2] But many of the early settlers in the United States brought with them a medieval faith in Thomas Aquinas' natural law theory and John Locke's 17th-century notion of natural rights (i.e., rights are not *given* by governments but *secured* by them), along with a belief in multiple and diffused authorities and power that might check and balance each other (Huntington, 1968). Therefore, Huntington maintains, the American Constitution ratified in 1789 was not a revolutionary document but, rather, a document that "in large part simply codified and formalized at the national level practices and institutions long in existence on the colonial level" and that "has changed remarkably little" since (p. 98) (also see, for example, Kirk, 2002, who cites Burke in maintaining that Americans merely were reasserting rights threatened by the British government). In the process, the US Constitution made a visible concentration of state power difficult, something the English mixed government system did well. The multiplicity of authority afforded by Tudor government produced a system premised on ambition counteracting ambition according to Newtonian principles and requiring compromise to work well.

For colonists, concentrated power had, since ancient times, meant domination, so power had to be checked by consent and representation of the governed. This, as posited in the Gregorian revolt against state dominance of the Catholic Church in the Middle Ages and its expansion to medieval representational parliaments (Moller, 2019). Otherwise, concentrated power's "endlessly propulsive tendency to expand itself beyond legitimate authority" would prevail (Bailyn, 1992, p. 56). And the natural "prey" of power was "liberty, or law, or right." Although power was not inherently a malignant force, the "nature of man [*was* malignant]—his susceptibility to corruption and his lust for self-aggrandizement" was unbounded (p. 59). Informing this perspective was the history of the ancient Greeks, the Roman Republic, the English Civil War, and earlier despotic kingdoms in, among others, Egypt, Europe, and Turkey.

Not everyone embraces all of Huntington's perspective. For example, Bailyn (1992) argued that a revolution of immense proportions *had* occurred in America. Bailyn also dismissed critiques of the writings of pamphleteers as "mere propaganda" and challenged the arguments of a capitalist conspiracy proffered by Charles Beard (1918) in the early 20th century. Instead, Bailyn argued that the

> fear of a comprehensive conspiracy against liberty throughout the English-speaking world—a conspiracy believed to have been nourished in corruption, and of which, it was felt, oppression in America was only the most visible part—lay at the heart of the [American] Revolutionary movement.
>
> (p. xiii)

Known pejoratively as "Robinocracy"—and designating the chief ruler as a "Robinarch"—the King's magistrates and colonial governors were "maintaining the façade of constitutional procedures" while "load[ing] the people with taxes and with debts" and creating a "mercenary standing army . . . to perfect its dominance in just those ways" (p. 50).

This rising anger was most prominently expressed in John Dickinson's *Letters from a Farmer in Pennsylvania* (1767–1768), as well as in the incendiary "reporting" of early newspapers such as the *Boston Evening-Post*, the *Boston Gazette*, the *Maryland Gazette*, the *New Hampshire Gazette*, and the *New York Mercury*. Typical, and notoriously prone to "fake news" and incitement, was the *Boston Gazette* and its editor, Samuel Adams, who wrote, "awake my countrymen, and, by a regular & legal Opposition, defeat the Designs of those who enslave us and our Posterity" (Burns, 2006, p. 125). But Tory newspapers, such as *Rivington's New-York Gazette*, engaged in similarly incendiary language, calling on the colonists "to ignore the cries of the Whigs (revolutionaries), not to 'submit to their unreasonable, seditious and chimerical resolves' and insurrectional tendencies" (p. 176). As Eric Burns (2006) summarizes the views of scholars, the American press "libeled and exaggerated and berated; [it] specialized in foul-mouthed impertinence" (p. 8).

Largely a symbolic reminder of the Crown's policy and administrative authority, the duty on tea by the British Parliament and its administration soon became a symbol of the assault on colonists' liberty and a major focus of pamphleteers' wrath. When this was followed by the Parliament's enactment of the Intolerable Acts (1774) in the aftermath of the Boston Tea Party, anti-tax and anti-regulatory fervor dominated communication.[3] To this day, this fervor consistently drives

American political and administrative reform efforts and, thus, compensatory state building.

The timing of the Parliament's action could not have been worse. Prosperity in the colonies sharply increased a sense of independence from government and traditional authority generally. This, amid the fraying of familial ties and contractual relationships noted earlier, plus massive inflows of capital and credit from English and Scottish sources. These alternative sources of financial capital reduced the British government's previous paternalistic role as middleman in such investments. Nor was colonial antagonism limited to small artisan merchants in townships. Small farmers challenged the authority of larger landowners (even southern planters). No longer were they dependent on the latter, as they began drawing direct lines of credit from other nations and gained access to markets.

All this set the stage for revolutionary fervor among a vocal minority of colonists, as well as an embrace of the prowess of society—rather than government—to address problems. John Adams estimated that approximately one-third of the colonists favored independence from England, one-third favored staying in the British Empire and reforming the relationship, and one-third lacked an opinion. Many commentators also portray the uprising as a "civil war" between loyalists and revolutionaries where a variety of atrocities were committed (Philbrick, 2016). Regardless, this revolt came packaged in a series of events familiar to most readers, including the battles of Lexington and Concord, the Boston Tea Party, Thomas Jefferson's *A Summary View of the Rights of British America*, the convening of the First Continental Congress in 1774, the Battle of Bunker Hill in 1775, and the Declaration of Independence in 1776. These were followed by years of heroic, underfunded, and largely asymmetric warfare led by George Washington; by the British surrender at Yorktown in 1781; and by the Treaty of Paris ending the war in 1783.[4]

****

Another major source of the American Revolution (1765–1783), as well as American exceptionalists' belief in the virtues of individualism and Montesquieu's "checks and balances" in government (an idea originating with Aristotle citing humanity's selfish nature), was the powerful imagery of "faculty psychology" as a way to realize America's millenarian vision (Howe, 1979, 2009). The revolution's roots can also be traced directly to Enlightenment thinkers (and even earlier to the Age of Pericles in Greece and the Renaissance) who bequeathed to the founding generation of Americans a set of ideas that the scholasticism of the Middle Ages considered radical and impious (Tarnas, 1991). These included the questioning of existing authority structures (monarchies and clericalism), an embrace of human innovation and creativity, the view of humankind as master of its own fate, and the centrality to political freedom of property rights.

Faculty psychology referred to how best to control one's mental (or cognitive) faculties for a virtuous life and is akin to Plato's notion of the tripartite soul. Importantly, its principles were then extrapolated to identify the best means for Americans to organize society. As such, faculty psychology informed the state-building design of the American political system. Just as Plato had espoused in the classical period of ancient Greece that order in the soul and order in the polity were linked, and as Immanuel Kant in the 18th century saw life as a struggle between duty and pleasure, faculty psychology posited that individual self-development and self-development of the polity for virtue and order reinforced each other. In the case of individuals, and much like Aristotle's focus in *Nicomachean Ethics* on prudence and temperance, faculty psychology valued "self-construction" or "self-improvement" and emphasized citizens' obligations to control their emotions (interests, avarice, ambition, and licentiousness) with reason (self-reflection, conscience, and prudence). In this period, Benjamin Franklin's program for "moral perfection" in *Poor Richard's Almanac* embodies this psychology. Emotions and reason were faculties in steady conflict, with emotions always ready to overcome reason and virtue and to wreak havoc on others and society. Thus, passions had to be "checked" by a person's rational powers, and the duty of all citizens—and a manifestation of personal worth and success by Calvinists (including the Presbyterians, Baptists, and, later, the Congregationalists)—was to exhibit self-improvement, self-realization (reaching one's potential), and self-control of all faculties. However, as modern day evolutionary biologists contend, the lower passions could never—and should never—be eliminated; the "highest value was balance, that is, the proper expression of each human power [faculty] but the excessive indulgence of none"—including reason (Howe, 1979, p. 29).

More concisely, the sources of liberty for individuals and nations were order, control, and the offsetting powers of individual and national faculties. Critical for doing this for individuals was ensuring widespread literacy among Americans, as well as advanced education for its socioeconomic elites. This is not surprising; over 100 members of the original Puritan settlers had attended either Oxford or Cambridge universities (Burns, 2006). Relatedly, Neil Postman (1985) argues that "between 1640 and 1700, the literacy rate for men in Massachusetts and Connecticut was somewhere between 89 percent and 95 percent. . . [while] the literacy rate for women. . . [ran] as high as 62 percent in the years 1681–1697" (pp. 31–32).

Moreover, as refugees from European class, religious, and ethnic discrimination, the colonists brought with them the Enlightenment ideas of reason-driven or rationality-driven liberation that were then ripping through the European continent and Great Britain. Rationality is akin to a person's mind working toward an outcome using logic and objectivity. Chief among these were English and Scottish rationalism, as well as the Newtonian empirical approach to building knowledge that contrasted with the emotionalism and superstition of earlier ages (Beard & Beard, 1944, pp. 62–63).

Also present was a faith—that will be replicated throughout this book—in scientifically informed progress to improve all aspects of life, rather than a fatalistic acceptance of an unacceptable status quo. Accompanying these beliefs was the embrace of the natural rights of individuals—especially rights to private property and to freedom of contract among willing individuals—rather than those granted to them by sovereigns and clergy. Indeed, property and contracting rights were prerequisites to life, liberty, and happiness. These rights, in turn, would be tempered by obligations enshrined in antiquity's four cardinal virtues (temperance, prudence, justice, and courage), plus the theological virtues of faith, hope, and charity (Prior, 2018). Drawing extensively on Cicero's writings, republican virtue and ordered liberty would also be obtained by the pursuit of natural law: "True law is right reason in agreement with nature" (Kirk, 2002). Likewise, self-improvement on Earth was seen in religious terms as the legitimate aim of humankind. Actions rather than abstract notions of goodness measured the worth of individuals and societies.

The balancing forces of the "good life" for individuals (i.e., continual self-discipline and cultivation of higher virtues) applied equally to social and political systems. This meant checking the passions of executive rulers and, especially from the perspectives of such Founders as James Madison,[5] slowing down legislation and letting reason prevail over passions over time (what Weiner, 2012, calls "temporal republicanism"). Edmund Randolph, for example, argued that the "evils from which the country suffered originated in 'the turbulence and follies of democracy'" (Hofstadter, 1989, p. 6). Added Elbridge Gerry, "democracy [w]as 'the worst of all political evils,'" a position shared by William Livingston, who wrote that the "people have ever been and ever will be unfit to retain the exercise of power in their own hands" (p. 6). Likewise, Roger Sherman hoped that the "people . . . have as little to do as may be about the government" (p. 6). Alexander Hamilton also joined the chorus: the "turbulent and changing [masses] seldom judge or determine right . . . the imprudence of democracy" must be checked. Echoing thoughts of such ancients as Plato and Aristotle, and as later chapters in this book demonstrate, similar attitudes would be seen among various administrative reformers—and the corporate-social science nexus of interests—throughout American history.

As conceived by the members of the 1787 Constitutional Convention, all but six of whom came from the wealthier and educated classes, this check was republicanism. Charles Lindblom (1977) argues that the Founders' view of liberty did not involve direct citizen control of, or participation in, government. Nor, like the early Roman Republic (circa 509 BCE) and Ancient Greece that many Founders had studied, was liberty accorded non-landowning white men, women, slaves, and, in America's case, Native Americans. As Lindblom writes,

> in America, the revolutionists declared their commitment not to popu-
> lar control but to "certain Unalienable Rights" [e.g., life, liberty, and the

pursuit of happiness] . . . . The Constitutional Founders were fervent liberals but no more than timid democrats, some not democrats at all.

(p. 163)

Indeed, again like early patricians in the Roman Republic, as well as followers of Socrates and Plato in Ancient Greece, "fear of the mob" (or "democratic despotism") (see Kirk, 1986) was widely prevalent among the leaders. History (e.g., the reign of the "Thirty Tyrants" after the demos of the Age of Pericles in Greece and Oliver Cromwell's Commonwealth in 17th-century Britain) told them that democracy ultimately deteriorated into class struggles that required dictatorship to restore order. Instead, the linkage they made was between liberty and markets, as per John Locke.

Lindblom (1977) continues that, for Locke, the "foundation of the liberal constitutional state was property. The function of the state was property protection . . . a set of rights that consequently subsumes liberty under property" (p. 164). The system created by the Founders was designed to "win and protect certain liberties; private property, free enterprise, free contract, and occupational choice . . . the end is always individual self-help" (p. 164). To which must be added Voltaire's influence on the thinking of deist "free-thinkers" such as John Adams, Benjamin Franklin, Thomas Jefferson, and James Madison regarding religious liberty and tolerance (the 16th-century philosophy of Jean Bodin was also an influence), freedom of speech, and separation of church and state (Noyer, 2015). Likewise, Americans' focus on freedom of speech and the press traced its roots to, among others, the 17th-century poet John Milton's argument against censorship.

Some went even further, especially those who later became known as the Anti-Federalists (Storing, 1981). Thomas Jefferson, for example, joined Thomas Paine philosophically (albeit not in practice as president) in offering the Rousseaunian argument that government stood in the way of the natural tendencies of the common citizen to "love and care for one another" (Wood, 2006, p. 210). Embodied in this contretemps was the spirit of civic republicanism. Thus, although some churches encouraged this tendency for religious reasons, others such as Jefferson sought to secularize human compassion in Kantian terms as an inherent moral sense discernable by human reason, if only government got out of the way. Paine (1995) put the matter succinctly in two deft phrases: (1) "society is produced by our wants, and government by our wickedness," and (2) society "promotes our happiness *positively* by uniting our affections, [government] *negatively* by restraining our vices" (p. 1).

Thus, as Burns (2006) writes more broadly of the Founding Era in words today's citizens and commentators do well to appreciate:

the Founding Fathers were not . . . a single entity, a group of men bound together by genius, good will, and identically defined concepts of love of country; in fact, they were not a group at all, but individuals in the most cantankerous sense, of men at odds with one another, often contemptuous of one another. The nation they bequeathed to posterity was more the result of the compromises they made grudgingly than the points to which they acceded with grace.

(p. 241)

And as John Roche (1961) earlier argued, the Constitution they created was less about principle than about instrumentalism (e.g., the three-fifths compromise regarding slaves in order to gain support in the South, but give the South less representation and electoral votes than if free men and slaves were counted equally).

In the end, these state-building compromises institutionalized in the US Constitution produced a federal government stronger in power by addressing the weaknesses of the Articles of Confederation. The latter had supplanted the dysfunctionally weak Continental Congress after the Revolution. The Articles of Confederation had included no power to impose taxes, facilitate interstate trade, or combat claims of state sovereignty, and it had impractically combined executive, legislative, and judicial tasks in one body, as had the Continental Congress. In more normative terms, and consonant with faculty psychology, Madison (echoing Montesquieu) wrote in Federalist 47 that "despotic power" would occur if the "accumulation of all powers legislative, executive, and judiciary [were put] in the same hands" (Wills, 1999, p. 89). This embrace of the idea of "mixed government"—touted by Aristotle, the Athenian statesman Solon, and Roman republicans—later served as the predicate for attacks on the federal bureaucracy in the 20th and 21st centuries. This, because agencies perform legislative, executive, and judicial functions. It also foreshadowed the persistent ability of opponents to thwart the building of administrative capacity commensurate with agencies' spiraling responsibilities.

The idea of emotional balance dominated by rationality was also central to creating a system of separation of powers (or different institutions sharing power), a bicameral congress, checks and balances, courts, and federalism. Not all the Founders believed in this governance framework. For example, Adams later chided Jefferson (and others such as Franklin) for initially "ridiculing" checks and balances, much as progressive reformers in the early 20th century would do. Their opposition was grounded partly in the thought of Enlightenment thinkers such as Anne Robert Jacques Turgot and Nicolas de Condorcet. But Adams joined Montesquieu and Locke in seeing checks and balances as "our only Security" against tyranny (Noyer, 2015).

Nonetheless, in this institutional framework, the theory was that passions and emotions were reflected in the House of Representatives (with representatives' two-year terms), reason was lodged in the US Senate (by senators' six-year terms), and virtue and wisdom in the federal courts (Howe, 2009). Not surprisingly, reality did not often comport with this theory. For example, between

1801 and 1835 under Chief Justice John Marshall, the wisdom of the courts did translate into answering debates over the meaning of the "separation of powers, the breadth of federal power, the relationship between the national government and the states, and the place of the Supreme Court in the government of a young nation" (Toobin, 2008, p. 86). Yet, the next 12 decades saw the Supreme Court showing a lack of wisdom in certain notable cases (e.g., racial bias in *Dred Scott v. Sandford* in 1857 and *Plessy v. Ferguson* in 1896, and corporate bias in *Lochner v. New York* in 1905).[6] Moreover, politics was hardly excluded from court decisions. For example, the Marshall court skewed heavily toward expanding the power of the federal government, while the Taney court lurched heavily toward restoring state power (Rehnquist, 2004).

Nor did debate over these divergent perspectives on governance end before or after adoption of the Constitution. Again, newspapers such as the *Boston Gazette* and the *Pennsylvania Gazette* dissembled the truth and served as provocateurs to advance the Whig and Loyalist causes during debates over ratification in the pre- and post-Revolutionary period. Elevating the discussion appreciably, the *Federalist Papers* (1788) were comprised of 85 essays serially published by Madison, Hamilton, and John Jay (under the pseudonym of "Publius") to support ratification of the Constitution.[7] But, after ratification, the dark side of reporting continued in newspapers, reaching levels of scurrilous political vitriol during the presidencies of George Washington and Thomas Jefferson.

Basically, two papers—the *Gazette of the United States* and the *National Gazette*—became political arms of the Federalist and Republican parties, respectively. Indeed, Hamilton and Jefferson funded and funneled succor in various forms (e.g., government printing contracts) to these outlets to serve as mouthpieces to advance their respective visions of governance and to undermine each other's reputation (Burns, 2006). They were joined in Anti-Federalist barrages by the *Philadelphia Aurora*, a paper founded by Benjamin Franklin Bache, the grandson of Benjamin Franklin. Writes Burns in words that should resonate—sadly—with contemporary readers:

> The atmosphere was toxic. . . . Americans were discouraged by the future, by the prospect that their government would not live up to their hopes, and they were discouraged by the present, by the acrimonious nature of the times, by a divisiveness that seemed to validate their pessimism about the years ahead. . . . As a result, men "who have been intimate all their lives, cross the streets to avoid meeting, and turn their heads another way, lest they should be obliged to touch their hats."
>
> (p. 245)

The application of faculty psychology principles to citizens and society also had another dark side. Part and parcel of the ascriptive tradition, not all citizens were deemed capable of personal development. This sentiment was ensconced in the Constitution's three-fifths compromise regarding slaves. This ensured the dominance of southern states in Congress until more territories entered the union and threatened that dominance. Compromises were sought in 1820 and 1850, but the Kansas–Nebraska Act of 1854 renouncing them led ultimately to the secession of the South from the Union and the Civil War in 1861.

Especially in the South, slaves were viewed as incapable of personal development and women as incapable of realizing the highest faculty of reason. Consider the fate of African Americans in the 18th and early 19th centuries. Congress passed legislation allowing only free, white males to vote or to be hired by the US Postal Service, a major source of federal employment during this time. Nor could women vote in this era (and they would not gain the franchise nationally until enactment of the 19th Amendment in 1920). As the feminist and transcendentalist Margaret Fuller later wrote, the problem at the core of traditional views of women was that the "gift of reason, Man's highest prerogative, is allotted to [women] in much lower degree" (Howe, 2009, p. 231). Women were stigmatized as "slaves to passion," a perception that began shifting in the early 19th century with the ideal of "Republican Motherhood" (see more below). For first- and second-generation Americans sharing this cultural view, women "were bearers of spiritual, moral, and aesthetic values" that they conveyed to their sons (p. 229).

Relatedly, as Fuller's unitarian and transcendentalist compatriots argued, the problem with faculty psychology was its focus on hierarchy and balance. They distinguished between "understanding" and "reason." Understanding was associated with knowing material things, while reason was associated with "self-transcendence" (or self-realization) that overcomes—not balances—understanding. Both were necessary, but reason (or rationality) had to triumph. Not surprisingly, Fuller not only felt that women had just as much capacity for self-transcendence as men, but they also were *more* predisposed to this trait.

Another aspect of ascriptive hierarchy associated with faculty psychology's emphasis on rationality and reason was the then dominant view regarding who qualified for public service. Only white males with property could vote, and public service was suitable only for the well-heeled, educated, and connected white male gentry. The preference was for individuals who no longer had to work, because they had already earned their fortunes. Men such as these would be more likely to work for the public interest, as opposed to their own parochial interests. Appropriately, until Andrew Jackson became president in 1829 and brought the idea of "rotation in office" to Washington, this period of American history was known as the "era of gentlemen."

****

Americans' self-conception of independence, individualism, anti-statism, and limited government was also most immediately advanced by the rise of evangelical fervor during the First (circa 1730–1760) and Second (circa 1800–1830) Great Awakenings. Certainly, these had their roots in the Protestant Reformation in the 16th century, which was itself a "radically libertarian revolution" against the all-encompassing authority structure and corruption of the Catholic Church hierarchy (Tarnas, 1991, p. 237). But during the First Great Awakening, a new view relating to state building arose of virtue and the role of government (McLoughlin, 1978; Noyer, 2015). Although the traditional churches stressed the role of government as denying "immoral" private interests and inculcating temperance and communal values among citizens, the First Great Awakening envisioned government acting "as the public's agent and not merely its disciplinarian" (p. 78). Also, New Light Presbyterians, Separate Baptists, Methodists, and itinerate preachers linked the "religious tyranny" of established churches (e.g., the Anglican Church) to "civic tyranny" (p. 78). Ironically, many of them did so while imposing religious tyranny on those who did not share their ecclesiastical views (Noyer, 2015).

Afoot at the same time during the pre-revolutionary evangelical era was a "Commonwealth Tradition" or "covenantal sensibility" that, itself, could be traced partially to the Hebraic tradition of the Israelites (Kirk, 2003). This religious tradition again stressed the superiority of society over government in meeting citizens' needs (material and spiritual). This early form of civic republicanism was community-oriented and focused on local self-help through voluntary efforts: "In the [civic] republican view, the colonial and Revolutionary ideal lay, not in the pursuit of private matters, but in the shared public life of civic duty, in the subordination of individual interests to the res publica" (Morone, 1998, p. 16).

Leaders of the American Revolution such as Jefferson—although often Deists themselves (e.g., Benjamin Franklin and Richard Henry Lee)—plugged into these evangelical sensibilities for their political ends. They told semiliterate citizens that they no longer needed to suffer old distinctions separating them from the landed gentry. The knowledge they acquired from their personal experiences—plus their exposure to newspapers, pamphlets, and evangelical preachers—gave them both the common and moral senses of traditional elites (McLoughlin, 1978). Wrought was an assault on the authority of "fathers, ministers, and magistrates" and a belief that "uncoerced cooperation and voluntary efforts could do the work of central government and established churches" (Appleby, 2001, p. 22). Both themes would play recurring roles in attacks on government and in calls for administrative reform from America's political Right over the next two centuries. In the interim, the obligations of citizens in this collective impulse of civic republicanism were profound—and sometimes disturbing. Wrote Benjamin Rush, citizens were "public property" with their "time and talents—[their] youth—manhood—old age—nay more, life, all belonging to [their] country" (Wakelyn, 2006, p. 953).

All this continued during the Second Great Awakening. During this evangelical revival, an "old Protestant ethic stressing rationality and order was superseded by an emotional version of the Christian doctrines of signs" (Appleby, 2001, p. 192). Itinerate lay evangelical preachers traversed the South and the Appalachian backcountry decrying organized religion and stressing personal relationships with God. Promoted implicitly in the process were the ideas of rugged, disciplined individualism and resistance to strong institutions, including government.

Evangelicalism thus established what cultural anthropologist Clifford Geertz calls a "cultural system," one that "synthesized Americans' ethos . . . the tone, character, and quality of their life . . . and their most comprehensive idea of order" in society (McLoughlin, 1978, p. 102). The consensus emerging from the Second Great Awakening was one of "self-help," volunteerism, and the idea that "government is best that governs least." Bequeathed to generations up to this day was what James Morone (1998) calls the "democratic wish" in America: there is little need for expertise; echoing David Hume, "common men with common sense" are sufficient for meeting the nation's challenges.

Also promoted were the foundations of Americans' millenarian self-conception that would play a major role in the future evolution of American administrative reform and compensatory state building. Both pre- and postmillennialist expectations flourished among evangelicals and 20th-century Pentecostals in America from the time of its earliest settlements. Premillennial expectations portrayed the return of Christ as necessary before the end of the world and the ushering in of heaven on earth. In contrast, postmillennialists saw "human effort contributing to the realization of God's providential plan" without the intervention of clerical or other intermediaries—including government (Howe, 2007, p. 285).

The Second Great Awakening thus harnessed the postmillennial zeal for good works pursued through volunteerism and the passion of believers with the idea that America was the "vanguard for the millennium": Americans' "destiny was not Europe's or mankind's but their own," its people were of a "new and special world," and their institutions "were beyond the capacities of decadent Europeans" (McLoughlin, 1978, pp. 102–105). A general feeling emerged that "material improvements, political democratization, and moral reform all provided encouraging signs that [American] history was moving in the right direction," away from premillennial end-of-days predictions (Howe, 2007, p. 286). Central to this view was the evangelical concept of covenant theology. With origins in Presbyterianism and the otherwise intolerant New England Puritanism, covenant theology afforded a cosmology for placing day-to-day events and choices in religious perspective, a cosmology designating America as God's favored nation and its founding as God's design for "satisfy[ing] his ultimate aims" (Bailyn, 1992, p. 32).

The new narrative offered in the Second Great Awakening by leaders such as Lyman Beecher and Nathaniel Taylor helped create what Perry Miller has called a "romantic nationalism" in America (McLoughlin, 1978, p. 106). It was a nationalism that would echo throughout US history—for good and for ill. Americans—largely Protestant Americans, that is—were said to be a "new and special race" shorn of the incapacities

> of decadent Europeans, superstitious Roman Catholics, ignorant heathen, or "colored" races to imitate. God had created a unique people and elected them to establish [American] institutions throughout the world; they were to uplift inferior peoples who, lacking the innate capacity for republicanism, might at least be converted or adapted to it if they could learn to assimilate the ways of Christian America.
>
> (pp. 105–106)

Also informed by evangelical tenets were the foundations of the proxy component of the compensatory state in America. Interestingly, but not surprisingly given their marginalized status in society, women were the most ardent supporters of revivalism during the Second Great Awakening. They showed "entrepreneurial prowess" in fundraising for itinerant preachers' teaching, pay, and housing. Some evangelical activities took place in their homes—to the consternation of husbands who did not share their enthusiasm. In fact, their homes often became the location of new religious societies after the departure of circuit-riding preachers, paving the way for volunteer associations carrying on religious work and services in the community.

Thousands of voluntary associations were created during this time, including those dealing with slavery and temperance issues that governments at all levels refused to address (Appleby, 2001; Howe, 1979; Remini, 2008). These included the American Bible Society, the African Colonization Society, the American Temperance Society, and the Home and Foreign Mission District Association. At the same time, many local religious societies morphed—sometimes with government encouragement—into loose–tight networks of confederated national associations doing the work done by governments in other nations. Included among these were the American Bible Society, the American Sunday School Union, the American Home Missionary Society, the Peace Society, the Society for Bettering the Condition and Increasing the Comforts of the Poor, and the Ladies' Association for the Benefit of Gentlewomen of Good Family. So impressive was this effort that contemporaries referred to these interdenominational organizations as the "Evangelical United Front" or the "Benevolent Empire."

As such, evangelicals' philanthropic efforts often compensated for state gaps in services created by the otherwise positive social mobility of this era, and in effect, they became administrative reformers in the emerging compensatory state. Evangelicals won many supporters who were impressed with their focus both on self-reliance and on building "civic spirit" for realizing the millenarian ends of American exceptionalism. Joyce Appleby (2001) writes:

> Evangelicalism normalized ardor . . . not just by reviving religion but in summoning converts to be public witnesses to [civic republican] virtue. Women flocked to the churches, where they found activities inspired by high-mindedness and an authority greater than their husband's. Young people turned their clubs into surrogates for the families that many had left behind. Affinity became the great cement when ties of family and community frayed. Reformers were passionate; their imagery appealed to the sentiments [rather than business "rationality"]. With words they created a solidarity among lovers of justice and dispensers of sympathy. Toiling in the field of virtue created bonds of affection and support.
> (p. 235)

Likewise, de Tocqueville (2012) observed that, unlike European churches that were typically allied with conservatism and elite society, American churches stressed freedom. "The Americans," he wrote, "combine the notions of Christianity and of liberty so intimately in their minds that it is impossible to make them conceive the one without the other" (p. 306). These ideas also created the enduring appeal to Americans of the embrace of "common men and common sense" rather than elites having special insights. Thus, while the educated were reading Locke's *Essay Concerning Human Understanding* (in which he valued knowledge received through the senses rather than purely through intellectual reasoning or church dogmatism) and Plutarch's *Lives* (stressing personal virtue as the highest aim of leaders), the lower classes attending evangelical tent revivals were gaining a sense for the same ideas.

****

Yet another factor grounded in American exceptionalist values was the resolution of a fundamental split between Hamiltonians and Jeffersonians over how visible a role the federal government should play in Americans' lives (Caldwell, 1988). Among other things, Hamiltonians (who came to be known as Federalists and sometime sympathizers with the British crown) thought it best to make federal government initiatives very visible to citizens. They also stressed the need for a national vision that would gain the allegiance of elite citizens to the federal government rather than to their states.

Secretary of the Treasury Hamilton did so by, among other things, (1) assuming state debts incurred during the Revolution, thereby nationalizing them; (2) successfully advocating for the creation of a national bank to provide a reliable currency, manage the nation's finances, and provide loans to industry; (3) using temporary tariffs and import quotas to protect infant industries; and (4) promoting "mixed enterprises," whereby public and private funds were comingled to stimulate industrial investment. Hamilton did so most notably in his *Report on Manufactures* (1791). What is more, and reminiscent of some of today's supply-side economics proponents, he argued that any "public debt" incurred by the federal government was a "public blessing" (Wilentz, 2005, p. 48). Debt holders would have a stake in the new nation surviving.

Conversely, Jeffersonians thought it best to *hide* the visibility of government initiatives so as not to alarm citizens (especially Anti-Federalists) who embraced limited government. They also feared centralization of authority in Washington after decades of the dominance of localism, as well as a return to monarchical tyranny (Balogh, 2009). They viewed Hamiltonian Federalists as trying to concentrate authority, as favoring the upper classes over average citizens, and as a direct threat to individual liberty. Embracing localism over cosmopolitanism, individual rights over collective responsibilities, and common sense (amateurism) over elite expertise, Jeffersonians "linked local autonomous governance to concentric bands of allegiance, ultimately extending across the continent" (p. 113). It was such sensibilities that progressives in the 20th century later sought to end.

They also believed—in true Rousseaunian Romantic fashion—that society was naturally harmonious and grounded in agricultural virtue. They feared that the Hamiltonian Federalists' emphasis on industrial development would undermine that virtue. Primarily, they worried that industrial policy would

> ally the federal government to a particular class of speculators, create (through the national bank) a means to dispense bounties to political favorites and bribes to opponents, and introduce what Madison called the "corrupt influence" of "substituting the motive of private interest in place of public duty."
>
> (Wilentz, 2005, p. 48)

To be sure, both Jeffersonians and Hamiltonians embraced a national developmental vision for the nation, as well as a commitment to commerce. Moreover, as president, Jefferson took two major actions—the Louisiana Purchase (1803) and the Embargo Act (1807) against British goods—that flew in the face of Jeffersonianism. He also came to realize, as a consequence of his embargo, that the nation could not survive without a vibrant manufacturing system. But, initially, the question was how to reconcile government-led national development with a commitment to free markets and localism, especially in the midst and aftermath of the War of 1812 and economic crashes.

Enter James Madison. He offered the idea of a "commercial republic" (Elkin, 2006; O'Connor, 2014) as the sine qua non for a just American society and, thus, for avoiding the decline of earlier republics since antiquity.[8] For Madison, as for Locke, the essence of governance was to create a political regime that protected private property (meaning land and other concrete goods) as essential to political freedom. But that regime simultaneously had to ensure that the pursuits of the interests of the propertied would redound to the general welfare of all. Madison contended that the spread of commerce itself would create conflicting interests, which then would have to compromise by building legislative majorities to protect their self-interests.[9] Pitting the ambition of some against the ambition of others in a system of separate institutions sharing power, checks and balances, legislative bicameralism, and federalism afforded the best approximation of a public interest.

In taking this position, Madison challenged the conventional wisdom that private interests were bad and that republics must be limited in scale to be responsive to citizens. Madison argued that a better balancing of interests would take place in an extended territorial republic, as more interests—meaning wider perspectives, not interest groups—would have to be accommodated to gain governing majorities. This view contrasted with the Anti-Federalists, who argued that the inherent pluralism of extended republics (such as the Roman Empire) produced ungovernability, lack of fair representation, and ultimately tyranny by a narrow elite. Nonetheless, America's self-conception as a national (i.e., extended) commercial republic was born from Madison's premises, as was sealed the aforementioned link between commerce and democracy. This, again, to the consternation of conservatives and observers such as de Tocqueville that materialism would become crass absent a link to traditional moral values (Kirk, 1986).

But this still begged the question of how a nation ensconced in the self-conception of American exceptionalist values could best meet its growing domestic needs, as well as military threats from the British, French, and Spanish territories surrounding the United States. Consonant with American exceptionalist values, one critical answer was to eschew Hamilton's prescription after the Federalists lost office and to *hide* the visible size of government (although Federalist tendencies continued under Chief Justice John Marshall's leadership on the Supreme Court). Consequently, hiding the visible size of government by using proxy actors (i.e., subnational governments, the private sector, and voluntary groups) (Light, 1999, 2019) as part of a compensatory state has roots in the Founding Era, not in the late 20th century. The size, complexity, and scope of the federal government are much greater today but not as a percentage of what government tried to do or wanted to accomplish through subnational and cross-sectoral proxies and networks in the 18th and 19th centuries. Moreover, as subsequent chapters show, this tendency to address public problems with a compensatory state has been amplified ever since the nation's founding.

As noted in Chapter 1, the federal government did not levy a direct tax on citizens, relying instead on import tariffs and land sales (Balogh, 2009). It also, in effect, hid tax collectors (the bane of the colonists) by placing them at the nation's borders and coastlines only and relied on local militia while stationing the US cavalry out of citizens' sight (e.g., on the western frontier). In addition, it relied on grants, subsidies, quotas, mandates, and pressures for conformance to coax subnational governments, private companies, and volunteer groups to advance its agenda.

So well hidden was the role of the federal government, and so visible that of the private and voluntary sectors, that Americans persuaded themselves that their growing commercial success had little to do with government actions (Appleby, 2001). This connection was further abetted by the "democratization of credit," whereby banks—not government agencies—produced the financial capital to fund the entrepreneurialism at the heart of the nation's economic growth. The underlying premise of this democratization of credit was ensconced in faculty psychology, amateurism, and humanist sentiments: anyone with common sense, drive, and desire could create and manage a business. Again, observers such as de Tocqueville (1830) argued that this "absorption in getting and spending will undermine man's disposition to the infinite, to the spiritual, and so diminish his humanity. Such avarice also is harmful to the social structure that makes such a pursuit of wealth possible" (Kirk, 1986, ch. 6, passim). But their concerns went unheeded.

Internationally, a similar rationale consistent with Americans' millenarian vision existed. Robert Kagan (2006) writes that Americans tended throughout the 19th century to believe the Enlightenment's conceit that

> free peoples were less likely to make war, especially against other free peoples. . . [and] they believed commerce tended on the whole, to draw people closer and reduce the likelihood of conflict. . . . [They] believed a world reformed along [economic] liberal and republican lines would be a safer world for their liberal republic, and that a freer and multiplying commerce would make them a more prosperous nation.
>
> (p. 64)

This Enlightenment liberalism view has persistently jousted with "realists" in international relations theory who dispute this generalization as contingent on circumstances, and with the ideas of noninterventionism and isolationism, to drive US foreign policy to this day (Thrall & Friedman, 2016).

Regardless, by 1815, writes Gordon Wood (2009b), Americans were "one of the most highly commercialized people in the world. . . [exhibiting] the almost universal ambition to get forward. . . [and] nowhere in the Western world was business and working for profit more praised or honored" (p. 2). Nowhere, as well, were the fruits of this philosophy more abundantly realized than in America. Between 1790 and 1840, per capita income growth of Americans increased from .05 percent to 1.5–2.0 percent each year (Wright, 2003).

Most notable in this regard was the political economy discussed earlier whereby the federal government afforded subsidies for, and licensing arrangements with, private companies; issued bonds for internal improvements; and expanded loans to individuals by the state-chartered banking and finance industries of the day. For example, by 1820, a federal government "hidden in plain sight" used subsidies to speed communication and commerce and to build nearly 2,300 post offices and 4,400 post roads in America, creating thousands of jobs in the process (Robertson & Judd, 1989). Thus, from the nation's founding, distinctions between public and private actors were "blurred." What Barry Bozeman (1987, 2004) labeled "publicness" in the late 20th century undergirded America's compensatory state values from the nation's birth.

****

During the founding period, the legitimacy of the idea of a commercial republic as the way to escape history was buttressed by its creation of new occupations and few artificial barriers to class mobility in America (for white males). Writes Appleby (2001):

> Opportunity, mobility, and egalitarian zeal worked together to sap older ways of thinking about social position. A sprawling, inclusive American middle class composed of families known for their respectability, their material competence, and their identification with a progressive model of human endeavor came into power, drawing individuals from all the ranks of colonial society.
>
> (p. 21)

These occupations were called "professions," despite the largely apprentice-based training for them rather than formal certification. They included civil engineers, doctors, explorers, lawyers, politicians, printers, publishers, and schoolteachers. For example, the rise of the commercial republic prompted a dramatic increase in the number of schools and teaching jobs in America (Appleby, 2001). This, due to the centrality of literacy and statistical computation to a commercial republic. Teaching jobs also were avenues for personal independence, economic insurance, and social mobility into other occupations, especially for younger persons in rural areas outside the South. Moreover, because teachers earned low pay, turnover in teaching was high, as teachers moved into other professions as soon as an opportunity existed. This created the need for more teachers.

As literacy and humanism spread, demand for reading materials other than the Bible soared. By 1810, the number of books published by new publishing houses reached about 150—books on such commercially relevant topics as agriculture and horticulture, mechanics, and statistics. By 1822, the publishing industry had grossed between $2 million and $3 million (Burns, 2006). This growth came in no small part from federal government subsidies for both post roads and newspaper mailings (see more below).

The commercial republic also made lawyering an avenue for economic and social mobility and a conduit for challenging existing authority structures in America. The creation of new towns on the East Coast and west of the Appalachians created a sizeable need for lawyers to deal with bankruptcies, estate auctions, and the recording of land titles. Typically, and again consonant with the idea of faculty psychology, those interested in legal careers apprenticed with others and then read for the law, with many going into politics. The 25 state legislatures existing in 1820, for example, required the selection of nearly 3,000 legislators, while the reapportionment that accompanied the first five ten-year censuses increased representation in the House of Representatives from 105 to 240 (Crenson, 1975). In the process, lawyers in politics began replacing clergymen as the dominant authority structure in society, and the former political dominance of the eastern seaboard states shifted to the western states. Lawyers became the trusted interpreters of current events—until their corruption helped sow the seeds for the Jacksonian revolution discussed in the next chapter.

Also contributing to economic mobility and the questioning of established authority structures in the commercial republic was the attraction to careers in medicine. But this profession, too, fell into many Americans' infatuation with the idea of amateurism: "common sense" was all that was needed to practice medicine (see, e.g., Balogh, 2009; Crenson, 1975; Howe, 1979). To be sure, nine schools graduated 225 individuals as doctors in 1817. Many of these graduates created advanced medical techniques and revealed the absurdity of many prior medical claims. Meanwhile, educated Americans devoured articles on medicine, thus increasing the status of physicians. By 1823, nearly 10,000 physicians— mostly without any formal education—practiced medicine in the United States. And like many lawyers in this period, many turned out to be incompetent or corrupt—thus again sowing the crisis of moral authority among "professions" that helped later spawn the Jacksonian revolution.

****

The commercial republic and the compensatory state also created a need for skilled managers. But the "art of organizing, coordinating, and directing the work of many individuals toward a single end was in fact a 'mystery'" (White, 1948, p. 473). The businesses that existed did not operate on even the limited scale that federal departments of this time operated. Manufacturers having hundreds of employees were rare. Consequently, there were few lessons to be gleaned from them, other than the intuitive "virtues of individual enterprise and personal responsibility in the management of small affairs" (p. 473). This lack of management knowledge was also a limiting factor in several of the Founders' policy initiatives, including Hamilton not establishing branches of the First Bank of the United States (1791).

This is not to say that management skills needed in the federal government were not available. Transferable skills existed in the areas of financial administration, purchasing, and clerkships. Writes Leonard White (1948), the "job of middle-management, especially in the customs and internal revenue offices [that comprised the overwhelming proportion of federal jobs], was on the whole well done" (pp. 475–476). Also adequate from knowledge honed in the merchant and trade businesses were positions for managing supplies, as well as other clerk positions where only reading and writing skills were needed.

Still, because businesses lacked general administrative theories for large-scale organizations, they had considerably less legitimacy than the military did for giving management advice. Thus, the Army became the favorite organizational model for government managers and gained first-mover advantages. Army veterans from the Revolution onward were a primary recruitment pool for federal departments, as well as for business. These recruits brought with them what would later be called a Weberian model of bureaucracy (based on sociologist Max Weber's "ideal" model), incorporating clear rationality-centered ideas on structure, division of labor, hierarchy, and control as the best approach to gaining economy and efficiency in organizations.

Also propelling the IRP-based focus on bureaucratic administration during this era was what would become the enduring quest for accountability in public agencies, especially given Americans' negative experiences with their British colonial governors and administrators. Launched partially in the process was America's fixation on instrumental rather than constitutive perspectives on the role of public managers.[10] Specifically, the approach established by various congresses and presidents (as well as subnational governors, mayors, and legislatures) in the compensatory state was one favoring the hierarchical subordination of agencies to elected officials.

Yet, as White (1948, 1951) summarizes for the Federalist and Jeffersonian Republican years, although Congress gave minimal levels of discretion and detailed supervision of *subordinate officials* in departments and agencies, it gave presidents and their department heads wide discretionary authority. Department heads, after all, were approved by Congress. Still, and ever since, discretion also varied across agencies based on their tasks. For example, vast amounts of discretion were given to officials in customs houses and post offices (in what would become sources of rampant political corruption). Not surprisingly, given reasons related to why the Revolution was fought, decidedly less discretion was given to matters of taxation.

Significant institutional and party differences also existed regarding to whom public managers were most accountable. For its part, the Supreme Court paid scant attention to agencies per se during the Marshall court's reign. Instead, it quite logically focused on such things as establishing its own power as a co-equal branch to declare congressional laws unconstitutional (*Marbury v. Madison* in 1803); the federal government's power to regulate under the Commerce Clause (*Gibbons v. Ogden* in 1824), and the extent of federal power under the Necessary and Proper Clause (*McCulloch v. Maryland* in 1819).

Meanwhile, the Federalists worried less than the Jeffersonians about executive power, and they worried more about executive impotence. Although accepting reporting requirements to Congress on plans and proposals, their appointees vigorously fought what they saw as congressional encroachments on their authority, including the organization of federal agencies. Within federal agencies, however, both the Federalists and Jeffersonians mimicked the military approaches noted earlier. As White (1948) summarizes, for instance, the Federalists

> gathered all the activities of government into three departments so that nothing was left at loose ends. They insisted that single officials bear the responsibility for administration rather than boards. They provided everywhere for due subordination and for authority commensurate with responsibility.
>
> (p. 513)

When it came to personnel, the "moral standards of the Federalist public service were extraordinarily high" (White, 1948, p. 514). So impressive were they for the most part that the Jeffersonian Republicans "declined to undo the work of their predecessors or to delegate some branches of federal administration . . . to the states" (White, 1951, p. 551). This, despite their platforms of restricting federal power and transferring power to the states. Writes White, the "Jeffersonians . . . carried the Federalist administrative machine forward without substantial alteration in form or in spirit for nearly three decades" (p. 558).

As Brian Cook (2014) writes, this stress by both parties on an instrumental rather than constitutive perspective on the role of the federal bureaucracy did not come without debate during this period. Tracing the roots of the instrumental model to Congress' famous Decision of 1789 over the removal powers of presidents (resolved in *Marbury*), for example, Cook shows how the six days of debate surrounding that decision were comprised of both perspectives. He writes that an instrumental perspective "conceived of public administrators, both heads of departments and 'inferior officers,' as pure agents . . . of the 'political' branches . . . aid[ing] the president and Congress in the performance of their constitutional duties and . . . undertak[ing] any other tasks assigned to them" (p. 33). The second perspective viewed the bureaucracy as having its own constitutive powers. Cook notes that "administrative officials, or department heads at the very least, [were] constitutional officers in their own right and just as legal as political subordinates" (p. 33). Such a perspective at least "implied" that federal agencies were a "distinctive, semiautonomous institution in the constitutional scheme" (p. 33).

Still, despite efforts by congressional Republicans to increase oversight of the executive branch, as well as Jefferson's successful efforts to shrink the size of the federal government and reduce its administrative capacity, the hierarchical propensities of the instrumental perspective held over from the Federalists still prevailed in most instances. Conspicuously absent during these founding years, however, was any thought of direct citizen involvement; only indirect representation through elected officials was ever pursued, a pattern replicated for the most part in future chapters. Direct involvement came only by means of voluntary efforts as part of the compensatory state.

One irony of the triumph of instrumentalism was that the idea of dual control of the bureaucracy, when coupled with the necessary discretion wielded by agencies, revealed the essential "governing role" (i.e., the constitutive role) that agencies had to play in this period. This occurred as agencies often pitted their presidential and congressional "principals" off against each other, efforts replicated throughout American history. Examples of this dynamic abounded, from the constitutive policymaking role played by officials (naval officers, revenue assessors and collectors, and US attorneys) interpreting Jefferson's ill-fated embargo to the programs established by national Republicans later implementing Henry Clay's (Whig, National Republican, Democratic-Republican-KY) American System of economic development (see more in Chapter 3).

****

As noted earlier, women and blacks, on average, did not fare as well as white men in terms of economic and social mobility during this time.[11] But they also made notable gains and contributions to state development and administration. Many played key roles in the volunteer associations that were crucial proxy components of the compensatory state, a host of which started with the encouragement, if not prodding, of federal, state, and local governments.

Starting in the 1790s with the first women's academy and continuing through the early 20th century, the idea of Republican Motherhood necessarily meant that young women had to be educated. In the process, many women became teachers in academies, and some with family resources even started their own academies of learning. Doing so meant not just becoming proficient in reading, writing, and mathematics to prepare their sons for business and public careers. It also meant mastering the classics (that were so frequently quoted or referenced in political discourse) and the natural sciences. What many clergy *forbade* them to read, however, were fiction novels, which were very popular in this era. The clergy saw novels as working against civic virtue, because they degraded morality, were not factual, were too titillating, and "played promiscuously with the imagination" (Appleby, 2001, p. 178). Also, the clergy argued that, because women had less knowledge of the ways of the world, they would be especially vulnerable to calls from novels for placing "love over other obligations" and to the "sinful passions" recounted.

Amid all these opportunities and constraints, an early "old girl's network" began to flourish within the compensatory state, one that would amplify over the years. This, as academy graduates hired younger graduates, raised revenue for new schools and seminaries, and made other women aware of these opportunities. Also, a cottage industry of schools in homes developed, a forerunner of today's homeschooling movement. Other women became writers, editors, or publishers, with many jousting with their pens against such inequities as gender-based pay inequality, slavery, and the lack of women's suffrage.

Southern blacks did not gain similar immediate benefits. They, too, experienced family fragmentation, but this was not from government support of their individualism, entrepreneurialism, or economic betterment. Theirs came from the forced breakup of families by slaveowners. In its early years, the evangelical movement was most interested in addressing the slavery issue. This interest later waned in the early 20th century after the Scopes Trial brought secular disdain for their values and in the late 20th century after the Civil Rights Act, the Voting Rights Act, and the countercultural movement.

Part of their earlier position was sincere, but it also was motivated by a desire to increase church membership rolls by admitting blacks (McLoughlin, 1978). And, in attending evangelical revival meetings, powerful religious conversion experiences led many blacks—both men and women—to become itinerate preachers themselves. Perhaps the most famous of these preachers were Sojourner Truth, John Stewart, Richard Allen, and John Bishop. Respectively, they were noted for preaching against slavery, establishing ministries among Native Americans, becoming the first black bishop in the African Methodist Episcopal Church, and becoming the first black pastor at a white Baptist Church. Importantly, by effectively performing their roles as itinerant preachers, teachers, and writers, they (and other blacks) helped place slavery—state-enforced as it was in this era—at the heart of political discourse. Their activities sorely undermined arguments that blacks lacked the capacity to function effectively as citizens. In doing so, they added tinder to what would later flame into the South's secession from the Union, the Civil War, and, eventually, their emancipation.

****

This conversion of beliefs, somewhat ascriptive social mobility, and the rise of the compensatory state did not happen spontaneously. Ideas are important, but they need coalitions of actors to push them to fruition. In this case, the first element in this nexus of interests advancing the idea of the commercial republic were the investment bankers, businesspersons, and land seekers who also stood to benefit monetarily from an expansion of the compensatory state. To be sure, the First

(1791) and Second (1816) Bank of the United States created and renewed as national entities contributed to—and benefited monetarily from—the democratization of capital. But, more generally, financial, business, and property interests were central to promoting—and benefiting financially from—the compensatory state with its subsidies, deregulation, and protection of new industries. Central to their supremacy in the political economy that arose was the Founders' aforementioned choice to eschew a direct tax on income to hide the visible size of the federal government. Combined with Jefferson's retirement of the national debt and his fatally flawed and mismanaged embargo against the British (1807), plus the costs of the War of 1812, the federal government grew increasingly dependent on the wealthy and on state-chartered banks to finance American economic development.

The economic historian Gavin Wright (2003) summarizes the situation and implications of these resource-dependency dynamics:

> As in the financial revolution of eighteenth century Europe, prudent management of government debt contributed to the institutional evolution of the capital market, widening opportunities for public and private agents to raise funds for ambitious new products. Among the first to respond were state-chartered banks, whose securities were second only to those of the [national] government as objects of investment and trade. The constitution deprived the states of the power to issue money, but not the power to charter banks, an indirect means of expanding the money supply (through note issue) and gaining revenue (or credit on favorable terms).
>
> (p. 397)

Thus, the states' independent banking systems were vital, albeit somewhat constrained, compensatory levers for realizing the nation's expressive motives of economic development and continental expansion. But state banks also benefited financially and through infrastructure development within and across political jurisdictions. A geographically integrated and significant network of traders in US securities existed in America by the 1790s. Although only three state banks existed in 1790, by 1835, 584 banks had been chartered by the states (Sylla, Legler, & Wallis, 1987). In addition, beginning in 1815, improvements in transportation that meshed private and public interests were largely state-sponsored and subsidized. Moreover, much of the development money for state-owned or subsidized canal companies—most notably, the Erie Canal—was provided by overseas bondholders (Wright, 2003).

As Wright (2003) also observes, the constituencies joining the financial community to drive these programs were comprised of "coalitions of urban merchants competing for trade, and landowners hoping for capital gains on their property" (p. 397). These coalitions cut across state boundaries, allowing them to leverage federal and state capital for national purposes. In fairness, and aside from Hamilton, the national government did not always actively promote national economic development until 1816 to 1828, when it offered a protectionist response to the "British System" of free trade and laissez-faire that was sorely disadvantaging the United States.[12] That response was comprised of a national bank, tariffs, and federally subsidized infrastructure development. Jackson's opposition to this early "American System" led to successful efforts to revive it by Henry Clay and the Whig Party in the 1830s and 1840s (see Chapter 3).

Further advancing the compensatory state in the commercial republic, and central components of it, were the institutional mechanisms used to advance infrastructure development. Most prominent among these for their implications for the evolution of American administrative reform and state building were the rise of private and municipal corporations (Nelson, 1982). The idea of using these types of corporations was not inevitable, however. They, too, were pushed by commercial interests in response to the historical–structural mismatch they claimed.

As is common throughout the expansion of the US compensatory state over its history, federal and state-chartered corporations and quasigovernment corporations were "sold" rhetorically by commercial interests as administrative reform mechanisms. These reforms would afford greater economy, efficiency, flexibility, and agility than would government agencies. Proponents also claimed that they would allow greater availability of credit without spending public funds. In effect, these arguments were the first of subsequent administrative reform calls for "running government like a business" (e.g., the technocratic progressives in the early 20th century), for quasi-public corporations (e.g., the Tennessee Valley Authority), and for associationalism in the 20th and 21st centuries.

This corporate format was attractive to economic elites during these years for several reasons. It effectively delegated state authority to private actors to do inherently government functions—something that contemporary public administration scholarship typically treats as a late 20th-century phenomenon (e.g., Durant, Girth, & Johnston, 2009; Johnston & Romzek, 2010). As consciously scripted by governments as part of the compensatory state, these corporations exercised such powers as seizing property under eminent domain, printing banknotes as currency, suing parties, and hiring and firing contractors. These corporations also gained legal status as "persons" under the law, a status subsequently supported in a series of major US Supreme Court decisions beginning with *Dartmouth College v. Woodward* (1819).[13]

At the same time, Andrew Schocket (2007) argues,

> corporations could allow a small group of individuals to control vast resources with the power of the state behind them but with little oversight, and thus the corporate form could be a recipe for constructive entrepreneurship, for self-interested exploitation of the public trust, or

for downright rascality less likely with public institutions and on a scale far greater than with private institutions.

(p. 7)

Membership in state- and municipal-chartered corporations, after all, was given to disengaged investors buying private corporate bonds or paying taxes, in the case of state or municipal corporations. Corporate officers then set their own bylaws and administrative structures to advance their interests.

As Schocket (2007) summarizes, the power of corporate elites "stemmed from their control of large amounts of capital, mostly raised from stockholders or bondholders with little interest in how the money was administered, and corporate insiders' leverage over resources essential to others' economic success" (p. 9). By the early 1820s, evidence of abuse by private and public corporations involved in the commercial republic clearly showed a paradox of democratic capitalism: "democracy and opportunity on the one hand, consolidated power on the other" (p. 5). For instance, these corporations decided the location of infrastructure developments and disinvestment; toll rates (and, hence, commodity prices); to whom water power would be granted or withheld; and what kinds of boats could use waterways. These afforded opportunities for favoritism and favor selling that were often taken.

Moreover, even in policy areas where public charters still dominated, corporations used their economic power to advance public policies redounding to their benefit, build new coalitions of dependency on them, and curtail criticism of their actions by newspapers afraid to jeopardize their lines of credit at banks. Created or expanded in the process were family fortunes, institutions, and growing class divisions that helped shape politics, economics, and wealth gaps for decades to come—and, more immediately, set the stage for Jacksonianism. Those disadvantaged by this authority structure became convinced that "politics and administration must be taken from the hands of a social elite or a body of bureaucratic specialists [in corporations and government] and [be] open to mass participation" (Schocket, 2007, p. 66).

****

The second major element of the nexus of interests reinforcing ideas of individualism, challenges to existing authority structures, and the use of the scientific method borrowed from the natural sciences were the early precursors of social science thinking and methodology in America (Berlin, 1992). Proponents of these ideas relied heavily on Renaissance (circa 1350–1650) and (especially) "long 18th-century" (1685–1815) Enlightenment thinkers such as Francis Bacon, René Descartes, John Locke, Isaac Newton, Benedict de Spinoza, and Voltaire. In the process, they challenged the oppressive hand of authority in all fields, but especially in religion and politics.

Although American proponents of these ideas shared evangelicals' anti-authority sentiments, their focus (as noted) was on reason and knowledge acquired through experience rather than the Bible, superstition, divine revelation, emotionalism, or abuse of power. Previously, and despite Aquinas' efforts in the 13th century to link reason and religion, the Catholic Church contended that knowledge and truth of the natural and social world could be discerned only through mediators such as priests and royalty. Enlightenment thinkers such as Descartes in his *Meditations on First Philosophy* argued that rational thought alone allowed all persons to become knowledgeable. Needed only were objective "facts" from which to reason, facts undiluted by personal "desire, bias, and motivation" (Barrett, 2015, p. 60). Prior to them, Scholastics (circa 1100–1700) such as Roger Bacon, William of Ockham, and Duns Scotus offered a similar perspective. Their focus was on dialectical reasoning, albeit with different goals (creating and defending church dogma) and means (conclusions were drawn largely from abstract reason without the benefit of empirical grounding). Put simply for all, however, "reliable knowledge was to be the arsenal of reason, and reason would be the force which led to rational change" (Postman, 1999, p. 25; also see Berlin, 1992). Decoupled from religious purposes was the linkage of direct experience, observation, reasoning, and measurement.

Moreover, for American proponents of Enlightenment thinking, the "logic of mathematics"—a touchstone of both the physical sciences and the corporate–social science nexus of interests ever since—was the best "language" for acquiring such knowledge and understanding causality. Ordinary language could not capture objective reality accurately (some, such as George Berkeley, even argued that an objective reality did not exist). This, because mathematics' structure "coincided more precisely with the structure of reality" (Postman, 1999, p. 63). Stripping the ambiguity of spoken language away would leave the scientific enterprise with "testable questions concerning human social life" (p. 63). The answers to these questions would then help preserve American exceptionalism's millenarian vision. In the 18th and 19th centuries, those questioning the ability of inductive reasoning to explain causality (e.g., philosopher Arthur Schopenhauer and Russian novelist Fyodor Dostoevsky) would see rationality as the slave of emotions or persons' wills. This, in contrast to positivists such as Francis Bacon, Auguste Comte, and Henri de Saint-Simon, who claimed that only the scientific methodology of the physical sciences (informed by Descartes' "reductionism" of the world to what can be known mathematically) afforded objective knowledge and revealed causality. It thus had to be the "preferred form of knowledge" in America (Ross, 1991, p. 17), just as Bertrand Russell and Ludwig Wittgenstein would later argue in the 20th century.

This IRP-grounded perspective first gained traction in America during this time period with the advent of the Republican Arithmetik movement noted earlier (Cohen, 1999). For proponents, "mathematics [was] a form of logic, which stretched the mind and improved the faculty for reasoning" (p. 81). In the process, the common interests of the corporate world, administration, and emerging social science thinking took root. Prominent between 1800 and 1820 was a reaction against colonial impressions that mathematics was a "trivial amusement" (p. 117). As democratic capitalism exponentially expanded the number of Americans doing business, numeracy was added to school curricula traditionally limited to reading and writing.

As Cohen (1999) observes, the claim was that mathematics and statistics afforded a degree of uniformity among otherwise disparate and complex dynamics in society. This was a society that badly needed some way to reduce complexity and give it a semblance of order. As noted, the commercial republic had uprooted or split apart families, fostered growing income gaps, demolished existing authority structures, and rendered traditional trades obsolete. Cohen writes: "It is possible to add apples and oranges if the problem is to know how much *fruit* there is. Numbers and statistics also allow one to sort out narratives regarding causality and probabilities of events" (p. 43; emphasis added). This logic, as future chapters will illustrate, is redolent in the IRP pursued by social scientists and administrative reformers ever since.

Granted, calculation and bookkeeping were necessary in all commercial endeavors, thus making numeracy critical to the commercial republic. But the legitimacy of numeracy and statistical analyses as worthy skills and topics of study are actually traceable to ministers. They saw the regularities that aggregate mortality statistics revealed as confirming their fatalistic image of a God who controlled their fate. But when these data were disaggregated, or different localities did their own analyses, it became clear that death rates varied geographically. This suggested that environmental factors were at work, factors that could be affected through human intervention (e.g., better sanitation).

As Cohen (1999) also notes, the "idea that God had ordained the time of everyone's death and that one's life-span . . . was fixed in advance" was undercut by statistical analysis (p. 92). In the process, "fatalism and uncertainty began to give way to [the idea that] control and predictability [by humankind was possible], exercised through the medium of numbers" (p. 84). Thus, in terms of an American self-conception, a sense of human agency emerged via statistics, one that would later blossom into a nexus of business and social science interests linking the scientific method to social and administrative issues.

Again, however, women and minorities were still marginalized in this American self-conception due to the ascriptive hierarchy noted earlier. In an era of Republican Motherhood, "sons might well learn moral precepts at the mothers' knees, but Euclid's geometry could come only from Euclid" (Cohen, 1999, p. 141). Moreover, although basic mathematics needed to run households was appropriate for women, to move to the higher levels needed in business would have been an admission that "commerce, progress, and logical reasoning" were faculties held by both men and women (p. 140). Such a concession was anathema in this period. Preserving the separation of the ideal woman from the "crass materialism" of commerce was necessary. In the process, both rationality and commerce were "masculinized" mathematically in ways that today's women are still too often confronted by in business; in the fields of science, technology, engineering, and mathematics; and in leadership positions in public and private organizations.

****

The preceding has reviewed the "initial conditions" establishing America's self-conception during the first and second generations of the Founders. Reviewed have been the political, military, social, economic, psychological, philosophical, technological, and religious sources of this self-conception. This chapter has also presented this conception's grounding in American exceptionalist values, noted the contention over state building and administration, and explored the linkage of democracy, capitalism, and administrative reform in the building of a commercial republic and a compensatory state.

Spawned by 1824 was a relatively small but impactful compensatory state, one that hid the visible size of the federal government by using carrots, sticks, mandates, and nudges to pursue its aims through subnational public and proxy actors. This compensatory state blurred the line between the public and private sectors; relied heavily on networks of public, private, and/or volunteer actors and associations; and viewed the public-sector components of the compensatory state in instrumental rather than constitutive terms. Wrought also were emerging views that statistical analysis and the scientific method of the physical sciences were a means for realizing Americans' millenarian vision of themselves and their nation.

These outcomes had not occurred spontaneously, nor were they inevitable. A nexus of corporate and emergent natural science and social scientific actors helped propel and shape them. At the same time, social and economic inequities based on US constitutional provisions and prevalent societal norms propelled disenchantment and nascent political movements to remedy them. Consequently, the millenarian optimism surrounding these new authority structures had been tested and found wanting. Further exacerbating discontent was the spread of the commercial republic beyond the Atlantic coast and to the nation's backcountry. Combined, these produced the next round of perceptions that historical–structural mismatches existed in America. This, as three political inflexions rocked the nation: Jacksonianism, the Civil War, and Reconstruction. These each spawned calls for the next rounds of political and administrative reform linked to state building in America. Chapter 3 discusses how, why, and with what results this happened.

Notes

1. In the 1740s, about a dozen newspapers were published in the colonies. By 1754, estimates of daily newspaper readership varied among newspapers from 400 to 700. By the time of the hated Stamp Act of 1765, and stoking hostility against it as a

threat to press freedom, circulations ranged from 1,500 to 2,500 readers. These figures understate readership, as copies were discussed in coffeehouses and passed on to others (Burns, 2006).

2. Natural law is not a codified body of law but, rather, "a means for doing justice by referring to the general norms for mankind" developed over centuries (Kirk, 2003, p. 109).

3. The Intolerable Acts were a series of five actions (including, later, the Quebec Act) taken in 1774 (after the Boston Tea Party) by Parliament to show the colonies that violence would not be tolerated.

4. Not all Americans sought independence from Britain. Some historians have called the Revolution America's "first civil war," as violent attacks occurred between British loyalists and the minority supporting independence in many parts of the country (see Philbrick, 2016).

5. Madison's experience in the Virginia legislature convinced him that human nature was too driven by narrow, parochial, and dysfunctional self-interest. In the Constitutional Convention, he urged (unsuccessfully) that the federal government be able to veto state legislation. His vision was that slowing down the legislative process would give time for what de Tocqueville later called "self-interest rightly understood."

6. *Dred Scott* declared slaves property without constitutional rights, *Plessy* ratified apartheid in America, and *Lochner* declared state efforts to improve citizens' lives unconstitutional (in this case, by limiting work hours).

7. Seventy-seven of these essays appeared in the *Independent Journal*, the *New York Packet*, and *The Daily Advertiser* between October 1787 and August 1788. They were published as a collection in 1788 as *The Federalist Papers*.

8. Madison later joined Jefferson in fearing that Hamilton's system would consolidate the power of speculators and creditors.

9. As Garry Wills (1999, ch. 6) notes, Madison was not arguing for a proliferation of interest groups but, rather, for an acknowledgement that commerce would produce various interests (e.g., agriculture, banking, transportation).

10. As noted in Chapter 1, instrumental perspectives view federal agencies as "instruments" or "tools" of elected officials. Constitutive perspectives view the career civil service as partners in policymaking, implementation, and evaluation where influence is, and should be, a two-way street (Krause, 1999).

11. The discussion of women and blacks in this section relies heavily on Appleby (2001, ch. 4).

12. Although associated with Henry Clay, the American System was part of Alexander Hamilton's "American School" (or "National School") in APD. It was championed by John Q. Adams, Clay, and Abraham Lincoln. In addition to investing in infrastructure, the system was anchored by high protectionist tariffs and a national bank to promote growth of productive enterprises rather than speculation. Political rationality was also part of this endeavor. For instance, the Republican Party relied on protectionist tariffs to pay for Civil War pensions and, thus, adroitly linked the American System to both economic development and support of veterans (Bensel, 2000).

13. See, for example, *Santa Clara County v. Southern Pacific Railroad Company* (1886); *Smyth v. Ames* (1898); *Hale v. Henkel* (1906); the *United States v. Martin Linen Supply Co.* (1977); *Citizens United v. Federal Election Commission* (2010); *Burwell v. Hobby Lobby Stores, Inc.* (2014).

Chapter 3

Inflexion Politics, the Corporate–Social Science Nexus, and American Administrative Reform, Circa 1824–1880

The millenarian optimism surrounding the commercial republic was sorely challenged by what might be called "inflexion politics" in America from roughly 1824 to 1880. These inflexion points included, but were not limited to, strident class and sectional debates over commerce and slavery as the nation expanded. Produced, in turn, were the Missouri Compromise of 1820, the Panic of 1837 (followed by years of depression), the Compromise of 1850 regarding slavery in the Southwest territories acquired after the Mexican–American War (1846–1848), and the Kansas–Nebraska Act of 1854, which spawned, first, the Republican Party of Abraham Lincoln (IL) and, eventually, southern state secession from the Union, the bloody Civil War, and Reconstruction.

Propelling these events—and their impact on the evolution of American administrative reform and its reciprocal link to compensatory state building—were not only a growing sense of social class, social immobility, and sectional divides but also expansion of the vote to all white males, the settling of the western backlands, and dismay over moral decay in all sectors of society. Emerging from these factors was the election of Andrew Jackson (D-TN) as president in 1828 and the advent of the Jacksonian Era in American political development (APD), state building, and administrative reform.

Politically, Jacksonianism railed against economic elites, nationalization of policy, and federally financed infrastructure development. Administratively, Jacksonianism was packaged, and interpreted by some later historians, as the democratization of federal employment through "rotation in office." This, despite its downsides, could be seen as consistent with aspects of the substantive rationality project (SRP). But Jacksonianism also extended the principle of "personal organization" from the private sector to federal agencies and pursued administrative reorganization premised on bureaucratic administration principles. Nor, again, was anything automatic or inevitable about this pursuit of the instrumental rationality project (IRP). The role of a corporate-emergent social science nexus of interests continued, as it had during the Founding Era, to promote and shape administrative reform and its reciprocal relationship to state building for the expressive, material, and authority gains legitimacy confers.

Relatedly, *political* rationality by Jackson and his political heirs informed these initiatives. They used them to create a new political authority structure—known to scholars as the "patronage state" (Lowi, 1969). They did so by using appointments and contracts to build political coalitions supporting their agendas, expanding the proxy components of the compensatory state in the process. Also buttressed was an instrumental rather than constitutive view of the role of public agencies.

But, as in the Founding Era, disappointment with the results of the IRP in this historical period—including the corruption of Jacksonians—led to claims that a historical–structural mismatch had again arisen. These claims prompted the next round of calls for American political, policy, and administrative reforms. The most effective political reaction against Jacksonianism came from the Whig Party. Central components of the Whig Party platform between 1832 and 1858 were amplification of economic development, individualism, and evangelical tenets of capitalism as levers to societal improvement and individual redemption. The Whigs even referred to capitalism as a "stated policy of heaven" (Howe, 1979, p. 187).

The successor to Jacksonianism, the nemesis of executive-centered government, and the precursor to the Republican Party, the Whigs are often seen as a brief anomaly. But they actually enjoyed great electoral strength in Congress during those two decades (with personages such as Henry Clay and Daniel Webster) and in the states, and they had two short-lived presidential victories (William Henry Harrison [OH] and Zachary Taylor [KY]) (Howe, 1979).[1] Although drawing support in all regions until the slavery issue provoked irreconcilable divisions leading to the rise of the Republican Party and a Democratic South, the Whig coalition consisted of rising business and professional actors, workers who benefited from manufacturing jobs, and those individual and business interests sympathetic with Henry Clay's American System of national funding for internal development projects.

Culturally, the Whigs further amplified the individual and state-building aspects of faculty psychology, the virtues of capitalist entrepreneurialism, and a fear of executive "Caesarism" personalized in the Jackson–Clay maelstrom of this period. Whigs also sought a more centralized, federal government-driven, and more rational (i.e., planning) approach to development. As such, the Whig movement and its rhetoric were a precursor to the planning and economic development preferences of the later business and professional components of the Progressive reform movement in the early 20th century and beyond.

Given their distrust of executive power, the Whigs also pursued what David Rosenbloom (2000) would see in the 20th century as a "legislative-centered public administration." Whigs also emphasized and amplified American predilections for hiding the visible size of government in the forms of industry-protecting tariffs, subsidies for internal improvements, and (in a pitched battle with Jacksonians that they would temporarily lose) reauthorization of a national bank for regulating currency and making money available for business investments. The Republican Party would continue these goals.

The Whigs' focus on issues of morality and the redemption of society (e.g., temperance, abolition of slavery, and benevolent associations), although secularized by some later progressives, also incorporated evangelical shades of the Second Great Awakening. They also further layered into Americans' identity—in ways influencing the management-driven component of the later Progressive movement—the ideas that wealth accrued through industrialization and technological innovation could ameliorate social conflict. Redistributing wealth by legislative and administrative fiat was not necessary, so long as the economic pie grew.

Finally, they shared the Founders' fear of demagoguery and respect for custom, a direct political reaction to the emotionalism they argued Jackson aroused in the people. For Whigs, Jackson was an affront to the hierarchical relationship of reason, rationality, and conscience over emotion and superstition stressed by faculty psychology. Still, like the Federalists, Jeffersonians, and Jacksonians before them—and Republicans after them—the Whigs' administrative theory involved an instrumental rather than a constitutive view of the federal bureaucracy. And, most ironically given the focus of the Jacksonian Era, citizen distrust of government and estrangement was again sown during this period, leading to the next round of calls for administrative reform and compensatory state building.

But the nation was soon at war with itself, with the Civil War bringing, first, an amplification of all components of the compensatory state, followed by a retraction of the federal component as Reconstruction ended in 1876. Paul Fussell (2000) writes that romance and myths begin all wars, are ritualized, and end in disappointment leading to irony and parody. The Civil War was no exception. Begun naively and boisterously like the Revolutionary War and the War of 1812 before it, each side in the Civil War claimed the likelihood of a swift, nearly bloodless victory. By its end, Oliver Wendell Holmes spoke for many in his generation when he wrote that the Civil War "made me lose my belief in beliefs" (Menand, 2001, p. 4). Produced in its wake "was the proliferation of irony, of a posture of distance and doubt in relation to experience" (Faust, 2008, p. 194). Moreover, "this was more than just a loss of faith; it was an issue of both epistemology and sensibility, of how we know the world and how we envision our relationship to it" (p. 194).

Unsurprisingly, Civil War mobilization, conflict, and the Reconstruction era that followed brought yet another set of political and administrative reforms to America. Again, these exhibited some continuities and discontinuities with their predecessors, but all were driven, challenged, and constrained by America's exceptionalist values. Initially, discontinuities included an explosion of size and some capacity building for the "national governments" of both the Union and the Confederacy. Continuities, however, included the dominance of the IRP over the SRP in administrative reform, in this case (again) directed against the alleged "emotionalism" that led to the war. Increasing formalization of bureaucratic administration also occurred for both the Union and Confederate bureaucracies to mobilize and fight the war. This again was accompanied by a further amplification of the proxy components of the compensatory state, as well as a significant return after the war to Americans' rhetorical limited-government roots.

These dynamics were supported and informed once more by a corporate–social science nexus of interests in search of the expressive, material, and authority gains that drive the quest for legitimacy. Consequently, the past—especially its initial conditions discussed in Chapter 2—continued to affect the evolution of American administrative reform in paradoxical ways. So, too, did the IRP help spawn a return to embracing more limited government and administration. In this, it also set the stage for the next rounds of administrative reform and state building in America: the civil service, Populist, and Progressive movements in the late 19th and early 20th centuries discussed later in Chapter 4.

****

The 1820s through the 1840s in America witnessed new spikes in immigration and technological innovation that provoked both opportunities and challenges (e.g., Barone, 2013; Remini, 2008). These again prompted worries that existing institutions were not up to handling those challenges. Regarding immigration, nearly five million immigrants arrived from northern European countries (primarily Germany and Scandinavia), plus England and Ireland. Their exodus was prompted largely by religious persecution, political conflicts, and crop failures. Meanwhile, internal population movements from rural to urban areas occurred in the United States, bringing with them the usual social, economic, and safety disruptions that begged redress. At the same time, a so-called new economy developed. It was catalyzed by enhanced productivity from technological innovations in farm equipment, an increase in class and religious consciousness through the printing press and telegraphy, and railroads that allowed more rapid Western migration (Hofstadter, 1955).

With the share of urbanites rising from 7 percent in 1820 to 18 percent in 1850, the new economy in these areas boomed (Heilbroner & Singer, 1999). Prosperity was premised less on industry and more on commerce, with a special focus on sole-proprietor-skilled artisanship, financial services, real estate, and the law. Entrepreneurial spirits soared as the precision afforded by skilled artisans—always in short supply—was not offset in value by mass-produced goods (e.g., shoes). Although investment in textile factories required large amounts of capital, the same was not true of, say, clothing or shoe production.

These smaller, less capital-intensive manufacturers often contracted out aspects of their work to farms and fishing families in their off-seasons, as well as to seamstresses living at home or working in sweatshops developed to meet these needs (Appleby, 2001).[2] In the process, the conceit of the colonial and founding periods was not only adapted to this time period but further amplified. The idea again prevailed among average citizens that markets, individual effort, and equality of opportunity—i.e., the beneficence of society—trumped any efforts at social improvement that government might make.

Amid the abundance generated by America's commercial republic, however, poor immigrants lived on the outskirts of towns and cities, with no public transportation to get even the educated among them to jobs. Mob and gang violence among different ethnic groups competing for jobs soon followed, exacerbated by the development of a rowdy and tawdry "tavern culture" (Appleby, 2001). Thus, nativist elements were given fodder for attacks on immigrants, while class resentments anathema to the American exceptionalist millenarian vision brewed.[3] Meanwhile, as women migrated to the city from the farm, prostitution spiraled. Not only did the need for income create this situation, but brothels afforded safety to women in a pre-police force environment. Ironically, this form of "entrepreneurialism" created yet another sense of "rugged individualism" and helped further the idea of the suffrage movement among younger women (Appleby, 2001). This was due to the financial independence that prostitution afforded them—along with the employment of women in the service industry and textile mills.

The proximity of immigrants in rundown tenement housing also brought urban fires, deaths, and injuries. Absent government services, contracted volunteer fire crews compensated. However, they were quickly taken over by urban gangs who competed with each other in turf wars—sometimes while buildings burned. This continued into the early 20th century. Also, so bad were sanitation and nutrition services that the lifespan for urban-born infants in the North was lower than for slaves in the South.

Nonetheless, Americans' self-conception continued, abetted by networks of volunteer groups that compensated for a lack of government capacity. Again, the federal government fostered and supported many of these networks until the Civil War's sectional conflicts fragmented unity (Novak, 2001; Skocpol, Ganz, & Munson, 2000; Skocpol, Munson, Karch, & Camp, 2002). In the interim, the national government worked indirectly to address these needs through a variety of religious associations mentioned in Chapter 2. These included the expansion of the American Temperance Society, the American Education Society, the American Home Missionary Society, and a number of philanthropies. Likewise, by 1837, the Evangelical United Front (Foster, 1960) noted in Chapter 2, and led by the American Bible Society's 900-plus membership, encouraged local associations to serve their communities' needs.

****

Historians and political scientists differ over what caused Jacksonianism. They disagree over the relative weight of the developments just noted, plus sectional bias (e.g., Turner, 1920); class (Schlesinger, Jr., 1945); the "democratization of business" (Bowers, 1922); and the quest for restoring moral order (Crenson, 1975). But their combination produced a potent rhetorical mix that shaped the politics, policy, and administration of this period. Rural–urban sectional tensions between western frontier folk and eastern seaboard institutions were strongly held and were predicates for frontier support for Jacksonian Era reforms (much as such splits would drive populist movements in America ever since). Historian Frederick Jackson Turner (1920) argued that Jackson was the "idol and mouthpiece of the popular will" in the West, embodying the essential (sometimes exaggerated) western traits of an expansive frontier society. These included rugged individualism, freedom, the self-made man, volunteerism, and equality of opportunity. All these traits were consonant with the larger society's embrace of faculty psychology, helped affirm the appeal of American exceptionalist values, and produced a frontier mentality largely free from class distinctions among settlers. These settlers chose men such as Jackson (e.g., presidents such as Harrison, Taylor, and John Tyler [Whig-VA]) as their leaders, ascribing their commercial or military successes to these frontier traits.

But it was the Panic of 1819 that raised both sectional and class rivalries to their peak. It also led to the creation of the Democratic Party (formerly, the Jeffersonian Republicans), the eventual election of Jackson, and Jacksonian administrative reform. As Chapter 4 will corroborate, the Jacksonians were the predecessors in origin, style, and political philosophy of both the Agrarian and Populist political reform movements in America during the 1880s and 1890s, respectively. Like Jefferson initially, Jacksonians stressed the natural superiority of agriculture over manufacturing. They also saw the natural state of nature as classless rather than hereditary and opposed banks, public debt, high tariffs, and federally funded internal improvements (see more below). All this because of the economic hardships these created for southern and western interests. Westerners saw these as tools of eastern elites that disadvantaged their own capitalistic aspirations. Moreover, westerners viewed the rapaciousness, corruption, and legally privileged ethos of eastern elites as the reason for the perversion of the "natural" economic order. The Panic of 1819 convinced them of this and, thus, contrary to Americans' millenarian vision, explicitly pitted economic class against class for the first time since Jefferson and limited social mobility (Hofstadter, 1989, p. 66).

The absolute and relative growth of manufacturing in the North compared to the South, improvements in transportation technology, and the continuing democratization of capital had increased the dependence of would-be western entrepreneurs on banks, most notably the Second Bank of the United States. This, because delay in payment collections imposed by distances from the East Coast meant that westerners had to borrow working capital from financial institutions. When the Panic hit, these loans were called in by the Bank, as well as by wildcat banks that had spread throughout the American South and West. Tennessee was hard hit, and Jackson (a Tennessean) found himself in great debt. Wrote Missourian Thomas Hart Benton, "All the flourishing cities of the West are mortgaged to this money power. They may be devoured by it at any moment. They are in the jaws of the monster" (Hofstadter, 1989, p. 67). Even more galling, he said, was that these "proceeds may travel eastward, where the 'sceptre' [sic] of money has fixed itself" (p. 67).

Some scholars contest both the sectional and class-based origins of Jackson's political and administrative reform agenda. Even some proponents of the class thesis see all regions affected by the crash (e.g., Bowers, 1922; Hofstadter, 1989; Schlesinger, Jr., 1945). They view Jacksonianism as a "movement to control the power of capitalist groups, mainly Eastern, for the benefit of non-capitalist groups, farmers, and laboring men, East, West, and South" (Schlesinger, Jr., 1945, p. 307). Other dissenters from the class and sectional theses argue that democratic capitalism gradually eroded commercial dominance by an exclusive eastern mercantile class. This left widespread national exposure to the pain of the Panic of 1819 and, later, the Panic of 1837. Dissenters point to the observations in 1820 of John Quincy Adams' (Democratic-Republican and, later, Whig-MA) and Jackson's later Vice President, John C. Calhoun (SC), that an

> immense revolution in fortunes [occurred] in every part of the Union, enormous multitudes in deep distress, and general mass of disaffection

to the Government not concentrated in any particular direction, but ready to seize upon any event and looking out anywhere for a leader.

(Hofstadter, 1989, p. 67)

Although democratic capitalism and the infrastructural investments of the American System supporting it were net positives for the economy, a corporate concentration of economic power was nonetheless building in the Northeast that spawned growing anger. Thus, by the 1820s, it became clear that a new power elite of financiers was gaining economic power and political leverage as state building proceeded to replace the locally based economic elite of the Founding Era as the dominant authority structure in society. This meant a shift in America from personal influence exercised in face-to-face commercial relations to an impersonal institutional (and bureaucratized) dominance of citizens' lives. In the process, a shift occurred from a personalized book-credit to a cash-based economy responsive to commercial interests—a shift that then stimulated political push-back framed rhetorically as saving egalitarianism in America.

These economic grievances, plus the rising egalitarian overtones of this period, sparked a surge in westerners registering to vote and running for political office in their states. Debtors, in particular, "rushed into politics to defend themselves" in several western states (Hofstadter, 1989, p. 67). For the first time, they saw politics, administration, and their economic welfare intertwined. The number of voters tripled between 1828 and 1848 as the population doubled, many of whom were rural farmers, urban workers, and debtors (p. 65, fn. 3). Those elected pursued laws preventing debtors' imprisonment, affording bankruptcy protection, and revamping public lands policy to their advantage. With their victories came a stinging diminution of control by commercial interests over state governments in the emerging compensatory state.

Parlaying these dynamics at the national level, Jackson framed his two presidential campaigns as an assault on "preferment" favoring the most well-off, be they in society or in government. He was elected president in 1828 after he controversially lost the election of 1824. Jackson won a plurality of the popular vote in 1824 but lost the presidency to John Quincy Adams. This happened when the Speaker of the House, Henry Clay, threw his support to Adams in what critics called a "corrupt deal" to secure Clay the role of Secretary of State (a presumed steppingstone to the presidency at the time).

For Jackson, the most egregious perception of class-based preferment in administration and state building involved the allocation of federal jobs by his predecessors. As noted in Chapter 2, until Jackson, government was portrayed as a calling or vocation for only the well-heeled, educated, and connected white, male, and propertied gentry. Granted, Jefferson removed Federalists from his new administration, but he replaced them with persons of the same class and background (Crenson, 1975) (see more below). Launched by the Jacksonians in reaction to these biases was a desire for a more egalitarian—although still property-owning, white male-dominated—conception of public service and administration. Consistent with earlier notions of American exceptionalism focusing on the lack of hereditary titles and artificial barriers to social mobility, Jacksonians reacted against government jobs becoming hereditary, as they sometimes were.

Jackson's major administrative innovation was the idea of "rotation in office," or, in William Macy's (in)famous phrase, "To the victor of elections go the spoils." Jackson argued that an upper-class-based public service that claimed de facto property rights to federal jobs was intolerable in a democracy. It also reduced government's responsiveness to the public and its legitimacy in the eyes of many citizens. Rotation in office was necessary to "democratize" the public service. Jackson argued that rotation would not be a managerial problem, because no particular skills were needed to perform government jobs.

As Jackson (1829) put it, public service jobs *"admit of being made,* so plain and simple that men of intelligence may readily qualify themselves" for appointment (emphasis added). In "this system [of job simplification through division of labor], individuals could be placed or replaced [after an election] without upsetting the integrity of the whole" (Jackson, 1829). Not surprisingly, and like his predecessors, Jackson's vision of the virtues of specialization through division of labor derived from his military career. It also served as the foundation for IRP-based arguments mounted by civil service reformers (implicitly) in the late 19th century and progressives (explicitly) in the early 20th century.

Only approximately 10 percent of federal jobs turned over as a result of rotation in office during Jackson's presidency. However, the rotation-in-office principle accelerated under his Jacksonian, Whig, and Republican successors. Under presidents James Buchanan (D-PA) and Lincoln, for example, roughly 53,000 positions were available at the end of the Civil War, while approximately 131,000 positions were available for patronage appointments when President James Garfield (R-OH) was assassinated in 1881 (Backgrounder on the Pendleton Act, 1883).

****

In reviewing the Jacksonian Era, Leonard White (1954) concluded that democratization of administration was the Jacksonians' most significant administrative reform. This was clearly true at the lower levels of the federal bureaucracy. But the very limited number of studies done on the social composition of Jackson's administrative appointments to high-level leadership positions indicates that his "common man" rhetoric did not apply to them. As Matthew Crenson (1975) discusses, Jackson's appointees to the higher civil service were hard to distinguish from those of John Adam's (Fed-MA) or Jefferson's. Citing prior research by Sidney Aronson (1964), he argues that no significant difference existed in social backgrounds across the three presidencies, including on education, occupation, and professional training. Indeed, similar numbers of professionals existed (e.g., agriculture, commerce, manufacturing, and the ministry), with lawyers the most represented. Importantly, however, Aronson included federal judges in his analysis and thus may have skewed his findings.

This did not mean that Jackson's appointees held the same political or policy preferences as their predecessors in prior administrations. They did not. But to the extent that social background helps shape philosophy (as much of today's research on representative bureaucracy indicates), no major differences in leadership composition are apparent. Moreover, the Jacksonians, Whigs, and Republicans who succeeded him in the White House were no less cognizant of the political advantages that patronage and rotation in office could bring to enhancing their political power. Like their predecessors, the Jacksonians relied on political parties (voluntary associations in their own right) as parallel systems to appoint clerks and to help them concentrate executive branch power in an otherwise "calculated [constitutional] system of dispersed power" (Wood, 2009a, pp. 32–33). The centuries-long quest by administrative reformers in America ever since to shift legislative and judicial power to the executive branch had begun.

A conjunction of material and authority motives drove patronage during the Jacksonian Era. These included the continuing need for presidents to attain their goals through the newly founded "second party system" (circa 1824–1854) (McCormick, 1966); for party machines to maintain their power; and for citizens in this democratizing period to have an SRP-premised stint in government administration. Patronage and rotation in office also afforded a degree of mass political mobilization, agenda control, and intergovernmental coordination. Jacksonians tried to "weld party and [administrative] office" into a new authority structure to pursue and coordinate their policy agenda within the otherwise fragmented federal system (Nelson, 1982, p. 24; see more below).

But there were other, more expressive motivations for administrative reform driving Jacksonianism. For starters, it was focused on restoring the moral integrity and institutional authority that had withered away during the second generation of Americans due to malfeasance and corruption in the emerging professions (see Chapter 2). Jackson also wanted to restore to federal agencies the moral integrity and sense of virtue of high-level agency appointees associated with the Washington, Adams, and Jefferson administrations. He hoped to appoint men of moral character to his administration, assuming that when citizens saw this, their morality and that of other institutions would increase.

A second expressive aim of patronage and rotation in office was to increase citizens' sense of the federal government's legitimacy. This SRP-based initiative was badly needed in an age when Americans' deference to institutional authority in general plummeted, the New England states had earlier threatened to leave the union because of the War of 1812, and resistance (passive and active) to federal government authority in the West was common. It would be even better if those placed in federal government jobs were liked and respected by fellow citizens in those estranged communities.

****

Still, the Jacksonians in many ways amplified the Federalist–Republican trends associated with the "organization methods of carrying on the public's business" (White, 1954, p. 562). In this vein, two other administrative reform initiatives are important to consider. The first, ultimately doomed to failure, was called "personal organization" and stemmed again from Jackson's military experience (Crenson, 1975). The second was to apply continental European-inspired administrative reform measures to counter the failures of personal organization. Combined, they prefigured a consistent philosophy of administrative reformers pursuing the IRP throughout American history: If you do not like the ways that public administrators are exercising their discretion, the solution is a combination of more ethical leadership, hierarchy, political control of discretion, and marketizing of responsibilities (contracting).

As noted, formal theories of administration did not exist in America (although elements of such did exist in Europe), so administration was experientially based. "Personal organization" was precisely such an experiential concept, with its immediate philosophical roots in the small businesses spawned by democratic capitalism in the Founding Era. As such, it became the "stock-in-trade of American business administrators" (Crenson, 1975, p. 72) and, with military models, gained a sequential, first-mover advantage in government agencies over later alternatives that were more democratically or constitutively based. In the process, the SRP aspects of administrative reform were diluted in ways consistent with Adams' (1992) pentimento effect.

Personal organization was premised on the idea that "men who headed organizations simply performed their functions according to their own aptitudes and preferences, and these personal inclinations, as well as the nature of the relationship chiefs and subordinates [fostered], determined administrative structure and procedure" (Crenson, 1975, p. 72). Thus, no abstract theory of organization guided businesses or the early federal agencies that modeled their administrative schemes on them. Instead, all organizations "reflected the whims, preferences, imaginations, and idiosyncrasies" of their respective department heads and chiefs. In theory, and reflecting tenets of both individualism and faculty psychology, leaders who were "honest, diligent, and upright" would develop organizational structures by their own lights and would monitor their subordinates to ensure those same qualities in their work. Thus afforded was a foretaste of the late 20th-century's call for entrepreneurial leadership in public agencies.

"Good administration"—defined as "honest and efficient" administration—would emerge, Jacksonians believed, if one ensured the "moral character of public servants" in leadership positions (Crenson, 1975, p. 77; McCormick, 1966). As

Jackson saw it initially, public administrators were to become "guardians of the government's legitimacy" by winning the "good will and affection of the people [for] the government . . . by faithful, prompt, and polite performance" of their duties (Crenson, 1975, p. 172). To this end, written proclamations to their staffs by federal agency leaders, such as the powerful Postmaster General Amos Kendall, were common. They tried to impose the "strict, puritanical rule of republican virtue—as they saw it"—in their departments (Crenson, 1975, p. 78). Kendall even tried to limit office conversations to work issues and enacted a series of prohibitions on reading materials in the office, use of office supplies, and receipt of gifts or gratuities. But, as always, the moral qualities and skillsets of human beings were uneven, meaning that personal organization readily became bad or corrupt administration. It also produced a maze of structural arrangements within and across departments and agencies that compromised coordination.

Even if proclamations and monitoring worked in Washington, not enough monitors of behavior existed to do the job effectively in agency field offices. Field personnel in the burgeoning compensatory state (see below) included subnational government actors, contractors, and even persons who worked part-time as civil servants in agencies and part-time in private businesses. Some of these even owned or worked in businesses that presented conflicts of interest for them (e.g., in customs houses and land offices). Thus, the distinctions between public- and private-sector employment not only continued to be blurred but also became unintelligible in many cases as the compensatory state expanded.

The shortcomings of personal organization as a means for restoring civic virtue to administration became clear, leading to a more structurally based, IRP approach to coordination and oversight of lower-level employees between 1829 and 1854. As Leonard White (1954; quoting the then Secretary of the Navy) summarized in ways contradicting Jackson's egalitarian instincts:

> The rapid growth of the country produces a corresponding accession to the duties of every department of Government and every public servant. The multiplication and complexity of laws involving new powers, new restraints, and new duties, call for additional labor and circumspection. The great increase of public records and documents . . . and the frequent calls from Congress imposing a necessity for researches, which comprehend the history and transactions of the department from its first organization, all contribute to render the duties of every officer and every clerk more difficult, complicated, and laborious.
>
> (pp. 7–8)

The fastest-growing federal departments experiencing major expansions of their workloads during the Jacksonian Era were the Post Office and the General Land Office under the Department of the Interior (see White, 1954). For example, the number of land patent permits issued by the General Land Office spiked from 7,000 to 25,000 between 1830 and 1831 alone, as western development spiraled under Clay's American System. However, the opportunities for corruption multiplied in the process of the compensatory state expanding to meet mounting responsibilities. Granted, the overall number of federal agency employees rose enormously from approximately 3,000 in 1800 to about 50,000 in 1860. Yet, that increase partly reflects pre-Civil War mobilization efforts (including the Mexican–American War of 1846–1848) in the late 1850s that would wane dramatically after Reconstruction (see more below). But, again, agency staffing, quality, and moral character never matched these responsibilities and normative standards, because, aside from wartime, hiding the visible size of the federal government from citizens continued apace.

At this point, and contrary to Woodrow Wilson's claim in his seminal 1887 centennial essay, members of Congress and leaders of executive departments began looking to Europe for administrative models and principles. Wilson was correct that the *systematic* study of continental European models and the explicit building of a self-conscious study of administration had not yet occurred in America by his day. That said, White (1954) reports that inquiries were made of European governments regarding revenue management, steamship regulation, postal service, and administrative organization (pp. 531–533). Grounded in the IRP, those shared by Europeans included specialization of effort (i.e., division of labor), devolving responsibilities to bureaus, and converting clerks to bureau chief positions. This, to relieve inordinate clerical and administrative burdens on top executives.

Introduced, too, were professional supervision and inspections into the bureaus and field offices of departments. Kendall's reorganization of the Post Office was typical of the IRP-based reforms of the Jacksonian Era: "Each administrative activity was lodged in its own pigeonhole, and there it stayed. No haphazard shifting of responsibilities was permitted to mar the precise division of the department's responsibilities into functional jurisdictions" (Crenson, 1975, p. 24). Concepts of bureaus, divisions, and offices were formalized, with responsibilities for subordinates written down for the first time.

Later, in the early 20th century, progressive reformers would focus on structure to maximize efficiency (defined as social efficiency). But the Jacksonians' structural formalization of bureaucratic administration was predicated on preventing "centralization and concentration of power and to institutionalize pluralism" (Nelson, 1982, p. 5). Indeed, separation of powers was their constitutional lodestar for designing federal administration. They saw organizational design as best pursued by replicating the checks and balances and federalism of the US Constitution, with each component of an organization "checking and balancing" the actions of the others. This very early pluralist conception of the role of actors in the federal government gave somewhat of an early foretaste of Carl Friedrich's (1940) notion of professional "inner checks," Norton Long's (1949) arguments regarding power in administration, and Matthew Holden's (1966) concept of "bureaucratic imperialism" as coordinating and accountability mechanisms.

Immediately, though, new problems arose. In a refrain familiar to contemporary readers aware of current bureaupathologies and subsystem politics, White (1954) notes that the "bureaus tended to become autonomous principalities, pursuing their own policy with support drawn from beyond the boundaries of the department to which they belonged" (p. 538). Indeed, Congress often opposed the creation of bureaus, largely because they meant higher spending levels and growth in departments. Still, once created, administrative structures with a decided military (and business) bent (e.g., divisions and regions) continued. Corruption in contracting also increased, as did links to congressional committees and interest groups rather than to the chief executive, with much the same happening in states and localities in the compensatory state. As some would later characterize as essential to agency survival and relative autonomy (Carpenter, 2001; Long, 1949), the predicate was set during the Jacksonian Era for what Woodrow Wilson (1981) later characterized in the 1880s as a corruption-addled "congressional government."

Congress' meager response to the corruption of the Jacksonian "spoils system"—plus its participation in it—thus fostered an amplification of administrative checks that only further ensconced the domination of bureaucratic administration in agencies. As throughout the history of administrative reform, this IRP dynamic, in turn, not only increased operational complexity and stovepiping of functions but made coordination, efficiency, and effectiveness more difficult. When sought, it also brought less effective legislative oversight of agency operations.

Also prevailing in the Jacksonian Era were IRP management images that built on prior beliefs and that were later amplified in various later rounds of American administrative reform. First, management in the public and private sectors was viewed as essentially alike—what today's scholarship calls "generic management." Proponents believed that effective public administration required the same skills, structures, and temperament as private management. This, despite its very different aims, values, and environment. Second, discretion by administrators needed to be limited, because it would result in venality, at best, and moral turpitude, at worst. As Crenson (1975) observed, the "aim of all these administrative arrangements was the effective regulation of bureaucratic conduct—to make administrators feel that the eye of their department 'was constantly upon them, not only collectively, but individually'" (p. 115).

****

As noted earlier, the Jacksonian period of American administrative reform also involved the amplification of the proxy government components of the compensatory state. A conjunction of emerging corporate and social science-based interests propelled this expansion. Moreover, despite American exceptionalism's aim of economic and social mobility as inoculation against the fate of earlier republics, the amplification of the compensatory state that took place brought significant economic class differences and obstacles to mobility.

Granted, the philosophy and legislative agendas of Jacksonians and Whigs differed in this period (see more below). The Jacksonians, for example, offered more solace to debtors and attacks on banks than did the Whigs. But the needs of the commercial republic propelled a continuing thread of "American radical entrepreneurialism" among both parties (Hofstadter, 1955). This characteristic reflected a persistent effort by varying economic class-based segments in society to sustain the ideals of individual self-sufficiency, faculty psychology, and material gain. For both parties, this desire soon merged with political aims. For example, with 11,000 employees, armies of contractors, and discretion over the kinds of materials sent through the mail, the Post Office became a key focus for pursuing partisan agendas and building loyalties to the Jacksonians as the compensatory state amplified (Carpenter, 2001).

In 1835, the Post Office relied on contractors to deliver the mail, contracts worth nearly $2 million and producing 20,000 additional patronage jobs. Kendall reissued existing contracts based on political agreement with Jackson's policy agenda. Also reminiscent of the Founding Era, local postmasters used the granting and withholding of their franking privileges to curry favorable newspaper coverage for the Jacksonian agenda. They also charged more for mailing opposition tracts in order to sway public opinion toward Jacksonian policy aims (Carpenter, 2001; Crenson, 1975).

Even more potent in creating a party-based authority structure by means of IRP-based administrative reform was the political advantage gained through control of the nation's customs houses and land offices. As William Nelson (1982) documents, the "number of employees in customs houses in port cities alone was a formidable patronage boon to [Jacksonian] political support and coordination." But the "real power . . . was their control of the speed with which imported goods cleared the post and the appraisal and classification of goods and hence the tax imposed on them" (p. 26). With discretion key to such actions, the threats to businesses not toeing the Jacksonian party line were unambiguous.

Equally well positioned for corruption were the nation's 62 land districts in western states and territories. These districts relied heavily on contractors to handle their workload. For example, Congress appropriated over $250,000 for surveying alone in 1819, a figure that grew greatly as new territories entered the nation during the remainder of the 19th century. Consequently, a reciprocal resource-dependency relationship again developed between government and business in the compensatory state. Business sought government contracts for succor, influence, and legitimacy, while growing increasingly dependent on them. Governments, in turn, depended on contractors to compensate for the ever-widening gap between growing administrative responsibilities and agencies' politically designed incapacity to carry them out to hide the visible size of government. In the process, the prior building of superior administrative capacity in business relative to government agencies further amplified the gap established during the Founding Era.

Business was indirectly assisted in this endeavor by the pursuit of legitimacy from some of the emergent, though still amateurish, social science interests of the day. As Dorothy Ross (1991) summarizes,

> given the roots of American exceptionalism in the debate over modernity and its dialectic of consensus and conflict [in European scholarly circles], America was fertile soil for the new social sciences. Interest in developing [what passed for] the social sciences [in this era (see below)] appeared both among those anxious to define and maintain the American exceptionalist vision and those anxious to modify or refute it.
>
> (p. 30)

Thus, and not unlike business, the social sciences sought to enhance their legitimacy through association (i.e., ties) with government and business.

As discussed in Chapter 2, a faith in mathematics and statistical analysis was already well established in America prior to the Jacksonian Era and laid a foundation for the further development of the social sciences in America. Yet, the social sciences of this period were not the professionalized and institutionalized social sciences that would develop in the last quarter of the 19th century. Instead, they were a steppingstone to them. Moreover, their methodologies were akin to what Charles Lindblom (1990) in the late 20th century called "probing." Probing is comprised of a "variety of method rather than formal technique" (p. 34) and

> does not seek the degree of conclusiveness of knowledge to which [natural] scientists have conventionally aspired; instead it seeks enough knowledge to warrant this volition instead of that [volition] in a world in which one must choose while knowing one's own fallibility.
>
> (p. 35)

As Thomas Haskell (2000) notes, this time period saw the development of a cadre of more amateurish social scientists. These "genteel men of [social] science" (or "gentry intellectuals") (see Ross, 1991) had no certification and only held a general interest in "human affairs."[4] Partly in reaction to what they saw as the emotionally driven devastation of the Civil War, many (but not all) of these gentry intellectuals would later create and join the American Social Science Association (ASSA) in 1865 (see more below and in Chapter 4). In the interim, they stressed the objectivity of their probing. Their authority would be premised on "accumulating and systematizing" esoteric knowledge that was beyond the intellectual ability of average Americans to comprehend in an age of growing complexity, class conflict, and societal interdependence (Haskell, 2000, p. 87). Their expressive goal was the production of an overarching science of society pursued as a "gentlemanly vocation" (p. 68) to remedy a significant historical–structural mismatch. Only then could what passed in the day as expertise-based objective knowledge protect the millenarian vision of American exceptionalism from nonrational thinking, superstition, and emotion-based politics.

Thus, once founded, ASSA's stated aim was to afford "sound" and "authoritative" research to a public that could not understand the underlying laws of the universe that members assumed existed. They asserted that, due to their education and overall gentrified upbringing, only they could understand the existing laws of nature. But, at its base, amateur social scientists were involved in a conservative "movement to defend the [eroding] authority of a gentry class, whose sturdiest foundation lay in the professions" (Haskell, 2000, p. 87). The gentry intellectuals thus sought to regain their standing by claiming unique expertise that could answer the questions others could not. Moreover, their claim of rationality appealed to larger segments of society who knew that their traditional world was changing, and this was all profoundly confusing to them.

More precisely, the immediate cause–effect understandings about how the world worked in everyday life held in small communities were losing legitimacy as the nation was becoming more interdependent. Among other things, interdependency was spawned by population movements and advances in transportation, communication, and emerging industrialization. Remote causation rather than immediate causation defied traditional common or community sense, a feeling that would be amplified later in the 1890s by the Progressive movement (see Chapter 4). Put most simply, there was more there than met the eye. Anticipating the arguments of structuralists in the early 20th century in anthropology, linguistics, and sociology, only experts could see the underlying structures of events that laypersons could see only as unrelated events.

Not surprisingly, however, established authority structures in the clergy had already pushed back against these upstart social science entrepreneurs prior to the Civil War. They did so by reframing the study of the social sciences in colleges as "moral philosophy" to be informed by the "fundamental truths . . . embodied in Christianity" (Ross, 1991, p. 37). This was especially true in older, clerically led and funded institutions such as Harvard and Yale where the sons of the nation's "old wealth" were educated. This was a reframing that played to ecclesiastical skills rather than to those of the gentry intellectuals of social science. Social science was "understood as a *science* of the principles and obligation of [moral and ethical] duty" (p. 36, emphasis added).

But newer colleges founded in the 1850s also developed courses in the social sciences. Although they were often clerically affiliated, these colleges catered to the sons of the more secularly and business-oriented wealthy merchants. They embraced Francis Bacon's empiricism and Auguste Comte's positivism, holding a belief that "empirical observation would yield, through rational reflection upon its evidence, the highest truths of [natural and social] science" (Ross, 1991, p. 37). The foundation builders of the liberal tradition in America, the

> originators of social science were members of the social world of the [more secular and] reform-minded aristocracy and educated middle class, functionaries, professors, doctors, lawyers, and clerics who wanted to throw off the traditional restraints [like religious dogma] placed on reason and initiative.
>
> (p. 10)

Nor did it hurt that commercial business leaders pressured New England colleges—dependent on their financial largesse—to add these kinds of rationality-based social science courses to their curricula.

In sum, traditional elites (and their authority structures), stressing the moral bases of the social sciences, were using higher education to advance what "was essentially a parochial defense of class [their own], an attempt to find a new basis for deference in a society no longer deferential" to them (Haskell, 2000, p. 89). In contrast, proponents of a more secular social science were trying to increase their legitimacy as an alternative authority structure by claiming the whole of human affairs as their domain of expertise. Thus, in a historical period where Jacksonians valorized the "common sense of common men," the genteel members "of the social sciences" claimed they held unique, and badly needed, expertise that could take emotion out of politics and could be used for the advancement of Americans' millenarian vision. Consequently, and predating the progressive reformers in the early 20th century, they envisioned what later became known as the politics/policy–administration dichotomy.

In claiming this, the emergent social sciences argued that Jacksonian democracy represented a historical–structural mismatch. It had produced an authority structure with "too much quackery," "demagoguery," and "emotionalism" to deal with the complex issues of the day. Remedying this situation required the establishment of an accepted hierarchy of knowledge—a recognized "community of competence" like themselves—to guide society better (Haskell, 2000). Also nurtured by such attitudes, however, were the seeds for perceptions of the conservative elitism of the social scientists and their genteel class, perceptions that would alienate many citizens from expertise-based agencies and state building throughout American history—and that would be repeatedly exploited by opponents of activist government.

****

Questions about the wisdom claimed by these amateur social scientists also arose. Like today, they disagreed about the hidden "realities" they identified and the policy prescriptions for dealing with them. Consider, for example, a major issue of the day: the economy. Not surprisingly, some social scientists either working or aspiring to teach in colleges largely funded by the economic elite advocated for laissez-faire markets. But there were others among them who supported protectionism. For example, Daniel Raymond's widely used text, *American System*, articulated the logic and specifics of a tariff system and how it benefited capitalism, as did popular publications by Henry Charles Carey, Matthew Carey, and Friedrich List.

As Raymond put it, only national tariffs could save capitalism from the inequalities and class divisions it would otherwise spawn and, thus, advance exceptionalism's millenarian promise. They would also allow markets to avoid Thomas Malthus' and David Riccardo's scenarios of economic and natural resource collapse, while still allowing the "natural laws of the market" to operate and "America to lead the world to Christian redemption" (Ross, 1991, p. 44). As Henry Carey put it in his *Principles of Political Economy*, tariffs would afford "habits of kindness and good feeling [that will] take the place of the savage and predatory habits of the earl[ier] period" (p. 45).

Nonetheless, most of the genteel men of social science came down on the side of laissez-faire economics. Perhaps the most influential in academia on a variety of topics during this time was jurist and philosopher Franz (Francis) Lieber. He contended that the mission of historians was "social analysis": the "separation of the permanent and essential from the accidental and superficial so that it becomes one of the keys by which we learn to understand better the present" (Ross, 1991, p. 41). He also embraced limited government and the importance of conscientious action as a duty of all citizens. The fundamental challenge facing modern states, Lieber argued, was "to last long—[but] to last with liberty and wealth" (p. 41). America would realize the American exceptionalist project because of democratic capitalism, its focus on free trade, and its republican institutions.

Two other notables of this period—Francis Wayland and Amasa Walker—were free-market proponents who, like Jean-Baptiste Say and Adam Smith, stressed "moral consumption" (Wayland, 1837) or "right consumption" (Walker in Ross, 1991, p. 43) as the way America could prove exceptional in history. Consumption—by individuals or governments—not only created wealth but was also a moral enterprise. It created a "community of exchange" rationally by means of its invisible hand that governments could only make inefficient by interference. This was a community where workers would be paid what they deserved based on their ingenuity and talents, unless they were engaged in immoral activities. But, for this to happen, the business and financial classes had to be respected, and government should not regulate them or limit their property rights.

****

As the Civil War grew closer, additional cleavages occurred among the gentry practitioners of the social sciences based on sectional differences. Again, this demonstrated that "objective" social science premised on the IRP often gave way to political rationality. In this instance, the combatants all framed their positions in American exceptionalist terms. Leading the charge against any philosophy furthering the nationalization of policy issues such as those proposed by the Whigs were social theorists who came from the most "exceptional" region of the nation—the South. Again, more than tariffs were involved; southerners feared that if any issue could be "nationalized," slavery might also be put at risk.

What Ross (1991, esp. pp. 30–37) calls "pro-slavery" economists borrowed selectively from Malthus and Riccardo, as did a so-called sacred circle of southern intellectuals. This circle is examined in greater depth later in this chapter regarding their influence during the runup to the Civil War and, later, during Reconstruction. Presently, it suffices to note that their analyses were clothed in the methods of historicism rather than Comte's positivism: they stressed the decline of the Roman Empire (Gibbon, 1776–1789), using it as the empirical foundation for their arguments in favor of preserving the South's slave-based plantation economy. In this, they offered "distinct conservative versions of political theory, political economy, and sociology" (Ross, 1991, p. 30).

These southern intellectuals also used American exceptionalist values to support their argument. The South's slavery-based economy, they contended, was a bulwark against an attack on the economic elites' property rights nationally, as well as the low-wage exploitation of immigrants happening in the North. Northern workers, they claimed, were essentially slaves themselves. Some, such as social theorist and apologist for slavery, George Fitzhugh (1854), called capitalism and free labor a "little experiment" that was ultimately doomed (p. 70). They also labeled northern capitalism and any links to the social sciences as aberrations in history rather than as accelerating, positive forces for American exceptionalist purposes.

Not all southern social scientists took this position. Those embracing Comte's positivist school of sociology acknowledged the class divisions that capitalism was generating in the North. America was "reproducing the class system of Europe" (Ross, 1991, p. 33). But these critics said that monopoly capitalists were to blame and were disturbing capitalism's "natural" order. Capitalism was not inherently flawed.

Some amateur social scientists even thought Jacksonian political and administrative reforms would end these distortions. But non-sectional disagreements also challenged the "Jacksonianism-as-savior" of the capitalist system perspective. Criticizing Arthur Schlesinger's "democracy-advancing" interpretation of Jacksonianism, Bray Hammond saw the Jacksonian idea of "frontier democracy" as a rhetorical fig leaf masking an "unprincipled scramble for power" among the usual economic suspects (Crenson, 1975, p. 20). Jackson embodied the "moral feelings of an age," but Jacksonianism was "not the philosophy of a radical leveling movement that proposes to uproot property or to reconstruct society along drastically different lines. [It would, rather, reestablish] equality before the law" for its citizens and unleash the "creative enterprise" of its people (Hofstadter, 1989, pp. 79–80). It was, added Marvin Meyers (1957), a philosophy "drawn fatally . . . to the revolutionizing ways of acquisition, emulative consumption, promotion, and speculation" in America's commercial republic (p. 15).

Contemporaries of Jackson, such as Henry Carey, took another approach to disabusing the Jacksonianism-as-savior perspective. One of the foremost American economists of his day, Carey turned on its head the Founders' view that economics was grounded within democracy. Instead, he argued in his three-volume *Principles of Political Economy* that "democracy was not the causal agent, but rather the result of the more basic conditions of American political economy" (Ross, 1991, p. 45). Thus, rather than government actions shaping markets, markets shaped democracy, including Jacksonian democracy (see Polanyi, 1944, for the classic challenge to this argument).

Still others, such as labor leader Thomas Skidmore, took a more radical position in questioning the ability of Jacksonianism to correct for excesses in the market (Wilentz, 1984). They joined with a range of working-class reformers in taking the position of European socialists. Jacksonianism was not up to the task, regardless of its call for political or administrative democratization. Needed, instead, was a fundamental redistribution of income, an end to inheritance, and equal educational opportunity for all. Only these would be enough to steer the nation back to its millenarian vision.

****

As happened to the administrative legacy of the founding generation, the Jacksonian administrative reform era created disappointments and, oddly enough, some citizen estrangement from government. These, as noted, led to perceptions of a historical–structural mismatch that helped propel the Whigs to power and, then, the Republican Party. As Crenson (1975) observes, Jacksonians "revealed a vague inclination to conduct public business through explicit rules and regulations," especially in the codes of conduct issued by some (e.g., Amos Kendall) (p. 160). Early on, the codes of conduct and accounting systems designed for personal administration had certainly changed the relationship between superiors and subordinates in public agencies in the compensatory state. In the process, the shadow of what Max Weber much later called the "iron cage" of bureaucracy and markets grew evident to some critics of Jacksonian administrative reforms. And, like Adam Smith (1776) and, later, 20th-century industrial psychologists citing the anomie of employees spawned by specialization (e.g., Elton Mayo, 1945), Jackson's political opponents in the partisan press even began referring to federal employees as "mechanical automatons" (p. 160).

Leonard White's (1954, passim, ch. 28) view on the Jacksonians' efforts also made clear the problematic relationship between images of democratization of politics and the realities of their administrative reform initiatives. He wrote that even the "rising spirit of democracy" had minimal consequences on the day-to-day operations of government inherited from the Federalists and Jeffersonians. Democracy imposed changes on the executive branch "from without," and the consequences of these changes mostly altered relationships between the federal bureaucracy and other branches of government. In the process, White's "art of administration" was "absorbed by the art of politics" (Crenson, 1975, p. 168).

These realities also further amplified the subsystem politics begun in the Founding Era. In addition, they expanded a growing compensatory state (as noted, through heavy contracting) and inflamed many citizens' feelings of exploitation and marginalization from decision making. They also further spawned discontent among elites—especially German immigrants and the educated in the Northeast—who saw only Appalachian ignorance and corruption and demanded reform.

Enter the aforementioned Whig Party and its successor after the split over slavery, the Republican Party, in 1854. As noted, the Whigs' legislative-centered version of public administration would prevail in the post-Civil War era and, because of its corruption, would later become a basis for the civil service reform movement and, then, the early Progressive movement. But before the civil service reform movement gained momentum, the nation experienced its greatest calamity: the Civil War.

****

Like Jacksonianism, scholars continue to debate the causes of the Civil War (see, e.g., Beard & Beard, 1933; Foner, 1995; Hofstadter, 1989; Schlesinger, Jr., 1949; McPherson, 2007; Pollard, 1866; Riccards, 1997). Regardless of cause, the Civil War's impact on Americans' self-conception was profound. The Civil War sorely challenged the conceit of American exceptionalism's millenarian vision as God's exemplar. How could God let such an atrocity happen? President Lincoln's answer in his second inaugural address was that Americans were reaping God's wrath for condoning slavery since the nation's founding. Long before this, Lincoln set the predicate for these words when he attacked what David Greenstone (1993) called "humanist liberals" who believed that the purpose of the state was "to satisfy human preferences" rather than "to develop human potential" regardless of race (pp. 50–62). In fighting the *Dred Scott v. Sandford* (1857) decision and the Kansas–Nebraska Act of 1854, Lincoln framed his argument in faculty psychology terms: "tolerating white racism as a politically acceptable preference [constituted] a barrier to the fulfillment of human potential" (Howe, 2009, p. 145).

That said, the war sparked a major amplification—and then rollback—of national centralization in the North and South and of bureaucratic administration. It also produced a further expansion of the proxy component of the compensatory state, subsystem politics, and the influence of the corporate–social science nexus on the administrative reform movement in America. As Balogh (2009) observes, "many of the [federal government] institutions created during the war were swiftly swept aside. . . . This was not the case, however, in the voluntary and private sectors, where the Civil War proved to be a catalyst for national consolidation" in the compensatory state (p. 277).

Likewise, Theda Skocpol (1992) argues that the Civil War did not leave as its legacy a "permanent autonomous federal bureaucracy as the U.S. 'Tudor Polity' reemerged after the South reentered the Union" (p. 68). Nor did things improve for federal administration in the post-war era. As White (1958) observed, the

> federal system from [presidents] Grant through McKinley was generally undistinguished. The moral climate after the Civil War was unfavorable, and only slowly improved; the technological arts useful in large-scale administration were undeveloped; executive talent tended to be drained off into railways, steel, manufacturing, and urban utilities.
>
> (p. 1)

Throughout, however, the power of the IRP over competing SRP alternatives once more prevailed.

****

As Drew Gilpin Faust (2008) vividly demonstrates, the Civil War wrought a calamitous "republic of suffering" for Americans. Proportionally, the war produced the largest wartime loss of American life in US history. Comparing the ratio of deaths to combatants (approximately 620,000) to total civilian populations, the Civil War incidence of death was six times more than in World War II. Its death rate of 2 percent of all soldiers extrapolates to about 6,000,000 deaths today (Faust, 2008, p. xi).

Its looming horrors aside, the immediate consequence of the Confederates' attack on Fort Sumter in 1861 placed the nation on war footing. The North and South both perceived the other as a "foreign nation," thus leading each side to fight the war accordingly. In political terms, without southern representation in Congress, the South could no longer stymie a Republican agenda to expand the number and capacity of federal agencies and to pursue further the Whig's (and now Republicans') American System.

With costs spiraling to nearly $2 million a day during the war, Congress authorized the use of paper money, the first of its kind in the United States. At the same time, it outlawed slavery in the District of Columbia and afforded compensation to those who freed their slaves. Congress also passed the Homestead Act (1862), launching the resettlement of approximately 25,000 settlers on three million acres of land in the West. Also enacted was the first Morrill Land-Grant

Act (1862), designating 30,000 acres in each state to create public agricultural and mechanical institutes, as well as land-grant universities, as part of the proxy component of the compensatory state. And instantiating the nation's Manifest Destiny ethic, Congress also passed the Pacific Railway Act (1862). Historian Richard Bensel (1990) argues that the "Civil War, even more than the end of the British colonial rule, represents the true foundational moment in American political development" (p. 10).

Bensel also contends that the need for war mobilization in the North made the nation's earlier failures to build adequate national state administrative capacity clear to the heirs of Jeffersonianism and Jacksonianism. Southern antipathy to building national administrative capacity also diminished, as the Confederacy lacked the administrative capacity to meet its warfighting needs. As Bensel writes, the building of administrative capacity and centralization were needed to consolidate "national" authority in both the Union and the Confederacy; perform recordkeeping during the war; memorialize Union (but not Confederate) war dead afterwards; establish a pension fund for widows; and pursue reconstruction after the war. In doing so, both the Union and the Confederacy amplified earlier administrative reform trends embracing IRP-based bureaucratic administration, instrumentalism, and the expansion of the compensatory state.

The Civil War required two full-scale mobilizations: one in the North and the other in the South. Taking the North first, the visible size of the federal government in Washington grew appreciably during war mobilization and fighting. This growth tried to rectify a "state of [administrative] impotence" at the war's beginning (Beatty, 2008, p. 58). The Union budget rose to over $1 billion from $63 million in 1860, and its administrative workforce expanded to 53,000 employees from 16,000 at the beginning of the war (Foner, 2015, p. 10).

A major part of this expansion was the addition of women to the federal workforce in Washington between 1860 and 1870 (Ziparo, 2017). This expansion came out of necessity, was informed by notions of a "separate sphere" for women, and became grist for opponents of government activism after the war (Ziparo, 2017). With clerical staffing needs mounting and men off fighting the war, educated women applied for jobs in the federal government, especially in the Department of the Treasury. Most clerical jobs were in the printing room, the cutting and separating room, and the dead-letter office in Treasury. These jobs were attractive to women for a number of reasons, but especially because they paid more than jobs in the private sector.

Nonetheless, jobs were not awarded based on female applicants' qualifications but, rather, on how well their applications stressed dire circumstances emphasizing traditional Republican Motherhood themes (e.g., financial need to raise children). Political connections were also necessary. Thus, only about 20 percent of women applicants were hired and, then, at considerably lower pay than men doing comparable jobs. Conditions were also placed on their employment. For example, they could not become part of the suffrage movement, thus helping to hold back the cause of women's suffrage for half a century.

Granted, as financial strains grew on budgets during the war, the hiring of women became an attractive way for agencies to save money. But, as young women came to Washington and lived in boardinghouses, their unaccustomed presence in such numbers on the streets prompted rumors that federal workers were prostitutes and pimps and that their boardinghouses were bordellos (Ziparo, 2017). These portrayals were commonly spread by newspapers. So effective and enduring were these characterizations (along with other cultural norms) that as late as 1920 (and passage of the 19th Amendment), women were excluded from about 60 percent of all federal jobs. Furthermore, until 1923, unequal pay for women was permitted but not mandated by law, while married women were discriminated against until 1937 (Rosenbloom, 1977). As Chapters 4 and 5 will discuss, this narrative—adding themes of effeminate administrative reformers and government workers—would be revived during the Progressive Era at the turn of the 20th century and during the Second Red Scare in the 1950s. And they would have similarly pernicious effects.

Nevertheless, by 1865, the federal government was the largest single employer in the North. It became so partly by expanding an administrative army of customs house officials and internal revenue agents, clerks, and inspectors (Foner, 1995). Initiated largely by Lincoln, Congress enacted economic policies that promoted corporate expansion and created a national banking system. The Union also imposed new and higher tariffs and taxes on consumption, promoted agricultural development, and established a bureau to facilitate immigration to replace soldiers leaving the workforce. Federal spending increased from 2 percent of gross national product (GNP) at the beginning of the war to 15 percent of GNP at its end (Balogh, 2009, p. 303). Thus, in wartime, the bonds of limited government in state building were broken in reaction to crises, as they would be later in the 20th and 21st centuries.

By the same token, the far more impoverished, less-educated, and laggard industrially based economy of the Confederacy mimicked these developments as best it could. Ironically, given its historical opposition to federal centralization, the Confederacy created an even stronger "national" state than the Union, "eventually crafting all-encompassing economic and social controls" (Balogh, 2009, p. 285). Initially lacking a comparable industrial and transportation base, the Confederate government in Richmond relied on mandates, coordination, and even property confiscation. It seized control of factories and constructed state-owned enterprises in the absence of private businesses. Moreover, its Sequestration Act went so far as to seize properties of family members living in the North, to declare that debts to northerners be paid instead to the Confederate government, and to require southern banks to reveal any property their partners and clients had in the North.

Bensel (1990) finds that the net effect for the South was to "replicate the administrative design of the ante-bellum Union throughout the confederacy" in the early years of the war and to expand the power of the national Confederate state as the war progressed (p. 103). The Confederacy also adopted a constitutional framework nearly identical to the US Constitution. In addition, it absorbed all the southern branches of federal agencies, adopting the bureaucratic administrative structures and accountability tools that already characterized them.

Thus, in a pattern of administrative "withdrawal and reestablishment" (Bensel, 1990, p. 101), both regions saw slightly more post offices than prior to the war, while the "federal courts, customs houses, arsenals, and lighthouses" of the compensatory state continued their work with the same personnel. In reaching its apogee of approximately 70,000 government employees in the South, 80 percent worked in the Confederate States' War Department (pp. 101–102). At the same time, further centralization and amplification of the military blueprint of administration occurred in the North and South in ways temporarily flouting Americans' self-conception of the need only for "common men and common sense." Bowing to a perceived need for expertise, this period witnessed some depoliticization of appointments to the military and the creation of a temporary civil service system (e.g., Balogh, 2009; Bensel, 1990; Foner, 1995).

****

The end of the Civil War in 1865 brought not only a vanquished South but also another expansion of national administrative capacity within the compensatory state. For starters, citizens wanted to account for loved ones killed in the war (Faust, 2008, p. xvii). During the imbroglio, incomplete and inaccurate records existed of who died, where, when, and how. This was partly a function of the magnitude of the killing and of the sorry condition of soldiers' remains. But it was also a function of battlefield psychology, strategic considerations, and morale building. For instance, at times, the greater the number of deaths reported, the easier it was to portray the efforts of surviving soldiers as heroic. At other times, understating deaths kept the enemy in the dark about military strength.

By war's end, however, dead soldiers lay unburied and piled atop each other on battlefields, thousands remained unidentified and unaccounted for, and others received hasty burials that offended Christian and Victorian sensibilities. As Clara Barton lamented, a "distressed class of sufferers [existed] all through the land waiting, fearing, hoping, watching day by day for some little tidings of the loved and lost" (Faust, 2008, p. 212). When soldiers did not return, families longed to learn that they had died heroically. This led nurses, chaplains, and friends to make up stories to relieve families' concerns that a "good" death— heroic, brave, or calming—was experienced by their loved ones. Also, enough stories existed of finding living soldiers amid piles of dead to give families hope that their loved ones might still be alive. Perhaps most important, the religious notion that friends and relatives would reunite in physical form in the afterlife—and that life in heaven was but an extension of life on earth—exploded in America during the war (Faust, 2008).

This sense of duty to the dead resulted as well in the need to memorialize the sacrifice of, at first, victorious Union soldiers and, much later (after 1903), Confederate soldiers. "Naming the [Union] dead"—and increasing the number of jobs for doing so—became widely understood as a duty of the federal government (Faust, 2008, p. 229). Absent federal concern about memorializing the Confederate dead, this also set off voluntary efforts by southern women and a number of private and state government initiatives to account for southern war dead. These efforts were later institutionalized in the national government as well.

In this context, two actions were taken that expanded the visible size of the federal government and other components of the compensatory state: the creation of national cemeteries for Union soldiers and the provision of pensions for Union veterans or their survivors. Both required a huge administrative effort to document what eventually became known as the Compiled Military Service Records. An army of federal clerks was hired to search among the fallen dead and collate on index cards the rosters, casualty records, and other documents necessary for proof of military service. Given Americans' predisposition for limited government, however, the visible size of the federal agency tasked with processing an eventual 36 million soldier entries for the Union had (once again) to enlist compensatory networks of volunteer, private, state, and local workers.

The gap between federal administrative capacity and the scope of the tasks involved was even worse for building national cemeteries. These (originally 17 in number) were established by Congress in 1867, a direct result of the work of Barton and volunteers led by Edmund Whitman. They argued that systematic efforts were underway to "obliterate and destroy all traces of the graves of Union soldiers" in the South (Faust, 2008, p. 226). Their memorialization mission involved disinterring tens of thousands of bodies, actions that some churches opposed. The extensiveness, costs, and administrative burdens were so formidable that they, too, overwhelmed federal capacities.

Thus, building national cemeteries also required the establishment of collaborative public–private–volunteer partnerships. These included postmasters, military commanders, and the US Sanitary Commission prodding and working with willing local churches, Christian commissions, local governments, and former soldiers. Faust (2008) puts the scope of these compensatory state-building efforts well:

> Whitman's request for information uncovered an army of record keepers [among the citizenry], waiting to be asked for details they had carefully

gathered and preserved . . . and [his call alone] . . . connected their individual efforts to the policies and actions of the state.

(p. 221)

By 1871, 300,000 Union soldiers were reinterred in 74 national cemeteries at a cost of over $4 million, a fact not lost on irate southerners whose war dead were not included in these efforts. Not only did this further help to propel states' rights' revivals in the latter Reconstruction era (see below), but, as noted, it also sparked voluntary expeditions led by church women to identify and rebury Confederate soldiers. Church and civic groups and ladies' aid societies took on the gruesome task of reinterment. These groups included the US Christian Commission, the Confederate Memorial Association, the Ladies of Richmond, the Ladies Memorial Cemetery Association (later renamed the Vicksburg Confederate Cemetery Association), and the Ladies' Memorial Association for the Confederacy.

A different kind of suffering—grinding poverty among the survivors of deceased Civil War soldiers—also helped expand the visible size of the federal government by providing pensions to soldiers and their families. The Union's Grand Army of the Republic (itself a large voluntary association of veterans) lobbied successfully for the creation of soldiers' pensions for Union (but not Confederate) soldiers in the post-Civil War era. However, as Skocpol (1992) notes (and as will be discussed further below), many of the financial, logistical, and administrative capacity problems of affording pensions on such a scale led to corruption and politicization of benefits. Led, in theory, by the under-resourced US Bureau of Pensions, implementors had to rely on a loose network of private and volunteer providers. In the process, pensions for widows became for Liberal Republicans and, later, early 20th-century progressives a "prime example of governmental profligacy and electorally rooted political corruption" (p. 2). This feeling, in turn, reinforced American exceptionalism's historical belief that government corrupts and that society flourishes when government gets out of the way.

****

That the Civil War amplified the proxy components of the compensatory state in these ways is not surprising given the historic capacity gap in federal agencies. Equally unsurprising given the dynamics in previous chapters was the amplification of the power of corporate and financial actors who associated themselves with government action (Roberts, 2012). As noted, the Civil War years saw spiraling increases in subsidies to railroads and for internal improvements, as well as federal tariff reductions for industry (e.g., on iron prices). Corporations also successfully pursued rights of way for transcontinental railroad development, an augmentation that soared above the already higher levels of subsidy wrought between 1850 and 1857 (Balogh, 2009, esp. pp. 288–290). Moreover, contracting and profits multiplied exponentially for the railroads (to transport troops and supplies), meatpackers (to feed the military), and mills (to produce wool for making uniforms).

In the wake of these successes, this period also produced the nation's first national trade associations (e.g., the American Bureau of Shipping, the National Association of Wool Manufacturers, and the National Paper Manufacturers Association). Along with reliance on the voluntary sector as part of the compensatory state, even more sinewy subsystems emerged with access and ties to government officials. These included the American Freedmen's Aid Societies, the aforementioned Grand Army of the Republic, and the consolidation and nationalization of several organizations. For instance, the US Sanitary Commission was a voluntary, cross-class, and confederated association that would become a model for other commissions later in the Progressive Era in the 20th century.

As Foner (2015) writes, the war boom in the North had immense political implications. It accelerated the "emergence of an American industrial bourgeoisie" and, thus, "tied the fortunes of this class to the Republican Party and the national state" (p. 9). But the greatest amplification of the political economy during (and after) the war was the ascendancy of the financial community and the federal government's dependence upon it. Importantly, the financial sector became a major source of resistance to maintaining and building federal administrative capacity in the compensatory state.

All aspects of the war depended on raising enough capital for expenses, thus making the Union and the Confederacy dependent upon these financiers. As such, Civil War mobilization "permanently chang[ed] . . . the relationship of the central state [i.e., the federal government] to finance capitalists" (Bensel, 1990, p. 238). Amplified in doing this were the dominance of New York City financial markets and the "rapid growth of a new, national class of finance capitalists" (p. 238). This dependency on finance capitalists grew even more in the post-Civil War era, abetted by the collapse of the southern financial system.

Some scholars argue that by the end of the war, "interests of finance capitalists and the American state were probably more closely linked than at any other point in the 19th century" (Bensel, 1990, p. 238). Although challenged by other scholars, what is not disputed is that this linkage was a double-edged sword for American state building. On the one hand, the federal government–financial capital link proved critical to funding the war and restoring the legitimacy of business interests (lost in economic recessions), more generally. On the other hand, financiers saw the US Department of the Treasury and its intrusion into financial markets as incompetent because of a lack of administrative capacity. They could have pushed for improving that capacity but instead opposed it.

To understand why this occurred, several factors are important to consider. First, the financial demands of the war forced the federal government to abandon temporarily the gold standard that had been the foundation of the US economy. Combined with reliance on federally unregulated markets, the government depended on financial capitalists as part of the compensatory state to, among other things, market debt securities, manage currency values, and maintain circulation of capital. At the same time, because of limited federal administrative capacity, anti-tax fervor, and the need to pay for the war as fast as possible, the Union financed the war through debt.

Major banks in New York (as well as consortia of banks in Boston, New York, and Philadelphia) distributed Treasury bonds. Granted, as the war progressed, a substantial internal revenue system and income tax were created. By the end of the Civil War, however, only about 10 percent of all households paid any tax (Balogh, 2009, p. 289). Thus, reliance on the financial community further amplified from earlier time periods what today is called "crony capitalism." For example, in 1862, nearly 80 percent of the bonds issued went to persons or firms in New York, while half of what was left over went to a single broker (Jay Cooke & Company).

Second, the uncertainties and vicissitudes of the war almost dried up European investments in the United States, investments that the nation relied on for growth. Into this vacuum rushed a host of new financial institutions and brokers in the country. Over a ten-fold increase occurred (from 167 to 1,800) in New York City bankers and brokers between 1864 and 1870 (Bensel, 1990, p. 239). This consolidation of financial prowess and power—often leveraged, tied to, and facilitated by the federal government—was unprecedented in size and scope.

Within this context, financiers witnessed the Department of the Treasury's aforementioned lack of administrative capacity and, hence, lack of competence. Blunders in money market operations, inefficiency, and fraudulent revenue collection by Treasury became apparent. Moreover, the financial community conflated this perception to include most agencies of the federal government. These feelings reached their apex during the Reconstruction era. The financial class saw Radical Reconstruction being implemented, in their eyes, by an administratively incompetent and corruption-riddled federal government that was not up to the task but, nonetheless, was becoming ever more intrusive into financial markets. Financiers lobbied heavily to end Reconstruction on these grounds. Before examining these dynamics, however, one needs to appreciate the role that Reconstruction itself played in the ebb and flow of state building and administrative reform that might enhance the capacity of the federal government in the compensatory state.

****

With the South vanquished, Radical Republicans in the Congress felt empowered to eradicate slavery while simultaneously restoring a sense of national identity. The two aims were inherently contradictory. Lincoln was unclear about the path he would take in his second term, but several thoughts gelled before his assassination. For starters, he wanted to readmit states that had seceded from the Union as quickly as possible. And just as he had acted first and consulted later with Congress during the war (e.g., invoking his war or military powers and ignoring or superseding the courts), he saw himself determining readmission standards. This, despite knowing that he would face strong opposition from Radical Republicans, who believed that speedy readmission would restore power to secession leaders and squander the North's victory.

Lincoln also expected that Congress—and the Radical Republicans within it—would have greater political leverage over him once the war ended. Nonetheless, he equivocated before war's end about the fate of freed blacks. Alternatively, he considered offering blacks colonization back to Africa, compensating slaveholders for freed slaves, and a phased-in emancipation. For Radical Republicans, these were unacceptable alternatives. They doubted that freed slaves would fare well without jobs, education, civil rights, representation in governments at all levels, redistribution of wealth, and banning former Confederate leaders from office.

Before war's end, Lincoln gave a general pardon to Confederates and the nucleus of reentry to the Union for "restructured" state governments. As part of these initiatives, he allowed states to rejoin the Union as soon as 10 percent of their voting population in 1860 agreed to establish a republican form of government that was loyal to the United States. He also left political and administrative "models" and precedents in several Union-occupied states (e.g., Louisiana) and hoped they would show how leaving reconstruction in his hands alone could occur "with minimum dislocation and without lasting bitterness" (Riccards, 1997, p. 275).

Fearing that the invasion of northern "carpetbaggers" into the South would rile the defeated southerners, Lincoln successfully pushed for state and congressional elections in Union-occupied Louisiana. Once elections took place, however, some in the state refused to recognize the new government. Soon, Arkansas and Florida followed suit. In reaction, Radical Republicans proposed in the Wade–Davis bill that no former Confederate civil or military person could vote or hold political or administrative office. Neither could anyone who fought in the Confederate army or aided it in creating a new Confederate constitution. Lincoln argued the bill was too punitive and undermined reconciliation.

After his assassination, most expected Lincoln's successor—Vice President Andrew Johnson (D-TN)—to follow the general outlines of Lincoln's agenda (Foner, 1995).[5] Moderate Republicans were also comfortable with the idea that Johnson alone would set the actual terms of Reconstruction. Like Lincoln, he envisioned a speedy reconstruction of the Union. As such, the first two years after the war are known as the "presidential reconstruction" era. Johnson did not even call Congress back into session as he rushed to put a reconstruction plan and pardon system into place.

But his initiatives were unacceptable to Radical Republicans. Their anger increased when Johnson restored all property to Confederate landholders, except slaves, and ended any possibility of creating a landed class of former slaves. Johnson also vetoed the Civil Rights and Freedmen's Bureau bills passed by Congress and asserted that Congress should pass no Reconstruction bills until all the southern states were reinstated into the Union. This state-rebuilding effort would have killed meaningful reform by creating a Southern state voting majority in Congress.

Aside from Johnson's impeachment by the House and acquittal by the Senate, the results of these actions were profound for Reconstruction.[6] As historian Peter Hoffer (2013) summarizes:

> Returning Confederate veterans, including their officers, were averse to their former slaves gaining title to the land. . ., much less treating slaves as equals. Freedmen and women were harassed, belittled, and cheated . . . as whites tried to "redeem" the South from the influence of the Republicans and their black allies. Newly reconstructed state governments no sooner ratified the Thirteenth Amendment [freeing slaves] and fulfilled the other terms required for their readmission to the Union than their legislatures passed vagrancy laws effectively re-enslaving the blacks.
>
> (p. 137)

Essentially, Johnson pursued a "restoration" rather than "reconstruction" strategy for his native region. He opposed federally guaranteed rights for blacks and insisted that the South was "white man's country," because blacks throughout history "had shown a constant tendency to relapse into barbarism" when left on their own (Riccards, 1997, p. 287). Emboldened, southern leaders demanded a restoration of all their previous rights. Moreover, Deep South states did not think Johnson's proposals went far enough, and many flouted them. Some added reservations to the 13th Amendment to the US Constitution freeing slaves, while others considered rejecting any responsibility for war debts. Moreover, an overwhelming majority of those elected to office in the region were former Confederate leaders.

At the same time, many southern states began adopting Black Codes in 1865 and 1866 that institutionalized segregation, reinstated criminal parts of the former slave codes, and prevented former slaves from leaving lands without permission. As Frederick Douglas observed at the time, the "work does not end with the abolition of slavery, but only begins" (Foner, 2005, p. 67). Looking back at the period 1860 to 1880 in both political and administrative terms, W. E. B. Du Bois wrote in his 1935 classic, *Black Reconstruction*, that "little effort has been made to preserve the records of Negro effort and speeches, action, work and wages, homes and families. Nearly all of this has gone down beneath a mass of ridicule and caricature, deliberate omission and misstatement" (Foner, 2005, p. xi).

Meanwhile, and unsurprisingly, Radical Republicans (led by Charles Sumner and Thaddeus Stevens in Congress) attacked what Johnson was doing. They wanted to use the Union's victory to destroy slavery on moral grounds but also to end what slavery produced: the "greatest concentration of economic wealth and political power in the entire country" among financial and corporate capitalists (Foner, 2005, p. 42). By 1867, Radical Republicans—accompanied by moderate Republicans incensed by Johnson's actions—heightened federal efforts to realize the former slaves' primary objectives: improvements in education, transportation, and public accommodations; elimination of the Black Codes; and economic uplift.

They did so partly by passing the Reconstruction Acts of 1867 over Johnson's veto. These acts stipulated that "lawful governments did not exist in the South, and that Congress [absent southern state representatives] could govern the region until acceptable ones had been established" (Foner, 2005, p. 121). Initiating the "congressional Reconstruction era," the acts divided the South into five military-administered districts, thus further ensconcing military models of administrative reform in Americans' self-conception. They also provided a process for how each would be governed and stipulated that leading Confederate officials were precluded from voting (as were women).

In prioritizing funding for public education during the congressional Reconstruction era, proponents had to overcome southern states' historic opposition to it. Lack of education funding was designed to preserve the plantation aristocracy's dominance over both slaves and poor whites. National spending for education in the North tripled between 1860 and 1870. But, in the South, state budgets for schools plummeted, with the highest reductions made in black schools. Drastic cuts in social services also hit poor blacks and whites inordinately hard, but especially blacks. This, amid southern states reversing the nascent and improved civil society that states, localities, northern philanthropists, and women and black groups had put together and helped fund to advance the life chances of slaves during the Civil War.

In practice, Republican military governors and their administrators pressured states to expand the existing public-school system while maintaining segregated schools. Even blacks supported this approach, being more concerned with gaining access to education and ensuring equitable funding between white and black schools. At the same time, military governors and administrators afforded blacks access to public accommodations and imposed antidiscrimination protections on business. With black influence growing in the Republican Party, a majority of southern states had laws guaranteeing "full and equal rights" in these areas by 1870.

Although difficult to implement administratively, these laws nevertheless began partially to meet the aspirations of blacks and, thus, sparked indignation from members of the southern white aristocracy. Yet, even former slaves were also disappointed. Many felt that the best way to advance their economic opportunity was through land redistribution. Opponents pejoratively labeled Radical Republican supporters of this idea "confiscation Republicans." But blacks remembered General William T. Sherman's famous pledge to give each former male slave "40 acres and a mule" and felt this promise had been broken.

Moderate Republicans in both the North and South argued that regional economic development was needed and should benefit blacks and poor whites alike. Nonetheless, they also believed land transfers in the South threatened their national focus on "free labor" and individual personal development. But what they feared most was the occurrence of the same kinds of demands for land redistribution in the North. This, as labor unrest in this industrializing region mounted and new waves of immigration occurred in northern cities to fill assembly-line jobs. Both developments lowered wages and undercut natives' job prospects. Northerners also worried that labor leaders and former slaves would form a powerful political coalition threatening their political dominance.

Thus, consonant with the Whig's American System, moderate Republicans focused instead on railroad construction in the region, a focus that was unprecedented in scope and scale from pre-Civil War investments. Their aim, consistent with the Madisonian vision of a commercial republic and exceptionalists' embrace of equal opportunity over equality of outcome, was to "create [in the South] a far larger and more integrated railroad network, to spur the emergence of a diversified economy of booming factories, bustling towns, and diversified agriculture freed from the plantation's dominance" (Foner, 2005, p. 165). But, again, the political triumph of this less aggressive approach was not inevitable.

As in earlier times, moderation was pushed, shaped, and instituted by the power of burgeoning corporate capitalism in America, plus the financial community that had gained dominance during the Civil War. The former stood to expand the financial gains they had made from the American System, including subsidies and contracts for internal improvements and railroad building. Financiers were anxious to reestablish high levels of cotton production immediately—a primary basis for trade—and, thus, enhance the importation of foreign commercial species. As noted, they also saw Radical Reconstruction efforts as delaying the dismantling of the massive internal revenue system developed during the war, which they opposed as growing the size of an administratively incompetent federal government. Continuing military occupation of the South on the scale envisioned by Radical Republicans also required sizeable increases in federal taxes that they would have to pay, growing the federal government and its administrative capacity in the process.

****

Without question, the Civil War and Reconstruction had profound implications for the visibility of the federal government as a component of the compensatory state, most especially enactment of the 13th, 14th, and 15th amendments to the

Constitution. Still, the visibility and vigor of the federal government was short-lived. It ended officially in 1876. This, after presidential candidate Rutherford B. Hayes (R-OH) made a deal swapping the support of four contested southern-state congressional delegations for his election over Samuel Tilden in return for ending Reconstruction.[7]

The end of Reconstruction sparked not only black cynicism but also a further amplification and institutionalization of the proxy components of the compensatory state that had occurred before and during the war and Reconstruction. As Du Bois lamented, the "slave went free; stood a brief moment in the sun; then moved back again toward slavery" with the advent of the Jim Crow era (Foner, 2015, p. 254). This, despite blacks' exemplary record of military service during the war. More than 180,000 black soldiers were killed in the war, along with 24,000 more in the Navy. Twenty-three blacks received the Congressional Medal of Honor (p. 52).

Equally misguided was the conventional southern narrative—perpetuated in the early 20th century by the Dunning School of Reconstruction History at Vanderbilt University—that Reconstruction was marred excessively by political and administrative corruption and misrule by blacks, southern "scalawags," and northern carpetbaggers (Foner, 2015, p. 248). Just how far off base were such characterizations was clear to anyone familiar with the associational movement that free blacks (and women) had created for themselves in the South, with prodding and help from the federal government. Recall that blacks had established and administered their own schools and mutual aid societies to meet unaddressed community needs. They also built their own "government out of sight" during the Civil War and then expanded it significantly during Reconstruction. This addition of proxy components to the compensatory state was comprised of efforts to compensate for state-sponsored and administered discrimination even before Jim Crow laws were enacted. These ascriptive obstacles included poll taxes, residency requirements, pig laws, and arrests for joblessness.

Moreover, as the federal government retreated, the role of voluntary organizations—especially those begun either outside or inside the black community—expanded and grew in importance. True to the commercial republic, faculty psychology, and American exceptionalist values, self-help, not government help, became the mantra of the day for black leaders. The "parallel" efforts and institutions built by blacks—often encouraged and supported by private foundations and the federal government as part of the compensatory state—were free from white supervision. They also created opportunities for blacks to gain leadership and organizational experience, as would the War on Poverty nearly a century later in America. These associations also worked collaboratively with state and local governments to try to advance blacks' place in a new social order.

These efforts again resonated with American exceptionalism's view of the superiority of society over government capacity building, as the sometimes hidden hand of the federal government continued. And despite encouragement from or even partnering with government, proponents argued that because of this administrative arrangement, society was "protected morally from" the possibilities of government corruption (Skocpol, 1992, p. 21). Roy Lubove (1986) writes that "voluntary association provided an alternative to politics and governmental action. It enabled groups of all kinds to exert an influence and seek their distinctive goals without resort to the coercive powers of government" (p. 2). In the process, a veritable "charity organization society" model flourished that was easier sold to elected officials and citizens because of its perceived link to civic republicanism (Balogh, 2009, p. 302). In addition, and as harbingers of the settlement movement in the early Progressive Era of the late 19th and early 20th century, these voluntary, mass-based, and cross-class associations were SRP-inspired schools and laboratories for citizen engagement in politics (Novak, 2001).

But, reiterating, this growth in the proxy component of the compensatory state did not happen by accident or merely bubble up, in Burkean terms, from "little platoons" of volunteers. As later chapters will detail, a powerful synergy exists between major wars and the growth of voluntary associations as part of America's compensatory state. The national government also needs and *encourages* these entities to compensate for its own administrative limitations, while the new associations seek to gain, retain, or enhance legitimacy and its expressive, material, and authority benefits by assisting state institutions (Skocpol, 1992; Skocpol et al., 2000). Thus, although growth in private-sector contracting is widely and correctly associated with war and leaves sinewy subsystems in its wake, it is less appreciated how the same occurs for voluntary associations. Indeed, as Jocelyn Crowley and Skocpol (2001) also demonstrate, voluntary associations with ties to the victorious Union effort were more likely to survive and expand until the present day through their association with government and (later) the tax incentives for donations permitted by federal law (also see Skocpol et al., 2002).

****

As in prior and subsequent time periods, the still amateur-based social sciences also helped to shape, and benefited from association with, Civil War campaigns and Reconstruction. Most prominently, the aforementioned ASSA joined with the National Civil Service Reform League, financial capitalists, the National Association of Manufacturers, and Liberal Republicans to push for civil service reform (Haskell, 2000). As the National Association of Manufacturers argued at its first meeting in 1868, the absence of civil service reform was costing business too much (Nelson, 1982, esp. 120–121).

For abolitionists such as Wendell Phillips, civil service reform was necessary to thwart the decline of civic virtue in America and to build a national community. Indeed, their aim was no less than to "reconstruct the moral foundations of American politics," an aim "second in importance [only] to the abolition of slavery" (Nelson, 1982, p. 121). One reform leader, Carl Schurz (1871), argued in SRP terms that civil service reform was not a purely administrative issue: "The question whether the Departments at Washington are managed well or badly, is, in proportion to the whole problem, an insignificant question" (also see Nelson, 1982, p. 121). The issue, instead, was ending a political and administrative system that "perverts public trust into party spoils . . . prostitutes election into a desperate strife for personal profit[,] and degrades the national character" (p. 121).

Among the most telling indictments of immorality and the need for civil service reform pursued by this corporate–social science nexus of interests was the aforementioned Veterans Pension system. As noted earlier, Republicans had used the pension system to reward and build the party's electoral base. Many deserving poor were excluded in the process, and receipt of benefits even got decoupled from actual military service. Given Americans' limited government predilections, the development of "partisan social networks" rather than federal administrative capacity to manage the pension system prevailed.

Thus, the end of Reconstruction certainly concluded an era of federal activism and firmly cemented the instrumental over the governance perspective of public administration. The difference with Jacksonianism, as well as later 20th-century reform efforts, was that this instrumentalism was congressionally—not presidentially—based. Thus, as alluded to earlier, the position taken by the Whigs was a legislatively anchored theory of public administration, one stressing instrumental responsiveness, accountability to Congress, and representation of interests (Rosenbloom, 2000).

As Leonard White (1958) observed, Republican presidents from Ulysses Grant (IN) to William McKinley (OH) embraced not only the theory of presidential subordination to Congress but also that the "President ought not even to be master of his own administrative household" (pp. 20–21). As Senator John Sherman (R-IN) (1896) wrote, the "executive department of a republic like ours should be subordinate to the legislative department. The President should obey and enforce the laws, leaving to the people the duty of correcting any errors committed by their representatives in Congress" through elections. In turn, and as noted earlier, congressional dominance created a series of politically and administratively weak presidents until Theodore Roosevelt (R-NY) at the turn of the century and in the aftermath of the Spanish–American War (1898).

In the process, congressional government only further amplified administrative corruption during the ensuing Gilded Age. This helped seal the victory of the civil service reform movement in 1883 with the passage of the Civil Service Act (aka the Pendleton Act) pushed by financiers and social scientists of the era. But the failures of congressional-centered administrative reform would—in consort with the continuing corruption of the Gilded Age, the slow pace of civil service reform, and emerging societal challenges—create the next perception of major historical–structural mismatches. This, as Chapter 4 chronicles, set the stage for, first, the Granger, Bellamy, People's Party, and Populist political and administrative reform movements and, later, the early Progressive reform movement.

Notes

1. This discussion relies heavily on Howe (1979); Remini (2008).
2. This discussion relies heavily on Appleby (2001).
3. Some scholars contend that the kind of economic class struggle emergent in the United States was quite different from what American exceptionalist proponents saw as economic class division. First, no hereditary aristocracy existed in America at its founding. Second, egalitarianism was not premised solely on income differentials: "Citizenship appeared to have given even the humbler members of society access to the knowledge and cultivation elsewhere reserved for the privileged classes" (Appleby, 2001, p. 59). Of course, not all were considered "citizens" in the United States, calling this argument partially into question.
4. Some feminist scholars have argued that the American Social Science Association (ASSA) was a feminist organization bent on advancing women's suffrage (e.g., Leach, 1980), especially within the local branches and affiliates of the organization. More recent archival research by scholars of intellectual history challenges this argument (e.g., Haskell, 2000).
5. This discussion relies heavily on Bensel (1990); Foner (2005, 2015); Riccards (1997).
6. Johnson was impeached by the House for violating the Tenure in Office Act by replacing Secretary of War Henry Stanton. But the real issue involved his actions on Reconstruction.
7. Hayes is the only president selected by a commission of congressmen and Supreme Court justices appointed to rule on contested electoral ballots.

Chapter 4

Industrial Agonistes, the Corporate–Social Science Nexus, and American Administrative Reform, Circa 1880–1920

Writing originally in the *American Economic Review* in 1925, noted economist Wesley Mitchell (1999) observed that "as in other sciences, we desire knowledge mainly as an instrument of control. Control means the alluring possibility of shaping the evolution of economic life" (p. 372). He also made it clear in his 1924 presidential address to the American Economic Association (AEA) that the means to that control was the creation of a "new science of economics" premised on behavioralism, statistical analysis, and institutionalism (Ross, 1991, p. 411). Other neoclassical economists who opposed institutionalism, such as John Bates Clark, nevertheless argued the same: "The whole modern movement may be interpreted as a demand for procedure which appears more adequately scientific"—meaning more like the natural sciences (p. 412). This, despite dissents from other scholars epitomized in the work of German philosopher and phenomenologist, Wilhelm Dilthey, and, later, British philosopher, Isaiah Berlin, and Austrian philosopher, Karl Popper, that the two sciences required different methodologies.

As noted in earlier chapters, efforts to link understanding of natural phenomena to rationality, mathematics, and morality stretch back at least to the Homeric epics and the Pythagoreans in the pre-Socratic era in Greece (Tarnas, 1991). With differences in focus and interpretation, all believed that a discoverable order underlay the surface chaos of the natural world. Millennia later, proponents of the Republican Arithmetik movement (later, members of the American Statistical Association and, then, the American Social Science Association [ASSA]) extended this belief in underlying order to the social and economic world. And circa 1880 to 1920, this viewpoint informed what became known as the Progressive reform movement in the United States.

Mitchell and Clark wrote and spoke their words after the Progressive Era ostensibly waned as an administrative reform movement linked to a state-altering project. Reformers sought to counter the negative externalities of the Gilded Age and its aftermath. Perceptions abounded that yawning historical–structural gaps existed between the needs of the nation (created by industrialization, immigration, and the first era of economic globalization) and the institutional structures bequeathed to it by American exceptionalist values. Moreover, in a period of uncertainty, a static view of economics and history must give way to a more dynamic view allowing greater control (meaning the shaping of these forces by human reason). Mitchell (1999) added that "even in days of reaction [to these dynamics], we cannot regain implicit faith in the stability of our prewar institutions" (p. 375). History was error-filled, and future millenarian progress required scientific rationality to guide public policy, state building, and administrative reform. Marginalized were competing Hegelian precepts of the messiness of history, learning from historical errors, and the dialectical non-linearity of progress.

This sense for a need for control was central to the Progressive movement. The progressives were a motley coalition of actors that included a coterie of emerging professional occupations and a now more professionalized group of university-based social science scholars. Many of the former represented a new wave of administrative professions spawned by the Industrial Revolution of the late 19th and early 20th centuries (e.g., accountants, managers, and industrial engineers). The latter were part of a generation of American scholars who studied in German universities and assimilated many of their professors' views of higher education, methodology, activist government, and the role of scholars in society.

They felt that universities were not for spreading ecclesiastical principles but, rather, for eliminating scientific amateurism such as offered by the ASSA. For them, studying societies' dynamics in systematic, logical-positivistic, and empirically grounded ways (as per the so-called Vienna Circle in Austria in the early 20th century) was the only viable path forward for realizing America's millenarian vision in an era of ever-growing societal and international interdependence. Moreover, picking up on European socialist thought, scholars had to become activists in society applying scientific rationality as a cure for society's formidable social, economic, and political ills. Only later would robust dissent from this activist perspective arise. Conservatives lamented the "loss of veneration" of traditional institutions, norms, and values that progressivism advanced (Kirk, 1986). Meanwhile, social scientists and the emerging field of public administration debated whether they should merely "investigate" social, political, and administrative ills or "investigate and instigate" for change.

Many in the social science professions also imbibed from their German experiences an abiding skepticism for key components of American exceptionalist values. Philosophically, they questioned the "natural state" of free markets, the invisible hand said to guide these markets, and claims of their inherent social efficiency. These, they argued, were metanarratives or "stories" with no empirical basis that served only to justify wealthy corporate interests and upper social class privileges. Corporations also were beginning to operate nationally and internationally, making subnational regulation structurally deficient. Thus, as in Europe, Americans' penchant for localism had to give way, in a mature urban–industrial society, to national governments playing an activist role in markets. They had to offset the negative externalities of markets rather than protect the wealth of corporate capitalists spawned during the Gilded Age by the Industrial Revolution. These capitalists, previously and positively seen as the captains of industry, were now seen as robber barons and threats to American exceptionalist aspirations for social mobility.

Yet, these emerging social science disciplines in America lacked the same kind of legitimacy that German professors enjoyed in their fields. Consequently, they sought to advance their legitimacy as authority structures in society by showing—individually and collectively—how their methodological prowess mimicking the physical sciences could attenuate mounting social strains that, again, belied the tenets of American exceptionalism. Like business, they saw affiliation with government activities—and especially federal activities during World War I—as the path to legitimacy and its expressive, material, and authority gains.

The assembly lines of the Gilded Age and the early 20th century caused the acceleration of earlier corporate concentrations of wealth and massive income inequality. Once again, the latter provoked repeated and sometimes violent actions by, and against, the oppressed, impoverished, uneducated, and non-English-speaking immigrants, this time from southern and eastern Europe. Fleeing poverty, they were also lured to America by the promise of assembly-line jobs. Also threatening were attacks against southern blacks fleeing farms for a better life in northern urban areas. These concentrations of people in urban areas also spawned social needs for services such as police, fire, health, and sanitation not provided directly by government but still by private contractors. Meanwhile, rural poverty increased, as did now familiar perceptions that northern industrialists (especially the railroads) and financiers, abetted by the Republican Party's tariff system, were again exploiting the labor of southern and western settlers for personal financial gain.

Amid these strains, a yearning developed again among American opinion leaders for bringing order to a world that looked out of anyone's control. For those in the American West, this yearning produced the Granger movement, followed by the Populist movement. In the industrializing East and urban areas, and among the more educated, it produced, first, the creation of "nationalist clubs" inspired by Edward Bellamy's socialist utopian novel, *Looking Backward* (1888), and, then, the People's Party. Both advocated the nationalization of industry run by a bureaucratic elite. Produced later was the aforementioned Progressive reform movement, which reflected the German idealist philosopher G. W. F. Hegel's view that new ideas needed new institutions in order to survive. This, also to counteract socialist, syndicalist, communist, and anarchist movements in America (Kramer, 2015).

Once again, however, the early Progressive movement was not an automatic or intellectually cohesive response to claims of a historical–structural mismatch. For example, three different perspectives on the best way to reform administration competed for ascendancy within the early Progressive movement. These were technocratic progressivism involving the amplification of a "science-based claim to social authority and policymaking" (Alchon, 1985, p. 175), the settlement movement predicated on "critical emancipatory" action research and citizen participation, and associationalism animated by notions of corporatism.

Collectively, nonetheless, they advocated for what became known as the "new" liberalism challenging the "old" liberalism of laissez-faire economics. In founding the American Economic Association in 1885, prominent economists such as Henry Carter Adams, John Bates Clark, and Richard Ely said they "regard[ed] the state as an educational and ethical agency whose positive aid is an indispensable condition of human progress" (Balogh, 2009, p. 352; see Ely, 1886). Social and economic problems that challenged the millenarian vision of American exceptionalism were not inevitable; "they were the effects of an unstable, ill-managed, but improvable corporate capitalism" (Alchon, 1985, p. 2).

Thus, many in the Progressive movement were decidedly more accepting than their predecessors of government intervention into markets and social affairs. As such, the visible size of an expertise-based federal bureaucracy grew, even before World War I amplified its growth. But the trajectory of this historical period meant that the national government continued incentivizing, working with, building on, and expanding the proxy component of the compensatory state. Thus, despite building up the federal government component of the compensatory state, reformers still heavily "parcel[ed] out [its] authority to interest groups, professional associations, the voluntary sector, corporations, and eventually even to labor unions" (Balogh, 2009, p. 355).

Conventional wisdom in public administration posits that the technological progressives dominated this reform period because that was what was needed to, for example, eliminate corruption and run government more like a business. Also dominant is the image of a radical transformation of the state through political and administrative reforms informed by the instrumental rationality project (IRP) with its emphasis on scientific management, planning, and scientific philanthropy. Aspects of this perspective are true to an extent, especially if one starts from the "peculiar stateless origins" thesis (Chapters 1 and 2). But if one views the state from an infrastructural perspective, one sees both the amplification of earlier technocratic administration (the IRP) and the building of the compensatory state. Moreover, its ascendancy over state-building and administrative alternatives was neither inevitable nor complete. Rather, alternative reform ideas fell before the growing legitimacy and power of the corporate–social science nexus of interests, although important aspects of some alternatives became part of the compensatory state. Like earlier amplifications of the IRP, however, its triumph contributed to citizen fatigue and estrangement from activist government and administration. This again led to the next rounds of calls for political and administrative reform in America, first, in the 1920s in the form of a "return to normalcy" and, later, once those reforms failed to alleviate the Herculean challenges of the Great Depression (see Chapter 5).

****

The 1880s witnessed the most dynamic period of economic growth in the United States since the Civil War. Between 1865 and 1873, national markets, reliable labor, technological advances, and a 40 percent increase in average real wages buoyed the economic and cultural spirits of the beneficiaries of a commercial republic. Even before the Civil War, "factories, railroads, and telegraph wires seemed the very engines of a democratic future." They were the means toward realizing "republican values, diffusing civic values, and enlightenment along with material wealth" (Trachtenberg, 2007, p. 38). Such feelings continued among many elite opinion leaders for the remainder of the century, manifested in two international expositions flaunting the wizardry of the machine (Philadelphia in 1876 and Chicago in 1893) and its links to America's millenarian mission.

The late 19th century also saw the embellishment of earlier trends regarding trade associations of businesses, though, even then, nowhere near the proliferation that came later during the first two decades of the 20th century. These included the Indianapolis Monetary Commission, the National Association of Manufacturers, the National Foreign Trade Council, and the US Chamber of Commerce. Reminiscent of how democracy and capitalism were linked in the early 19th-century image of a commercial republic, "commerce and courage" were initially linked by high society with the manly virtues jeopardized by an "overcivilized" Gilded Age and Victorian society (Lears, 2009, p. 32). As historian Richard White summarizes, high society worried about the declining place of masculine virtues in a "newly industrialized and seemingly effete order" (McPherson, 2007, p. 87). In the process, businesses—especially the captains of industry—became heroes to many Americans. And no more powerful symbol of this heroism was the consolidation of industry in vertically integrated and administered corporations in the Gilded Age (Chandler, 1993).

As noted in earlier chapters, the quasi-public and private incorporation mechanisms of administrative reform and state building went back to the colonial era in America. Indeed, the colonies themselves were the product of joint-stock companies, such as the Dutch and British East India Company. What changed during the Gilded Age, however, was the pretense of the pursuit of a public interest by these entities. This, despite the capture of those original public corporations by private interests (see Chapter 3). Businesses now had the right to incorporate for profit with no further justification needed. Many states also lowered the requirements for incorporation, viewing corporations "as the product of market forces that required political protection only from those who dared to interfere with [the] natural law" of the marketplace (Balogh, 2009, p. 16). But, to be sure that "natural law" prevailed, corporate contributions to political campaigns soared.

During the Gilded Age, American businesses needed access to copious amounts of capital. Governments' weakening requirements for incorporation afforded businessmen access to that capital through the selling of shares in companies. At the same time, the courts protected such laissez-faire principles as private property rights, limited government, and "freedom of contract." They did so partly by claiming a distinction between public and private affairs that barred government intrusion. Especially potent in protecting corporations was the doctrine of freedom of contract supported by the US Supreme Court. Justices found that it was unconstitutional to deny employers and employees the right to enter employment relationships, no matter how detrimental to employees (Rehnquist, 2004). With some exceptions, this doctrine also undermined minimum wage, maximum labor, and child-labor restrictions enacted later in this time period (e.g., in *Adair v. United States* in 1908 and *Hammer v. Dagenhart* in 1918).

With business protected in these ways, a "corporate reconstruction of American capitalism" transpired (Sklar, 1988, p. 46). This reconstruction began in the 1880s, with its most profound consolidation occurring between 1898 and 1904. In 1883, only 20 corporations were listed on the New York Stock Exchange; by 1904, estimates are that nearly 300 trusts existed, with a capitalization value of about $7 billion (Sklar, 1988, p. 46; also see Gordon, 2004; Weinstein, 1968). Between 1897 and 1904, 4,227 firms merged, creating 257 combinations (e.g., International Harvester and United States Steel) (Eisner, 2000b, p. 29). Doing so meant the dwarfing of the states' power to constrain corporate concentrations of capital that violated American exceptionalist values related to free markets and individualism.

This reconstruction of capital nonetheless prompted vibrant economic growth during the 1880s and 1890s and business expansion into new markets, albeit with a devastating depression from 1893 to 1897 in America. Amid this growth, basic management issues such as preventing overproduction had to be addressed. As Marc Allen Eisner (2000b) summarizes the situation, "corporations had to discover some means of coordinating expansion and managing competition to exploit growing economies of scale while maintaining stability" (p. 29). Their solution was both vertical integration within their business supply chains and horizontal integration in product lines through the building of such legal entities as the American Cotton Oil Trust, the Standard Oil Trust, and the Sugar Trust.

The organizational, administrative, and financial acumen needed by these corporate titans—plus the managerial workforce they put together to run these businesses—was stunning. For example, as late as 1840 in America, no middle-management positions existed in business (defined as managers who supervised others and reported to their own superiors in the organization) (Chandler, 1993, p. 3). As business historian Alfred Chandler (1993, p. 1, passim) wrote, "in many sectors of the economy, the visible hand of management replaced what Adam Smith referred to as the invisible hand of market forces." The dominant characteristics, Chandler wrote, of the new multi-unit corporation—which would become the organizational model for government agencies—were "distinct operating units" coordinated by a "hierarchy of salaried executives" (i.e., middle managers). Markets "remained the generator of demand for goods and services, but modern business enterprise took over the functions of coordinating flows of goods through existing processes of production, and of allocating funds and personnel for future production and distribution." Wrought was the rise of "managerial capitalism," with the "modern business enterprise. . . [becoming] the most powerful institution in the American economy and its managers the most influential group of economic decision makers."

Amplifying earlier iterations of the IRP, the modern multi-unit business enterprise, wrote Chandler (1993, pp. 6–7), was appealing because the transaction costs of coordinating multiple units administratively in a single organization were lower than the transaction costs of markets trying to coordinate independent units in the production chain. But those attributed advantages (e.g., greater productivity, lower costs, greater profitability) could only be attained if a managerial hierarchy were created. However, as in prior iterations of the IRP, modern business units and management systems took on lives of their own, meaning that the managerial hierarchy became a "source of permanence, power, and continued growth" (Sombart, 1930, p. 200). As future chapters will illustrate, the same dynamics occurred when the IRP lessons of the multi-unit business enterprise were applied to multi-unit public and nonprofit agencies in the compensatory state.

For now, and in inefficient path-dependency terms, this continued emphasis on building administrative capacity in the private sector greatly amplified the historical first-mover advantages of private- over public-sector administrative capacity. This, in turn, helped "lock in" the logic of business and the IRP in future administrative reform efforts (Trachtenberg, 2007, p. 134; also see Brands, 2010; Gordon, 2004; Lears, 2009; Weinstein, 1968). In 1901, for example, only 21 percent of all federal employees (N = 239,476) could be classified as administrators, with nearly 80 percent of all employees working in the Post Office or the War and Navy departments.

As Eisner (2000a) puts it, until the 1900s, the "federal government remained something less than a functioning administrative entity and something more than a support system of a post office" (p. 23). Adds William Becker (1982):

> In comparative terms of the development of managerial structures, the large-scale corporation was more highly developed bureaucratically than the executive departments of the federal government. The specialization, the division of labor, and the economic rationality of the larger corporations made them fundamentally more advanced. . . . By World War I, major American corporations employed many thousands of employees worldwide. The levels of bureaucratic control were greater and the scale of operations more complex than anything undertaken by the U.S. government at the time.
>
> (pp. 182–183)

These developments, in turn, had significant political consequences for the evolution of American administrative reform and compensatory state building. By the 1890s, a new, self–conscious middle class of professionals arose, one that built on earlier trends in the United States. As historian Robert Wiebe (1967) writes, this new class had two broad categories:

> One included those with strong professional aspirations in such fields as medicine, law, economics, administration, social work, and architecture. The second comprised specialists in business, in labor, and in agriculture awakening both to their distinctiveness and to their ties with similar people in the same occupation. In fact, consciousness of unique skills and functions, an awareness that came to mold much of their lives, characterized all members of the class.
>
> (p. 112)

Not surprisingly, the new professional class embraced the changes under way in society, seeing them as opportunities for social mobility, enhanced status, and greater legitimacy. These changes "offered them respectable and profitable positions" and a security that allowed them "to look beyond today's work and try to locate themselves within a national system" or community (Wiebe, 1967, p. 112). In an increasingly interdependent world, their expertise became even more prestigious and financially lucrative as this period progressed, a development their associations enhanced by raising needed educational entrance requirements for their professions.

These efforts to control supply through cartelization for expressive and material gains also further promoted the legitimacy of these professions as authority structures in society, albeit not to the extent anticipated much later by Trotskyite-turned-conservative James Burnham (1941) in his classic, *The Managerial Revolution*. And, like the captains of industry, this rising managerial elite also sought employment opportunities in and professional links to the public sector to advance their aims. Consequently, they, too, advocated the creation of public agencies that would be organized to allow for "technical, fact-finding, and promotional" activities that played to their professional strengths (Wiebe, 1967, p. 112).

****

But the development of a managerial class in business was not the only economic class-based development of the Gilded Age. As in prior economic booms, the benefits and burdens of wealth creation were unequally distributed among Americans, further inflaming social class consciousness. For starters, industrialization in the North sparked a huge demand for unskilled workers on assembly lines, a need largely filled by a new type of immigrant to America: southern and eastern Europeans (rather than northern Europeans) (Barone, 2013; Heilbroner & Singer, 1999; Lears, 2009). Between 1860 and 1900, the industrial working class—consisting heavily of these types of immigrants—increased by five-fold, from 1.5 to 5.5 million workers. This rate increased further during the first decade of the 20th century. From 1900 to 1910 alone, southern and eastern European immigrants comprised nearly 70 percent of emigres to America. Thus, by 1910, one-third of Americans were foreign born or had one parent who was foreign born.

Many immigrants had fled Europe to escape abject poverty, a fate many attributed to discrimination against them by their governments. Much as in prior periods, many were also lured to America by false promises of streets paved with gold. In this case, they were bilked by unscrupulous recruiters (known as padrones) hired by corporate industrialists to fill low-skilled positions on factory assembly lines. Fear and derision of southern and eastern Europeans for taking jobs away from earlier emigres were amplified in the early 20th century when new arrivals clustered by themselves in ethnic neighborhoods (e.g., "Little Italy" and "Little Hungary").

These communities offered new arrivals a connection with others from their homeland. But they also segregated the immigrants from mainstream American society. In these enclaves, immigrants often continued to speak their native languages, maintain their religious preferences (often Catholic and Jewish), and maintain their own traditions. Fears of their not assimilating in America also stemmed from each ethnic group starting its own foreign-language newspapers, food stores, restaurants, social clubs, and separate educational facilities (Hebrew and Catholic parochial schools).

Ghettoization initially made sense for immigrants. But this isolation helped inspire a "fear of the other" towards them that would help spawn violence by and against immigrants, the "First Red Scare" (1919–1920), and, ultimately, immigration law restrictions. Further ratcheting up these fears was a series of dynamite bombs mailed to American establishment figures in 1919 and 1920. During two months in 1919, 36 bombs were mailed by anarchists to politicians, corporate chieftains, and administrators across the nation (Clements, 2010; Jones, 2012). Targets included the US Attorney General, A. Mitchell Palmer; John D. Rockefeller; other business persons; sponsors of immigrant restriction and deportation legislation; and newspaper editors.

While immigration from southern and eastern Europe was raising fears and bringing Americans' self-conception into question, a conjunction of other events occurred to spark social and class conflict. Notably, between 1807 and 1914, the real wages of laborers rose only about 1 percent every two years. Neither did working conditions improve, meaning that high rates of deaths and injuries prevailed. Simultaneously, another massive migration into the cities from rural areas occurred, the product of yet another round of mechanization of agriculture. Those displaced from these jobs emigrated to urban areas in the northeast and Midwest to get assembly-line positions. But like southern and eastern European immigrants, they found themselves living in already overcrowded, unsafe, and unhealthy urban tenements. They were also badly in need of social, health, sanitation, police, and fire services not provided by local governments. Instead, political machines, their private contractors, and volunteers provided them at their discretion, with the first two groups doing so often on a discriminatory or ability-to-pay basis.

Moreover, this rural-to-urban relocation expanded further to include blacks during the first two decades of the 20th century. Fostering what became known as the Great Migration beginning in 1916 were a southern sharecropping system that offered little economic opportunity to blacks, the revival of the Ku Klux Klan and its violence, and wages in northern manufacturing that were nearly triple what blacks could earn in the South. Also helping to push blacks out of the South was the aforementioned institutionalization of Jim Crow racism between 1877 and 1920.

As Kimberley Johnson (2010) points out, among the atrocities committed against blacks during this era, southern whites used the legal and administrative systems to supply convict labor to private firms. This generated enormous profits for the firms, as well as for state treasuries. She writes that the "thinnest layer of legality and profit motive separated the convict leasing system from slavery. . . . Because blacks could not serve on juries, their peers did not judge them" (p. 13). Moreover, a biased trial leading to quasi-servitude was a positive outcome given the alternative: lynching. Indeed, by failing to pass state and national anti-lynching laws during these years, lynching became, in effect, state-sponsored vigilantism. Moreover, individual state government administrators legitimized withholding the vote from blacks through poll taxes, literacy tests, and vagrancy laws and, thus, played an active role "in shaping, maintaining, and defending Jim Crow" (p. 4).

But as discussed shortly, the role of World War I cannot be ignored in stimulating rural-to-urban/southern-to-northern black migration and the need for urban service provision. When the war began in Europe in 1914, European immigration slowed dramatically, leading northern industrialists to begin heavy recruitment of blacks as replacements. Black newspapers were filled with advertisements luring blacks to manufacturing jobs, including fictitious stories of black economic success in the cities.

Another "pull-factor" for blacks was their service in segregated US military units during World War I. They felt they deserved greater economic opportunities for their service and tried to seize them by flocking into northern cities for work. Between 1910 and 1920, the black population grew nearly 66 percent in New York City, 148 percent in Chicago, 500 percent in Philadelphia, and 600 percent in Detroit (Barone, 2013; Heilbroner & Singer, 1999; Lears, 2009; Trachtenberg, 2007). As white soldiers returned after World War I and experienced the recession of 1920–1921 (see more below and in Chapter 5), however, earlier racial tensions between blacks and whites flared as they were again pitted against each other for jobs and housing. For example, 1919 and 1920 witnessed race riots in large cities such as Chicago, New York City, Philadelphia, Tulsa, and Washington, DC.

In the process, the largely white Protestant elites reacted as they had to earlier immigration eras by fearing that the nation's identity and values were at risk, much as one hears today from vocal quarters of the US population. Even more worrisome to them was the "vigorous defense displayed by many African American communities" during the Red Summer riots of 1919 (see more below) (Johnson, 2010, p. 27).[1] This fear and unease was exemplified by racist writers such as Lothrop Stoddard who wrote in his popular book, *The Rising Tide of Color Against White World-Supremacy*, that "dark-skinned races constituted a worse threat to Western civilization than the Germans or the Bolsheviks" (Allen, 1931, p. 55).

Nor were American exceptionalist millenarian visions helped by rising corruption in government, corruption led by urban political machines. These were dependent on recent immigrants for electoral support in exchange for the provision of jobs and social services. A de facto part of the compensatory state, these machines filled a vast policy and administrative gap in meeting social needs that Americans' historical conception of limited government had bequeathed to the Gilded Age. As the muckraker Lincoln Steffens (1969) wrote in *The Shame of the Cities*:

> Franchises worth millions were granted without one cent to the city . . . companies which refused to pay blackmail had to leave; citizens were robbed more and more boldly; pay-rolls were padded with the names of nonexistent persons; work on public improvements was neglected, while money for them went to the boodlers. . . . [M]en of wealth and social standing, who, because of special privileges granted them, felt bound to support and defend the looters. Independent victims of the far-reaching conspiracy submitted in silence.
>
> (p. 9)

Nor did the corruption of political machines stop in the cities. With its roots in the Jacksonian age, it stretched across levels of government. Federal agencies— such as the Department of Agriculture, the Department of the Interior, the Postal Service, and the Department of the Treasury—became satrapies of state and local political machines in the compensatory state.

****

Simultaneously undermining the legitimacy of Americans' self-conception of classlessness, social mobility, and comity was economic hardship in the nation's agrarian heartlands (Hofstadter, 1955, esp. ch. 1). As noted, beginning in the late 19th century, many white and black farmers had been lured to the heartlands by false claims. This time, the perpetrators were real estate promoters and the federal government's further efforts to settle these lands. In terms of the latter, the Homestead Act of 1862 (mentioned in Chapter 3) lured farmers to unproductive lands and encouraged land speculation by farmers and corporate interests. Many farmers lost that bet, especially when gold production fell during the Gilded Age, thus limiting the nation's (and the world's) money supply. Nor were they helped when foreign competition for selling grains and textiles surged.

Produced was a doubling of farms, but "farm income . . . declined from one-fourth to one-fifth" of "total national income" (Sanders, 1999, pp. 101–102). Railroads and other speculators then rushed in to buy lands with failed mortgages at bargain prices. This, as banks that had lent money to settlers at exorbitant rates were quick to foreclose on the properties. But, as political scientist Arthur Bentley concluded, the

> farmer may often have suffered from excessive interest and grasping creditors; but. . . [farmers were] too sanguine and too prone to believe

that [they] could safely go into debt, on the assumption that crops and prices [for food and land] in the future would equal those in the present.

(Hofstadter, 1955, p. 55)

Blame aside, social inequalities spiraled and spiked the ire of western farmers. As Elizabeth Sanders (1999) puts it: "So large an interest [i.e., agricultural interests]—broadly enfranchised, undisturbed by sharp cultural differences, and imbued with a long-standing republican ideology—was strongly predisposed to political action when confronted with" these economic and social dislocations (p. 101). All of which in the late 19th century led, first, to the Granger movement and, later, to Populist revolts in the American heartland.

Legislatively, the primary administrative ideas of the Grangers were regulating railroads, reforming the civil service, and ameliorating what they called a corrupt economy. Consonant with American exceptionalist values, the "state" meant state government to the Grangers and led to so-called Granger laws in individual states, some of which were later repealed or weakened. The Grangers and (later) the National Farmers' Alliance racked up some regional political victories, but they never had a major national impact.

Subsequently, in the 1890s, farmers turned to a still grassroots Populist party. Unlike the Grangers, Populists advocated for an activist national government. Akin to the prescriptions brought back from Europe by young Americans who had studied there (see below), Populists called for the federal government to intervene in markets to advance the public interest. Yet, consonant with Americans' self-conception, they worried about handing too much power to the federal executive branch and the bureaucratization of administration that might accompany it. Thus, unlike the national Progressive movement that followed on its heels, Populists were not focused on the "unique coupling of a reform agenda with a faith that scientific and social-scientific knowledge could be applied constructively to address social problems" (Eisner, 2000b, p. 34).

The Populist agenda aimed instead "to tame capitalism, to deconcentrate" its power, not to end it (Sanders, 1999, p. 133). This did not stop corporate interests and their defenders from successfully labelling Populists "socialists." However, the Populists' agenda did not include the nationalization of industries as socialists desired. Moreover, many of the then left-of-center Populists' ideas were absorbed by the national Republican and Democratic parties throughout the 20th century.

****

Also amplified in the wake of the inequalities and concentration of wealth in America produced amid the major benefits of capitalism were efforts to organize workers into labor unions. These began in 1869 with the creation of the Knights of Labor, followed by the Federation of Organized Trades and Labor Unions in 1881 and the American Federation of Labor in 1886. But these efforts spiked in the wake of the Panic of 1893. They were also animated by the adverse social consequences of corporations' focus on "efficiency." Greater efficiencies, through what was called "scientific management" (see below), were sold to workers as able to increase profits that would be shared with them. But, instead, most industrialists lowered wages and fired employees. Still others saw scientific management as an effort to shift power from skilled artisans to the growing managerial class (Kanigel, 1997).

In response, this period saw violence-ridden strikes quickly ensue. These strikes involved hundreds of thousands of unskilled industrial workers, with the peak years of unrest occurring in 1877, 1886, 1892, and 1893. In 1886, for example, the Haymarket affair (or massacre/riot) sparked a national phobia regarding unions and their "foreign elements." After the killing of several strikers by Chicago police the day before, some 1,500 workers in Chicago held another labor demonstration matched against approximately 300 police. A bomb was thrown, prompting police to fire on the crowd, killing and injuring protesters. Led by German-born radicals, eight individuals were put on trial, seven were sentenced to death, and one was given a 15-year sentence. In its aftermath, hundreds of foreign-born radicals were arrested across the nation.

Then, amid the financial Panic, the Pullman Strike occurred in 1894, bringing violence and government suppression in its wake. The Pullman workers had recently joined Eugene Debs' newly formed American Railway Union. After fighting broke out between strikers and scabs in Illinois, most public opinion leaders—including the clergy—attacked the strikers for their "inhuman and brutal selfishness. . . [which] disgraces modern civilization" (Churchman, 1894, p. 7). Arguing the strike was a threat to national mail delivery, President Grover Cleveland (D-NY) sent in federal troops to stop the fighting, a federal court injunction ensued against strikers, and Debs and others were jailed.

Chastened in the 1890s by corporate and government suppression, some in the union movement tried to build coalitions with other interest groups. After Samuel Gompers organized the American Federation of Labor (AFL) along craft lines that informally discriminated on ethnic, racial, and gender grounds, the AFL did not seek to destroy corporations but, rather, to get more benefits out of them for artisans. The AFL traded more managerial control of the workplace in exchange for higher pay and shorter workdays for laborers. Certainly, the links between the concerns and interests of labor and agricultural organizations also held the potential for an alliance against corporate and financial interests in America. Yet, the "political weakness of the farmer–worker coalition often made it impossible to overcome capitalist resistance in the executive and the legislature and to override the Supreme Court's constricted view of national legislative powers" (Sanders, 1999, p. 5).

Labor–management conflict continued unabated during the first two decades of the 20th century. As alluded to earlier, this spawned a set of immigration restrictions favored by nativists. Daniel Tichenor (2002) writes that a "monumental battle" between nativists and proponents of immigration was ultimately resolved between 1910 and 1920 in favor of nativism (p. 116). Nor did the sentiments of Irish and German immigrants against entering World War I help the situation. And with the arrival of the Industrial Workers of the World (or Wobblies), fears of socialism and anarchism further stoked nativist fires (see, e.g., Chace, 2004; Sanders, 1999). Set off by the aforementioned wave of anarchist bombings in the Red Summer of 1919, as well as the Boston police strike that same year, nearly 30 race riots and repeated other strikes occurred in 1919 and 1920. Amid this turmoil, the Palmer Raids on suspected radicals deported many immigrants from the country without due process (see more below).

These developments fomented questions about not only the ability of existing political institutions to handle industrialization's social and economic challenges but also their legitimacy. As historian Gabriel Kolko (1977) writes, the Gilded Age and its 20th-century legatees in business created a widespread perception that corporate capitalism produced a society "out of control." The economic growth celebrated earlier as a natural extension of the Founders' vision of a commercial republic constrained only by limited government was, by the 1880s, a problem rather than an asset. Some even called democracy itself into question (as would others later in the 1930s and 2010s). In fact, by the first two decades of the 20th century, the idea of a historical–structural mismatch grew further amid commercial and military threats from European nations with nimbler governance systems than those afforded by the US Constitution.

****

As referenced earlier, similar perceptions of a historical–structural mismatch and remedies for it were also abreast in Europe in the late 19th century and were carried back to the United States by many American students studying abroad. As Daniel Rodgers (1998) chronicles, an entire generation of American elites studied in Europe before graduate schools existed in America, and especially in Germany, between 1870 and 1890.[2] Aside from the virtues of studying in another culture at the best universities in the world and (unlike in American colleges and universities) being encouraged to discover knowledge through science and positivism rather than accept religious dogma, tuition and living costs in Europe were less expensive than in the United States (Ross, 1991, p. 58).

Born and raised with rugged individualism and free markets as their credos, many American students came home immersed in the continental idea of social "interdependence," or what some German intellectuals called "solidary." As noted, the ASSA had similar notions, but its members wanted to restore the legitimacy of the gentry class and mostly preserve laissez-faire economics. But the continental European version of interdependence came to far different conclusions. Interdependence meant that free markets produced both positive and negative externalities. It followed that an activist nation state was imperative for managing these problems and the social unrest they caused. Students witnessed these externalities from industrialization and urbanization in Europe during their matriculation and saw them happening in the United States upon their return. Many of them not only became university professors but also leaders of the early Progressive reform movement at the state and federal government levels.

Economists in Germany, who were many Americans' professors, were seeking at the time to overturn what they termed the "tyranny" of the English economic doctrine of laissez faire, self-sufficiency and self-help (as per faculty psychology), and personal responsibility for one's fate. Much earlier, economists and commentators such as Friedrich List had argued that free trade only exacerbated economic gaps between the developed and the developing world. They also joined Alexander Hamilton and Henry Clay in supporting protectionism for infant American industries. Others, such as economic historian Arnold Toynbee, later challenged laissez faire on moralistic grounds. In this same vein, these younger European economists—known as "historical economists"—argued that laissez faire was an "ideology" or "narrative" conjured by British manufacturers to maintain their power over nations with less economic capacity.

Two of the leading historical economists of the American students' days in Germany were Adolph Wagner and Gustav von Schmoller, both proponents of a school of economics known as "State Socialism." Offering what he called the "law of increasing state activity" in the face of market failures, Wagner argued that state intervention into markets was necessary and meant the nationalization of key industries to "remoralize" economic life (Rodgers, 1998, p. 91). In particular, Wagner also advocated for limits on profits and a redistributive tax system.

Likewise, von Schmoller joined Wagner in dismissing general theories of economics such as laissez faire as merely "social constructs" rather than "natural states" of being. But although Wagner's antipathy to laissez faire was grounded in Marxist perspectives, von Schmoller's disillusionment also included the free market's exaltation of "individual egoism" (Rodgers, 1998, p. 92). His critique was based on the failure of classical economists to incorporate history into their thinking and their lack of focus on context and empirical study. Moreover, although students garnered a justification of state intervention in markets from Wagner, von Schmoller brought "home to [them] the historical relativity of all economic doctrines" (p. 92). Both scholars, however, also left them with an appreciation of how empirical research using the positivist scientific methods of the day should impact economic policy and government administration. Investigation and instigation were their models for the social sciences.

From critiques such as these grew an organization of historical economists in Germany called the Verein für Socialpolitik or, more simply, the Verein. At their meetings, leaders of the Verein emphasized direct action and policy and administrative influence by the professoriate. In doing so, they held debate forums that brought together historical economists with business owners and managers, as well as journalists. The audience then took a vote on key social questions of the day, with the arguments and votes reported in the press. The Verein also sponsored summer camps with courses in "social economics" for policymakers, students, and clergy. Moreover, they gave widely heralded weekly public lectures where they expressed their opinions on social, policy, and economic questions.

Perhaps their most impressive accomplishment, and the precursor of what progressives did even more effectively in the early 20th century in America, was the production of monographs read by policymakers. Thus, by the late 1890s, the Verein had offered a positive-state, market-interventionist vision and policy agenda. In the process, the Verein became a "factory of social fact-finding and was cautiously and *professionally* building the empirical rationale for the socially active state" (Rodgers, 1998, p. 93, emphasis added). This, building upon Otto von Bismarck's "welfare state" project in Germany (created, ironically, to thwart socialist political gains in the country).

Not all Americans who studied in Germany ascribed to the Verein agenda, in whole or in part. Nor did all like the way German instructors ridiculed what they called the unbridled commercialism and anti-statism in the United States (using the classical definition of the state as the federal bureaucracy). Most also were not sympathetic to the autocratic aspects of Bismarck in Germany (or elsewhere) or to Marxist theories of history. What they *did* agree with and brought home to US universities, however, was the European fear of the mob (much as in the Roman Republic and among many of the Founders of the United States). They also embraced state activism; had confidence in the use of scientism and reason to make policymaking and administration more rational (i.e., logical and objective), with a focus on state administrative planning; and believed in professional, university-based social sciences participating in statecraft (Rodgers, 1998, p. 89). Put bluntly, their aim was to make themselves the successors to earlier and, in their eyes, failed authority structures in America and, thus, to use the IRP to change American exceptionalist values to "save" the nation's millenarian vision.

Initially, their impact was minimal. The historical economists among them were attacked, not surprisingly given their intellectual lineage, as "socialists" and "collectivists." Most of these charges came from industrialists who, by then, financed many universities. Several social scientists lost their jobs, leading eventually to the establishment of tenure for faculty to avoid political retaliation. Indeed, the reaction of corporate and private foundation donors to universities and the professions led the nascent American Economic Association reluctantly for a time to abandon overt policy formulation and to dissolve its various committees on "social questions."

But, slowly, economists such as John Bates Clark, John Commons, and Richard Ely successfully advocated for the "social possibilities of the state" in the United States. They, in turn, imbued a similar vision among their students in such elite schools as Columbia University and Johns Hopkins University. Their students imbibed the idea that "institutions could be rationally designed to restrain, control, or redirect the social and economic changes that the nation was encountering, and thus improve the human condition" (Eisner, 2000b, p. 34). In addition to the AEA, they also helped found other professional associations premised partially on the Verein model (see below). Thus, through their activism, they helped amplify the IRP in America, while making universities and their social science graduates important components of America's compensatory state. Before seeing how and why this occurred, the rise of the professional social sciences in American universities needs attention.

****

As mentioned in Chapter 3, the pre-professionalization world of the amateurish ASSA argued that gentry intellectuals of social science would find answers to the complexities and challenges facing Americans. Some members of the ASSA even strangely shared the vision held by sociology's founder, Auguste Comte, that a "hierarchical, authoritarian society integrated by the scientific construction of organic institutions" was also necessary for American exceptionalist goals to be restored (Ross, 1991, p. 12). Similar claims (absent references to American exceptionalism, of course) went back to Plato's time. It was also resplendent among Enlightenment thinkers such as Francis Bacon, Nicolas de Condorcet, and René Descartes; 18th- and 19th-century thinkers such as Jeremy Bentham, Karl Marx, and J. S. Mill; and 20th-century socialist activists such as Harold Laski and Sidney and Beatrice Webb in Great Britain. More recently, economist and social theorist Thomas Sowell (2007) and psychologist Steven Pinker (2002) refer, respectively, to this as an "unconstrained" or "blank slate" vision of human beings. This vision sees human nature (and, thus, society) as malleable and perfectible through reason alone while ignoring social evolutionary and biological constraints on behavioral change (also see critics such as Berlin, 1992; Kirk, 1993; Lindblom, 1990; Oakeshott, 1962).

In contrast, and since antiquity (e.g., the Greek historian, Polybius), philosophers and political economists such as Friedrich Hayek, Richard Hooker, Michael Oakeshott, Jean-Jacques Rousseau, and Ludwig von Mises were highly skeptical about a "scientifically guided society" (Lindblom, 1990) dominated by bureaucratic experts (also see Aron, 1955). Experience, tradition, and ideas (what Kant called "a posteriori" knowledge) rather than pure reason (what Kant called "a priori" knowledgeand Hayek called "epistemic humility" about governments' abilities) should be the basis for governance. Their skepticism, doubt, and outright opposition to scientifically guided and expertise-based societies founded solely on reason were rooted in their belief in a "self-guided society" (Lindblom, 1990).

Such a society aggregated "personal" or "tacit" experience, tradition, and knowledge (Polanyi, 1958) into beneficial social knowledge. Experience, observations, and the consensus of generations—that is, the rationality derived through trial-by-error learning over the ages (or "social evolution")—were safer for society than the IRP. This, not only because of the limitations on human reason imposed by complexity but based on Kant's notion that the "crooked timber of humanity" and its will to power would produce disastrous results if left unconstrained. In addition, complexity heightens the possibility that IRP-based initiatives in one policy area can produce negative consequences in other areas. Others (e.g., British journalist and economist Walter Bagehot) attacked Bentham's and J. S. Mill's utilitarianism (with its felicific calculus) as substituting equations premised on pain and pleasure for religious values in policymaking and creating a pernicious leveling tendency for society (Kirk, 1986). In what Sowell (2007) calls a "constrained" vision of society—and ever since do traditional conservatives—faith in "distributed intelligence" (rather than centralized intelligence) and Burkean ideas prevailed: the individual is foolish, but the species is wise (also see Oakeshott, 1962).

Nonetheless, as noted earlier, the ASSA's aim had been to establish "communities of the competent" and to put them to work on policy and administrative problems. Like the Verein, they would do so "by rebuilding [their] authority on the foundation of functional expertise" that was beyond the ken of average citizens (Haskell, 2000, p. 22). Authority could no longer "be left in the hands of the incompetent . . . there were truths that no honest investigator could deny" and that only experts could discern (p. 87). Henceforth, decisions should only be informed by those with special knowledge rather than "raw self-assertiveness, or party patronage, or a majority vote of the incompetent" (p. 87).

By the 1890s, however, the ASSA had collapsed as younger scholars found its still-amateurish claims unsuited to explaining the dynamics of a full-blown urban industrial society. This, amid infighting in the association about what constituted "legitimate" research. This dynamic, one that has dogged the social sciences ever since, afforded an opening to university-based professional researchers pursuing legitimacy of their own. In universities, European-inspired, bureaucratic organizational models premised on knowledge specialization were taking hold. Led by presidents at Brown University, Cornell University, Johns Hopkins University, the University of Chicago, and the University of Michigan, universities were soon transformed from their religious roots "so that [they] could confer authority upon [a striving new] elite class of leaders for American society" housed in specialized academic fields (Haskell, 2000, p. 76).

As in the world of business professions noted earlier, the next two decades saw the creation of equally specialized academic associations that eventually institutionalized disciplinary fragmentation. Joining the American Statistical Association created in 1839 were the American Bar Association (1878), followed by the American Historical Association (1884), and then the aforementioned American Economic Association (1885). Next came the American Political Science

Association (APSA) in 1903, the American Sociological Association in 1905, and the International Psychoanalytic Association in 1910. Each sought legitimacy for its profession by hiving off perceived ancillary research topics to other fields and applying the methodologies of scientism to government, administrative, social, and psychological issues—much as they have done ever since with some variations (Haskell, 2000; Ross, 1991).

Many argued that only the construction of the "American university and a system of [full-time] professional and semi-professional elites built upon it" could—and should—speak authoritatively to government (Haskell, 2000, p. 121). In contrast to the ASSA's focus on integrating various areas of expertise, and consonant with the logic of bureaucratic organization, academic specialization was—as noted—key to this endeavor. For proponents, "specialization was relatively easy to effect and carried the status rewards of institutional and disciplinary independence" (Ross, 1991, p. 283). Thus, by 1900, this norm prevailed and prompted decentralized university systems organized by disciplinary specialization. This division of mental labor has since wrought enormous benefits to society, including greater prosperity, medical breakthroughs, technological advancement, and better quality of life. But it has also been the source of many problems. These include difficulty in reaggregating knowledge to take a holistic view of one's education and society, constraining cross-pollinizing of research information, and bureaucratic fragmentation.

This focus on specialization also institutionalized a fragmentation *within* disciplines over the proper role of the social sciences, as well as over appropriate methodologies and competing theories. For example, although most historians saw no room for building an applied component into their profession, political scientists initially saw application of their research as critical to gaining legitimacy and improving society. Meanwhile, economists such as Ely pushed for applied statistical analysis in university curricula as basic to addressing social ills and restoring American exceptionalism. Ely contended that his field should not "look so much to [deductive] speculation as to the historical and statistical study of actual conditions of economic life" (Nelson, 1982, p. 82). Fellow travelers envisioned the application of inductive economic methods (i.e., data collection and analysis) to social problems in a united effort, "each in their own spheres," by the church, the state, and the social sciences. Likewise, younger political scientists, though not historians, "coalesce[d] around their interest in administration and the opportunities it opened [for them] to act as experts on the problems of government" (Ross, 1991, p. 282). Political scientists at Columbia, for example, were active in urban politics in the 1880s through the 1890s and joined (as noted in Chapter 3) with the ASSA and corporate interests to enact the Civil Service Act (CSA) of 1883.

Meanwhile, in the emerging field of sociology, splits emerged over the extent to which research should be basic or applied. Albion Small, chair of the

Department of Sociology at the University of Chicago and founder of the *American Journal of Sociology* (1895), promoted "Statistical Sociology." It would discern the "equilibrium of a perfect society" (Ross, 1991, p. 125). In this latest iteration of Republican Arithmetik (see Chapter 2), sociology needed rigorous "inspection and induction, not . . . speculation" (p. 125). In pursuing this "Dynamic Sociology" of theory building and hypothesis testing, sociologists would "change the actual into the ideal" society (p. 125).

Small and his colleagues also saw sociology offering a kind of "scientific morality." They argued that sociology could "bring back that better era of the republic [the founding 'era of gentlemen'] in which [public servants] utterly abnegated all selfish purposes," in this instance, when confronted with statistical realities (Nelson, 1982, p. 87). But sociologists would not get *directly* involved in public affairs, partly for fear of political retribution. Instead, they would offer their scientifically derived laws of probabilities and let politicians do with them what they would.

As Dorothy Ross (1991) argues, Small's vision entailed a "sociology of social control." Moreover, a strong element of sexism also underlay this vision. Ironically, this form of ascriptive hierarchy would spawn yet another amplification of the proxy component of the compensatory state. As she writes:

> In part as a reflection of the prejudices that still dominated academia, those outside the respectable male white Protestant class were often denied access to professional careers. Between 1890 and 1900, the number of women taking graduate courses in all fields nearly doubled, to 30 percent, and a larger proportion than formerly were undoubtedly now enrolled in regular degree programs. Sociology matched the national average and most likely claimed a larger share of women than economics and political science. [But] by and large these women graduates were steered to social work and reform [i.e., advocacy] activities or to the women's colleges, precincts the men were defining as outside the scientific and academic mainstream. There, despite pressure to adopt the trapping of science and professionalism, women social scientists sometimes managed to keep open the lines to social democratic activism and to explore heterodox [policy and administrative] ideas.
>
> (p. 158)

Women also were only to study the "'simpler forms of social life' while men studied the 'larger' ones" (Deegan, 1988, p. 194). For instance, the University of Chicago adopted a separatist approach to men and women faculty members that eventually led to the new field of social work and what Camilla Stivers (2000) later called "settlement women." Such female sociologists as Edith Abbott, Jane Addams, Sophonisba Breckinridge, and Florence Kelley were to start or work in settlement houses (e.g., Hull House in Chicago) outside of academic departments, while males were to join the professoriate (see below). Moreover, this occurred despite women often outperforming their male counterparts during their education and in terms of publication productivity. Jane Addams (the cofounder of Hull House), for example, wrote a dozen books and published over 500 articles that stressed the interplay of experience and critical reflection, a philosophy also made popular by the American pragmatic tradition of John Dewey, Charles Peirce, and William James. Yet, beginning in 1892, her work was "airbrushed" out of the field for a time by her male colleagues (Deegan, 1988, p. 14).

Gender differences also worked their way into social science methodology during the late 19th century and, later, into public administration in the early 20th century. Female sociologists tended to focus on "critical–emancipatory" research, while men stressed a "social–technological" approach. More on these differences will follow, because they played roles in creating splits in the early Progressive reform movement. Notable now is that these differences manifested themselves in arguments regarding the use of scientific analysis. Women stressed using analysis to improve the life chances of their subjects, whom they interviewed extensively and with whom they frequently co-published research. In contrast, men embraced the social–technological approach that was more focused on theory building and hypothesis testing. The critical–emancipatory approach also involved more bottom-up, citizen-driven research and activism. This, just as feminist scholars in public administration and other fields more recently have argued against the privileging of quantitative empiricism as inherently sexist and racist by marginalizing these and other interpretative research methodologies (Stivers, 2019).

One sociological landmark of the critical–emancipatory approach incorporating "investigation and instigation" is the extensive volume of maps and associated essays (or notes) contained in the *Hull-House Maps and Papers* (HHM&P) published in 1895.[3] This publication was designed "to present conditions rather than to advance theories—to bring within reach of the public exact [and accurate] information" for action. As one of the contributors to the HHM&P—Agnes Sinclair Holbrook—wrote:

> to merely . . . state symptoms and go no further would be idle; but to state symptoms in order to ascertain the nature of disease, and apply, it may be, its cure, is not only scientific, but in the highest sense humanitarianism.
>
> (HHM&P, p. 58)

Social analysis and advocacy had to be integrated, a research approach that challenged the cannon emerging in sociology and that would be dismissed by the 1920s as inadequate for a career in the academy. For reasons discussed later, however, natural science-based methods triumphed as the best way to ensure a continuation of American exceptionalism.

****

Although the social sciences pursued legitimacy in this fashion, the predicates for emulating the "hard" sciences to gain legitimacy came from the professions of industrial and mechanical engineering, plus statistics. The American Society of Engineers was initially the dominant force in this movement. In turn, engineering exercised considerable influence on the emerging profession of public administration during the first two decades of the 20th century. This was not surprising; many of the problems of urban America involved infrastructure, which required engineering expertise.

But the highly influential minority of progressive engineers' aims went well beyond these problems. They became key promoters of applying their IRP (most notably, systems analysis and scientific management) to the whole nation, in a confluence of expressive, material, and authority gains for their field. As historian Joan Hoff Wilson (1975) argues, their aim "was [for the engineering profession] to employ technology in a manner both humane and efficient to improve economic conditions . . . while generally enhancing the social status and power of engineers generally" (p. 36).

Progressive engineers tended to be mid-career and well-established engineers such as Herbert Hoover and Morris P. Cook. They believed that "engineers could justify greater prestige for themselves only if they accepted collective responsibility for the well-being of the public in their attempt to organize a more efficient society" (Wilson, 1975, p. 36). Moreover, as Hoover wrote in his *Memoirs*, "their professional training in impartial logic uniquely qualified engineers for this responsibility; they occupied a position of disinterested service" and "want nothing . . . from Congress. . . [but] . . . efficiency in government" and societal justice (p. 37). Thus, engineers were an "economic and social force. Every time [one] discovers a new application of science, thereby creating a new industry, providing new jobs, adding to the standards of living, [that engineer] also disturbs everything that is . . . He is also the person who really corrects monopolies and redistributes national wealth," not government (p. 37).

The growing corporate, economic, and political clout of this minority propelled the progressive engineers' vision to ascendancy in the field and, more broadly, in the economy. Between 1880 and World War II, engineering grew faster than any other profession in the United States, with its numbers soaring between 1880 and 1930 from approximately 7,000 to 226,000. Engineers also had the highest rate of social and economic mobility within organizations. As Wilson (1975) summarizes, the "truly prominent engineers almost invariably ended up as corporation executives" (p. 34). With them came the application of what became known as "scientific management"—the ultimate IRP.

The father of scientific management at the shop-floor level was the engineer Frederick Winslow Taylor. In an early version of what today is known as "principal–agent" theory, he disparaged the "rule-of-thumb" thinking that characterized industrial relations in the early 1900s. He thought it gave shirking workers in industry the power to control industrial productivity. In his view, unskilled workers took advantage of this situation by "soldiering"—that is, taking it easy and, thus, controlling worker output. Instead, Taylor envisioned a "science of work" led by experts trained in statistical analyses of work processes and outcomes.

The heart of these analyses was "time-and-motion" studies, where work analysts studied how workers did their jobs. They then figured out how to do them more efficiently by identifying the minimal number of actions needed for completion and the time required. Discerned would be the "one best way" to organize work processes and, thus, maximize efficiency through control by professional managerial experts. A rising tide of profits from these actions could then be shared with workers, thus reducing labor–management tensions administratively and regaining the millenarian dream of American exceptionalists.

The initial attractiveness of Taylor's work was the control, objectivity, and thus legitimacy it would give to these specially trained work planners. Both managers and their subordinates would have to follow specific procedures to improve productivity, regardless of a person's partisan connections, personality, or subjective evaluation of a situation. Attractive to attain, as well, was what Mary Parker Follett called an impartial "law of the situation" that would be discernible from these time-and-motion studies. Consensus on administrative and policy actions would result. Once objective, data-driven research by experts was initiated, decisions would result based on objective facts rather than power and emotion. From these, "creative conflict" would result: reasonable people with different interests would come to a solution that was different from their initial position and that would refocus the debate in a more constructive, objective way. In effect, Follett was articulating the philosophy of rationalists prior to her time and ever since. However, like them, she, too, heavily discounted "confirmation bias," organizational politics, issue framing, and humanity's will to power.

The irony of scientific management was that it sparked more, not less, labor–management conflict. Not the least of the reasons for this was that it allowed low-skilled or unskilled female and child workers to work assembly lines. By 1920, nearly 20 percent of all manufacturing workers were women and 13 percent of all textile workers were younger than 16 years old. As noted, many employees of both sexes also lost their jobs through mechanization. Moreover, those not terminated worked at least a ten-hour day, yet earned 20 to 40 percent less than the minimum wage necessary for a decent life.

Thus, as southerners had argued in the runup to the Civil War, many workers believed that industrialization and scientific management actually reduced "free men" to "wage slaves."[4] Scientific management "meant less autonomy, more surveillance, more quantified timing and measurement of output. . . . [Moreover,] sensing a subtle imprisonment, they [workers] harbored fantasies of escape." Gaps in wealth inherited from the Gilded Age also grew wider. By 1900, 10 percent of Americans owned over three-fourths of the nation's wealth. Thus, contrary to American exceptionalism's millenarian vision of social mobility, many once again saw the country on the brink of violent class warfare. Sparked was more fodder for perceptions of a major historical–structural mismatch, one leading to the most impactful American administrative reform movement of the 20th century—the Progressive reform movement. And the scientific planning vision of the progressive engineers was central to this movement.

****

The Progressive reform movement was hardly a cohesive one. It was launched by an eclectic Baptist–Bootlegger coalition of small business (which disliked the dominance of corporate capitalism threatening their existence), agrarian, anti-vice, suffragette, temperance-leaning, anti-immigrant, urban-educated, and now professionalizing cadre of social scientists. The movement thus "breathed life into a new fragmented and issue-oriented politics in which often-contradictory reform movements" existed side by side (Tichenor, 2002, p. 114). Each member of this coalition tried to advance its respective cause by linking it to those of the other members.

Hinting at both the transitory nature and effeminacy of this movement, political machine leaders dismissively revived older tropes that progressive reformers were "morning glories" who would "wilt in the noonday sun." This, as they had argued earlier with gender stereotypes during and after the Civil War and would later do in the 1950s during the Second Red Scare. Nonetheless, progressive reformers from well-to-do backgrounds—such as Senator Henry Cabot Lodge (R-MA) and future president Theodore Roosevelt—jumped into elected politics and administration with more than civil service reform on their minds. At the root of their reform efforts was the threat still posed by political machines to political morality, as well as to their class interests.

Roosevelt argued that progressives must demonstrate to immigrants that the corruption of the political machines was not needed to get jobs and other services. Although possessing the same moral indignity that civil service reformers had demonstrated in working for the CSA of 1883, progressives concluded that just providing more qualified persons for government agencies was not enough to improve their operations and legitimacy. That effort had proven inadequate to the task. Moreover, the CSA affected only about 10 percent of the federal workforce, with this percentage growing to only about 30 percent by the early 20th century. Civil service reform spread even slower in the state and local government components of the compensatory state.

Instead, more fundamental structural changes were needed to embrace political and administrative reforms and, hence, reshape state building and power. As

Karen Orren and Stephen Skowronek (2017) contend, progressives sought to change governance from the US Constitution's "containment structure" for preserving "ordered liberty" to an "entrepreneurial structure" that unloosened the historical bonds of limited government. That is, for the Founders, government was to afford a structure for individuals' pursuit of life, liberty, and property as they defined it—not as defined by government. Politically, progressives called for election reforms that were populist in nature in that they were designed to diminish party power, including nonpartisan elections, direct primaries, citizen referenda, secret balloting, and direct elections of US senators. The Progressive Party platform in 1912 even included a plank *ending* national political parties altogether (Pestritto & Atto, 2008, pp. 21–22).

Important elements of the Progressive movement also went so far as to challenge the US Constitution as anachronistic, a hindrance to good governance, and calibrated by the Framers to prevent majority rule and protect elite interests. As Rohr (1986) puts it, the progressives' view of "Public Administration . . . was conceived out of wedlock with the Constitution of the United States" (p. 4). In making this historical–structural mismatch argument, they claimed that America's Madisonian system of checks and balances, separation of powers, bicameralism, and federalism was too cumbersome, corrupt, and amateurish to cope with the nation's challenges. Specifically, the constitutional design placed the United States at a commercial and military disadvantage against its European competitors because of its slowness of action compared to parliamentary systems. Moreover, its defused power made it impossible to address economic inequality on a national scale.

Campaigning successfully in 1912 for the presidency, Woodrow Wilson (1913) made this case thusly, challenging the Founders' principles:

> The makers of our Federal Constitution read Montesquieu with true scientific enthusiasm. . . . Politics in their thought was a variety of mechanics. The Constitution was founded on the law of gravitation. The government was to exist and move by virtue of the efficacy of "checks and balances." The trouble with the theory is that government is not a machine, but a living thing. It falls . . . under the theory of organic life. It is accountable to Darwin, not to Newton. . . . No living thing can have its organs offset against each other, as checks, and live.
>
> (pp. 46–47)

As Wilson (1908) put it earlier, "synthesis, not antagonism, is the whole art of government, the whole art of power" (p. 106). This, contemporizing the thoughts of early 18th-century critics such as Condorcet and Turgot who found checks and balances unnecessary and pernicious, and dismissing Lord Acton's warning in the mid-19th century about concentration of power as corrupting absolutely.

Progressives such as Wilson contended that what checks and balances did was to preclude any branch of government from "claiming a true position of national leadership" and to leave the people "without a clear, accountable leader" (Pestritto & Atto, 2008, pp. 16–17). In addition, although separation of powers made sense prior to the Progressive Era, it no longer did: the Founders held an "obsessive fear of majority tyranny," but now the "people were no longer a danger to themselves" (p. 15). As reviewed in greater depth below, the answers to this dilemma were to reject the logic of the Founders that constitutional constraints on majorities were necessary to temper and tame the fleeting and often dangerous passions of majorities in pure democracies. More precisely, progressives offered a "stewardship theory" of the presidency (Arnold, 2009) (see more below), a separation of politics from administration, a view of the Constitution as a "living document," and agencies as having executive, legislative, and judicial powers.

But for many progressives such as Herbert Croly (1914), Wilson did not go far enough. Citing a primary difference between civil service reformers of the late 19th century and progressives, Croly wrote that both "official Republicanism" and the Democrat Woodrow Wilson were too conservative in their aims. They inappropriately embraced Jeffersonian individualism and engaged in the "superstitious worship of the Constitution" (Pestritto & Atto, 2008, p. 295). True progressivism, Croly averred in Verein fashion, was "committed to a drastic reorganization of the American political and economic system, to the substitution of a frank social policy for the individualism of the past" (p. 15), and had "to replace the old order with a new social bond" that would become the "rock of which may be built a better structure of individual and social life" (p. 25). And the positivist extremes of the emerging social sciences, with their focus on societal interdependence and impersonal forces, had already started the attack on individualism by arguing that citizens were acted on by these forces rather than helped enact them (Haskell, 2000). Human nature also was inherently malleable by (re)shaping the culture of society (Will, 2019).

Similarly, one of public administration's founders, Frank Goodnow (1916), argued that an inordinate "fear of political tyranny through which liberty might be lost [and] which led to the adoption of the theories of checks and balances and of the separation of powers" was anachronistic (p. 41). He was joined later by political scientist Charles Merriam (1920), who referred to the "hide-and-seek" nature of politics occasioned by the Madisonian system and its propensity to promote irresponsibility to the electorate, graft, and corruption. Merriam wrote that the

> conclusion was widely reached [by progressives] that the check and balance system[,] instead of supporting liberty, endangered it; that instead of serving as a barrier against tyranny, it became the bulwark of special privilege and interests lurking in its complications.
>
> (p. 142)

Merriam also reported that a "notable effort" was made unsuccessfully during this period to obtain a constitutional amendment to Article 1, Section 6. This, in order to advance a more parliamentary-like system whereby members of Congress could serve simultaneously in administrative posts.[5] Relatedly, in 1912, the Progressive Party of Theodore Roosevelt offered failed proposals to make the Constitution easier to amend (by requiring only simple majorities in Congress).

Nor were existing laws barriers to change for many progressives, because they were crafted by corrupt patronage machines, Thus, they were unjust in an Augustinian sense ("a law that is not just does not seem to me to be a law") and lacked legitimacy (Prior, 2018, p. 73). As Peri Arnold (2009) observes, progressives such as James Garfield, Gifford Pinchot, and Theodore Roosevelt "saw ethical principles and scientific information as fully adequate substitutes for laws" (p. 120). Also consonant with the emerging orthodoxy of scientism and pragmatism discussed earlier, they believed that the "right ends justified efficacious administrative means, even if it required playing loose with the law" (p. 121). Meanwhile, academic leaders such as Wilson and Leonard D. White began redefining public administration as a field of business and management rather than law (Moe & Gilmour, 1995), in ways that would prove ironic by the 1980s (see Chapters 7 and 8). Meanwhile, the Supreme Court occasionally used scientific analysis (along with commission reports) to diminish the importance of judicial precedent in what became known as a "Brandeis Brief." This approach was named after future Supreme Court Justice Louis Brandeis, who used it in *Muller v. Oregon* (1908) to establish that the right to contract had limits (Rehnquist, 2004, pp. 110–111). And were all this not enough, progressives such as Roosevelt unsuccessfully proposed that judicial decisions be overturned by majority votes.

****

With a critique and agenda so bold and contrarian to both the US Constitution and American exceptionalist values, progressive reformers in this period (and ever since) tried to reframe those values to legitimate their claims. For example, Goodnow critiqued the Declaration of Independence's focus on natural rights theory as empirically unfounded, misguided, and anachronistic (as did progressive economists such as John Commons, Richard Ely, and Simon Patten). Influenced by his mentor at Columbia University, John Burgess, and reflecting the sentiments of the Verein and the ASSA regarding the interdependency of society, Goodnow argued that "man is regarded now throughout Europe . . . as primarily a member of society and secondarily as an individual" (Pestritto & Atto, 2008, p. 57). Moreover, reminiscent of 19th-century German philosophers such as Johan Herder, rights are not conferred upon an individual "by his Creator, but rather by the society to which he belongs" (p. 57) and as discerned by government. Added Follett (1918) in setting out a "rights agenda" that reached its heyday later in the Rights Revolution of the 1960s and 1970s (see Chapter 6), the

> truth of the whole matter is that our only concern with "rights" is not to protect them but to create them. Our efforts are to be bent not upon guarding the rights which Heaven has showered upon us, but in creating all the rights we shall ever have.
>
> (pp. 137–138)

Thus, the Founders' idea of limited government protecting natural rights—especially property and contract rights—had to be replaced on moral grounds with the creation of positive rights for human economic fairness and development. The original "containment" structure of government intervening in markets only on salutary grounds—for example, ensuring fair market exchanges and protecting individual liberty—that the Constitution afforded had to be breached. And with this breach came a moral justification for unlimited government activism and for particular goals (e.g., wealth redistribution and government planning by administrative experts).

Goodnow's ideas (as well as Croly's) were well aligned with historian Frederick Jackson Turner's (1893) now classic "closing of the American frontier" thesis.[6] Goodnow contended that migration to the cities in the late 19th century ended the viability of individualism as a pillar of society and governance. Moreover, the stress on personal rights emerged in the 18th century before the insights provided by evolutionary biology. As in evolution, societies—and the rights they define—were not static, because they had to adapt to changing circumstances such as those facing America at the turn of the century. The social evolutionary basis of "fit societies" meant that individual rights could only be secured if citizens discounted the commercial republic's valorizing of self-interest in favor of a focus on social duties, community, and collaboration.

Progressives also saw traditional religious doctrine as placing too much emphasis on individual salvation in the next world, rather than on the social duties of this world. Walter Rauschenbusch, a leading proponent of what is known as the Social Gospel movement, argued for a "Christianizing of the social order" that would jettison traditional "self-centered piety" (Pestritto & Atto, 2008). Exhibiting a somewhat Nietzschean perspective, he felt that the dominant religions of his day unwisely taught men "to seek the highest good of the soul by turning from the world of men" and toward the hereafter (p. 113). A variant on this theme was offered by Jane Addams. She called for a return to the early Christians' understanding that one finds Christ within all men but not without fellowship with others (Pestritto & Atto, 2008). While true to an extent, this view ignored the evidence noted in this book that religious orders and evangelical movements had been consistently involved in moral and social causes and civic responsibility since the nation's founding (also see, e.g., Neuhaus, 1986). Paralleling these perspectives were devotees (e.g., Croly, 1909, 1914) of Auguste Comte's positivist vision of a "religion of humanity" supplanting traditional religions. Collaboration, deconstruction of the capitalist system, and social planning by experts would replace the rapacity of competition and markets.

Another redefinition of individualism came from the engineering profession mentioned earlier, most notably by the Founder Societies. Believing that it was essential to harness private corporate interests to the public interest for expressive and authority reasons, its progressive members argued for a "higher individualism" or "cooperative individualism." This would occur through coordinated and self-directed group action by business associations to engage in industrial and societal planning (Wilson, 1975, p. 70). Consonant with traditional faculty psychology, they would balance or check the unbridled materialist passions of individuals and corporations using reason informed by data collection and analysis. If individuals and corporations adopted this broader definition of individualism, they would gain "increasing quantities to share [i.e., to redistribute]," as well as "time and leisure and taxes with which to fight out proper sharing of the 'surplus'" (p. 71).

Key elements of the Progressive reform movement also reconceptualized the Founders' idea of property rights. Calling the idea of property rights a "fiction," they argued—as elected officials such as US Senator Elizabeth Warren (D-MA) did later in the 21st century—that a "private business that employs thousands of people, uses the natural resources of the nation, enjoys exemptions and privileges at law, and is essential to the welfare of great communities is not a private business" (Pestritto & Atto, 2008, p. 123). Such a company "is public, and the sooner we abandon the fiction that it is private, the better for our good sense" (p. 123). Put differently, an "organizational society" was underway, one in which "industrialism had shifted the context of economic decisions from personal relationships among individuals to competition among well-organized groups" (Hays, 1995, p. 70). Moreover, the American exceptionalist ideals of individualism and property rights had led only to economic disparities and class conflicts that could be healed solely by a national government-driven redistribution of wealth.

Progressives also tried to reframe the idea of which institutional body—the president or the Congress—best advanced democracy. They lauded the moves by presidents Theodore Roosevelt, William Howard Taft (R-OH; on rare occasions), and Woodrow Wilson to act based on the plenary rather than the enumerated powers of presidents. After Jackson and prior to Roosevelt, if the Constitution did not expressly grant presidents power to do something, they would not do it. Roosevelt flipped this around: if the Constitution did not forbid an action, a president could do it. This aforementioned stewardship theory effectively portrayed presidents as the embodiment of Rousseau's "general will," since they were the only political officials elected by all the people. Challenging the Founders' fears of demagogues and popular passions, and clearly in line with progressives' view of leadership, this idea of a "personal presidency" or "plebiscitary presidency" (Lowi, 1985) appealed to many citizens in the wake of the corruption of Congress, state legislatures, and local governments, as well as the courts' still business-oriented conservatism. For Croly and other progressives, it was also a way to reconcile Hamilton's vision of a strong national executive with Jefferson's original emphasis on decentralized democracy. That is, Hamiltonian means could be used to pursue Jeffersonian ends, a progressive view later shredded in the 1960s and 1970s by the Vietnam War and the Watergate scandal, respectively (see Chapter 6).

Progressive historians also began negatively redefining the motives of the Founders and the US Constitution. These historians were led by Charles Beard of Columbia University and Carl Becker of Cornell University. Becker argued that there were two revolutions involving contests over ideas, one against England and the other concerning class warfare in America. Beard elaborated and extended Becker's argument. Steeped in the emergent scientific methods of historians of the time, his work undermined, first, the popularized image of the Founders as larger-than-life characters. Next, it attacked historian George Bancroft's more impersonal narrative of the Revolution as a "providential fulfillment of the American people's democratic destiny" (Wood, 2002, pp. xxiii–xxiv). Beard argued that the Constitution was really a counter-revolution set up by rich bondholders against farmers and planters. Reversed in the process were the democratic and Jeffersonian tendencies unleashed by the American Revolution among debtors and non-landholders.

Still other progressives such as Croly (1914) contended that the "best way to popularize scientific administration and enable the democracy to consider highly educated officials [i.e., bureaucratic experts] as [their] representatives [more so than elected officials] was to popularize higher education" (pp. 376–377). Thus, progressives worked to establish universities and graduate schools, touting especially the "Wisconsin Idea" of universities becoming central collaborators in governance (Orren & Skowronek, 2017, p. 155); that is, becoming a recognized part of the compensatory state. The further amplification of the corporate–social science nexus was afoot in these reform and state-building efforts, given their potential for legitimacy gains.

Finally, to advance their ends, nativist elements in the progressive coalition spoke openly about who was "fit" to engage in policy and administrative processes. Portraying a Hobbesian society of struggle against all, and distorting Charles Darwin's theory of evolution, they embraced both the mental inferiority of nonwhites and supported limiting their numbers through eugenics. Relatedly, nativists argued that ethnic diversity could complicate the efficiency and effectiveness of governance if immigrants participated. These notions were premised on the widely popular book by the English philosopher Herbert Spencer,

Social Statics, which embodied the doctrine of Social Darwinism. Yale sociologist William Graham Sumner became America's most noted popularizer of Spencer's notion of the survival of the fittest. He, plus eugenicists citing World War I IQ tests, thus gave "scientific" legitimacy to discrimination (ascriptive hierarchy) by advocating Social Darwinism as the intellectual justification for it.

****

Reframing American exceptionalist values rhetorically is one thing; operationalizing the political and administrative reforms sought by this motley coalition of progressives was another. Two of the most significant operational challenges to state building they faced involved permanently shifting policymaking power from states and localities to Washington (i.e., the nationalizing of policymaking power), as well as shifting it from legislatures to unelected professional experts located in public agencies. Because of the national scale and negative externalities of the newly emergent industrial economy in the United States, many progressives claimed that a national democracy was the only way to salvage Americans' millenarian vision as a beacon to the world (Eisenach, 1994; Rodgers, 1998).

The published case for doing all this had been made, first and most famously, in 1887 by then professor Woodrow Wilson in his aforementioned centennial essay. Comparing the state of administrative theory in the United States to that of European nations, Wilson argued that a science of public administration was way overdue and badly needed in America. As preceding chapters have shown, since the Founding Era, Americans had sought out European models of administration. These had been applied through the business and military experiences of Jacksonian administrators and during the Civil War. Wilson's essay, however, called for the *systematic* study and adaptation of administrative principles to American government, something that had not been done before.

Arguing, among other things, that even continental European autocracies understood how critical efficient service delivery was for maintaining their legitimacy and power, Wilson contended that Americans had not learned that lesson. He argued that they had focused on *political* theory rather than *administrative* theory. He averred that it was getting easier to "write a Constitution than to run one." For Wilson, developing a science of American administration was both critical and possible, because public administration was, at its essence, a field of business. And in a nod to a constitutive perspective, he argued that experts in public agencies could—and should—be given "large powers and unhampered discretion" to apply that science.

Accountability to the public, Wilson contended, could be maintained through bureaucratic administration. Those higher up in the hierarchy would be held accountable for their subordinates' actions. To give them smaller powers (i.e., to limit their discretion inordinately) would invite lethargy rather than Alexander Hamilton's energy in the executive. Looking ahead briefly to what actually developed in the 20th century with its labyrinth of bureaucratic rules, regulations, and reorganizations, bureaucracy and a constitutive perspective were actually incompatible. Moreover, so complex organizationally and inter-organizationally would this system become that finding out who was responsible for problems was difficult. In the process, the idea of "systemic failure" became the norm, meaning no individual was responsible.

That said, prescriptions such as Wilson's sparked a four-decade-long search by public administration and business scholars for principles of administration to guide the public and private sectors. This generic approach to administrative theory included organizing by function, eliminating overlap and duplication, establishing appropriate spans of supervisory control, designing clear lines of authority and responsibility, and making responsibility commensurate with authority. Citizens were viewed as largely passive and untutored, with a one-way flow of communication from agency experts to them the epitome of instrumental rationality.

But could a democracy embrace principles of administration borrowed largely from autocratic European nations without risking autocracy for itself? Wilson claimed American values were not endangered, because elected officials *set policies* while administrative experts merely carried them out. He famously wrote that "if I see a murderous fellow sharpening a knife cleverly [meaning autocrats], I can borrow his way of sharpening the knife without borrowing his probable intention to commit murder with it" (1887, p. 220).

Likewise, in 1900, Goodnow claimed that public administration was about "truth," not emotionalism. Experts staffing public agencies would discern this truth by means of their analytical talents. Thus, they needed freedom from politics to save the republic from the "polluted" atmosphere of special interest politics that had developed during the 19th century. He wrote that, as in business, public administrators could and should be a "force . . . free from the influence of politics" (Pestritto & Atto, 2008, p. 20). What became known as the politics–administration dichotomy was born, a separation that was conflated into a politics/policy–administration dichotomy premised on the same logic. This, because those private foundations funding early public administration research felt that figuring out how to "run government like a business" was politically less controversial and threatening to their own interests in a period of social unrest (see more below) (Durant, 2014b; Lee, 2013; Roberts, 1994; Rosenbloom, 2008).

The founders of public administration, however, were not naïve when they envisioned a politics–administration dichotomy. For some, politics was related solely to eliminating the patronage system. Moreover, most believed that politics should be separated from administration *as much as possible* but understood that it could *never be totally eliminated*. After all, "administration is policy," because the discretion public agencies wield is policymaking and has political implications.

Moreover, "politics follows discretion"; those affected by policy will seek to influence that discretion wherever it is exercised to advance their interests. Public administrators' concern, then, was over *where* politics might better be played to advance the public interest—legislatures captured by corrupt political machines or the executive branch of government throughout the compensatory state. They embraced the latter.

Nor would shifting policymaking power to experts in the executive branch be a problem in a democratic republic: public managers would be "bridge builders" to the public and, thus, fuse "true" efficiency with "true" democracy (Waldo, 1984, p. 133; also see Lee, 2008; Raadschelders, 2017). Consistent with the thinking of the earlier ASSA and the university-based social science professions and their associations, experts would make the policy choices that citizens and their elected representatives would make had they the time, inclination, and expertise (Cook, 2014; Durant & Ali, 2013). Doing so would "link administrative expertise, political habits and traditions, public thought, and political experience in a grand, creative synthesis that would fortify and enrich democracy—make it more democratic—in the only way possible under the conditions of modernity" (Cook, 2014, p. 7). Added Frederick Cleveland in 1913, "mak[ing] agency administrators more efficient was synonymous with asking how to make them more responsive" to the public interest (Schachter, 2010, p. 83).

Not unlike in earlier periods discussed in this book, however, the progressives' dreams of nation state building—as well as those of their corporate and social science allies—were not without ethnic, class, and gender biases. Only professional experts were eligible for public jobs, meaning that the uneducated or underedu- cated could not qualify. This shifted political and policymaking power to the rising middle class of professionals noted earlier and away from legislatures and recent immigrants. In addition, claiming that administrators merely carried out policies that elected officials enacted created the image that voters were still in control. Thus, "reforms that blended what the Constitution separated, that unified its oper- ation and integrated the work of policy making, received their [the progressives'] certificate of 'good governance'" (Orren & Skowronek, 2017, p. 154).

Granted, most early progressives took a "social evolutionary" view of immi- gration (Cook, 2007). As Wilson put it, over time, immigrants would acquire the tools of education and citizenship by participating in local government and the work of settlement houses (see more below) and civic associations. In the interim, however, the national administrative apparatus had to be sheltered from their influence—much as the patrician classes in the Roman Republic isolated the plebeians to "protect" their interests. But, with nativists part of the Progres- sive reform coalition, and pointing to Wilson's early publications, nativism also could be linked to this rationale.

For example, in the 1912 presidential election, the Hearst newspaper pointed to Wilson's strong and consistent anti-immigrant and anti-labor bias. In his *A History of the American People* (1902), Wilson had written,

> now there came multitudes of men of the lowest class from the south of Italy and men of the meaner sort out of Hungary and Poland . . . and they came in numbers which increased from year to year, as if the countries of Europe were disburdening themselves of the more sordid and hapless elements of their population.
>
> (Chace, 2004, p. 136)

Wilson protested during the 1912 presidential campaign that his derogatory comments were taken out of context and that he was merely talking about "certain lawless elements" among them. Still, his views and actions regarding race and ethnicity as president, plus the underlying objective of the politics–administration dichotomy, undermine his "clarification" (see Chapter 5).

****

In combination with the social schisms and unrest of this era, progressive arguments initially set the stage for the creation of a host of state and local public agencies to implement the legislation they enacted. As in earlier time periods, this expansion of the subnational component of the compensatory state produced agencies premised on bureaucratic administration (albeit in commission format), an instrumental view of the public service, and the need to shift policy-making power from legislatures to the executive branch. These efforts included the creation of 13 state bureaus of labor by 1888; state railroad regulatory commissions (begun in Massachusetts earlier in the 1870s); the city manager–council form of government (1906 in Staunton, Virginia); and state public utility commissions. At the local government level, urbanization sparked a flurry of new responsibilities and agencies. Detroit was typical, creating nearly 228 new administrative activities in its portfolio, "including the 'development of zoning plans, inspection of food handlers, public health nursing, community centers, electrified street lighting, motorized fire and policy services, public airport facilities, dental care for school children, mandatory grade school—and later high school education'" (Stillman, 1998, p. 125).

Agencies such as these often became models for federal agencies, prompted by reformers' view of the need to nationalize and rationalize previous state and local responsibilities through federal legislation passed during the Roosevelt and Wilson eras. As noted, these often started as commissions with overlapping terms and rotating partisan leadership. Legislators throughout the compensatory state favored this organizational format (and continue to do so today), because divided partisan leadership gave them more opportunities to influence policy decisions. It also prevented chief executives from making wholesale changes in leadership and agency policy direction (Moe, 1985). This was especially true for the regulated community of business interests. They, and proponents in the legal profession in the late 19th century, envisioned these agencies as driven by "lawyerly habits of mind, respect for the legal process, and personal [i.e., legal] training" (Hoffer, 2007, p. 171). Moreover, if all else failed, they could appeal agency decisions to courts staffed by conservative lawyers sympathetic to their interests.

So accurate was this view that the caseloads of the courts spiraled between 1880 and 1920. After Reconstruction, the Republican Party expanded the grounds for moving state cases into the federal courts in the Jurisdiction and Removal Act of 1875, and the federal judiciary faced a crushing burden of appeals. Intended originally to help blacks, the act instead was used by corporations seeking more sympathetic venues for their cases and appeals of regulatory decisions. In response, Congress weighed two approaches in the 1890s. One, ultimately unsuccessful, limited corporate access to the courts. The second was a successful effort to reorganize the federal system to reduce case burdens on the Supreme Court. The Judiciary Act of 1891 reduced direct appeals to the Supreme Court by creating federal appeals courts to review district court decisions.

Against this evolving backdrop, Roosevelt and Wilson differed initially over how best to deal with corporate size and power, with Roosevelt advocating regulation by agencies and Wilson advocating trust-busting. Trust-busting occurred during the Roosevelt administration (and even more so during the interregnum of the Taft administration). But regulation—and the creation of regulatory agencies— carried the day in ways that were significantly amplified later during the New Deal and the Great Society (Chace, 2004). Joining federal agencies created earlier in this period (e.g., the US Geological Survey in 1879, the Interstate Commerce Commission in 1887, and the Department of Labor in 1888) were the Department of Commerce and Labor (1903), later changed to the Department of Labor in 1913; the US Forest Service (1905); the precursor of the Food and Drug Administration (1906); the Federal Reserve System (1913); the Federal Trade Commission (1914); and the National Park Service (1916).

Amplifying earlier trends in administrative reform and promoted by what Stivers (2000) calls "bureaucratic men," the IRP prevailed as a state-building premise over other alternatives offered by progressives (see more below). Its success was advanced by three interrelated campaigns by so-called technocratic progressives operating at the local government level of the existing compensatory state. The first was the launch of Bureau of Municipal Research (BMR) movements. BMRs were nonprofits organized *outside* of city government agencies to advance the technocratic vision of economy and social efficiency. The second involved the establishment of bureaus of efficiency (with variations on this name) *within* urban government agencies (Lee, 2008). The third effort involved the creation of "training schools."

The most formidable of the BMRs in terms of leadership and innovation was the New York Bureau of Municipal Research (NYBMR). Chartered in 1907, it was led initially by a triumvirate of icons in the emerging field of public administration: William Allen, Henry Bruère, and Frederick Cleveland. The bureau focused mainly on executive-centered budgeting and made efficiency the prime value to be pursued. In the end, the NYBMR was credited with "transmit[ting] the doctrine of efficiency to hundreds of American towns and cities" (Lee, 2008, p. 18). Then, in 1911, the NYBMR founded the Training School for Public Service (TSPS) to prepare trainees for public-sector jobs at all levels of government. The TSPS then affiliated with the NYBMR to create the National Institute of Public Administration. Graduates of these programs were expected to start new BMRs, staff them, or apply their skills in existing and new agencies throughout the compensatory state, as well as in bureaus of efficiency.

With the aim of making public agencies "run like a business," BMRs and bureaus of efficiency sought to recruit "able and disinterested men" who would become "experts in the study of government" (Lee, 2008, p. 18). They would "conduct studies and surveys (i.e., audits) of city government agencies, collect objective information, and then recommend 'scientific' approaches to improve [their] efficiency" (p. 18). Joining these training and educational efforts were similar programs pursued by a growing number of newly formed professional associations before 1930. These groups included the International City Managers Association (1914), the Government Finance Officers Association (1906), and the American Society of Municipal Engineers (1894). By the late 1920s, many of these associations would link arms to create the Public Administration Clearing House (aka "1313") in Chicago.

****

As noted, although IRP-based technical progressivism largely prevailed in the Progressive Era, major alternatives to it existed *within* the Progressive movement. One such alternative—based on the substantive rationality project (SRP) and (as noted) led by what Stivers (2000) calls "settlement women"—fell to the growing political clout of the corporate–social science nexus of interests pushing technocratic progressivism in their campaign for legitimacy. As discussed, the still-prevalent "separate sphere" ideation in American life and in academia meant that most college-educated young women—including those in academia—joined the settlement movement in the United States (Knight, 2010). This movement was partly modeled after Toynbee Hall, established by Canon Barnett in 1884 to cope with the extreme poverty produced by industrialization in London's East End. Five years later, in 1889, Jane Addams and Ellen Starr extended Barnett's vision to American cities by creating Hull House in the impoverished northwest side of Chicago.[7] In this case, however, it was university-educated, largely single women who lived with the poor. So successful was Hull House that, by 1900, 22 settlement houses were established in the United States, and, by 1920, over 200 settlement houses existed. In the process, a women's network compensating for the lack of government capacity and pushing through their research for greater government activism was again amplified.

In contrast to technocratic progressives, settlement women favored democratic administration and explicitly value-infused research over value-free research, the bête noire of the objectively based social sciences. An important variant of the SRP, Addams' approach was to try to obtain social policy and administrative reform through research informed by "sympathetic knowledge," "standpoint epistemology," and "critical pragmatism." She wrote that

> we know at last, that we can only discover truth by a rational and democratic interest in life, and to give truth complete social expression is the endeavor upon which we are entering. Thus, identification with the common lot that is the essential idea of Democracy becomes the source and expression of social ethics.
>
> (*Stanford Encyclopedia of Philosophy*, 2014)

Stivers (2000) discerned a general difference between bureau men (i.e., the technological progressives promoting the IRP) working at municipal research bureaus and settlement women. She considered bureau men's interests to be largely on administrative improvements, such as budgeting and cost accounts, that would lead to better efficiency and, hence, less corruption. In contrast, settlement women focused on improving living conditions through research directed at social change (i.e., "investigate and instigate"). In the process, settlement women were much more applied, citizen-centered, and participatory in focus than were technocratic progressives. Their focus was on *praxis* (*praxeology*) or action-oriented research grounded in the SRP.

At one level, Stiver's view of separate spheres has been confirmed by other researchers. At another level, however, other researchers question a clear distinction between the two camps (Schachter, 2010), making this a question of extent rather than kind. Most notably, Hindy Lauer Schachter (2010) argues that some women were active in the scientific management or "technocratic progressive" movement and that some men participated in the settlement movement. Moreover, efficiency, statistics, and empirical analyses were central to the writings of women involved in settlement houses and, by extension, the National Consumers League.

For example, Addams, Florence Kelley, and Lillian Wald all insisted on gathering data and doing statistical analyses—as the aforementioned HHM&P demonstrated. Indeed, many women reformers were drawn to scientific management for tactical and expressive reasons: to couch their "softer" societal concerns in statistical (and, hence, more technical and masculine) language and, thus, gain professional legitimacy in a male-dominated political and social science milieu. As such, data analysis might become the great equalizer in policy debates for both sexes, as well as an Archimedean point of leverage for the women's world-view (Schachter, 2010).

Nevertheless, the gender-based and epistemological-based split in the social sciences over the value of applied versus basic research gave the bureau men and their IRP a significant power advantage over settlement women. Moreover, the financial support for public administration research from private family foundations such as the Rockefeller philanthropies was critical to the triumph of technocratic progressivism (Roberts, 1994; Rosenbloom, 2008; Schachter, 2010). Using fortunes amassed during the Gilded Age to offset negative family images, these foundations still felt it was not in their economic and political interests for researchers at, for example, the NYBMR to explore socially charged issues. They did not want to fan further the flames of labor–management strife already underway in America lest it undermine their business and class interests.

In the case of the NYBMR, these views eventually forced William Allen off its three-member board of directors in 1914. As Mordecai Lee (2013) observes, Allen was a vocal but abrasive advocate for "efficient citizenship," democratic administration, and an activist role for public administration in social issues. Later, between 1927 and 1936, the Rockefellers' continuing largesse and public administration's quest for legitimacy cemented the demise of Addams' and Allen's version of SRP-informed democratic administration (Roberts, 1994). Looking ahead briefly to show their path-dependent nature, Lee (2013) saw the same resource-dependent dynamics later accompany the founding of the American Society for Public Administration (ASPA) in 1939. Public administration legends Louis Brownlow and Luther Gulick wanted to create a research organization that would be more "scientific" than the by then dominant Governmental Research Association (GRA), which was primarily comprised of BMRs. The GRA sought Rockefeller money to pay for a secretariat and central office, but Brownlow convinced the foundation to refuse. He then used Rockefeller money to undercut GRA by generating a report showing that GRA-style research was not the kind of research needed by public administration. The GRA collapsed when Brownlow, William Mosher, and senior federal practitioners (such as Harold Smith and Donald Stone) seceded from GRA to create ASPA.

These resource-dependency dynamics created a shift in public administration research priorities. As Schachter (2010) argues:

> The concerns of the bureau [men] and settlement leaders before America's entry into World War I were quite different from the work of public administration experts in the post-war era. In the latter period, primary attention centered on internal structure and less energy devolved on substantive change to help the poor. This difference in orientation

accompanied the removal of women's reform endeavors from public administration texts—as well as the removal of the bureau role in citizenship education and substantive policy change in favor of emphasizing structural reforms.

(p. 91)

****

Curiously, public administration analyses of the Progressive reform movement stop with the bureau men/settlement women dichotomy. Less appreciated is a third source of friction and abrasion within the reform movement. Dubbed the "associative state" by Ellis Hawley (1997, p. 19), this alternative model of Progressive administrative reform was championed, most notably, by Herbert Hoover and best explained in his books, *American Individualism* (1922) and, later, *The Challenge to Liberty* (1934). Unlike the views of settlement women, proponents of the associationalist movement gained support from portions of the corporate–social science nexus of interests for the expressive, material, and authority gains conferred by legitimacy. Thus, it too amplified the proxy component of the compensatory state in consequential ways during this time period and beyond.

By the time *American Individualism* was published, Hoover already had achieved worldwide acclaim as the "Great Engineer" and the "Great Humanitarian."[8] He had done so as a millionaire businessperson turned public servant prior to and during the United States' entry into World War I. For example, his voluntary organizational and political feats were legendary in organizing food relief as chairman of the Commission for Relief in Belgium during World War I. In this effort, he created a private voluntary network of international government and business actors that fed over ten million starving Belgians and French in northern France during the occupation of the German army. Hoover, as head of the American Relief Administration (ARA), also led a post-war effort to address the starvation and devastation in Eastern Europe and Russia. He then transformed the ARA into the European Relief Council, raising millions of dollars in private contributions and building cross-national relief networks (Clements, 2010).

Hoover's Quaker-informed public philosophy of associationalism was premised on government-stimulated voluntary cooperation to address public problems. Direct government intervention was a last resort if private and civic volunteerism failed. He saw associationalism as a "third-way" alternative to rapacious capitalism (and free markets) and innovation-depressing and dignity-sapping socialism. For Hoover and his acolytes, properly educated and self-governing businesses, state and local governments, voluntary organizations, and professional associations informed by data analyses provided by federal agencies would willingly tackle any social or economic problems. Rather than regulate or provide direct assistance, technoscientific experts in the federal government would serve solely as sources of research and information, coordination, and national guidance.

Thus, as a social progressive, Hoover believed that an activist federal government was needed to address inequality and other social challenges in the compensatory state. For him, labor strikes and lockouts were "waste," just as poor planning and lack of coordination among businesses produced waste. This waste crushed human dignity, "hardened class feelings," and thus jeopardized the nation's economic and political health. America, he argued, needed a "New Era" of governance and a "new economic system"—a third way that avoided unprincipled laissez-faire doctrine *and* bureaucracy-based socialism (Leffler, 1981; Ziegler, 1981).

For Hoover, as for other progressive engineers and social scientists, "painful purges [i.e., depressions in the business cycle] were neither necessary nor inevitable. . . . Much of the difficulty lay in defective business organization, ill-informed decision-making, and improper uses of private power" (Hawley, 1981, p. 45). Hoover believed that a "cooperative system" among businesses "could save the nation from the triple evils of economic disorder, political radicalism, and statist regimentation" (p. 65). This, through "cooperative modernization and regulation" based on the "market information and statistical data needed to rationalize production, purchasing, and investment decisions" (p. 55).

Like bureau men (technological progressives), Hoover also saw bureaucrats in the federal government as a "national elite of technical experts." However, unlike them, he saw the role of federal agencies solely as "stimulat[ing] the private sector to organize and govern itself" in the public interest (Clements, 2000, p. 128). "Decentralization, voluntarism, and localism," data analysis, business-supported social science, and administrative reorganization animated his thinking (p. 96). Government agencies would afford "illumination, guidance, and cooperation" without "dictation or coercive [government] controls" (Hawley, 1981, p. 47).

As such, Hoover's associationalism was an early 20th-century version and amplification of the compensatory state and social science agenda that had been building since the nation's founding. It was also an important variant on today's scholarly focus on one form of "emergent" networks of third-party and federal government actors. In Hoover's mind, these associations would "work out bureaucratic arrangements that would *nourish* individual, community, and private effort rather than supplant them" (Hawley, 1974, p. 116, emphasis added). Although initially opposed by Republican conservatives in the business community, more socially liberal businesspersons allied with progressives in the social sciences to advance Hoover's governance and administrative vision once he became Secretary of Commerce in the 1920s (see Chapter 5).

****

After World War I began in Europe in 1914, and before the United States entered the war in 1917, debate raged in America over the role the nation should play in it. Aside from national security and moral debates, many recently arrived immigrants from Europe still held allegiances to their native countries, and President Wilson did not want to exacerbate these tensions. For these and other reasons, he successfully ran for reelection in 1916 promising to keep the United States out of the war.

As for progressives, many were reluctant to support entry into World War I, partially because they feared the war would drain resources from domestic needs. Noninterventionists such as Addams were roundly criticized by the government as being radical Bolsheviks (Deegan, 1988). She and 61 others were put on a US War Department list sent to the US Senate, accusing them of holding "dangerous, destructive and anarchistic sentiments" (McGerr, 2003, pp. 307–308). Eventually, most progressives supported Wilson's call to arms after German U-Boats harassed US shipping, the Zimmerman Note surfaced positing an alliance between Germany and Mexico, and the Bolshevik Revolution of 1917 occurred. Some saw advantages in war planning, mobilization, and warfare. Younger progressives such as John Dewey calculated that these national planning efforts could translate into similar initiatives to address social problems in the post-war era. Dewey wrote of the "social possibilities of war" and thus argued that a precedent would be set that could be exploited later by progressives: "we [Americans] shall have to lay by our good-natured individualism and march in step" (Goldberg, 2018, p. 186). To witness this vision, however, progressives would have to wait until the end of World War II, and then only see it in Great Britain under Prime Minister Clement Atlee's Labor government.

Also buoying the support of technological progressives and associationalists were the "dollar-a-year" men from business, such as Bernard Baruch, who were leading war mobilization and applying scientific management principles in doing so. They looked favorably on Wilson's use of 5,000 "mobilization agencies" to ensure that all aspects of the economy marched in the same direction, his nationalization of industries (e.g., the railroads and telephone companies), and his domination of financial markets with Liberty Bond drives. If the United States could plan effectively during war, why could it not do so for social improvement in peacetime?

But, as noted, the dreams of social progressives (in contrast to those of technological progressives and associationalists) were soon dashed after the war. Indeed, even Wilson abandoned his impressive earlier social progressive stance and legislative record as he tried to appeal to conservatives for support of his League of Nations. This, as reform exhaustion occurred, displeasure mounted with Wilson's backsliding on entering the war, and his League of Nations proposal foundered (Clements, 2000; McGerr, 2003). Asked critic Walter Lippman, "Can anyone name a single piece of constructive legislation and administration carried through since the armistice?" (Burner, 1968, p. 5). Indeed, as war critic Randolph Bourne prophesied in 1917, and as Henry Bruère later concurred in 1919, "there isn't going to be any radical, quick reconstruction in America, . . . The tendency is toward reaction back to pre-war conditions" (McGerr, 2003, p. 310).

Indeed, conservative, pro-business Republicans wielding both technocratic and, especially, associationalist approaches took control of Congress in the 1918 midterm elections and the presidency in the 1920 elections (see Chapter 5). However, as during the Civil War, mobilization and warfighting buoyed the profits and legitimacy of the corporate–social science nexus through their affiliation with the federal government. This occurred as "expertise-generating organizations working in combination with or outside of the [federal government] carved out an important role in shaping the understanding of policymakers and the public of what constitutes a public problem while, at times, proposing potential remedies" (Hendrickson, 2010, p. 58).

In the process, World War I produced a quantum leap in the federal government component of the compensatory state. Included in this leap were a series of boards, such as the Food Administration, the National War Labor Board, the War Finance Corporation, and the War Labor Policies Board. Meanwhile, in the proxy component of the compensatory state, the federal government encouraged the building of commodity groups and war service committees that were certified by the US Chamber of Commerce as representatives of these groups in policymaking and administration (Eisner, 2000a). These industry-wide groups included the American Association of Advertising Agencies (as part of government efforts to sell the war to citizens), the National Restaurant Association (to help coordinate food conservation efforts), the American Farm Bureau Federation (1919), and the American Legion.

Thus, "while primary reliance continued to be placed . . . upon private initiative, the Government undertook to deal in respect to many matters, not with individual business concerns, but entire trades and industries" (Eisner, 2000a, p. 47). It was easier to deal collectively than individually with business entities. In the process, however, sinewy subsystem ties going back to the nation's founding were ratcheted up appreciably by the federal government. In effect, during the war effort, a reciprocal resource-dependency relationship was created favoring the business community over the federal government—just as happened during the Civil War and would happen again in World War II, the Cold War, and the War on Terror.

Similarly ensconced in several federal agency networks was organized labor, most especially the National War Labor Board (NWLB). Led by Samuel Gompers' American Federation of Labor (AFL), and against a continuing backdrop of the bitter and often violent labor strikes discussed earlier, more conservative labor leaders (such as Gompers) envisioned an associationalist management–labor relationship. In combination with the aforementioned business–government relationships, "varying numbers of legally equivalent institutions established temporary or permanent accommodations with each other through voluntarist action and looked to the state simply for ratification of these bargains" (Eisner,

2000a, p. 69). The invisible hand of the federal government was over all of the compensatory state.

As Eisner (2000a) summarizes, World War I

> resulted in a hasty creation of new state capacities. . . [but] new policy tools had to be developed with some care if the state was going to exercise extraconstitutional powers over private economic interests. . . [thus] requiring some significant compromises and a blurring [again] of public and private power that would have some weighty implications.
>
> (p. 46)

Practical realities involving the new "organizational society" (including "financial institutions, corporate bureaucracies, and functional or occupational organizations"), plus philosophical commitments to American exceptionalism, meant a "new reliance on the private organizational elites that had emerged in the prewar years," along with existing and new associations coaxed into existence by federal agencies and the Congress (Hawley, 1997, p. 16) (see more below).

Yet another aspect of the expansion of the proxy component of the compensatory state produced by World War I involved the voluntary sector. As Mark Hendrickson (2010) writes, the government consciously "spun off" to the voluntary sector (incentivized much later by favorable tax treatment) many highly charged issues such as racial discrimination. Also occurring was a "fluid movement of individuals, findings, and ideas" among the public, volunteer, and private sectors (e.g., so-called Negro labor experts in the National Urban League) (p. 58). These spin-offs of responsibility to the volunteer sector were often sought by its leaders for greater legitimacy and expanded the compensatory state. And although nowhere near as politically powerful as business or the social sciences during and after World War I, voluntary associations gained increased visibility, legitimacy, and "patriotic" recognition.

****

Not surprisingly, the inherited lack of government capacity combined with the amplification of the compensatory state produced principal–agent-type information asymmetries that, again, favored corporate interests and led to mischief during the war. Consider the War Industries Board's (WIB) Price Fixing Committee. Basically, pricing of key goods had to be negotiated with the very industries that were being regulated. The WIB, in turn, even conferred "quasi-official" government status on them as part of the trade associations and war services committees the conflict had created. This was the price that still capacity-short agencies had to pay to get access to business information.

As Robert Cuff (1969) writes, the "theme of decentralization [of the war effort] should be regarded largely as a rationalization for the Board's dependency on oligarchies of private economic power" (p. 130). Adds William Leuchtenburg (1964), the "outstanding characteristic of the war organization of industry was that it showed how to achieve massive government intervention without making any permanent alteration on the power of corporations" (p. 129). In the process, both existing and newly created associations and industries "were greatly strengthened. . . . After the war, many of these [business] associations continued to represent the interests of their sectors and actively sought to nurture close relationships with policy makers and key agencies" (Eisner, 2000a, p. 47).

Also, as in earlier periods of needed networking building,

> national officials attempted to append to the [federal government] the capacities of more developed private-sector institutions such as corporations, trade associations and agricultural associations. Their cooperation was secured . . . through the . . . incentive of the purse . . . private interests collaborated in the expectation that cooperation would carry financial benefits (e.g., restrictions on market entry; a high rate of return; access to licenses, contracts, or subsidies) [from the federal agencies created to implement this approach].
>
> (Eisner, 2000a, p. 40)

Still needed to realize technological and associationalist progressives' vision and war victory, however, were empirically grounded data and statistical analyses done by experts within and outside the federal government. To these ends, and like corporate interests, the social sciences were both needed and sought to link themselves to government, not only out of patriotism but due to their continuing quest for legitimacy and its expressive, material, and authority benefits. Moreover, they often worked in tandem with the corporate sector in this endeavor.

As discussed earlier, and prior to World War I, many social scientists did not view poverty, disease, unemployment, and social discontent as the inexorable result of an unjust social order. Rather, they resulted from an unstable, ill-managed, but improvable corporate capitalism (Alchon, 1985; also see Kolko, 1977; Weinstein, 1968). Their leaders argued that new administrative and technical "machinery of some sort had to be invented [and] new standards . . . created" for addressing America's ills (Adams, 1918, pp. 280–281). Technical and associational progressives argued that the nation would be rescued from "moral anarchy" by placing human affairs where they "never yet have been placed, under the control of trained human reason" in the social sciences and other professions (Nelson, 1982, p. 82). Moreover, during World War I, social scientists worked inside and outside federal agencies, gaining a reputation as "disinterested professionals" who used scientific methods and were dedicated to a public "service ideal" (Alchon, 1985, p. 10).

Social scientists especially gained an institutional toehold in the Wilson administration's Central Bureau of Planning and Statistics and the WIB. But their migration to government agencies was not sufficient for realizing wartime mobilization. Consequently, professional associations of social scientists partnered with those in agencies to complete a good deal of the surge of war-related research. Their efforts were impressive. Even Bourne (1917) wrote that the "War has revealed a younger intelligentsia . . . immensely ready for the *executive ordering of events*" (p. 696, emphasis added). They showed elected officials and citizens the value of "seeing," understanding, and ordering a chaotic world through statistical and econometric eyes.

More broadly, statisticians and economists amplified their earlier claims that "business cycles could be measured statistically, possibly predicted, and perhaps even controlled" (Clements, 2010, p. 133). Addressing a joint meeting of the AEA and the ASA in 1918, noted economist Irving Fisher proclaimed that economists and statisticians were the "logical arbiters of an impending class struggle" (Alchon, 1985, p. 38). That struggle could be recast favorably by treating social problems as "hypotheses in terms that allowed for precise statistical illumination and verification" (p. 40). The institutional economist Thorstein Veblen even spoke of a "directorate" of engineers that would lead a revolution for a "more competent management of the country's industrial system," a revolution to replace an existing regime that "has most significantly fallen short" (Barry, 1997, p. 266).

Upon these pleas for rationality, the war's aftermath saw the creation of the National Bureau of Economic Research (NBER) in 1920 and the Social Science Research Council (SSRC) in 1923. This proxy approach again was taken instead of building a commensurate in-house capacity in government in part to hide the visible size of the federal government. Led by social scientists, embraced by Hoover and his associationalist allies in the business community, and funded by corporate donors, the SSRC became an "important catalytic agent, . . . stimulating research, encouraging the improvement of scientific method, and facilitating interdisciplinary communication and cooperation" to address public problems (Alchon, 1985, p. 116).

Thus, although a "gnawing [sense of] social science illegitimacy" existed among social scientists at the beginning of the war, by war's end a "higher and more secure status for the social sciences" developed (Alchon, 1985, p. 34). Seizing on this momentum, many social scientists and their associations in the compensatory state argued that an "expansion of technocratic data and authority" was now needed for the further development and implementation of policy addressing all kinds of social problems. Although expressive motivations prompted these arguments, social scientists also correctly assumed that expansion would bring to them even "more wealth and income for everyone [material gain], . . . a narrowing of the gap between technocratic vision and [political] competence [expressive gain], and . . . a higher and more secure status for [the] social science[s]" [authority gain] (Alchon, 1985, p. 34).

It is also important to understand that social science advocates were not alone in pressing this case. The success of this campaign was the product of a "managerial constellation of business, foundation, social science, and government elites" (Alchon, 1985, p. 51). Especially critical financially were the Rockefeller trusts (again) and the Carnegie Corporation. Both funded major studies and gave institutional support to the NBER. Meanwhile, Henry Jones Ford (1920), the president of APSA, argued that the work of political science "was to clear away the wreck" of the war and apply its knowledge of organizations, jurisprudence, and government forms to rebuilding the world (p. 2). His pleas were amplifications, of course, of both Enlightenment thinking and, in turn, the ASSA in the post-Civil War era.

Likewise, during World War I, the American Psychology Association linked over a dozen committees to the Department of War to do such things as IQ testing for soldiers and developing the "new" science of personnel management. This deft fusion of military, social science, and business actors boosted the legitimacy prospects of the psychology profession to unprecedented heights during and after the war. In true compensatory state fashion, however, these contributions were often done through private consulting firms. Regardless, the corporate–social science nexus of interests "facilitated the transfer of public policymaking from the political to the administrative arena, a process that began a generation earlier with the rise of the modern corporation" (Alchon, 1985, p. 51). This, in turn, meant that the "production of social knowledge was made routine," and this routinization produced an expanded financial "subsidization of the data competence and scientific legitimacy of social science" (pp. 51–52).

****

In the end, progressives left a mixed legacy of state-building accomplishments, administrative reform, and important social legislation. They also left significant negative externalities that would be amplified in the longer term by valorizing the IRP, amplifying an expertise-based compensatory state, and reaffirming an instrumental rather than constitutive view of public managers. The metes and bounds of that state were powered and shaped by a corporate–social science nexus seeking what they sincerely thought to be a better approach to policymaking and administration—but also material and authority gains—by affiliating themselves with the federal government and marginalizing nonexperts from the policymaking process. But, in Barry Karl's (1983) elegant phrase, it was an "uneasy state" that, arguably, could be nothing more, given the tenets of American exceptionalist values except in times of crises. Thus, again, and as Chapter 5 analyzes, its very nature set off the next two competing rounds of calls for administrative reform in America. This occurred, first, during the Roaring

20s and, then, after perceived historical–structural deficiencies spawned by the Great Depression of the 1930s.

Notes

1. The Red Summer of 1919 involved race riots in over three dozen cities and in one rural county in Arkansas.
2. This section relies heavily on Rodgers' pointing to the roots of reform coming from Europe.
3. The full name of the HHM&P publication was: *The Hull-House Maps and Papers: A Presentation of Nationalities and Wages in a Congested District of Chicago with Comments and Essays on the Problems Growing Out of the Social Conditions.* The research was done between 1892 and 1894.
4. All data in this paragraph are taken from www.apstudynotes.org/us-history/topics/rise-of-unions/.
5. Article 1, section 6 of the US Constitution precluded legislators from holding executive positions.
6. Turner's thesis was critiqued in the 1960s as failing to consider regionalism and as exaggerating frontier democracy and egalitarianism.
7. This discussion of Addams relies heavily on Knight (2010).
8. This discussion of Hoover relies on Burner (1979); Clements (2010); Hawley (1981); Hoover (1922); Leuchtenburg (2009); Nash (1988, 1996); and Wilson (1975).

Chapter 5

Post-War Boom and Bust, the Corporate– Social Science Nexus, and American Administrative Reform, Circa 1920–1940

World War I had brought impressive economic prosperity to America. Between 1915 and 1920, the United States experienced the largest five-year increase in gross national product (GNP) in its history to that point (McGerr, 2003). Still, as noted in Chapter 4, historians portray the end of the Progressive Era in approximately 1920. Its demise is frequently attributed to Americans tiring of the turmoil of the era, the social and moral proselytizing of reformers, and the burgeoning scale of federal, state, and local intervention into their behavior. As Martin Shefter (2002) summarizes, "wartime policies brought government into the lives of ordinary people so intrusively [that] the United States experienced a 'general postwar reaction against active government'" (p. 121).

As also noted, social progressives' hopes were dashed when war planning did not morph into comprehensive social planning in the post-war era, especially after the Bolshevik Revolution in October 1917 had presumably put Russia on a path toward such a rationality-guided Marxist–Leninist society. Nor were their social equity concerns helped by revelations of corruption in wartime contracting and the discrimination and violence that accompanied the suspension of Americans' constitutional rights and freedoms by the Woodrow Wilson administration and Congress. These included the Sedition Act, the excesses of the Committee on Public Information, and the Palmer Raids during the First Red Scare (1919–1920) (Clements, 1999, esp. ch. 10).[1]

The Wilson administration also had demonized immigrants by promoting a "100-percent America" campaign against so-called hyphenated Americans (e.g., German-Americans) (Goldberg, 2018, p. 186). This, as Wilson claimed that "any man who carries a hyphen around with him carries a dagger that he is ready to plunge into the vitals of this Republic whenever he gets a chance" (p. 186). The Wilson administration also had created a vigilante-like group called the American Protection League that used violence and intimidation against war protesters. In addition, the Red Scare helped throttle down the momentum of the labor movement. This transpired as business placed the Bolshevik label on strikers and social progressives and as anti-union sentiment spiraled in large segments of the public (Allen, 1931, pp. 47–48). Although over 2,000 labor strikes occurred between 1919 and 1922, the labor movement was set back immensely in membership to pre-war levels (Hawley, 1997, esp. pp. 39–42). Diminished were labor leaders' hopes that World War I gains in legitimacy would continue after the war.

But the war also provoked disillusionment and disenchantment more broadly. Many opponents of the war were disillusioned with the sacrifices of blood and treasure, while others lamented the creature comforts they gave up during the war (McGerr, 2003; Watkins, 1993). As T. H. Watkins (1993) summarizes some of these sentiments, the

> thousands of Americans who had died on the battlefields of Europe, and the billions of dollars that [had] been loaned to the allies by [the United States] . . . [were] . . . bad investments—wasted on nations who could not control their own people.
>
> (p. 27)

Just as after the Civil War, cynicism set in, with many feeling that US citizens had once again been sacrificed for the gauzy abstractions, naïve dreams, and unrealized aspirations of their leaders.

Others, such as economist John Maynard Keynes, warned accurately that the 1919 Treaty of Versailles ending World War I was too economically punishing and demoralizing to the Germans and would be a setback to peace (but see MacMillan, 2002, for a counterargument). After a period of economic prosperity fueled partly by American loans calmed things in Germany, the Great

Depression hit Europeans especially hard after US banks called in those loans. Thus, in several ways, the treaty did contribute to Hitler's rise, Nazism, World War II, and the Holocaust. So, too, did the war negatively "color much of middle-class America's attitude toward the torn and bleeding nations of Europe" (Watkins, 1993, p. 27). Specifically, it helped promote a return to Americans' historical isolationist temperament. Moreover, after a physically disabled and distracted Wilson ordered rapid war demobilization, the recession of 1920–1921 occurred, stoking further labor unrest in America.

Also unleashed by World War I was a legislative resurgence of American nativism limiting the immigration into America of southern and eastern Europeans, as well as Chinese. In the process, virulent strains of ascriptive discrimination were unleashed against blacks, Catholics, and Jews, with violence promulgated by the revival of the Ku Klux Klan that President Ulysses Grant had largely crushed militarily in the 1870s.[2] This, while President Wilson "defended segregation and disenfranchisement [of blacks] . . . whom he saw as 'ignorant and unfitted by education for the most usual and constant duties of citizenship.' " His administration also opposed anti-lynching laws, did little to try to stop race riots between 1917 and 1919, and segregated federal offices (Clements, 1999, p. 101).

Given this conjunction of factors, the 1920s became known as an era of conservative, minimal-state, Republican leadership. This, as President Warren Harding (R-OH) proclaimed a "return to normalcy" in the country after defeating the Democratic ticket of James Cox and Franklin D. Roosevelt (FDR). Harding died in 1923 but left behind a record with implications for administrative reform and state building that has been overshadowed by scandals (e.g., Teapot Dome). His record included disarmament treaties, lowered taxes, national debt reduction ($26 billion), and falling unemployment (from 12 percent to 3 percent). His administration also abolished the 12-hour workday, created the Bureau of the Budget (BOB) and the General Accounting Office (since 2004, the Government Accountability Office) as part of the landmark Budget and Accounting Act (BAA) of 1921, and passed the inaugural federal highway bill (Pietrusza, 2007, pp. 423–424).

But, at the same time, the 1920s saw nearly 6,000 independent companies "swallowed up" in 1,200 corporate mergers. By 1929, approximately 200 corporations controlled half of all American industry (Watkins, 1993, p. 46). This prevailed until the Great Depression and 1932 landslide election of Democrat FDR with huge Democratic majorities in Congress. Also unleashed after the 1920–1921 recession was the Roaring 20s of economic growth. Harding's successor, Calvin Coolidge (R-MA), left a similarly formidable conservative economic record. During his presidency, the national debt fell from over $22 billion in 1923 to $17 billion in 1929; taxes were cut in four of his six years as president, with 98 percent of the population not paying taxes in 1927; and taxes were cut for those earning under $10,000 from $130 million to under $20 million between 1923 and 1929. Meanwhile, the nation's gross domestic product (GDP) grew an average of 7 percent annually during Coolidge's presidency (Pietrusza, 2007, p. 431).

Sparking this economic growth during the Republicans' "return to normalcy" was pent-up demand for goods and services restricted by the war. Unleashed by the advent of installment buying, a wave of seemingly insatiable consumerism occurred. Consumer credit debt skyrocketed from $2.6 billion in 1919 to $7.1 billion in 1929. A level of libertinism seldom witnessed in America before the 1920s was also unleashed, with conventional social norms of behavior, including sexuality, seemingly suspended until a brief reprieve (amid exhaustion!) in the late 1920s (Allen, 1931; Eisner, 2000a; Heilbroner & Singer, 1999).

But focusing on Harding's and Coolidge's pro-business, minimalist agenda in the 1920s ignores the flourishing of one element of the Progressive movement's administrative agenda—the linking of Herbert Hoover's associationalist brand of administrative reform with compensatory state building (see Chapter 4). It also ignores how three important cabinet appointees had strong ties to the Republican Progressive movement. These included Hoover as Secretary of Commerce, Charles Hughes as Secretary of State, and Henry C. Wallace as Secretary of Agriculture. They all believed that "properly staffed and delimited, government [agencies] could serve as a catalyzer and coordinator of cooperative endeavors, a gatherer and clearinghouse of needed information, and a consulting service for groups in need of organizational and technical expertise" (Hawley, 1997, p. 48). With the support of business, private foundations, the social sciences, and the nonprofit world, Hoover and his allies pushed associationalist remedies that helped catapult him to the presidency in 1928.

Likewise challenged by more recent research is the notion that Hoover's associationalism died after it proved inadequate to handle the challenges of the Great Depression (see, e.g., Hart, 1994; Hawley, 1997; Karl, 1983). To be sure, FDR's New Deal significantly amplified the size and regulatory scope of the federal government in Washington using the instrumental rationality project (IRP)-based tenets of technological progressives. But FDR also amplified the expansion of the corporate and voluntary components of the compensatory state. Thus, as David Hart (1994) summarizes, in the "shadow of the welfare state and the warfare state, the associative state has survived" and "advocacy [has occurred] on its behalf in virtually every Administration" since (p. 30).

FDR's efforts were buoyed by the now familiar progressive refrain that a historical–structural mismatch existed: America's Madisonian system could not meet the challenges, this time, of the Great Depression. But, more structurally, many in his administration inaccurately argued that the United States was entering a permanent era of economic and natural resource scarcity requiring a stronger national bureaucratic hand to plan for and navigate. Many opinion leaders also held these positions, including public intellectuals and the by now more legitimized social sciences. Social science associations picked up their historical refrain that "only a few were truly capable of understanding human and social problems" in periods of scarcity, and thus, the average person was "incapable of making sound decisions or wise policy choices" (Hawley, 1997, p. 144).

Other opinion leaders also admired the relative efficiency, speed of action, and planning capabilities of Fascist Benito Mussolini in Italy and Communist Joseph Stalin in the Soviet Union. Additionally, in a familiar claim, they feared that the United States was severely disadvantaged by the cumbersomeness of American democratic institutions. History, some said, was on the side of strong leaders and bureaucratically led governance rather than democracy, a lament one hears today in some vocal quarters on the Right and Left. But FDR foiled calls for extreme political and administrative reforms by these doubters, as well as by socialists, anarchists, right-wing corporatists, and left-wing populists (Katznelson, 2013; Kennedy, 2005; Shlaes, 2007). Conservative business leaders also turned against him after his 1936 reelection campaign when he began excoriating them for greed and "corporate royalism." However, earlier, a more moderate corporate–social science nexus of reform interests helped shape his policy, administrative reform, and state-building agenda.

Given the durability of Americans' self-conception as an exceptionalist nation based on limited government, economic liberalism, and volunteerism, a strong conservative backlash constrained FDR's aspirations. The stubbornness of high levels of unemployment prior to the United States' entry into World War II also buttressed this backlash, as did regulatory, judicial, and administrative over-reaches by FDR. The latter occurred after FDR tried to pack the US Supreme Court with judges more amenable to his activist state agenda,[3] after he campaigned in 1936 against members of his own party who did not support the New Deal agenda, and after his President's Committee on Administrative Management (PCAM) recommended increasing the power of the president relative to the Congress. Moreover, in a by now familiar pattern, FDR's emphasis on the IRP also aroused perceptions among some that average citizens were marginalized from the expertise-based agencies that blossomed during his presidency. This again set the stage for further enhancement of the compensatory state and subsequent calls for the next rounds of administrative reform in the 1950s through 1970s discussed in Chapter 6.

****

Martin Shefter (2002) argues that "World War I greatly strengthened firms capable of operating in global markets" (p. 121). It also instigated massive losses of capital among US European allies and skyrocketed their debt, which the United States largely financed. Simultaneously, the Austrian–Hungarian, German, and Ottoman empires were physically, economically, and socially decimated and were replaced by smaller, more impotent nations with boundaries set up for colonial gain by the 1919 peace treaty. The British navy, along with its merchant shipping, was also depleted.

All this left the United States as the primary economic and military power in the world. As Robert Heilbroner and Aaron Singer (1999) argue, prior to the Wall Street Crash in 1929, the overall economic situation in the United States was robust:

> Between 1922 and 1929, national income rose from $63.1 billion to $87.8 billion. Per capita income had jumped from $517 for the period 1909 to 1918 to $612 for the period of the 1920s. Despite generally shorter working hours, output per worker was up by 30 percent. Industrial production nearly doubled between 1921 and 1929. . . . [I]inflation and unemployment were virtually nonexistent. The average annual rate of increase in prices between 1923 and 1929 was less than 1 percent and unemployment averaged only 3.7 percent of the labor force.
>
> (p. 256)

In addition, between 1925 and 1929, the United States was responsible for nearly half the world's industrial production.

Great ironies also existed, however, amid this abundance. First, the 1920–1921 recession in many ways discredited the legitimacy of the federal government rather than the private sector. Fault lay not only with too rapid demobilization after World War I but also with unwise federal fiscal and monetary policy.[4] Unemployment hit nearly 12 percent in 1920 as American soldiers returned from Europe, while GDP declined nearly 17 percent. Second, the war (again) created a "lost generation" of Americans, one that was cynical of sacrifice based on calls by their political leaders to "duty, honor, and country." The carnage suffered by both sides in the war in the wake of political and military strategic/tactical blunders (e.g., at the battles of the Somme and Verdun) could not be compensated, forgotten, or forgiven. In total (including US losses), approximately 8.5 million soldiers died, and total casualties approached 37 million soldiers. Third, psychic fatigue with progressivism and World War I combined with pent-up demand after years of wartime sacrifice to rekindle an extreme embrace of Americans' individualism, consumerism, and laissez-faireism (Allen, 1931; Hawley, 1997; Watkins, 1993, 1999).

More precisely, the "lost generation" launched attacks on authority structures of all kinds in America. Importantly, the natural and social sciences indirectly abetted this revolt. Developments in both catalyzed a questioning of traditional morality and afforded justification for unprecedented personal freedom. Critical to this was the popularizing—sometimes inaccurately—of earlier science findings and theories by new methods of mass communication, just as happened later in the 2010s with social media. Popularized from psychology (and, especially, the work of Sigmund Freud), for example, was the idea that repressed sexual drives produced mental health problems. Freud, an atheist, also ridiculed religion as superstition. Likewise, popularization of biologically based theories—notably evolution—implied that humankind was not God's creation and history was not guided by a divine power. Rather, evolution was random, and humans evolved from animals. Thus, some claimed, shared animal instincts were "natural" to satisfy.[5] This, in contrast to faculty psychology's emphasis on integrating these instincts (what psychologist Carl Jung called humankind's "shadow archetype") with more noble ones. Concomitantly, falsely conflating Albert Einstein's theory of special relativity as legitimating value relativism helped unloose the bonds of traditional standards for many in the younger generation.

All this cast existing norms, values, and ethics into question as mere products of place and time (i.e., the "historicism" challenged later by Leo Strauss [1953] and others in the 20th century) and as metanarratives used by the powerful to pacify the masses. This, much as today's postmodernists contend, as had Sophist value relativists in 5th-century BCE Athens and the Romantics in the 18th and early 19th centuries. Paradoxically, although denouncing the triumph of rationality over emotion in citizens' personal lives, the rationality of the scientific method was embraced to justify overthrowing existing norms and values. For example, traditional norms regarding women's wear, the use of cosmetics, and sexual abstinence were set aside by many. Concurrently, birth control and abortion were proselytized by Margaret Sanger and others, while newsstands and movies touted sexual freedom. In the process, the lost generation inverted faculty psychology's stress on reason and balance over emotions, much to the consternation (and sense of secular ridicule and societal alienation) of religious fundamentalists.

More broadly, the relative prosperity that assembly-line manufacturing brought (see more below) once more persuaded many Americans that markets should be the ultimate authority structure in society. Although informing Americans' self-conception since the Founding Era, the idea of America's commercial republic was amplified once more with a vengeance. As one student of the 1920s colorfully put it:

> from early 1923 to late 1929 (and the Wall Street crash) . . . nearly seven years of unparalleled plenty [occurred] . . . during which men and women might be disillusioned about politics and religion and love, but believed that at the end of the rainbow there was at least a pot of negotiable legal tender consisting of the profits of American industry and American salesmanship: nearly seven years during which the businessman was. . . "the dictator of our destinies," ousting "the statesman, the priest, the philosopher, as the creator of standards of ethics and behavior."
>
> (Allen, 1931, p. 138)

Moreover, and just as in the early 19th century, business and religion were linked in many minds. This, as books and pamphlets lionized corporate leaders and businesses in conventional religious terms (e.g., *Moses, Persuader of Men* and *The Man Nobody Knows*) (Allen, 1931, pp. 154–155). In addition, as college enrollments soared, universities began offering business and management courses, beginning a campaign for legitimacy by business schools that would pick up during the 1930s and 1940s (see more below). However, not unlike earlier eras when market appetites were unleashed (e.g., the Gilded Age), this happened despite repeated corporate (and public) corruption scandals. During the 1920s, these included the aforementioned Teapot Dome Scandal, graft at the Veterans' Bureau, revelations of war profiteering by companies during World War I, and multiple other contracting scandals.

Nonetheless, and partly responsible for buoying support for business and its administrative model amid these scandals, conservative newspaper editors started impugning the motives of muckrakers, congressional investigators, and administrative reformers. For instance, in commenting on the Teapot Dome Scandal, the *New York Times, New York Tribune,* and *New York Evening Post* called investigators "assassins of character," a "Democratic [Party] Lynching Bee," and "contemptable and disgusting" (Allen, 1931, p. 134). In a by now familiar red herring, they were joined by many in the corporate community who questioned the patriotism of investigators, characterizing their efforts as international conspiracies led by socialists to topple the US government. Thus, as prosperity blossomed, many readers again believed that government, not business, was responsible for scandals and should stay out of business.

Sparked by the mass production of goods that lowered prices appreciably, consumerism was also an escape for workers from the tedium and drudgery of Taylor's scientific management of the assembly line. Ironically, the same assembly line that bored them as workers also allowed them as consumers to purchase goods previously enjoyed only by the more affluent. For instance, although a car cost an average of two years pay prior to 1914, one cost only three months of wages by the late 1920s. Moreover, General Motors' launch of the consumer credit industry was adopted by banks for all types of purchases, making nominal disposable income no longer a barrier to ownership. Thus, automobile ownership soared from 4,000 in 1900 to 400,000 by 1929. Radio advertising also relentlessly encouraged citizens to spend to keep up with their neighbors, efforts ridiculed in the 19th century as dangerous by novelists such as Gustave Flaubert and Charles Dickens. This, as the science of propaganda developed during World War I by George Creel to "sell" the war to, and stymie the dissent of, Americans was applied to the selling of commercial goods.

The demand for trucks and cars also led to a rapid growth in the construction of all-weather surfaced roads to facilitate commerce and recreation. In addition, rapidly expanding electric utility networks to power homes and assembly lines led to new consumer appliances and new types of lighting and heating for homes and businesses. Meanwhile, the invention of the radio lessened (but did not eliminate) feelings of rural isolation, as did the expansion of local and long-distance telephone communications. Additionally, recreational activities—such as traveling, going to movies, and professional sports—became major businesses.

Aside from a better quality of living for the average worker, the assembly line also improved women's life chances. New appliances meant they could escape a good deal of housework drudgery, as did the smaller size of homes. Mass production allowed more women to choose to work outside the home in gainful employment—especially the ever-amplifying number of college-educated women who wanted to do so. They also could escape traditional "women's work" (e.g., clerical work, teaching, and nursing) by taking their degrees in such new fields as advertising and real estate.

At the same time, the impact of the automobile on housing patterns and passenger rail travel was profound. Though suburbs had been growing since the late 19th century, their growth had been tied to rail or trolley access, and this growth was limited to the largest cities. Cars changed this, accelerating the growth of suburbs and serving as the beginning of urban sprawl, a problem ever since in America that would later in the 20th century help create fiscal stress for inner cities across America.

At this point, a paradox of consumer-based economic abundance developed. US bank deposits climbed during the 1920s, giving banks more to lend to consumers. As bank deposits grew from $17.4 billion on the eve of America's entry into World War I in 1914 to $52.7 billion by 1928, banks funded a wave of speculative financial investments that ultimately crashed the entire economic system in 1929 and triggered new calls for state building. This was accompanied by real estate speculative booms and busts, first, in southern California and, later, in Florida (see more below).

****

But, as in other post-war eras, not all Americans reaped the gains of the Roaring 20s before the Depression. Once again, blacks who served in the military in World War I were disabused of their hopes for equal treatment when they returned from Europe after the war. By 1919, approximately one million blacks had migrated from the South into northern manufacturing cities hoping to realize these benefits. As in the past, however, racial tensions flared between blacks and ethnic immigrant populations over competition for jobs and living space. These tensions were, of course, exacerbated by the aforementioned 1920–1921 recession. Nor did it help that rumors circulated about how Europeans had treated blacks as equals and how white women in France had sexual relations with black soldiers. In 1919 and 1920, race riots occurred in New York City, Philadelphia, Tulsa, and Washington, DC, as well as in smaller cities such as

Longview, Texas, and Elaine, Arkansas (Johnson, 2010, p. 27). And by failing to pass anti-lynching laws during these years, this heinous practice continued apace.

In addition, the end of the war also rekindled nativism directed toward immigrants. Between 1919 and 1924, over 250 million southern and eastern Europeans entered the United States. By the end of the 1920s, the nation's population had doubled since 1890, with a third of the increase attributable to immigration from these areas (Kennedy, 2005, p. 14). Nearly one-tenth of the population were immigrants and nearly 20 percent had at least one parent born outside of the United States. Additionally, the concentrations of immigrants in urban ghettos discussed in Chapter 4 expanded to constitute what David Kennedy (2005) calls a "kind of polyglot archipelago in the predominately Anglo-Protestant American sea" (p. 14). Not surprisingly, all were viewed as sources of cheap labor for companies, cheap labor that undermined white employment and helped spark the riots noted above (pp. 14–15). Jews fleeing pogroms in the Soviet Union and Eastern Europe were falsely and despicably excoriated for causing all of America's ills as part of an international Jewish and Bolshevik financial cabal for world domination (Allen, 1931, p. 56).[6]

In short order, a crackdown on immigration occurred legislatively between 1920 and 1924, limits that amplified those begun by the Immigration Act of 1918. That act was based on faulty science and pursued by "Progressive Restrictionists" (including eugenicists) trying to purify the American race. Nativists called immigration the "Great American Problem" and aimed to create a "national regulatory system that excluded immigrants of national and ethnic groups they deemed inferior" (Tichenor, 2002, p. 115). Most notable in this regard were the Emergency Immigration (or Emergency Quota) Act of 1921, followed by the Immigration (or Johnson–Reed) Act of 1924.[7] The 1921 act included a quota system per country, placing annual limits on total immigration (355,000 per year). The 1924 act then capped the number of "insufficiently Anglo-Saxon or Nordic Protestant" persons entering the country. Each of these acts, of course, required under-resourced public agencies to implement them faithfully.

Amid this social strife, despite immigration restrictions as a function of illiberal nationalism (i.e., with the idea of the nation premised on ethnic homogeneity and international isolation rather than what Frederick Douglas once called a "composite nation" (Lepore, 2019), and with technology placing unskilled workers out of jobs, unemployment surged. Sparked was a ramping up of earlier efforts to organize workers into unions, including new efforts by the communist-affiliated Industrial Workers of the World (IWW, or Wobblies). Splits soon occurred within the IWW and with other more radical labor reform groups, as well as among socialists and anarcho-capitalists who believed that the private sector could provide all government functions more efficiently than government (Rothbard, 1974). Some believed in direct political action, while others did not (e.g., the Socialist Labor Party members and anarcho-syndicalists who thought that the state was the tool of capitalists). Drained in the process were the treasuries and membership of this movement. What did emerge, however, was the Communist Party/USA. Taking its orders from Moscow, it did not gain significant traction until the Great Depression, despite furtive efforts to do so.

The ongoing cries of "Bolshevism" leveled against them notwithstanding, various ethnic groups and black leaders continued to resist. Established in 1913, the Jewish Anti-Defamation League fought anti-Semitism. It was joined by the continuing efforts of both the National Association for the Advancement of Colored People (1909) and the National Urban League (1910) to fight for black and other ethnic issues, as well as the Brotherhood of Sleeping Car Porters (1925), the most powerful black union in the country. Efforts also materialized to unionize Mexican-Americans in the southwest of the United States, efforts presaging similar efforts later in the 1960s. However, the work of these and other groups, plus the social struggles of the 1920s that they fought to redress, were largely ignored by the media until the Wall Street Crash of 1929 and Great Depression of the 1930s.

****

Prior to the 1929 Wall Street Crash, a major question was how best to deal with the continuing social and economic challenges unleashed by corporate capitalism. Pledging relief from the federal activism of the Progressive movement, Harding relied on economic growth to address unemployment problems and, by implication, racial and ethnic divides. In so doing, during his brief tenure, Harding focused less on creating new public agencies than on economic growth and revamping existing administrative processes. After his death, the equally pro-business, limited government, and anti-union Coolidge followed much the same agenda.

Harding's most famous achievement administratively was congressional enactment of the aforementioned BAA of 1921. As early as 1900, even profligate members of Congress realized that federal spending was unsustainable, especially after budget authority was decentralized to congressional committees during the Gilded Age. Aside from recentralizing budget authority in Congress, the early progressives felt that an executive budget was needed, a budget that chief executives at all levels of government in the compensatory state would submit for legislative approval. The bureaus of municipal research discussed in Chapter 4 built on the recommendations of President Theodore Roosevelt's Keep Commission (1905–1909) in making such proposals. But it took the piling up of additional debt from World War I for Congress to enact the BAA. This, despite earlier administrative reform success in cities and states.

As noted, the BAA also created the BOB, placing it in the Department of the Treasury to ensure congressional influence. This, until it was moved to the Executive Office of the President (EOP) in 1939 (created by FDR pursuant to the Reorganization Act of 1939) then later renamed the Office of Management and Budget under President Richard Nixon (R-CA) in 1970. Harding's first budget director, Charles Dawes, focused on cutting federal expenditures and post-auditing agencies for efficiency and to ensure money was spent according to statute. Typical of the coevolution of institutions in American politics, the BAA also created the General Accounting Office, giving Congress a way to counteract the power of the BOB through post-audits of agencies.

Harding also created a few other agencies (e.g., what became the Federal Highway Administration and the Bureau of Aeronautics). However, it was Hoover's "forgotten progressivism" of associationalist state building and administrative reform that ultimately triumphed during the 1920s. In the process, the proxy components of the compensatory state were again amplified, as the corporate–social science nexus of interests worked actively for, and benefited from, them. Before discussing the dynamics of the political economy of interests involved, however, it is important to understand how Hoover's associationalist principles triumphed over alternative administrative reforms.

Before accepting Harding's invitation to become Secretary of Commerce, Hoover obtained the President's assurances that he would (1) have a voice in foreign affairs, (2) be authorized to create a voluntary standardization program dealing with manufacturing industries, (3) work with the Department of Labor to reduce labor problems, and (4) have authority to "call for voluntary services of men and committees of inquiry [including social scientists] to discuss social and industrial currents" (Gaddis, 2005, p. 11). As Secretary of Commerce, Hoover took a previously backwater agency and, through adroit bureaucratic entrepreneurship, catapulted it into the leading force of progressivism in the 1920s (Hart, 1994; Hawley, 1974; Hofstadter, 1989; Nash, 1988, 1996; Wilson, 1975). Curiously, public administration has largely neglected this feat.

Still, Hoover faced staunch opposition from conservative Republicans in the Harding and Coolidge administrations (e.g., Secretary of the Treasury Andrew Mellon), as well as from critics in the antitrust division of the Department of Justice who argued that associationalism violated antitrust laws. Thus, Hoover's efforts to build a "new scientific and economic frontier" were stymied initially by Harding's free-market conservativism in dealing with the 1920–1921 recession. Hoover advised Harding to increase government spending to stimulate the economy (a foretaste of Keynesian economics). Instead, Harding—guided by Mellon—halved the size of the federal budget and reduced the national debt by a third. However, as things worsened, Hoover successfully advocated for the non-statist technocratic planning that was the essence of his social science-based associationalist perspective on administrative reform (Alchon, 1985, p. 50).

Hoover put his associationalist vision to use, first, in convening the 1921 Conference on Unemployment in Washington, DC. The conference consisted of approximately 100 attendees. Members included representatives of the most troubled industries (railroads, coal mining, and construction), 12 (largely conservative) labor leaders, and the public. The conference was staffed by an advisory committee of 22 economists and statisticians, complemented by the National Bureau of Economic Research (NBER) noted in Chapter 4 and the National Research Council begun in 1916 to coordinate scientific findings. Consonant with associationalism, Hoover insisted that no major government initiatives occur—especially unemployment insurance, that "most vicious of solutions" (Clements, 2010, p. 134). Instead, he focused on mobilizing the "fine cooperative action of our manufacturers and employers" (p. 134).

Ultimately, the conference's recommendations "reflected the traditional ideas of its [conservative] business members rather than suggestions from its social science advisers" or the public (Clements, 2010, p. 135). This was not surprising. Although economists embraced Wesley Mitchell's argument that business cycles could be predicted, and possibly controlled, by means of statistical analyses, Mitchell's idea still was not widely known among the public. More broadly, social scientists differed over the causes of and cures for social phenomena, as had the 19th-century members of the Verein and their successors ever since. Nevertheless, and with little empirical evidence offered to connect his associationalist approach with the economic recovery that ensued, many credited Hoover for it. Nor did it hurt that Hoover relentlessly took credit publicly for ending the recession (Leuchtenburg, 2009).

But it was not until 1925 that Hoover's associationalist vision of administrative reform was clearly a "major force in shaping public policy" (Hawley, 1997, p. 84). This occurred as Hoover deftly got associationalist allies into key agency positions across the federal government that affected or served as obstacles to his vision. These included the Antitrust Division of the Department of Justice, the Department of Agriculture, the Federal Reserve Board (FRB), the Federal Trade Commission (FTC), and the Interstate Commerce Commission (ICC) (p. 84). Hoover also marshalled external allies for his agenda by engaging with networks of associations and private philanthropies he had worked with earlier in his career in China, Europe, and Russia.

Throughout his tenure, Hoover also used Commerce's Division of Simplified Practice and Standardization to address the problems of underperforming industries (e.g., the textile industry) or newly developing ones (e.g., the airline industry). In addition, he convened nearly 1,200 efficiency conferences on the elimination of waste in industrial design, production, and distribution. These efficiency conferences involved nearly 900 trade associations and 7,000 corporate firms (Wilson, 1975). He also created a business cycle committee of the President's Conference on Unemployment in 1923 to assess current economic conditions and to project the short-term future. Subsequently, in 1928, he formed a committee of businesspersons and the NBER to do the same. The latter produced a two-volume study entitled *Recent Economic Changes in the United States* (Clements, 2010, pp. 358–359).

To the chagrin of Mellon, Secretary of State Hughes, and Secretary of Agriculture Wallace, Hoover's network of acolytes pushed the associationalist agenda in other agencies. At the FTC, for example, his allies allowed businesses to define what constituted unfair ethical practices, and at the FRB and the ICC, his followers regulated "by devolving power and responsibility on private groups" and "eventually bring[ing] their 'regulators' into the larger Hooverian 'cooperative system'" (Hawley, 1997, p. 85). Likewise, his allies in the Department of Justice politically outflanked critics in other agencies who, as noted, argued that associationalism violated antitrust laws.

The influence of Hoover and his allies in the Coolidge administration led some to call him the "undersecretary of everything." As a reporter at the *New Republic* summarized:

> It is certainly not generally recognized . . . how extraordinarily extensive is his impress upon the government outside of his own Department. There is no reason to doubt whether in the whole history of the American government a Cabinet officer has engaged in such wide diversity of activities or covered quite so much ground. The plain fact is that no vital problem, whether in the foreign or the domestic field, arises in this administration [Coolidge's] in the handling of which Mr. Hoover does not have a real—and very often a leading—part. There is more Hoover in the administration than anyone else . . . more Hoover . . . than there is Coolidge.
>
> (Leuchtenburg, 2009, p. 63)

But an irony also emerged because of realpolitik: one of the era's utmost proponents of free enterprise ("businessmen deserve high public esteem"), Hoover was also "most responsible [during the decade] for [building] swollen government agencies" (p. 65). This was especially true for his Commerce Department, as he sought to enhance its power relative to other agencies.

At the same time, Hoover's associationalist onslaught led many citizens to link the broader economic dynamism of the 1920s with him. This, in turn, helped marginalize more radical alternatives such as socialism and syndicalism, as had been Hoover's "third way" plan. Also facilitating this were the analyses he directed out of the Department of Commerce that led to progressive legislation. These included elimination of the 12-hour workday, natural resource conservation initiatives, and promotion and regulation of radio and aviation. But it was the Great Mississippi Flood of 1927 that catapulted Hoover (R-CA) and his associationalist administrative reform vision to the presidency.

As historian John Barry (1997) notes, Hoover saw the disaster as a test case for bringing to his hoped-for presidency the philosophy that "government should help individuals indirectly, by providing leadership without coercion" and that "society's strong men—outside of government—had . . . the leverage to move a society" once engaged (p. 370). As such, Hoover mounted a campaign for financial support from bankers and foundations across the country. As in all his efforts, and counter to his later public image of aloofness, his style was one of "endless 'jawboning,' behind-the-scenes stimulation of public opinion, and the manufacture of pressure [on the strong men] from all directions" (Nash, 1996, p. 190).

But Hoover's associationalist vision was even broader than rebuilding the Delta. Many blacks saw the flood's destruction as an "emancipation" from both being sharecroppers and the explosion of racial violence against them in 1927. As unsuccessful calls for federal anti-lynching legislation arose, Hoover purposely characterized his efforts as "reconstruction" to show their racial dimensions (and to appeal politically to black Republicans). He unsuccessfully proposed that all plantations be broken up, sold to blacks, and financed by a new private resettlement corporation (Barry, 1997). Hoover's civil rights vision, seen as politically cynical by some, was never realized. And in publicizing his associational efforts as successful, he failed to acknowledge that federal agencies were critical to his success or that two-thirds of the dollars raised came from the federal government. But on the flood's heels, the presidency was his.

****

Hoover, and his associationalism, was not the only shaper and beneficiary of the challenges and opportunities of the 1920s. As noted, the role of the social sciences in analysis and planning in the compensatory state during World War I had already boosted their legitimacy. Moreover, the economic boom of the 1920s continued it, especially for economics, giving it first-mover advantage among the social sciences that would later be amplified. As Stuart Rice, a leading proponent of scientific methodology for the social sciences and forerunner of similar evidence-based administrative reform advocates today, wrote: "civilization no longer has time to wait for undirected trial-and-error progress" (Ross, 1991, p. 399).

Although not advocating a "cold rationality" approach to policymaking, Rice argued that science itself must become the "object of emotional attachment" (Ross, 1991, p. 399). Added liberal economist and future New Deal notable Rexford Tugwell in 1924, the social sciences offer the "possibility of a remade world—no less" (pp. 399–400). In the process, the social sciences could defend America against the "radicalism, ideology, and totalitarianism" afoot in the world that threatened America's millenarian vision (p. 400). Little did they anticipate the horrific uses made later of scientism in Germany and the Soviet Union.

But, as during World War I and earlier times, the appeal of social scientific methods even in the professions was not automatic in the 1920s and 1930s. Private family foundations and philanthropies continued to play a critical role in their ascendancy. Exposing the view of foundations held by social scientists, noted English sociologist and cofounder of the London School of Economics, Graham Wallas, argued in 1923 that the "growth of the private foundations for scientific research offers a lucrative milch [milk] cow with a sedate temper when nothing pink [socialism] or red [Marxism] is in the same pasture" (Ross, 1991, p. 403).

Led by Charles Merriam, Wesley Mitchell, and Beardsley Ruml (director of the Laura Spelman Rockefeller Memorial), funding by the Social Science Research Council (SSRC) (see Chapter 4) as part of the compensatory state increased the social sciences' collective legitimacy and political power. It did so by providing an overarching institutional umbrella for advancing their interests politically. The SSRC board of directors included members from the American Economic Association, the American Political Science Association, and the American Sociological Association. By 1925, they were joined by representatives from the American Anthropological Association, the American Historical Association, the American Psychological Association, and the American Statistical Association.

Although Merriam was the intellectual founder of the SSRC, and the Russell Sage Foundation and the Carnegie Corporation also contributed to its operations, Ruml at the Rockefeller Memorial played a dominant role in promoting and subsidizing social science research using the scientific method. During his tenure, Ruml—a psychometrician by training and envisioning technocratic social sciences—funneled $40 million to the SSRC, the NBER, and the Brookings Institution. Combined, the period saw a 40-fold increase in philanthropic largesse for the social sciences, thus further buoying their quest for legitimacy as authority structures informing the public and private sectors in the compensatory state (Alchon, 1985). At the same time, the image of scientific philanthropy took root in America (Ross, 1991).

Much like philanthropies earlier in the century that quashed "controversial" research by bureaus of municipal research (e.g., the "efficient citizen" and settlement women movements), private foundation funding helped marginalize alternatives to the scientific methodology of the natural sciences (Ross, 1991, pp. 403–404). The experience of the New School of Social Research was typical. Founded in 1918, the New School was staffed heavily by Progressive social scientists such as Charles Beard, John Dewey, Wesley Mitchell, and Thorstein Veblen. Partly sparked by concerns over academic freedom, the New School embraced scientism but explicitly linked it to democratic philosophy and citizen participation. Shunned in funding by large, politically conservative foundations, the New School had to rely on much smaller gifts from Progressive (and largely female family member) donors. In the process, the school was chronically underfunded, lost faculty (e.g., Dewey and Mitchell), and, for a time, decided to abandon its social democratic focus (p. 404).

As Dorothy Ross (1991) writes, the growing "cultural authority and social power of scientism pushed the center of gravity in the social science professions toward a harder and more technocratic conception of social science" (p. 404). This new center of gravity, in effect, delegitimized methodologies that did not rely on the scientific methods of the natural sciences. It was a "rather striking and genuine intellectual revolution . . . characterized by a shift *from understanding phenomena to control*" of them (p. 404, emphasis added).

As in earlier eras, however, concerns also arose about the relevancy and social equity impact of the "quantitative" emphasis of the social sciences. For reasons that resonate with today's criticisms of this approach (see Riccucci, 2010), critics argued that a focus on testable hypotheses limited the kinds of problems that could be studied because of data deficiencies. They also were said to narrow abilities to identify the underlying causal mechanisms involved. In addition, some feared that a focus on only measurable social factors would follow (Schachter, 2010; Stivers, 2000), while others such as sociologist Karl Mannheim (1929) contended that both ideology and visions of utopia could (and would) creep into the presumed objectivity of the social sciences and humanities.

Still others foresaw the marginalization of average citizens from civic deliberation. As Ellis Hawley (1997) argues, the "sense of estrangement between scientific endeavor and the values held in other sectors [that is, non-social scientist, non-business, and non-foundational] of American society seemed to deepen and intensify" (p. 143; for similar arguments, see Hummel & Stivers, 2010). The social sciences' growing resource dependency on government and private funding would be amplified dramatically over ensuing decades. Its next amplification, as well as its reliance on linking the social sciences to the IRP in the federal government component of the compensatory state, would come during the Great Depression of the 1930s.

****

As noted, economic growth was extraordinary prior to the Wall Street Crash of 1929 and contributed to the attacks on authority structures in society other than business. Earlier in the decade, President Coolidge pronounced laissez-faire economics to be the golden calf of prosperity. Helping to operationalize Coolidge's dictum that the "man who builds a factory builds a temple," Treasury Secretary Mellon successfully pushed Congress to lower tax rates on the wealthiest Americans (the Revenue Act of 1926). But, just as in the Gilded Age, disturbing slow-moving, secular trends crashed that prosperity and bred economic distress.

Several interacting causal mechanisms stand out. For starters, shoddy and sometimes corrupt management in a spiraling number of US banks occurred, accompanied by an insufficiently risk-averse attitude among them. As prosperity boomed during World War I, and mimicking earlier historical periods, the number of state and national banks in the country doubled from approximately 14,000 to 31,000 between 1920 and 1930. But bank failures also spiraled, averaging over 600 per year between 1922 and 1929.

In the process, and once again in American history, the "share of disposable income going to the top 1 percent jumped from 12 percent in 1920 to 19 percent in 1929" (Watkins, 1999, p. 47). Also, although the economy was primed by mass marketing to millions of Americans, the masses could only buy so much. This caused demand to decline precipitously toward the end of the 1920s. Provoked was a severe decline in production, prices, and personal income as workers were terminated from their jobs. In the two months prior to the first Wall Street Crash in 1929, production fell by 20 percent, wholesale prices declined by 7.5 percent, and personal income fell by 5 percent (p. 47).

Still, money for speculation sloshed around in the pockets of wealthy Americans and their bankers. Having already provoked the two collapses in land speculation noted earlier, they now turned to stock speculation. This, as the value of corporate stocks rose significantly, fueled by increased profit margins due to productivity improvements from assembly-line production. Stock values went from $67 billion in 1923 to $87 billion (Heilbroner & Singer, 1999, p. 264).

Also fueling stock speculation was the previously mentioned advent of buying stocks on margins. Banks and stockbrokers encouraged investors "to buy stocks with loans [at 8 percent to 9 percent interest rates] covering the difference between the value of the shares and the amount of the[ir] down payment" (Heilbroner & Singer, 1999, p. 264). Stock loans soared from a billion dollars in 1920 to $8.5 billion by September 1929. Until then, 1.5 million investors were in the market, with the share of American families soaring from 15 percent in 1900 to 28 percent in 1929.

But, on October 24, 1929, the bottom fell out of the market. Sparking this fall was a massive sell-off in shares that began a vicious downward spiral of selling and defaults on loans as margin calls accelerated. Investors facing margin calls had to sell their stocks to pay off their loans, thus adding to falling prices and panic among other stockholders to sell their shares before stock values plunged further. A short-lived upturn in stock prices then occurred, accompanied by an announcement from the new Hoover administration and corporate heads saying that the economy remained sound.

However, prices soon fell again and bottomed out in mid-November 1929. This occurred as forced liquidations of capital continued, and banks called in more loans (including from Europe). By 1930, President Hoover still gave assurances that "all the evidences indicate that the worst effects of the crash upon unemployment will have passed during the next sixty days" (Watkins, 1999, p. 53). He then failed to veto the Smoot–Hawley Tariff act, thus raising tariffs to unprecedented levels on 20,000 products. The tariff provoked retaliation by trading partners, and the crisis worsened.

American's market losses were staggering, with the stock market losing 17 percent of its value—$74 billion—between 1929 and the election of FDR in 1932. This was three times what America spent fighting World War I (Heilbroner & Singer, 1999, esp. pp. 266–267). In the five months after the crash, unemployment doubled from approximately 1.5 to 3.2 million Americans and then reached approximately one-quarter of the workforce in 1933 (Watkins, 1993, p. 53). Under FDR, unemployment remained at nearly 15 percent on the eve of World War II, partly because of his efforts to cut the budget deficit after 1936 (Zelizer, 2012).

As for economic relief for Americans, Hoover's reliance on associationalism now seemed flawed. Absent federal government pressures to form associations, these presumably self-emergent and public interest-oriented industries refused to partner with one another. In addition, the trust necessary between business and labor waned amid a worsening economy and scandals. Associations quickly turned into self-serving oligopolies. Associationalism as administrative reform also contributed to an image of Hoover as aloof and passive. Yet, consistent with associationalist principles, he inaugurated "reconstruction finance corporations" to stimulate the economy through cooperative public–private associational investments pursued with off-budget financing. He also used the limited fiscal tools available to him.

As David Kennedy (2005) writes, "given the constraints under which he labored . . . Hoover made impressively aggressive countercyclical use of fiscal policy" (p. 57). These constraints were again directly attributable to American exceptionalism's historic embrace of limited government, economic liberalism, and civic republicanism. For example, 1930 was the first year in which systematic collection of employment data by the federal government occurred in the United States, so it was hard to know the scope of the problem. At the same time, the states—not the federal government—in the compensatory state were responsible for spending on construction projects, a major tool of countercyclical policy. Federal spending constituted only 3 percent of GDP in 1930 (Kennedy, 2005). Still, with Hoover's prodding, the net stimulative effect of combined federal, state, and local fiscal policy in 1931 was higher than at any other year of the New Deal era (until World War II) (p. 58).[8]

Nonetheless, in the 1930 congressional elections, Republicans lost eight Senate seats. Although still the nominal majority party (48–47, with one member of the Farmer–Labor Party), Republicans could rely on only about 40 votes on any bill. In the House, Republicans had no net loss of seats, but (amazingly) 13 members died between election day and the seating of the House in March, most of whom were Republicans (Katznelson, 2013). This left a Democratic majority, with John Nance Garner (D-TX) as Speaker of the House. Politically to the right of Hoover, and with an eye on the presidency himself, Garner's primary aim was to stop Hoover's countercyclical efforts for political gain. At the same time, Bull Moose Republicans such as Fiorello La Guardia (NY), Robert La Follette, Jr. (WI), and Burton Wheeler (MT) chided Hoover for not doing enough. Coupled with his opposition to federal aid for the unemployed, the public handed a landslide victory to FDR and the Democrats in 1932.

****

To appreciate the scope of the socioeconomic, political, and administrative perils facing the new Roosevelt administration in 1933, it is useful to turn, first, to a study commissioned by Hoover only four weeks before the 1929 Wall Street Crash. In commissioning social scientists to produce this report, he expected their findings to serve as a policy and administrative guide for America to cope with the dizzying social changes the country was experiencing (Kennedy, 2005). Once identified in this way, active management of social change would occur "through informed, though scrupulously limited, government action" (p. 11).

Entitled *Recent Social Trends in the United States*, the massive, heavily sourced, and statistically grounded report covering the 1920s took four years to produce, and Hoover disowned it before it became election fodder for his opponents in the 1932 campaign. The report stated that:

> Nearly forty-five million Americans lacked electricity and inside plumbing; huge farm surpluses had put farmers out of business and out of their homes; infant mortality rates for Southern Blacks were twice those for whites, the life expectancy for Blacks was 15 years less than for whites; the wealth amassed during the 1920s went disproportionally to the wealthiest Americans, who were located predominantly in cities; mass production was displacing skilled workers; professionals found job and income stability, while blue collar workers faced employment insecurity by constant lay-offs; one of every four women was gainfully employed, but these were largely unmarried and childless women; birth control among white female urbanites was high, and meant that poor Blacks and immigrants with high birth rates would overwhelm white WASPs; state and local taxes had soared in a vain attempt to handle social responsibilities that the federal government wouldn't deliver; federal taxes also increased significantly, but went largely to service WW I debt.
>
> (President's Research Committee
> on Social Trends, 1933, p. 29)

FDR ran on a contradictory platform to balance the budget while also promising action and experimentation. With the US economy on its knees, huge

Democratic majorities in Congress, and the legislature not in session until March 1933, the Roosevelt administration hit the ground running. It emphasized the familiar Progressive argument of the existence of a historical–structural mismatch of epic proportions. Reviving early Progressive arguments, FDR contended that American democracy could only be saved by shifting greater power to the executive branch.

FDR was aided by an overwhelming sense of what economist Frank Knight called "immeasurable uncertainty" (Katznelson, 2013, p. 33) and anxiety among Americans, not unlike what they felt at the turn of the century. They lived in fear from want domestically and fear of expansionist and militaristic nationalism across the globe. Specifically, the administration worried about Germany, with Adolf Hitler and the rise of the National Socialist Party (the Nazis); Italy, with Fascist Benito Mussolini and his Black Shirts; Spain, with Italian Fascist-aided Francisco Franco; Japan, with militaristic Emperor Hirohito and Prime Minister Hideki Tōjō; and the Soviet Union, with Joseph Stalin and the Communist Party.

Although cultural differences across nations produced different strategies and emphases in approach, each of these leaders believed, as Mussolini put it, that the "liberal democratic state is destined to perish" (Katznelson, 2013, p. 5). Sounding much like the early progressives, Mussolini argued that checks and balances, separation of powers, legislatures and parliaments, and a pluralistic party system were inefficient and mired in partisan and special interest conflicts and corruption. These strongmen saw themselves as embodying the national interest as leaders of mass-based parties. They contended that mass-based parties were more democratic, because they provided a direct line to citizens unencumbered by third-party intermediaries, such as legislatures, courts, and interest groups. They could also much better produce and implement long-term plans for addressing societal needs (Katznelson, 2013).

The economic and social woes of the United States that once again called American exceptionalism into question made these arguments intriguing to some citizens, including many intellectuals. For starters, as Ira Katznelson (2013) writes, these arguments appealed to recent US immigrants:

> Proud of their diaspora nationalism, there was much ethnic admiration, even loyalty, to German and Italian Fascism, ideological attachment to the USSR to the point of spying, and there was a good deal of anti-civil liberties counterpunching by Congress, the courts, and the executive branch.
>
> (p. 39)

Some even shared the idea that democracy was only a stage in history. Indeed, by late 1938, "only Britain, France, the Low Countries, and Scandinavia" were able to "preserve those 'liberal' freedoms that had spread across Europe since 1789" (p. 40).

By the mid-1930s, American sociologist Howard Odum saw "widespread confusion, unrest, distrust, and despair" plaguing the United States, as well as "movements toward violent revolution" (Katznelson, 2013, p. 43). Sensing the demise of American exceptionalism, journalist Walter Lippmann wrote that the "fixed points by which our fathers steered the ship of state have vanished" (p. 30). More broadly, Britain's Harold Laski argued as a socialist in 1939 that the "liberal society of the epoch before 1914 is unthinkable in our age if nations [are] to cope with the challenges—*and political advantages*—of totalitarian forms of government" (p. 40, emphasis added). Political scientist Harold Lasswell wondered "what democratic values can be preserved, and how?" (p. 45).

To many intellectuals, the idea of nationally led and bureaucratically informed planning by experts was alluring.[9] In 1928, for example, 112 articles on national economic planning were published, a figure that rose to 365 articles by 1933. Moreover, between 1920 and 1931, 80 books on Soviet planning were published in the United States. Indeed, 2,500 wealthy Americans visited the Soviet Union in 1929 alone and most came home impressed. Wrote muckraker Lincoln Steffens after a visit to the Soviet Union (and before the atrocities of Stalinist pogroms were known), "I have been over into the future, and it works" (Goldberg, 2018, p. 280).

Likewise, Mussolini's administrative reforms and corporatist organization of business–state relationships fascinated many scholars in the early 1930s. Among them was Charles Merriam of the University of Chicago, leader of the behavioral movement in political science and, later, a member of FDR's PCAM (see below). He found some of these reforms worthy of pondering for America, especially their "experimental nature, antidogmatic temper, and moral *élan*" (Katznelson, 2013, p. 93). So, too, did a second member of PCAM, Louis Brownlow. Both he and Merriam went to Italy to study Mussolini's "modern administrative methods" in preparing their report. Like Woodrow Wilson in 1887 when he advocated the use of continental European administrative "knives" without "borrowing the intent of those wielding them," Merriam, Brownlow, and others insisted they could reform administration without risking autocracy. And Merriam even thought that social science research would render authoritarian regimes like these relics of the past.

Some anti-New Deal and free-market social scientists, especially Austrian economists Ludwig von Mises and his student Friedrich Hayek (see more in Chapter 6), had escaped from European totalitarianism and condemned such thinking as naïve and dangerous. Other opponents of FDR reemphasized the ideas of the "marginalist revolution" of the late 19th century "to provide an intellectual defense for the social inequalities of [the] early 20th century" (Phillips-Fein, 2009, p. 38). Based on the work of economists such as Alfred Marshall and John Bates Clark, marginalist theory, with its "new mathematical neoclassical economics," offered a "more scientific sounding way of understanding the extreme division of wealth" (p. 39). Specifically, "both labor and capital received their 'marginal' product [of business], equivalent to what they contributed to production" (p. 39). Basically, they got what they deserved.

But the Great Depression produced in its wake a victory for economic theories (later to be called Keynesianism) that, like those of the Verein in Germany, saw the necessity of government intervention into markets, as well as the demise of Social Darwinism (see Chapter 4). Importantly for the amplification of the IRP, positivist social science, and compensatory state building, a cadre of economic experts and administrators were called on to design and implement the New Deal. Reviving the arguments of technocratic progressives and associationalists, proponents such as George Kennan argued that the United States had to be led by a "specialized elite who 'would have to subject themselves to discipline as they would if they entered a religious order'" (Katznelson, 2013, p. 32). This, to ensure what Carl Friedrich later called "inner checks" on expert discretion. A relatively abbreviated period of constitutive rather than instrumental views of public administrators was born.

****

Animating these dynamics, of course, were FDR's aggressive steps to address the economic plight of Americans. Many said his administration not only "saved capitalism from itself" but also saved representative democratic institutions in America (but see Burnham, 1941, as an example of those who thought he undermined capitalism). FDR faced a fundamental question: did dealing with the Great Depression require a vast expansion of presidential and, hence, executive branch administrative power? No dearth of public intellectuals, historians, and social scientists argued that it did, at least until the crisis passed.

Prior to the 1930s, many linked parliaments to a "post-rational politics" that had to be stopped through strong presidential and executive branch leadership (Katznelson, 2013, p. 105). Indeed, under Great Depression conditions, some felt that democracy could only be saved if more power was given to FDR. Invoking Lincoln, the economist Stuart Chase said that a "temporary dictatorship" was necessary, albeit one "that will not tear up customs, traditions and behavior patterns to any such extent as promised by either the Red [Communist] or the Black [Fascist] dictatorship" (p. 118). Absent was a similar concern for the US Constitution. More moderately, Lippmann told FDR that he should be given the "widest and fullest powers under the most liberal interpretation of the Constitution" (p. 118). The president needed "extraordinary powers" to not be "constrained by the usual checks and balances" (p. 119).

FDR—as an intellectual heir of such earlier progressives as his cousin, Theodore Roosevelt—also believed in shifting and expanding policymaking power from Congress to an expertise-based executive branch. In his inaugural address, FDR grounded his arguments and actions philosophically in William James' pragmatism (experimentation) and 1910 "moral equivalent of war" essay. FDR asked Congress to "promptly and decisively" grant him the "broad Executive power to wage a war against the [economic] emergency . . . that would be given to me if we were in fact invaded by a foreign foe" (Katznelson, 2013, pp. 121–122).

Invoking the constitutional duty of presidents to be commander-in-chief during wartimes, FDR said that "our Constitution is so simple and practical that it is possible always to meet extraordinary needs by changes in emphasis and arrangements" (Katznelson, 2013, p. 121). But, in this instance, he rhetorically rejected the idea of marginalizing Congress. Its role in governance had to be respected, so he sought Congress' approval when action was needed. Of course, with his party in the overwhelming majority, he received free reign during the first 100 days of the "First New Deal" (1933–1935).

In practice, FDR's actions created an unprecedented shift of authority from the legislative to the executive branch in Washington, one that earlier progressives would have envied. Sometimes, congressional approval came after the fact (e.g., his declaration of a "bank holiday" without prior congressional approval). As for the remaining ten major laws passed during the first 100 days, all were drafted by new executive branch agencies without congressional input (Katznelson, 2013, pp. 123–124).[10] Congressional debate was limited to four hours, and floor amendments were barred without prior approval by a congressional committee. In addition, the statutes' vagueness delegated immense discretionary power to existing and new federal agencies.

****

As noted, the New Deal produced a massive expansion of federal government policies, agencies, and personnel, dwarfing anything ever seen before in American history. In the process, contends Theodore Lowi (1969), the New Deal's expansion of the federal executive branch role—most especially, its devolution of authority from Congress to a bouillabaisse of regulatory agencies and independent regulatory commissions (IRCs)—reflected the founding of a "Second American Republic." Concurs Joanna Grisinger (2014) more recently:

> By the end of the 1930s, the bureaucrats were in charge. In expanding the federal government's field of play in the preceding decades, Congress and the White House had created dozens of agencies, departments, bureaus, and commissions to handle this new and staggering workload. With the vast growth of [federal] government responsibility during the Great Depression came yet more new agencies that complemented and often overlapped the jurisdictions of older ones. . . . Routine matters handled by more than 100 federal agencies and commissions . . . dwarfed the caseload of Congress and the federal courts.
>
> (pp. 1–2)

But the New Deal did not transform the IRP-based administrative strategies used to run agencies. And the corporate–social science nexus of interests had much to do with this. One sees the amplification of earlier trends as agencies and IRCs were organized on the basis of generic principles of administration. They also were viewed in terms of the IRP as machines to be fine-tuned, staffed with technocratic experts, and capable of aligning employees with agency goals. FDR's administration employed experts applying the latest insights from "good [administrative] science" to bring "ordered freedom" through hierarchy, rules and regulations, and departmentation by function (Smith, 2006, p. 23).

Continuity also existed in FDR's choice of agency heads and close advisors. Many leaders had served on World War I's War Industries Board (e.g., Bernard Baruch) or headed agencies (e.g., Brigadier General Hugh Johnson of the short-lived National Recovery Administration). FDR also turned to the academic community for assistance. These individuals included such technocratic progressives as lawyer Adolf Berle of Columbia Law School, legal scholar Felix Frankfurter of Harvard Law School, and economist Rexford Tugwell. Frankfurter, in turn, enticed a similarly inclined group of younger lawyers to Washington agencies (the "little hot dogs"). In the process, private and social science interests once again gained in professional legitimacy and material benefits. These benefits included funding for research by social scientists, as well as restrictions on market entry, higher rates of profits, and licenses, subsidies, or contracts for corporations (Eisner, 2000a, p. 40).

FDR also turned to social scientists to help organize his administration, especially those in the emerging subfields of industrial psychology, organization theory, and organizational behavior. For social scientists, this meant their already increasingly successful quest for legitimacy during and immediately after World War I, as well as during Hoover's associationalist tenure, was further amplified by ties to federal activities. Indeed, and despite contrarian voices discussed later in this chapter, the continuing ascendancy of the IRP over its competitors again was directly attributable to elements of social science research conducted in the 1920s and 1930s.

As William Scott (1992) describes, "by fact gathering and concept validation, however crude, [proponents of scientific management] established positive science as the epistemology of choice in management" (p. 28). This epistemology further reified the technological and associationalist progressives' equating of efficiency, bureaucratic administration, and the end of social unrest. They constituted the IRP "yardsticks that measured management success and legitimacy" rather than substantive rationality project (SRP)-based governance values (p. 28).

Meanwhile, so-called functionalist New Deal agencies plumbed past experiences and academic advice for organizational principles. During the 1920s and 1930s, functionalists focused on control of employees, behavioralism, and what executive leaders did in order to discern the skills needed for success. Researchers built on the pioneering work of industrial psychologist Henri Fayol (1930), who, in 1916, identified the functions of executives in *Industrial and General Administration*. He offered a five-fold categorization of executive functions: planning, organizing, commanding, coordinating, and controlling. In *Industrial Organization and Management* (1928), management professor Ralph Davis boiled these down, initially, to planning, organizing, and controlling but, later, added motivational skills. Some public administration practitioners also took a functionalist perspective based on their experience in public agencies. Building on the work of Fayol, Luther Gulick devised the most iconic mnemonic in the field's history: POSDCORB. The letters stand for planning, organizing, staffing, directing, coordinating, reporting, and budgeting. These became critical administrative constructs for FDR's appointees in agencies as New Deal state building expanded.

Finally, and continuing the IRP of technological progressivism, FDR's New Deal agencies applied structuralist perspectives to organizations (although FDR often ignored those principles, using competition among subordinates to get advice). In pursuing principles of administration for making organizations efficient, the reigning orthodoxy (see Chapter 4)—questionable empirically—was sustained that politics and policy should be separated as much as possible from administration. The work of James Mooney and Alan Reiley (1931), articulated in their book, *Onward Industry!*, took on crucial importance for management generally. And the publication of Luther Gulick and Lyndall Urwick's (1937) *Papers on the Science of Administration* specifically applied the generic principles of business to government agencies.

The "high noon of orthodoxy" and the legitimacy of a public administration profession began in 1936. At Merriam's urging, FDR asked him, Brownlow, and Gulick to advise him on how best to organize and coordinate the now 115 new agencies, independent commissions, and public corporations the New Deal created (Arnold, 1998, 2007; Dickinson, 1996; Newbold & Rosenbloom, 2007). They formed the PCAM, or the Brownlow Committee. Informed by five separate studies from subcommittees comprised of political science and public administration experts, their final report in 1937 took a decidedly Hamiltonian (rather than Madisonian) perspective informed by generic organizational principles.[11] Stressed, among other things, were "unity of command," "like functions aligned cheek-to-jowl," and "energy in the executive."

The PCAM report also shifted the early progressives' focus on neutral competence to *responsive competence* of the bureaucracy. Most importantly, responsive competence meant responsiveness to the president rather than Congress. The report famously argued that the "president needs help" and that an executive office of the president be created for this purpose. Opposed initially by Congress as a power grab, FDR fulfilled this recommendation in 1939 by creating the Executive Office of the President (EOP) pursuant to the Reorganization Act of that year.[12] But, given the relative loss of congressional power they entailed, most of the other recommendations of the Brownlow Report waited decades before their adoption (e.g., the Office of Personnel Management in 1979) (Lee, 2016).

The report also made 19 other recommendations to improve personnel management, including a significant expansion of the civil service system. This aspect of the IRP allowed FDR to extend civil service protection to persons who had been hired for their commitment to the New Deal (called "blanketing in"), making them largely impervious to removal by his successors. Other IRP-based recommendations were to give presidents total control over fiscal management, create better staffing in the BOB, and pursue better systems of auditing to enhance presidential control of the career civil service. And in trying to bring further unity of command to IRCs, as well as to private and public corporations created during the New Deal, the PCAM report unsuccessfully recommended that IRCs become part of the executive branch.

Significantly, the PCAM report made little mention of the Congress and state and local governments, despite the important role they played in the compensatory state. Even when mentioned in a subcommittee report on federalism, Congress and subnational governments were portrayed negatively as foiling unity of policy command in and from Washington. Granted, the PCAM subcommittees noted the importance of accountability to Congress, but they saw this as done best through unity of command under the president. Reminiscent of arguments in Woodrow Wilson's 1887 essay, the route to accountability was through strict functional controls. The most positively framed consideration of agency–congressional relations was a subcommittee report on agency rulemaking. But its recommendations were not highlighted in the final PCAM report.

Also consistent with earlier administrative reform efforts, PCAM (1937) justified this IRP-based consolidation of power in the executive branch in democratic terms: "without good management democracy itself cannot achieve its highest goals" (p. 18). But, not surprisingly, Congress demurred. Staffed by members of the Brookings Institution, the so-called Byrd Committee strongly contested the idea that the "president needs help." The committee argued that *balance* between presidential and congressional power was essential to good governance.

PCAM defenders responded disingenuously that the report's recommendations were based purely on scientific evidence. But, in choosing Brownlow, Gulick, and Merriam, FDR knew the presidentialist direction the PCAM report would take. Sidney Milkis contends that FDR's purpose was "to create a bipartisan 'administrative presidency' that would neutralize party politics and bypass the other two branches of government" (Scott, 1992, p. 21). Regardless, FDR's political critics certainly saw PCAM as yet one more move to aggrandize his own power at the expense of the other two branches of government. This, especially when combined with his reorganization of the executive branch, his later Supreme Court-packing efforts, and his aforementioned unsuccessful campaigning against

Democrats in the 1938 midterm elections who did not support all aspects of the New Deal. Ironically, Democrats lost 72 seats in Congress, leaving a cross-party "conservative coalition" in Congress that would stymie his goals.

****

Most scholarship correctly highlights the growth of bureaucratic administration in Washington during the New Deal. However, it has deemphasized the amplification of the proxy components of the compensatory state that took place alongside it. This was true at the subnational government levels, as well as in the private and nonprofit sectors. Moreover, as the compensatory state grew, the New Deal amplified the historical legacy of corporate-dominated subsystems inherent in Hoover's associationalist dream. David Hart (1994), for example, argues that the "associative undercurrents of the conservative 1920s [under Hoover] became the wellsprings of 'bold, persistent experimentation' in the 1930s. Without acknowledging it, 'Mr. New Deal' prescribed a hefty dose of the new, improved associationalism" (p. 13).

Similarly, Richard Hofstadter (1989) observed that the "first" New Deal was based on a strategy of "state-guided monopoly . . . advocated by the Chamber of Commerce, the Farm Bureau Federation, and the National Grange, and incarnated in the NRA [the National Recovery Act] and AAA [Agricultural Adjustment Act]" (p. 432). He added that Roosevelt's "basic policies for industry and agriculture had been designed after models supplied by great vested-interest groups" in those industries (p. 435). Adds Peri Arnold (1972), "both in business and agricultural policy the New Deal acted to place the tools of coercive power in the hands of private-sector organizations. The impetus was touchingly Hooverian" (p. 540). It was also infused with political rationality. New Dealers felt that this associationalist approach could produce broad political coalitions of corporations, labor, and farmers—in the process, creating clientele groups supportive of their agenda and of use in future elections (Eisner, 2000a, p. 305).

New Dealers were also convinced that, with the closing of the American frontier, the Great Depression, decreasing population growth, and declining investment, the United States would need planning and coordination by experts (as FDR described in his 1932 Commonwealth Club address). This, because economic growth might be over in the country. The United States, most economists argued incorrectly, was now a "mature economy," and slow growth was a new normal for the nation (Brinkley, 1995, pp. 132–133).[13] The day of what FDR called "enlightened administration" was upon the nation. Partially with this end in mind, largely self-governing industrial trade associations were charged by the National Recovery Administration with publishing and enforcing fair business practice codes that were Hooverian in intent. These included production quotas, the pace of plant modernization, and work-hour limitations. The FDR administration also hoped that self-governing code authorities comprised of cross-cutting industry representatives would eliminate overlap and duplication of research and development (R&D) efforts across the economy.

As in earlier times, however, it became clear that industries involved in setting building codes engaged less in cooperative R&D innovations and more in "defend[ing] collective stagnation" (Hart, 1994, p. 19). Created was a "system of industrial 'planning' . . . [that] vested power in 'industry-dominated code authorities, most of which were simply trade associations in public garb" (Eisner, 2000a, pp. 308–309). According to the liberal journal *Nation*, unleashed was a

> spectacle of chaos without a parallel, even in war time. . . [as] . . . not less than 2,000 trade-association lawyers whipp[ed] up their respective clients to rush in with codes governing trade practices, wages, and working hours—all of them impelled solely by a desire to escape the operation of the federal anti-trust laws.
>
> (p. 312)

Thus, reminiscent of the small business–big business tensions that began in the Founding Era, the NRA codes afforded an "opportunity for the more powerful and more profitable interests to seize control of an industry or to augment and extend control already obtained" (Eisner, 2000a, pp. 315–316). Not surprisingly, the largest gains in profits were made by the larger corporations, medium-sized firms amassed approximately one-quarter of the profits, and small firms gained only 4.4 percent of this business (p. 317). Thus, many of the regulatory agencies created with the best of intentions by the FDR administration, like their predecessors, became "cartel managers" or engaged in "corporate-dominated planning under the protective auspices of the state" (p. 344).

Granted, the Second New Deal (1935–1938) saw the FDR administration get tougher with corporate actors. Prosecution of antitrust laws, for example, spiked after a doubling of the budget and increases in numbers of prosecutors. Nearly one-half of all prosecutions under the Sherman Anti-Trust Act done up to then were taken during this period. But, in the end, FDR never lost his fear that federal programs would create citizen and industry dependency on them. He also never abandoned his balanced budget predilections. Hindered as a result were economic recovery, agency capacity commensurate with responsibility, and regulatory efforts after 1937 until US entry into World War II.

For example, the Securities and Exchange Commission (SEC), which was created to regulate the financial markets, suffered from implementation structures that still smacked of Hooverian associationalism. It did enforce disclosure requirements and regulated other financial activities, but huge elements of self-regulation were apparent. The SEC relied on trade associations to regulate stock exchanges and over-the-counter markets, while the National Labor Relations Board's certification process narrowed the discussion from general workplace management issues toward wage, hour, and benefit issues. It also turned the vocabulary of discussion into legalese, effectively precluding rank-and-file members from debates. This marginalization continued to be multiplied and amplified whenever regulatory agencies were created. More generally, government-supervised self-regulation and voluntary cartelization designed to protect the status quo dominated—just as Woodrow Wilson had originally predicted in the 1912 presidential election (Eisner, 2000a, esp. pp. 89, 108–112).

Concomitantly, the grants awarded by New Deal agencies in Washington further expanded both the compensatory state and Democrats' political fortunes. As the first director of the Works Progress Administration and FDR confidante, Harry Hopkins, candidly saw it, the New Deal state-building and administrative reform effort was a political machine that could "tax and tax, spend and spend, and elect and elect" (Smith, 2006, p. 6). Grants to businesses for large- and small-scale public works projects were part of the succor that held this coalition together, as it had since the nation's founding. Much of this was needed and still serves today as the bulwark of America's fading infrastructure. Still, FDR needed to couch his initiatives rhetorically in American exceptionalist values, always aware that he had to convince Americans that his agenda was "not alien to their values" (Milkis & Nelson, 1999, p. 267).

****

Nonetheless, perceptions of FDR's intentions were steadily attacked by conservative corporate leaders and other conservatives on expressive and material grounds, beginning with the Second New Deal. One might think that the Great Depression would have soured the public's view of the legitimacy of private management and its corporate associationalism. But it did not. In no small part, this was because of the influence of the Harvard Graduate School of Business (HGSB) and the vision of its second dean, Wallace B. Donham (Scott, 1992).[14] HGSB became a hub of the corporate–social science nexus, seizing on the agency incapacity gap wrought by Americans' historical self-conception of limited government and economic liberalism.

From 1919 to 1942 under Donham, the HGSB linked business and social science as alternatives to reform extremists on the Left and Right. Much like technocratic progressives in the previous two decades, and embracing Hoover's associationalism, the HGSB's goal was to develop a scientifically informed managerial state. That state was to be developed by an elite, interdisciplinary collection of scholars and business intellectuals. Founded in 1933 and known variously as the "Harvard Circle" and the "Society of Fellows," advocates at the HGSB included such social science notables as George Homans, Elton Mayo, Robert Merton, Talcott Parsons, Fritz Roethlisberger, B. F. Skinner, and Lloyd Wagner. Chester Barnard was also a frequent speaker at the HGSB. Thus, borrowing and adapting aspects of 19th-century Saint-Simonianism, they envisioned business leaders and social scientists as an elite governing body for society.

The Harvard Circle viewed society as an organic system, with a social science-informed management theory serving as an Archimedean point of leverage for bringing order out of societal chaos. Moreover, Donham believed that incorporating social science methodology into the emergent field of business management education was essential for attaining the legitimacy still lacked by schools of business and management in the 1920s and 1930s. This view was grounded partly in Robert Michels' "iron law of oligarchy" and Vilfredo Pareto's concept of the "circulation of elites." Harvard Circle members argued that traditional political elites and institutions could not deal with the challenges posed by the Great Depression and modern economies. This familiar historical–structural mismatch argument meant that business management schools had to produce "self-reflective" private-sector managers who were part of a new governing elite and who understood their responsibility to society.

Thus, like Hoover and other associationalists, Donham and his colleagues appreciated the centrality of government. But, again, they believed that a technocratic elite spanning the public *and* private sectors should lead society—a private–public partnership capable of "bridging" the imperative of expertise with democracy while avoiding socialism and laissez-faire extremes. Homans even argued that the "*governmental* elite includes not only those holding the higher posts in the administration [i.e., in government] but also . . . the powerful financiers [and] industrialists" in society (Scott, 1992, p. 22; emphasis added). Volunteerism coordinated by an expertise-based managerial elite, applying social science research methods, and having a strong ethical and moral sense was the way to bring "ordered freedom" to the compensatory state (p. 18). Once again, non-majoritarian meritocratic institutions would "save" the millenarian vision of American exceptionalism without threatening democratic values.

****

More broadly, by the 1930s, several foundational figures in the social sciences and public administration had urged agency experts to consider themselves a new "governing class" (see Waldo, 1984, p. 90), practitioners of the "master trade of all" specializations (see Mosher, 1939, p. 416), and "research technicians who possess the just, wise, and omniscient qualities of Plato's guardians" (see Pfiffner, 1940, p. 25). G. H. Durham made the boldest claim, urging experts to accept "their destiny as a Democratic Ruling Class" (see Waldo, 1984, p. 126). Although expressively motivated as promoting the public interest, such bold claims could readily be labeled as self-interested. They thus have fit easily into the narratives of opponents of activist government and administrative capacity building ever since. Indeed, as later chapters will make clear, they became fodder for Populist-informed movements in the late 20th and early 21st centuries that culminated in the election of Donald Trump in the 2016 presidential election.

But not everyone in academia was enamored by the HGSB's and New Deal's vision linking agency expertise, bureaucratic administration, and corporate capitalism. For example, James Burnham worried in his 1941 classic, *The Managerial Revolution*, that exploitation of workers could take place too easily in the private sector as investors deferred to managers. He wrote that "all class economies are exploiting . . . and the managerial society will be exploiting" as well (p. 123). Moreover, and further disparaging the sociotropic vision of a cross-sectoral management elite, the same would happen in public agencies in terms of the relationship between managers and political appointees.

Relatedly, Adolf Berle and Gardiner Means observed in their 1932 classic, *The Modern Corporation and Private Property*, that a managerial elite in corporations risked the "power of confiscation of part of the profit stream and even of the underlying corporate assets by means of purely private processes" (p. 247). Just as in the Gilded Age, the rise of scientific management, World War I, and the "return to normalcy" with business owners hoarding profits for themselves, corporate managerialism would result in further social inequality and worker exploitation.

Others in the academy called for various forms of democratic administration as more appropriate approaches to management in a democratic republic. More akin to the SRP, managers needed a "democratic impulse" or "imperative" that went beyond efficiency. Some, such as industrial psychologist Ordway Tead (1933), argued that "industrial democracy" was necessary at work lest democracy at large suffer. In their view, "both private and public administration were in an important and far-reaching sense false to the ideal of democracy [in] their insistence that [it was] something peripheral to administration" (Waldo, 1952, p. 87). Thus, organizations had to be "guided and controlled in ways calculated to allow all members . . . an opportunity to help formulate [their] objectives and, also, to realize for themselves . . . a sense of personal growth, development, and realization" (Tead, 1933, pp. 291–292). In the process, and amplifying the settlement women's SRP perspective, both private and public organizations in the compensatory state could—as in the voluntary sector—become "training school[s] for more democracy" (p. 292).

In the end, however, industrial democracy never gained enough traction in America to make a significant impact. As Chapter 6 will discuss, a counteroffensive by corporate interests in the post-World War II era stifled the cause of either industrial democracy, specifically, or democratic administration, generally. But its logic for the workplace, at least, set the stage for putting people back into the picture as more than automatons and presaged the "human relations" movement of the 1960s in motivational theory and the social equity movement in the 1970s and beyond.

The marginalization of citizens from public agency decision making also disturbed others in academia. They challenged scientism's claim for practical and moral authority in policy debates. For example, philosopher John Dewey eschewed his earlier view that collecting and analyzing data with scientific rigor alone would reveal fundamentals of society that could be addressed to advance American exceptionalism. For him, citizen involvement in policymaking was critical to understanding social problems and crafting appropriate remedies for them—a foretaste of the "argumentative turn" in the policy sciences in the 1990s and beyond (see Chapter 7).

Others worried that this marginalization was prompted by the growing power and expansion of interest groups and associations during the 1920s and 1930s. Citizens' participation was limited only to voting. Critics claimed that corporate dominance of associationalist reform prescriptions showed how naïve earlier pluralist social scientists (such as Arthur Bentley, 1908) were in seeing democracy at work in interest groups. Granted, some political scientists in the 1930s, such as Pendleton Herring, still saw interest groups as central to informing the constitutive role played by public managers. Herring (1936) wrote in his classic, *Public Administration and the Public Interest*, that agencies given broad discretion by Congress were bombarded with pleas from private interest groups to respond to their narrow parochial needs. As such, they dealt routinely with political pressures but, hopefully, balanced these pressures in ways advancing the public's interest. But he also conceded that this was not always the case.

Also causing perceptions of the marginalizing of citizens from agency decision making was the New Deal's otherwise beneficial amplification of the use of project-based grants to state and local governments. Legatees of intergovernmental "carrots and sticks" used since the nation's founding to pursue public purposes while hiding the visible size of the federal government, about 100 project-based grants arose from the New Deal. These grants paled in comparison to the number of categorical grants in the 1960s and 1970s (see Chapter 6) and, unlike them, were driven by state and locally defined needs. However, average citizens were already far removed from decisions over the nature and distribution of these grants, as they had been in earlier administrative reform periods.

It was also clear that two categories of citizens—blacks and women—were especially marginalized from the governance process. As noted, such was certainly the case during the Harding and Coolidge administrations, but FDR also gave them little overt (as opposed to less visible) support when it came to anti-lynching laws and other social legislation. This was because of the power of racist southern committee chairmen in Congress. These officials were largely populist when it came to supporting FDR's economic development initiatives, and they were some of his staunchest supporters in the war effort of World War II. But FDR knew that they would not support any legislation that benefited blacks and women, and their opposition could derail his policy agenda (Katznelson, 2013).

As Suzanne Mettler (1998) argues in *Dividing Citizens*, southern racism initially shaped New Deal programs and their administration in deleterious ways for both groups. Occupations held by white males were guaranteed benefits in programs such as Social Security, while occupations (e.g., farming and household maids) held by blacks and women were not. Ascriptive hierarchy was also present in the administration of such programs as aid to families with dependent children, unemployment insurance, and the Fair Labor Standards Act. Rights to these protections were not "nationalized" for blacks and women but, rather, left to the discretion of states. As today, state governments and their administrators could tighten eligibility requirements, payments, and enforcement levels, as well as impose excessive administrative burdens. Thus, this concession effectively allowed racism and sexism to prevail in certain states.

The same went for employment opportunities, although the record is more mixed. Indeed, FDR's relatively less visible administrative efforts began a realignment of blacks from the Republican Party (since the Civil War) to the Democratic Party that continues today (Katznelson, 2013).[15] For instance, blacks seeking federal government employment became members of FDR's Federal Council of Negro Affairs—known informally as Roosevelt's "Black Cabinet." And, by 1939, nearly all federal departments had a "Negro adviser," although their responsibilities differed widely. FDR also created 45 administrative and leadership positions for middle-class black men and women in federal agencies. Notable among those serving were Frances Perkins, Secretary of Labor; Mary McLeod Bethune, director of the Division of Negro Affairs of the National Youth Administration (NYA); and Robert C. Weaver, who began as an aide to Secretary of the Interior Harold Ickes and later became Secretary of Housing and Urban Development in the 1960s. More generally, the Hatch Act (1939) and the Ramspeck Act (1940) contained limited provisions against racial discrimination in federal employment.

Nearly 300,000 blacks were employed by Bethune's NYA led by Aubrey Williams. But, even then, the chances of receiving training and employment in the NYA were higher if blacks lived outside the South, where racist elements dominated local NYA boards. Still, such initiatives helped create a new generation of educated middle- and upper-class blacks. For example, the NYA established covert racial quotas for distributing over $600,000 in undergraduate and graduate student aid to over 4,000 black men and women (Kirby, 1980). Ickes, using administrative tactics that future presidents would emulate, also ensured that a nondiscrimination clause was part of every contract issued by the Public Works Administration and initiated the building of 49 low-income housing projects between 1933 and 1937. Of these, 14 were black-only projects and another 17 were mixed-race (p. 23). However, the efforts to advance more inclusive democratic administration and combat ascriptive hierarchy were again resolved in favor of the politically more potent technocratic and associationalist progressives. Their successful framing of administrative reform in terms of American exceptionalist values helped in this regard.

****

Equally contentious in the 1930s from an SRP perspective was the role of public agencies versus private charities in the compensatory state. Elisabeth Clemens (2010) writes that a battle occurred over reconfiguration of the voluntary sector. After the Civil War, private charities opposed public funding for poverty relief, preferring separate public and private spheres to enhance their legitimacy. Institutional care was a government responsibility, while charity was the responsibility of private and nonprofit organizations. In other words, each compensated for the other's shortcomings.

As earlier chapters have indicated, the practice of allocating funds and tax benefits to private charities as extensions of governance for federal purposes was established long before the beginning of the 20th century. Moreover, these transfers were justified on the grounds that private charities were more consistent with American exceptionalist values, especially civic republicanism and limited government. As Clemens and Doug Guthrie (2010) argue, the "great episodes of 20th century state-building were always already embedded in complex relationships between associational and governmental means for organizing social efforts" (p. 26).

Indeed, by the 1930s, the strict legal division of the sectors was quite muddled in practice. But, in New York, the Association for Improving the Condition of the Poor (AICP) pressed for a "complete welding in the power and prestige of the public agencies with the initiative and elasticity of private agencies" to bring about the "increased efficiency of both" (Hopkins, 1999, p. 83). Although such partnerships were not the position of all private charities, the AICP also saw the link to government as a survival and legitimacy-enhancing strategy for itself and the sector (pp. 97–103; also see Lubove, 1986). Moreover, the increasing professionalization of social workers meant that "careers cross-cut the sectors; growing requirements for incorporation and oversight of private organizations also generated pressures toward common understandings of what should be done and how" (Clemens, 2010, p. 83).

Basically, however, a bureaucratic and political turf war related to compensatory state building soon ensued. FDR wanted expertise-based federal government agencies to handle social issues, including welfare. As such, Harry Hopkins (1999), head of the Federal Emergency Relief Administration, argued that the "unemployed must apply to a public agency for relief, and this relief must be furnished direct to the applicant by a public agent" (p. 83). The administration's justification was that private charities could not cope with the needs generated by the Great Depression. However, it also reflected the Progressive dream of turning private charity into a public right. In addition, it was designed to draw a political bright line between FDR's agenda and aspects of Hoover's associationalism. During the height of the Dust Bowl drought in the early 1930s, Hoover fought tenaciously against defiant Democratic members of Congress to appropriate tens of millions of dollars for the Red Cross. Concurrently, he opposed any federal programs for drought or unemployment insurance. In contrast, FDR, as New York Governor, urged those in need to apply for aid to the government as a "right" rather than seek charity, because their situation was not their fault.

This effort to create a bright line distinction with Hoover had unanticipated results for FDR. His efforts sparked the ire of major corporate leaders. Addressing the Greater New York Fund in 1938, John D. Rockefeller, Jr., foretold a successful counteroffensive by the corporate community to ensure a return to charitable (rather than government) redress of social needs. Rockefeller argued in classic American exceptionalist terms that

> failure to support adequately these privately-operated health and welfare agencies may mean ultimately the taking over by government of their functions. . . . This country was developed by men . . . prizing liberty above all things. How they would have scorned the thought of bartering liberty for security.
>
> (Clemens, 2010, p. 108)

What occurred as a result, according to Clemens (2010), was a

> less-[politically] conflicted incorporation of voluntarism into the national project and the organization of governance . . . a novel synthesis that would develop into the nonprofit sector of the postwar decades, nurtured both by expanded tax exemptions and multiplying "partnerships" with government.
>
> (p. 81; see Chapter 6 for greater detail)

In the process, "transformed charitable organizations [became] vital partners in the expansion of public intervention during the 1960s" and 1970s (Clemens & Guthrie, 2010, p. 20; also see Smith & Lipsky, 1993).

****

By the mid to late 1930s, FDR faced yet another political and administrative conundrum with implications for state building and administrative reform: the possibility of a second world war. Mussolini was mobilizing to invade Ethiopia, the Spanish Civil War was underway, and massive German and Russian rearmament was occurring. In addition, Japan had invaded the Chinese mainland and

Hitler had invaded several Balkan nations. But FDR had to face these developments as the legatee of the total demobilization pursued after World War I, demobilization fostered by war weariness and disillusionment with government and abetted by many Americans' isolationist tendency.

Resistance to war mobilization and involvement came earlier legislatively in the Neutrality Acts of 1935, 1936, and 1937. Then, in 1938, Hoover returned from a 14-nation tour of Europe and "urgently warned the United States not to join the formation of any democratic alliance with Britain or France against the Fascist dictatorships" (Katznelson, 2013, p. 299). Eying another presidential run in 1940, Hoover said that the "forms of government which other peoples pass through in working out their destinies is not our business" (p. 299). Undeterred, but still publicly demurring from intervention, FDR first used the cash-and-carry provisions of the 1937 Neutrality Act to afford support to Great Britain and, later, the Lend-Lease Act.

By 1939, FDR faced a rapidly deteriorating situation, leading him to argue publicly that the neutrality laws were really benefiting the Axis powers. As Katznelson (2013) observes, he:

> spoke nearly 10 months after the Anschluss had swallowed an all-too-pliant Austria into the Third Reich, nine months after both Mussolini and Hitler had rebuffed his call for a declaration of nonaggression to last for ten years, some six months after the Evian Conference had failed to cope with the growing problem of stateless Jewish refugees, just over three months after the Munich agreement had conceded the Sudetenland to Germany, two months after Kristallnacht, and in the context of alarming press reports about growing Nazi influence in Latin America. Moreover . . . Hitler had just greeted the New Year by pledging to accelerate the buildup of German military might and by committing his government to "forging the complete National-Socialist unity of the German people."
>
> (p. 300)

FDR persuaded Congress to drop the arms embargo provisions of the 1937 Neutrality Act. He did so with continued opposition from isolationists but with the support of southern Democrats. Among the former was the celebrated aviator Charles Lindbergh, who warned that joining the Allies risked "los[ing] a million men, possibly several million—the heart of American youth" (Katznelson, 2013, p. 303). He added that the United States would be "staggering under the burdens of recovery during the rest of our lives" (pp. 303–304). Lindbergh was joined by many "America Firsters," such as Henry Ford and historian Charles Beard, plus many in the diaspora of Germans and Japanese in America. But, as Chapter 6 will discuss, American intervention into World War II came with the

Japanese bombing of Pearl Harbor in 1941, followed by the Cold War after Germany and Japan surrendered. Their consequences for the evolution of American administrative reform and compensatory state building would be profound. So, too, would the impact on reform of the corporate–social science nexus of interests and, reciprocally, on its legitimacy. Produced in the process of taking their IRP-based recommendations to heart, however, would be resounding calls by the 1960s from both the Left and Right in America for massive administrative reform and state building.

Notes

1. As Clements also notes, Wilson made less extensive use than Lincoln of wartime powers and relied less on government agencies than on private and volunteer efforts because of the influence and friendship of Hoover.
2. Grant sent federal troops to enforce the three sets of civil rights bills known as the anti-Ku Klux Klan acts.
3. Most irritating to FDR were Supreme Court decisions in 1935 that declared the heart of his New Deal efforts unconstitutional. In *A.L.A. Schechter Poultry Corp. v. United States*, the court ruled the National Industrial Recovery Act of 1933 unconstitutional. It did the same to his petroleum code system in the *Panama Refining Company v. Ryan* case. Both were deemed violations of the nondelegation doctrine by Congress.
4. In terms of the Federal Reserve System, its members—operating largely without reliable data on unemployment or GDP estimates—decreased rather than increased the money supply to offset reduced government spending. In terms of the gold standard, problems immediately occurred in establishing appropriate currency exchange rates.
5. This section on morality and consumerism relies heavily on Allen (1931).
6. Earlier Jewish immigrants worried that they, too, would be associated with these facetious claims.
7. This discussion of immigration relies on Tichenor (2002).
8. Interestingly, Keynes agreed with Hoover. He argued that public works' approaches in the United States were too unlike those in Great Britain to work well.
9. Data in this paragraph rely on Shlaes (2007), pp. 116–117.
10. These included the Agricultural Adjustment Act, the Economy Act, the Emergency Banking Act, the Emergency Farm Mortgage Act, the Emergency Railroad Transportation Act, the Farm Credit Act, the Federal Emergency Relief Act, the Home Owners Loan Act, the National Industrial Recovery Act, and the Unemployment Relief Act.
11. The five studies were conducted by prominent public administrationists and included: Floyd Reeves and Paul David's study of personnel administration in the federal government; Arthur Buck and Harvey Mansfield, Sr.'s study of fiscal management; Robert Cushman's study of IRCs; and Arthur W. Macmahon, James Fesler, and Herbert Emmerich's study of the administrative rulemaking process.

12. Although the EOP was originally comprised of four offices, it has expanded over the years to include varying numbers of agencies. Most notable among these are the Office of Management and Budget, the Council of Economic Advisers, the Domestic Policy Council, and the National Security Council.
13. Similar "limits to growth" arguments exist throughout US history. The National Resources Committee in a 1938 report assumed incorrectly that declining population growth in the 1930s would become the new normal and afford little economic growth for the remainder of the century.
14. This discussion relies heavily on Scott (1992).
15. This discussion relies on Katznelson (2013); Kirby (1980); Krislov (1957); McCluskey and Smith (1999); Sitkoff (1978); Reiman (1992).

Chapter 6

World War II, the Cold War Nexus, and American Administrative Reform, Circa 1940–1980

"States make war; war makes states," wrote political scientist Bartholomew Sparrow in 1996 (p. 3). These words aptly summarize the observations of scholars such as Ira Katznelson, Charles Tilly, and Martin Shefter. Observes Sparrow (1996):

> The Declaration of Independence brought the United States into being; the Civil War established the politics and government of the United States for much of the nineteenth and early twentieth centuries; and the First World War spurred the development of the twentieth century American state. But most important for understanding American political development in the latter half of the twentieth century is the Second World War. World War II jolted a moribund national economy out of the Depression, led to the creation of international

systems of trade, investment, foreign exchange, and diplomacy, and
established the United States as a political, economic, and military
superpower.

(p. 2)

The imprint of World War II is also apparent on domestic institutions, politics,
and authority structures of all kinds (e.g., business, economic, political, professional, religious, and social science). In turn, the inefficient path dependency of
the historical–structural mismatches created by the war helped shape the evolution of American administrative reform in this period. Just as they had done earlier, administrative reformers used World War II and the subsequent Cold War
to justify the further nationalization of policy and continuing shifts of legislative
power to the executive branch. These state-building initiatives again wrought a
consistent amplification of the instrumental rationality project (IRP), despite
alternatives to it, as well as of the proxy component of the compensatory state
in America.

Apparent, too, is how Americans' self-conception of limited government, economic liberalism, civic responsibility, and ascriptive hierarchies informed American administrative reform and its link to state building. And, once again, the
ascendancy of the IRP as an administrative reform strategy was influenced by the
relative power of elements of the corporate–social science nexus of interests. They
did so for what they believed would be a more rational policy and administrative
process that might also enhance their legitimacy and, thus, further their expressive, material, and authority goals.

It is also noteworthy that, prior to World War II, American exceptionalist values rolled back the visible size of the federal agency component of the compensatory state in post-war eras. But the end of World War II defied this pattern due to
the advent, first, of the Cold War and, much later, the war on international terrorism (see Chapter 7). This, as war footing and fighting became a new normal in
America. For nearly the next five decades, the United States built domestic and
international institutions structured on the premises of market-based free trade,
bureaucratic administration informed by the IRP, and instrumental perspectives
of the career bureaucracy.

The defense and foreign policy components of this effort collectively, and
sometimes pejoratively, have been called the "national security state." It is comprised of such agencies as the Central Intelligence Agency (CIA), the Department
of Defense, and the National Security Agency. Moreover, in the name of national
security, bureaucracy's natural tendency for secrecy was progressively amplified.
This, at a cost of transparency, as criteria for classifying government documents
were considerably relaxed (e.g., in national security directives unavailable for
decades) and response times to Freedom of Information Act requests were inordinately delayed by cumbersome processes and redactions.

Internationally, the United States—led by both Republican and Democratic presidents—helped found and heavily fund collective security arrangements such as the United Nations, the North Atlantic Treaty Organization (NATO), and the Association of Southeast Asian Nations (ASEAN), as well as financial institutions such as the World Bank and the International Monetary Fund. In the process, Eisner's (2000a, p. 12) characterization of World War I dynamics was amplified: existing federal "state capacity was [again] expanded by appending the [administrative] capacities of private-sector associations on to the [compensatory] state." In addition, not only were bureaucracies involved, but the federal government's role would expand "with respect to labor-management relations, income taxation and public borrowing, and defense spending" (Sparrow, 1996, p. 9). As in the Civil War and World War I, World War II and the Cold War also amplified the "formation of quasi-corporatist government–business–labor partnerships" that operated "largely out of sight" of average citizens and their elected representatives (p. 9; Brinkley, 1995; Fleming, 2001; Kennedy, 2005).

These were deliberate political choices by President Franklin Roosevelt (FDR) and his successors. As historian Alan Brinkley (1995) writes about FDR's political and tactical motives regarding expansion of the proxy component of the compensatory state:

> Roosevelt feared that entrusting the war economy to existing [federal] agencies would create damaging partisan divisions [over exceptions to limited government]; and he believed that [conservative] businessmen would respond more readily to direction from other businessmen than to orders from what they considered a hostile federal government.
>
> (p. 190)

A similar amplification of an IRP-driven compensatory state also took place in the domestic social policy arena during the 1945 to 1980 period, one building on and expanding FDR's New Deal agencies and structures. Most important was President Lyndon Johnson's War on Poverty in the 1960s, an effort driven by Johnson's turn to the social sciences for program development. Like FDR, Johnson and a Democratic Congress added new programs and agencies to the federal government that did two things consistent with minimizing as much as possible the visible size of the federal government. First, his administration prodded, mandated, and helped fund subnational governments and third-party actors to act in pursuit of federal policy goals, and second, it created bureaucratic implementation structures for these programs that relied heavily on both subnational governments and third-party actors. These implementation structures, of course, also shaped policies within statutory constraints.

Johnson's refocus on the Vietnam War after 1966 from domestic policy left the so-called Rights Revolution as the central driver of the amplification of the compensatory state. This revolution incorporated a shift in legislation from what David Schoenbrod (1983) calls "rules statutes" to "goals statutes." Rules statutes are relatively precise in wording, identify specific risks and behaviors for agencies to curb, and provide them with information on implementation strategies. In short, they focus on "thou shalt not" goals. In contrast, goals statutes reflect highly laudable but ambiguous social goals specified in "thou shalt" language (e.g., make the waters fishable and swimmable). These are largely open-ended and, thus, devolve immense discretion to agencies as to where to bound their actions.[1] The safer political and legal route for expertise-based agencies in this environment was to expand those boundaries, especially as the precedent set by the US Supreme Court decision in *Chevron USA, Inc. v. Natural Resources Defense Council, Inc.* (1984) gave huge deference to agencies whenever statutes were ambiguous. This, until the last five of six *Chevron*-related cases (the exception being *Gundy v. United States*, 2019), saw a more textualist-oriented court slowly erode that deference (Wood, 2019). Unless *Chevron* deference is limited or rejected by the Supreme Court in the future, a perverse political incentive exists for legislators to not act and count instead on judges to affirm regulations that agencies promulgate. Likewise, when a statute is silent on an issue, an agency can regulate with decidedly less fear that it lacks the authority to act.

In the process, goals statutes further (albeit temporarily) advanced the long-standing quest of social scientists to legitimize themselves as authority structures in American policymaking. As Theodore Lowi (1995) writes, goals statutes were—and remain—premised on systems thinking (a key aspect of the IRP and of the aforementioned Harvard Graduate School of Business) informed by econometric social science methodology and theory. As he also argues, goals statutes reinforced "traditional European administrative state theory" and the early progressives' faith "that experts know best and will exercise their judgment neutrally" (p. 60). International rules of law were also later imported into US Supreme Court deliberations (e.g., regarding the death penalty), much to the consternation of conservatives opposed to activist state building and worried about an erosion of national sovereignty (Toobin, 2008).[2]

At the same time, goals statutes were unlike their rule-oriented predecessors in rationale: legislative debate shifted from "consequentialist" reasons for action (as per the pragmatists noted in earlier chapters) to moral grounds (e.g., everyone has an undefined right to clean air). Regardless of the merit of the arguments made, and as the Founders predicted, the idea of positive "rights" also made legislative compromise less possible and pushed elected officials to turn their attention to administrative reform to advance their policy goals. In placing an unlimited "duty" on agencies to remedy injustices (Lowi, 1995), pressure mounted on the courts to review agency rules more synoptically on substantive policy choices when challenged, thus making the ideological composition of the courts more important.

But a paradox also began that would haunt the Supreme Court to this day. As Karen Orren and Stephen Skowronek (2017) observe, the activism of the court "enhance[ed] [its] institutional position" (p. 146). But it also "made it more difficult for it to set itself apart from policy conflicts and protect the integrity of its [original] mission to ensure that policy conforms to the law" (p. 146). Conservative activists argued that liberal judges were no longer interpreting the law but, rather, making it to suit their liberal impulses (Teles, 2008). What ensued (see Chapter 7) was a multi-decade-long fight by conservatives to put persons on the federal courts who were variously called "strict-constructionists," "textualists," or "originalists."[3] Judges and legal scholars holding this philosophy argued that courts must adhere to the words of the Constitution and statutes as written, rather than interpreting their intent to meet contemporary situations.

Against this backdrop, public agencies also (again) became the target of attacks from the extreme Right and Left of the political spectrum. From the Right, conservative private corporations and business associations joined with social conservatives to mount aggressive campaigns against them. They portrayed regulation—and the agencies that implemented them—as un-American and a threat to capitalism, democracy, and liberty—charges amplified in seriousness by the anti-communism of the Cold War. This campaign also included the funding of conservative "think tanks" in Washington to counter what critics saw as progressives' capture of the bureaucracy and the policy debate. These were designed to reduce the monopoly on expertise held by federal agencies, justify their downsizing, and insert conservative voices into political, legal, and administrative debates in Washington.

Meanwhile, various elements of the Left likewise claimed that historical–structural mismatches existed that could not meet the nation's exceptionalist goals. They characterized public agencies as self-serving, overly bureaucratized, and inimical to flexibility and innovating. Agencies also stigmatized clients, were captured by corporate or other interests, and even propped up a capitalist system that should fall. By the 1970s, more mainstream research and spokespersons also questioned the effectiveness of many programs in this system, blaming bureaucratic resistance for disappointments and failures.

All this, in turn, further amplified the early progressives' focus on ensuring that the bureaucracy's "neutral competence" shifted into using administrative reforms (largely the IRP) to gain "responsive competence" to chief executives. Also, with the rising costs of the Cold War and domestic programs, administrative reformers tried to rationalize the budget process, as well as reform agency personnel policies, bureaucratic structures, and decision rules. Produced, however, was a now familiar pattern: *political rationality* frequently diluted or trumped the technocratic rationality of these efforts. Moreover, these IRP-based reforms amplified the earlier marginalization of average working-class citizens lacking the expertise to become involved in what was soon called the "procedural republic"

(Sandel, 1998). This, while large businesses, their associations, and upper- to middle-class liberal interest groups gained influence in legislatures and agencies. Collectively, as the next chapter discusses, these dynamics again brought cries for the next round of administrative reform that began in the 1980s and continued despite their disappointing results with various IRP-based emphases through the Obama administration.

****

As noted in Chapter 5, Americans' isolationism in foreign policy prevented overt US intervention into World War II until the Japanese sneak attack on Pearl Harbor in 1941. FDR believed that US neutrality would mean a win for Germany in World War II and would spread the totalitarian Third Reich world-wide. By 1940, the United States had quietly begun a military buildup, bringing total military spending to a then unprecedented level. With contracts to defense industries booming at approximately $1.5 billion per month, both business and labor supported the buildup. And despite World War I's bad experience with noncompetitive bidding for arms contracts, the United States used the same contracting format to speed up war production. These contracts were administered through a reconstituted Reconstruction Finance Corporation associated with Herbert Hoover. Also consistent with earlier wartime efforts, the federal government turned to corporate leaders and associations, as well as to the voluntary sector and state and local governments. This, to compensate for inadequate administrative and policymaking capacity in federal agencies bequeathed to them from history.

As James Evans (2010) observes, "World War II forced a union of science and invention as the United States put university scientists and corporate engineers together in government projects for the rapid invention of radar, nuclear weapons, and other defense technologies" (151). From all this, a system of government-supervised self-regulation amplified earlier trends and "took on oligopolistic tendencies." It did so by "reducing the number of competitors, favoring the best organized competitors, specializing politics around agencies, [and] ultimately limiting participation to channels provided by pre-existing groups" (Lowi, 1969, p. 63).

Thus, as Sparrow (1996) demonstrates, the "U.S. government became the new locus of exchange [as] a result of [World War II], [but this] did not mean that the [federal] government, by itself, necessarily had greater authority. The jointness of the wartime state-building implicated nominally private actors in the expansion of the government and at once constrained the scope of federal authority. The private became public, and the public included the private; both built the state"—and were part of it (p. 311). Amplified in doing so was the "publicness" of organizations, publicness that stretched back to the nation's founding.

Still, various procurement investigations launched by Congress during and after World War II (e.g., the Truman Committee hearings between 1941 and 1948) identified some of the same misfeasance and contractor favoritism that had historically plagued contracting and associationalism. On balance, however, the private–public partnerships, combined with the United States winning the war and directly providing veterans with the GI Bill, produced positive perceptions of both government and business that lasted until events in the early 1970s (see below).

Mobilization by means of the proxy component of the compensatory state also, again, gave large suppliers a key advantage over smaller competitors, an advantage magnified during post-World War II demobilization. Given what had happened after World War I, FDR began thinking about demobilization in 1943. As Marc Allen Eisner (2000a) illustrates, an early

> decision to free up resources in the final stages of the war would have permitted many of the smaller firms . . . to make a transition into civilian production, thus providing the structural preconditions for a decentralized competitive economy after the war. Yet early reconversion was opposed by the larger industrial concerns, who had great influence in the war mobilization agencies . . . and the Joint Chiefs of Staff.
>
> (p. 358)

FDR's instincts were also stymied by a coalition of the Department of War, the uniformed services, and other agencies seeking to lead reconversion. They joined large corporations in opposing production cutbacks and efforts made to ensure small business inclusion. Large corporations had already received most war contracts during the conflict, as thousands of small businesses were "shut out" of war production. Nor did corporations want this contract spigot turned off. Thus, in the end, "small firms were left to languish until the end of the war. Many found it impossible to compete with the larger firms, which entered the post-war economy with large reserves of capital derived from war contracts" (Eisner, 2000a, p. 358). Larger firms "quickly secured new defense contracts and were given preferential status in acquiring the facilities and stockpiles the government had financed, often at fire-sale prices" (p. 358). As such, larger corporations reaped the benefits of this new—and now permanent—expansion of the proxy components of the compensatory state.

These World War II and early Cold War dynamics also spawned demographic shifts that planted the seeds for major political shifts that would later have important administrative reform and compensatory state-building consequences in the 1980s. Sun Belt migration from the North and Midwest started the rise of Sun Belt conservatism. Migration into California and the Sun Belt states began initially in World War II with mobilization and support efforts. The war transformed California "from a distant regional center to a national economic dynamo" (Barone, 2013, p. 196).[4] Washington's attention to the state was sparked initially by the aforementioned attack on Pearl Harbor and the presence of a Japanese submarine that fired on an oil tanker near Santa Barbara, California. These, in turn, led to FDR's infamous establishment of Japanese internment camps. California already contributed 20 percent of the nation's oil and housed much of its aviation industry (e.g., Lockheed and Northrup). It also contained several military bases enlarged to house millions of military personnel en route to battle in the Pacific theater. Cities such as San Diego flourished, and about 100,000 defense workers resided in the Los Angeles Basin alone.

Enticed by the climate, many of these military personnel and defense contractors either stayed or returned after discharge from duty, making California into one of the fastest-growing metropolitan areas and economic engines in the country. Not surprisingly, a housing boom followed, and auto plants moved to California. As word spread, migration from the East and Midwest spawned a huge market for goods and supplies in California, prompting small business growth. Highway building also surged.

But these trends were not limited to California. More broadly, lower labor costs in "right-to-work," anti-union southern and southwestern states prompted many companies to establish or move existing facilities to the region after the war. Also created was the foundation for a post-Cold War network of arms manufacturers, military installations, and research laboratories stretching down the Atlantic coast and going westward across the South, Southwest, and California. This building of what today is known as the "Gun Belt" reflected conventional associationalist philosophy. This, as the latest in administrative reform initiatives— newly formed quasigovernment institutions (e.g., government-owned, company-operated installations) and think tanks such as the Rand Corporation—dotted the Gun Belt.

****

When World War II ended, the Soviets broke earlier promises made at the Yalta and Potsdam conferences to allow self-determination and democratic elections in Eastern Europe. Abandoned, first, were Soviet promises to create coalition governments in France and Italy and, then, free and fair elections in Poland. The Soviets also tried to increase their influence in Iran, Greece, and Turkey—just like they had already done in Estonia, Latvia, and Lithuania—while pressuring Finland and Norway to sign mutual-assistance treaties. They also cut off land and train services to western-controlled sectors in Berlin, bringing about the famous Berlin Airlift (1948–1949).

But fearing "war exhaustion" by Americans after four years of fighting and loss of blood and treasure, the United States (after great debate) opted to "contain" rather than reverse Soviet gains in Eastern Europe. Containment, an ultimately successful strategy, involved the United States reacting to Soviet intransigence economically (e.g., the Marshall Plan succeeding the discarded Morgenthau Plan to deindustrialize Germany), politically (e.g., by creating NATO and ASEAN), and administratively by building and repeatedly amplifying the capacity of the national security state. Conservatives on the far Right, led by Senator Robert Taft (R-OH), were strongly opposed to this option and to the United States becoming the "world's policeman." This feeling broadened to wider audiences later after the nation participated in undeclared wars (called "police actions"). These occurred, first, under UN auspices in Korea (1950–1953) and, later, in Vietnam (1955–1975). The Korean War ended without US victory, and the Vietnam War ended in defeat and military demoralization. The doctrine of containment, however, was not officially abandoned until the Reagan administration applied concerted economic, political, technological, and strategic pressures in the 1980s on an already collapsing Soviet system (see more in Chapter 7).

But, after World War II, most Americans, joined by internationalist leaders, concluded that the massive number of casualties in both world wars stemmed partly from the hasty and inadequate training of soldiers. They also realized that they were no longer protected from military aggression by two great oceans. It became clear to them that Soviet bombers could cross the oceans and, later, that medium range and intercontinental ballistic missiles could deliver nuclear bombs in a matter of 15 to 20 minutes to the United States and its allies from launch pads and submarines. Clarity on these threats was also given by the creation of the Warsaw Pact, comprised of the Soviet military plus the troops of Moscow's by then satellite governments in Eastern Europe. And along with US soldiers stationed in Germany essentially becoming a trip-wire in Europe against Soviet invasion, the gradual ramping up of US military and industrial might— which the United States had done successfully in earlier wars of attrition— became problematic.

By the 1950s, what became known as the "vital center" of Republican and Democratic leaders also believed that every increase in Soviet military and nuclear arsenals required a similar buildup of United States and European forces. A staunch believer in balanced budgets, World War II hero and five-star general Dwight D. Eisenhower (R-KS) was elected president in 1952. Eisenhower thought it cheaper and wiser strategically to rely on massive nuclear retaliation rather than continue the buildup of conventional forces. "Mutually assured destruction," or MAD, originated in this era and prevailed throughout the Cold War (see more below).

In 1960, then Senator John Kennedy (D-MA) ran for president partly on a platform falsely claiming that a "missile gap" favoring the Soviet Union had developed during the Eisenhower presidency. His opponent—Vice President Richard Nixon (R-CA)—felt that he could not rebut these claims without jeopardizing national security. Once in office, the Kennedy administration argued that no gap existed, but an overreliance on nuclear arms *did* exist. Developed was a "flexible response" doctrine combining conventional and nuclear forces. A massive arms race with accompanying growth in size and administrative infrastructure geared toward containment and MAD continued throughout the Cold War era, with occasional efforts at arms control. In the process, the arms race significantly expanded the relative size of the military budget, put severe strains on the domestic policy budget, and amplified a vast military–industrial–university complex to support and maintain this buildup.

So worried was Eisenhower that he used his final national address to warn his successors about the need to contain the power of this complex. He readily conceded that a military buildup in weapons, administration, and university research ties was necessary to counter the Soviet threat. But he also feared (as the Founders did) that national security would overwhelm domestic needs, that corporate profits combined with the military's penchant for new weapons would allow a technoscientific elite to drive American policy, and that universities' increasing dependence on military research dollars would stifle "intellectual curiosity" in other policy areas. This, as the costs of the arms race soared, as top-secret classification of documents in national security agencies spiraled, and as fears of nuclear Armageddon grew.

Economist George Stigler argues, and as witnessed in earlier periods of contracting since the nation's founding, that a system of rent-seeking by contractors often developed. This, as a political system that railed against "privilege in policy formulation only . . . foster[ed] it quite systematically in the implementation of policy" (Lowi, 1969, p. 297). What is more, this *intra*national network of contractors and subcontractors in congressional districts made— and continues to make—contract termination nearly impossible in areas represented by high-ranking congressmembers sitting on oversight committees. Coupled with the building of the aforementioned network of national laboratories, government-owned and company-operated weapons facilities, and non-profit research institutes scattered across the country, what American political development scholarship calls "lock-in" ensued during the 1960s and 1970s (and beyond) (see more below).

****

The Cold War also expanded both domestic and international bureaucratic institutions and expert staffing within them. All applied the principles of the IRP to fight the Soviet threat. Congress first passed the National Security Act of 1947, which created the CIA to succeed the World War II Office of Strategic Services, as well as the National Security Council (NSC) to advise the president and the National Security Resources Board. It also placed the National Military Establishment (NME) (the three military services) under a single Secretary of Defense. In 1947, the NME became the Department of Defense.

Then, in 1958, the Defense Reorganization Act created the Defense Advanced Research Projects Agency (DARPA) in the Pentagon and clarified the chain of command from the president to the Secretary of Defense. Later, in 1986, Congress would pass the Goldwater–Nichols Department of Defense Reorganization Act taking operational command authority from the Joint Chiefs of Staff and giving it to combatant commanders in different parts of the world. It also established the office of Vice Chairman of the Joint Chiefs of Staff and made the occupant the principal military adviser to the Secretary of Defense, the NSC, and the president.

In the process, growth in the visible size of the federal government continued. Between 1933 and 1953 alone, the

> executive branch of the federal government grew from 600,000 civilian employees to 2,600,000. . . . [Moreover,] the proportion of federal, state, and local government revenues jumped to 24 percent of GNP by 1950 from 6 to 7 percent of GNP in the 1920s.
>
> (Ferrell, 1994, p. 195)

Concurrently, and reflecting Americans' traditional rationalist faith in international trade as an inhibitor of war, the United States developed a variety of rule-based multilateral institutions. Among the most significant were the World Bank (1944), the International Monetary Fund (1945), the General Agreement on Tariffs and Trade (1947), and (later) the World Trade Organization (1995). By 1970, economic globalization had recovered to pre-World War I levels as a product of these initiatives (Nye, 2017, p. 7). Created by the United States was an international order of institutions (including the United Nations), as well as a global economic world order that would go largely unchallenged in government until the early 21st century under the Trump administration. Meanwhile, although federal, state, and local governments employed approximately 4 percent of the civilian labor force in 1933, they employed approximately 10 percent of that workforce in 1950, rising to 14 to 16 percent in 1990.

Funding the Cold War's domestic and feverish national security ambitions was, of course, very expensive. American leaders had to contend with the intellectual power of Americans' reification of budget balancing. But, as noted in Chapter 5, a new intellectual justification of budget deficits emerged from the social sciences in the post-war era, a philosophy promoted by macroeconomists: Keynesian economic theory (Brinkley, 1995). Keynesianism was attacked by conservatives but was embraced by liberal corporate leaders as a way to reduce regulatory, trust-busting, or planning reforms that were more intrusive in the market economy. Reminiscent of the claims of the early progressive economists noted in Chapter 5, Keynesians argued that budget deficits (and surpluses) could be countercyclical tools for smoothing out and managing the business cycle.[5]

Deficits were not as bad as historically portrayed if they did not create structural deficits. Deficit financing also was attractive to corporate liberals, because it was perceived as a means for regulating the economy as a whole rather than industry by industry (Brinkley, 1995).

Moreover, corporate liberals were more positive about government agencies after working closely with them during World War II. Agency experts shared the same impression of corporate liberals. Together, they began supporting social programs *and* national security spending under the tenets of Keynesianism. Comprised of committed Keynesians, for example, the Committee for Economic Development was established (with links to the Business Advisory Council). Members believed that the "health of the postwar American (and world) economy was of more importance than the immediate market environments of particular sectors" of the economy (Brinkley, 1995, p. 173).

Keynesianism became official US policy with enactment of the Employment Act of 1946, setting an ambiguous target for unemployment interpreted widely as 4 percent unemployment. US fiscal and monetary policy were aimed at maintaining that level. The political appeal of Keynesian economics to elected officials was also palpable (Rosenbloom, 2000). Increased spending would go for projects in the districts and states of members of Congress, investments they would claim credit for delivering in reelection campaigns. Likewise, getting and retaining project funding were alluring to state and local components of the compensatory state, making them difficult to terminate.

As the size of the US domestic and national security budgets and administrative apparatus grew during this time period, worries also arose about their impact on personal liberty. As early as the 1940s, political scientist Harold Lasswell (predating Eisenhower) captured the spirit of anxiety of those who worried that the United States was becoming a "garrison state" (Lasswell, 1941, p. 455). Lasswell worried that a perpetual state of security fears and preparation for war was developing, meaning that "every aspect of life would eventually come under [nation-] state control" (Friedberg, 2000, p. 57).

As in earlier periods of reform, the increases in deference to the executive branch that Keynesianism necessarily wrought led to concerns about both halting that shift in foreign policy (e.g., the Bricker Amendment of 1954) and how best to hold all federal agencies accountable for their actions. Amid a range of administrative alternatives, reformers turned once more to the IRP with its inherent bias toward "outer checks" on agency discretion (Finer, 1941), rather than Friedrich's aforementioned inner checks of competing professionals and their consciences. Not unlike earlier efforts to enhance control and accountability of agency discretion in decision making, this otherwise beneficial effort also produced an amplification of what political philosopher Michael Sandel (1984) calls a "procedural republic" that privileged expertise and organized interests (see more below) and amplified the complexity of governance. As Sven Steinmo

(2010) argues, the solution to too much complexity was (again) *more* bureau-cratic complexity, this time in the rulemaking process.

The first congressional efforts to do so occurred in 1933, during FDR's first year in office, and culminated initially in 1940 with efforts to pass the Walter–Logan Act (see Grisinger, 2014; Karl, 1983; Rosenbloom, 2000). This effort was pushed by conservative business opponents of the New Deal and the American Bar Association (ABA). Although the motivation for conservatives and their cor-porate allies is obvious, the ABA's support is less so at first glance. But the ABA saw the New Deal as a threat to judicial power. The association felt the federal courts had been losing authority to the executive branch, thus also threaten-ing the influence (and legitimacy) of lawyers in policymaking in the executive branch (Dimock, 1980).

Aiming to restore their legitimacy, the ABA formed a committee in 1933 to do a series of reports on administrative issues related to New Deal agencies. Under the leadership of the noted legal scholar and jurist, Roscoe Pound, in 1937, the committee produced a ten-point indictment of the administrative procedures of New Deal agencies. Its recommendations became the basis for the Walter–Logan Act. The report highlighted the IRCs' frequent failures to hold hearings before issuing regulations, their exclusion of attorneys from hearings, their failure to base regulations on evidence "on the record," and their hearing only one side of various issues. The report's recommendations stressed the creation of formal hearings in cases of agency rulemaking and adjudication, a public rulemaking record, and judicial review of all agency rulemaking efforts. Judicial reviews of all rules, of course, placed an onerous analytical burden on agencies, one that would slow regulation of the economy by IRCs and indirectly foreshadow efforts at "paralysis by analysis" by conservatives in the 1980s and beyond.

Passed by both houses of Congress, the Walter–Logan Act was nonetheless successfully vetoed by FDR. Despite FDR's veto, his Attorney General, Robert Jackson, advised the president to commission a study identifying needed reforms in administrative law. He did so partly because administrative reform was needed and partly to head off adoption of more restrictive legislation of the executive branch by Congress. The nearly 500-page "Final Report of the Attorney Gener-al's Committee on Administrative Procedure" was released in 1941, again focus-ing its critiques only on IRCs.

During World War II, no formal legislative action was taken. However, in 1946, a compromise between progressives and conservatives became the Admin-istrative Procedure Act (APA) (www.legisworks.org/congress/79/publaw-404. pdf). This compromise basically meant the Republicans and their allies accepted the political infeasibility of rolling back the New Deal. Thus, Congress had little choice but to delegate broad swaths of its policymaking authority to agencies equipped to deal with complex issues. Basically, Congress conceded a constitu-tive role for government agencies, created agency administrative procedures akin to the legislative process in the hope of advancing a greater range of substantive rationality project (SRP)-based values (e.g., responsiveness, transparency), and subjected these to judicial review. With this acknowledgement, and based on the 1941 report, the APA also went beyond IRCs to include all federal agencies. Various statutes over the ensuing years added other procedural hurdles in the hope of regularizing and advancing SRP-based values (e.g., the "dialogue requirement"). In addition, "little APAs" were enacted in the states. Citizens and interest groups were to become "little attorneys-general" through court suits holding agencies accountable for their actions.

The APA represented an important advance in democratic constitutionalism in policymaking in public agencies, and as envisioned, its importance in protecting constitutional rights and projecting an SRP approach to administrative reform cannot be overstated. In this instance, the logic of administrative reform was this: if the problem was a lack of representation in the rulemaking process relative to the legislative process, the solution was to institutionalize more pluralism, transparency, and legal reviewability. But, less positively, the APA also was a victory for the courts and the legal profession in creating a judicialization of administration in the federal government and in states later adopting little APAs.

As administrative law expert Kenneth Culp Davis observes, the APA "brought back the decision of [policy and constitutional] controversies of all kinds to the judicial system" after seeing the courts marginalized by the New Deal (Dimock, 1980, p. 104). By judicializing both agency rulemaking and adjudication, it also "secured . . . the power and influence of lawyers" within agencies that have steadily advanced ever since (p. 104). Moreover, legal training's focus on procedural compliance rather than management accomplishment was antithetical to effective public management. Wrote Dimock, speaking for other critics, although "statistically the best way to become a government executive is to be a lawyer . . . law school may provide the worst preparation" to becoming one (p. 43).

Procedural compliance, although necessary for preserving constitutional values, nonetheless can also foster compartmentalization of thinking about the parts (of decision making) rather than on the synthesis of thinking required by high-level public managers. Thus, it is necessary to make a distinction between procedurally driven "red tape" (Bozeman, 1993) that is not linked to advancing organizational effectiveness and constitutional values and "green tape" that is linked to it (DeHart-Davis, 2008). This said, and as green and red tape accumulate, judicializing also can decrease efficiency and prevent the blending of managerial, political, and legal thinking required for policy decisions (Rosenbloom, 1983). Amplified, too, is "goal displacement"; complying with rules can reduce a focus on policy outcomes and sometimes stymies effectiveness (Wilson, 1989). Procedural compliance also can make public managers risk-averse, even though innovation is often required. At its best, however, procedural compliance protects important values that one does not want to see compromised or ignored in a democratic republic.

Created during the APA's implementation ever since has been the procedural republic noted earlier, a development that enhances the power of lawyers, the judiciary, and powerful organized interests such as corporations, while marginalizing most citizens even further from rulemaking. Granted, the APA's dialogue requirement sought to bring citizen input into the process, and often did so. But the APA and its progeny in the states require "resources, organization, and sophistication" that most citizens lack and corporate interests, social scientists, and other organized interests find less daunting to marshal (Kerwin & Furlong, 2010, p. 114). Research also suggests that the influence of business interests varies across stages of the regulatory process (e.g., business interests trump others in the vital regulatory agenda-setting and pre-proposal stages) (Kerwin, Furlong, & West, 2010) and under certain conditions (e.g., Yackee & Yackee, 2006). Thus, in practice, the pentimento effects (Adams, 1992) of the IRP noted in Chapter 1 bleed over onto the SRP initiatives.

****

Amid all this, corporate conservative criticism still abounded, and New Deal battles continued over expertise-based bureaucratic activism in Washington. This, as labor seemed to be gaining the upper hand legislatively over management. In response, Congress first passed the Taft–Hartley Act in 1947 to scale back labor's gains. Corporate conservatives (specifically, the steel and financial industry) gained significant relief from the regulatory power of such agencies as the National Labor Relations Board and the Securities and Exchange Commission (Storrs, 2013). This was followed during the 1950s by corporate conservatives, traditional conservatives, and conservative scholars continuously portraying labor unions as threats to individual liberty, the free market, and *Lochner*'s freedom of employees to contract with an employer as they saw fit.

These rollbacks were accompanied by a Second Red Scare that began in the late 1940s and early 1950s, one that again tarnished the legitimacy of federal agencies in the compensatory state. In 1938, Congress had created the Special House Committee to Investigate Un-American Activities, with its name changed to the permanent House Un-American Activities Committee (HUAC) in 1945. Relatedly, the Senate Internal Security Subcommittee and Senator Joseph McCarthy's (R-WI) Permanent Subcommittee on Investigations were also created. Members of these committees and their staff worked with the Federal Bureau of Investigation to identify alleged communist subversives. Also created was the federal employee loyalty program, reluctantly endorsed in 1947 by President Harry Truman (D-MO) to combat charges of communist subversion within the federal government (Ferrell, 1994; Rosenbloom, 2014).

Spurring on the Second Red Scare was the now ultra-conservative Hearst newspaper chain. The chain portrayed the federal civil service under FDR and Truman as permeated by communist sympathizers. And not unlike earlier instances of limited-government backlash against women serving in Washington during the Civil War, civil service reformers in the late 19th century, and the early progressives of the 20th century, these charges were laced with misogynistic, homophobic, and racist prejudices (Storrs, 2013). These editorials, plus a bestselling book published in 1951 by two Hearst reporters called *Washington Confidential*, portrayed the federal bureaucracy as a "femmocracy."

Historian Landon Storrs (2013) summarizes the vitriol of the book's tirade on the character of federal employees generally:

> The femmocracy consists of self-supporting women whose alleged unhappiness proved that the "emancipation of women is baloney." Staffing the federal bureaucracy, this femmocracy was an incubator of sexual depravity and communism. Women outnumbered men by one-hundred thousand, and "g-girls" (government girls) slept their way to the top, sometimes with the help of older female bureaucrats who procured ambitious prospects from the heartland for the few government men who weren't "eunuchs" or "pansies." Communists allegedly took advantage of the situation, using suave male Reds to recruit "sex-starved government girls," "white girls" to recruit the many "colored men" in government jobs, and "trained good lookers" to recruit "meek male clerks in soporific jobs at standardized subsistence pay."
>
> (p. 86)

As scurrilous and fallacious as these charges were, Cold Warriors and anti-labor elements of the conservative corporate world and their associations spread the idea that these "behaviors" in the federal bureaucracy were a microcosm of what the United States would look like under communism. Communism's antipathy toward religion and emphasis on egalitarianism would lead to licentiousness, lesbianism, interracial mating, and homoeroticism. Washington—and the federal civil service in general—was an "endless round of 'interracial, inter-middle-sex mélanges' and 'yachting parties' of black drag queens" (Storrs, 2013, p. 95).

Led by McCarthy, allegations of communist spies infiltrating government agencies (especially in the US Department of State) next shook the foundations of the progressive agenda and the image of federal employees. Although significant instances of Soviet spying were proven (e.g., Alger Hiss and Klaus Fuchs), the largely unsupported charges of disloyalty to America destroyed the reputations of thousands of civil servants—and the civil service as a whole. Many progressives who had joined the federal government during the Great Depression had been associated with socialist and even communist-related groups at different points in their lives. Recall, for example, many intellectuals' fascination with the five-year plans of Vladimir Lenin and Joseph Stalin (Chapter 5). Also, many progressive men in the New Deal (and in state and local governments) had either married or hired the rising number of university-educated professional women who heavily staffed the conservative-disparaged social service agencies at all levels of government and in the voluntary sector.

In doing so, the Second Red Scare further stoked Americans' historical attachment to a limited government, especially at the federal level. Granted, by the end of 1954, the brutality of McCarthy and his committee at least nominally ended the Second Red Scare. But fear of communism, the tradition of ascriptive hierarchy in America, and national security threats generally persisted during this period of the Cold War to undermine further the legitimacy and bureaucratic capacity of federal agencies in the compensatory state.

****

Destructive enough on its own, the campaign against the legitimacy of public agencies and their employees during the Second Red Scare was complemented by the efforts of the National Association of Manufacturers (NAM) and leaders of the US Chamber of Commerce. The NAM had previously joined the Liberty League in opposing the New Deal on constitutional, free-market, and personal freedom grounds (Phillips-Fein, 2009, esp. ch. 2). This effort had been comprised only of corporate elites and focused on business interests. By the 1940s and 1950s, a small coterie of these conservative corporate and Chamber of Commerce leaders thought it wiser to broaden the coalition to all businesspersons *and* even to workers.

Such corporate leaders as Jasper Crane (Du Pont Chemical), Sterling Morton (Morton Salt Company), and Leonard Read and William Clinton Mullendore (Chamber of Commerce officials) feared the upsurge of strikes by labor in 1946 (Phillips-Fein, 2009). So, this time, corporate conservatives launched initiatives to spread the free-market gospel through a business-funded public relations campaign. They heralded the threat that unions and the "nanny state" of bureaucratic administrators posed to US victory in the Cold War and to American exceptionalist values, such as free markets, private property, and individualism.

Read first created the Foundation for Economic Education (FEE), an organization publishing reports making this case. But Crane argued that success could only be won if the campaign had a "New Testament for capitalism" (Phillips-Fein, 2009, p. 30). He found that testament in the collective works of Austrian School economists Ludwig von Mises and Friedrich Hayek, plus Russian emigre Ayn Rand. Each had fled totalitarian governments. Von Mises' and Hayek's defense of free markets and "spontaneous" social order against government planning by agency experts harkened to proponents of free markets discussed in earlier chapters and pummeled the ideas of the Verein. Both also disputed the ability of mathematics, econometric models, and Keynesian macroeconomic analysis to capture the complexity of national markets, although Hayek was more tolerant of a limited welfare state.

Wrote Hayek (1988) acerbically in *The Fatal Conceit*, while neoclassical economists and social scientists concede that everything that now exists was "developed from a process of spontaneous order . . . they call on human reason—now that things have become so complex—to seize the reigns and control future development" (p. 22). Both economists also thought that embracing reason and theoretical abstractions ungrounded in experience (as the *philosophes* leading the French Revolution had done) was dangerous. Trial-and-error experience over the ages (or "social evolution") was the best guide to action.

Von Mises also excoriated state planning for killing innovation and creativity, derided unions as agents of "economic violence," and portrayed collective bargaining as "bargaining at the point of a gun" (Phillips-Fein, 2009, p. 105). In *Human Action* (1949), he wrote that free markets create a safe space where individuals' ideas could revolutionize—and had revolutionized—the world. Added Hayek, national social planning was impractical and dangerous. Contrary to the convictions of the American disciples of the Verein and the American Social Science Association in the mid- to late 19th century, the technocratic and associationalist progressives of the early 20th century, and the social planners of the New Deal, national markets were too complex for rational social planners to understand and steer wisely. Moreover, in an extended economy of this complexity, goal agreement was not possible. Ultimately, bureaucratic planners' views would have to be enforced by government coercion at the cost of the Founders' emphasis on individual rights.

Still, neither von Mises nor Hayek advocated unregulated markets or the virtues of laissez-faire capitalist greed. Not so Rand, who, like Friedrich Nietzsche before her, saw no morality higher than self-interest. She told corporate leaders that the existing moral code demonizing self-interest and individualism—not misguided economic policy—was *the* major threat to capitalism and had to be changed. Doomed, she thought, were such campaigns as the FEE's to evangelize capitalism, impugn government bureaucracy, and fight communism by distributing literary materials. So, too, were campaigns by the Christian Business Men's Committee and the Businessmen for Spiritual Mobilization (BSM) to link capitalism with Christianity. Nevertheless, to further their conservative agenda, the BSM in the 1950s mailed copies of Hayek's *The Road to Serfdom*, as well as *Christian Economics* newsletters, to 150,000 ministers for their sermons.

With this patina of academic legitimacy, and despite the Austrian School's distinctly minority stature relative to the dominant Keynesian School, the NAM also launched an education campaign to show managers how to combat union drives. Also spurred was the rise of anti-union consultants in the 1950s, foreshadowing the rise of union-busting consultants in the 1970s. Meanwhile, General

Electric tried to convert workers into supporters of corporate America's agenda. It did so by educating its employees on the virtues of capitalism and how workers, too, had a stake in preserving the free-market system from IRP-based state planning led by expertise-based agencies (Phillips-Fein, 2009, esp. ch. 2). Their best weapon on the shop floor and on television was a fading Hollywood movie actor and future president of the United States, Ronald Reagan.

Nevertheless, during the 1950s, a rift still occurred in the larger conservative movement among believers in the free market, religious values, and libertarianism (e.g., Russell Kirk, Robert Nisbet, Clinton Rossiter, Leo Strauss, and Richard Weaver). Some saw the decline of religious tradition (not free markets) as the key to the fall of the Western world and, particularly, the downfall of American exceptionalism. William F. Buckley, Jr., tried to heal that rift. Buckley's *National Review* proffered what contributor Frank Meyer called a "fusion" version of conservatism. This included preserving a "competitive price system," fighting corporate and union monopolies, embracing traditional religious values, and opposing the "Big Brother State" and its bureaucrats (Phillips-Fein, 2009, p. 78). Revived amid this in 1962 was a strain of libertarianism influenced most notably by Nobel Prize-winning economist Milton Friedman's (an admirer of Hayek's work) bestselling book, *Capitalism and Freedom*.

Buckley also convened a meeting in 1960 of 100 young conservatives to advance fusion ideas, one that produced a one-page document called the Sharon Statement. This statement became the template for creating the conservative Young Americans for Freedom (YAF) on college campuses. YAF remains today a pool of talent for conservative campaigns, administrations, and think tanks. The Sharon Statement was framed in American exceptionalist values such as individualism, markets, and limited government. It urged young conservatives to recognize that: (1) the "transcendent value" of an individual's "God-given" free will is paramount; (2) political liberty is impossible without economic liberty; (3) free will and liberty cannot be compromised by the coercive power of government and its agencies; (4) a government abuses its powers when it interferes in markets; (5) when a government redistributes income, it diminishes the moral autonomy of citizens; and (6) the criterion for evaluating US foreign policy is whether it serves the just interests of the United States, not the globe (www.yaf. org/news/the-sharon-statement/).

****

Still, pressures mounted for some type of government action to respond to the negative social externalities facing the nation, most of which were linked to an amplification of the migratory patterns noted earlier. And addressing them, again, had both political and administrative repercussions. Migration to the South and Southwest accelerated, first, in the 1960s when President Lyndon Johnson funneled federal investment into his economically underdeveloped native region.

Inheriting Kennedy's goal for the United States to beat the Soviet Union to the moon, Johnson located new space facilities at Cape Canaveral in Florida and at the Houston Space Center in Texas. He also distributed research and development funds and other federal contracts throughout the region. Second, he conditioned receipt of millions of dollars of federal grants on recipients' plans to integrate their workforces racially.

In the process, however, a further decline occurred in the steel, auto, and engineering industries in the North and Midwest Rust Belt states, followed by an increase in high-tech businesses and jobs in other Gun Belt states. Overall, this increased the South and Southwest Gun Belt's initially more conservative political clout in Congress. In California, for example, the state's representation in the House of Representatives rose from 23 members of Congress in 1940 to 43 in the 1970s, while Rust Belt states lost representation.

Importantly, as migration from the Frost Belt to the Sun Belt was occurring, familiar patterns resumed of migration of poorer blacks from the South to cities in the North in the 1950s and 1960s. This was accompanied by a shift in composition of immigrant populations into the United States. Like the Great Migration of blacks in the early 20th century, this south-to-north migration was prompted by shrinking agricultural employment for blacks in the South, by employment opportunities on northern assembly lines, and by a desire to escape Jim Crow laws.

Once again, paid boosters painted a falsely utopian picture of life for blacks in northern cities. So incentivized, nearly one-half of all southern blacks between 20 and 24 years of age migrated to northern cities such as Chicago, Detroit, New York, Philadelphia, and Washington, DC. From 1940 to 1960, the black population in the ten largest US cities nearly quadrupled to 4.2 million persons. By the 1970s, Detroit and Baltimore were nearly black-majority cities. Moreover, black families sent their children to northern cities for summer employment (Barone, 2013, p. 199). Thus, more liberal blacks became concentrated in northern metropolises, while more conservative ethnic elements fleeing state taxes and harsher weather conditions moved into the South.

Alongside these trends, immigration demographics from abroad both amplified and shifted in composition, with many immigrants mostly poor and uneducated who settled in urban areas (Tichenor, 2002).[6] The National Origins Act of 1924 had restricted immigration overall for decades. This changed for a time with the passage of, first, the Immigration and Nationality Act (also known as the McCarran–Walter Act) of 1952 and, later, the Immigration and Nationality Act (also known as the Hart–Celler Act) of 1965. The former allowed immigrants to become naturalized citizens without discrimination based on race, sex, or marital status. But it was the latter that shifted the ethnic composition of immigrants toward Asia (in stark contrast to the Chinese Exclusion Act of 1882), the Caribbean, and, especially, Mexico and Latin America.

Thus, despite growing calls from unions to restrict immigration to protect members' wages and jobs, immigration soared, especially from Mexico. The population of undocumented workers also began growing, fueled partly by a lack of administrative capacity to process those applying legally for work visas or citizenship. Since 1942, backing from the agriculture industry for cheap labor had earlier wrought the infamous Bracero Program for guest workers. Industry claimed that Americans did not want the kinds of jobs taken by immigrants. They also argued that food shortages would result without the help of immigrants.

Also contributing to increased numbers of documented and undocumented workers and shifts in immigrant composition was lax enforcement of restrictions by the Immigration and Naturalization Service (parts of its functions were transferred in 2003 to Immigration and Customs Enforcement, or ICE). The agency did deport criminal elements but failed to protect the rights of Mexican immigrants. The influx of the latter prompted guest workers to unionize in the 1960s under the leadership of Caesar Chavez (the United Farm Workers Union). But Democrats led by Senator Robert Kennedy (D-NY) and Senator Edward Kennedy (D-MA) were repeatedly unable to get strict protection for immigrants during the 1960s and 1970s.

As in all prior migrations, existing housing supplies and public services could not cope adequately with this influx. This resulted in overcrowding of black, brown, and Asian immigrants in dilapidated and disease-prone urban ghettos and poor rural areas. Conditions had improved after World War II, as post-war prosperity produced more affordable housing within cities and in what would become suburbs. Combined with the highway construction noted earlier, whites and industry began a decades-long exodus to the suburbs. But this also began the flight of urban taxpayers and jobs to the suburbs. Importantly, this flight was assisted by otherwise positive government policies and education loans (the GI Bill) given to white World War II veterans but, initially, not to blacks. These same highways also allowed suburbanites to commute to the inner cities for jobs without paying taxes for the city services they consumed (e.g., police protection). Diminished in the process were badly needed public services to the economically disadvantaged left in inner cities.

Since the Progressive Era, a series of presidents had tried to address social equity issues such as those spawned by these dynamics. They argued that states and localities lacked the will, wherewithal, or authority to deal with them. President Truman's efforts at compensating for subnational shortcomings faced major defeats in Congress, although he did make some progress by using executive orders (EOs) (e.g., on integrating the military) or the courts to push his agenda. As Truman's successor, Eisenhower had notable successes in some domestic policy areas, but his actions were largely reactive in nature on civil rights (Parrett, 2000).[7] Eisenhower's successor, John Kennedy, supported civil rights after television showed the brutal reaction to the movement to peacefully integrate the South led by Dr. Martin Luther King. However, he initially saw more aggressive legislative action as a threat to his reelection chances in 1964.

On the heels of Kennedy's assassination in 1963, his successor, Lyndon Johnson, seized an opening in the political opportunity structure to create the single greatest assault on black ascriptive hierarchy and poverty since Lincoln. Following up on US Supreme Court decisions (e.g., *Baker v. Carr* in 1962 and *Reynolds v. Sims* in 1964) to reduce the power of rural representation in state legislatures, Johnson pushed successfully for enactment of the Civil Rights Act of 1964 and the Voting Rights Act of 1965. In terms of the Voting Rights Act, Johnson accurately predicted (actually understated) how the previously solid Democratic South would be lost to Democrats for at least a generation—and, with it, support for federal government activism.

Johnson also turned aggressively to enacting what he called a War on Poverty as part of his Great Society project. In the process, and with large Democratic Party majorities in Congress, he established administratively run programs in areas such as community development, education, medical care (the creation of Medicaid and Medicare), rural poverty, transportation, and urban decay (e.g., the Model Cities Program). Created were over 400 categorical grant programs to address these needs, a presumed fulfillment of Herbert Croly's early progressive agenda. Johnson's philosophy was straightforward: it should not matter where a person is born or lives to enjoy basic human rights.

****

Johnson's Great Society efforts had four important dimensions that account for the further amplification of the compensatory state, the IRP, and conservative challenges to it. First, most programs were not developed within federal agencies. Johnson was acutely aware of bureaucratic inertia in federal agencies after his decades in Congress and did not trust local and state governments that had condoned or enacted racist policies. So, he turned to private foundations, universities, and, especially, social scientists to compensate for these inadequacies by developing most of his Great Society initiatives (Aaron, 1978; Califano, 1991; Caro, 2012).

This was but a further amplification of the legitimacy of social science-based research underway since the late 19th century, one actively sought out by social scientists and their associations (Aaron, 1978). Indeed, prior to the Johnson presidency, even President Kennedy had (erringly) echoed in an address at Yale University the progressives' dream of turning political questions into administrative ones:

> The fact of the matter is that most of [the nation's] problems, or at least many of them, that we now face are technical problems, are administrative problems. They are very sophisticated judgements which do not

lend themselves to the great sort of 'passionate movements' [of earlier eras] . . . they deal with questions which are beyond the comprehension of most men.

(p. 167, n. 1)

During the Great Society, social scientists offered programs often derived from quantitative- and econometric-based research, the conscious focus of private foundation funding since the early 20th century (see Chapter 5). In the process, a flood of research and program evaluation money was appropriated legislatively to government and independent researchers in universities. Indeed, Great Society legislation typically required that certain percentages of appropriations for programs be spent on researching these topics (Aaron, 1978, p. 170, n. 14).

At the same time, and not unlike at the dawn of the 20th century, a new class of professionals arose. This class, however, was comprised of a surge of baby boomers obtaining PhDs in the social sciences. Much like those earlier professionals who became the backbone of the Progressive movement, these research-oriented PhDs and their professional associations became vital electoral constituencies promoting increased spending for federally funded social science research (e.g., the National Science Foundation, the National Institutes of Health, and the Department of Defense). This, as a sincere (i.e., expressive) belief in the application of social science research to address society's problems combined with "publish-or-perish" university incentive structures.

Although progress was made in many areas (e.g., Head Start and Great Society program alumni who went on to elective office in the nation), the War on Poverty was framed by conservative business and noted intellectual conservatives (such as political scientists Edward Banfield and his student James Q. Wilson) as largely a failure and an insult to American exceptionalist values. Other experts sometimes characterized the utility of statistically based social science as unhelpful to practice and confusing to average citizens. These critics even included leading practitioners of this approach—most notably, the prominent program evaluation expert Peter Rossi and leading economist Henry Aaron of the Brookings Institution.

Donald Kettl (2009) compellingly argues that the shift from "hard" policy aims (e.g., building infrastructure) to "soft" social policy goals (e.g., ending poverty), where demonstrating short-term benefits is nearly impossible, contributed to this backlash. Less acknowledged by the field, however, was mention of the otherwise positive role that social scientists played in helping to expand the policy agenda to these types of questions as the Rights Revolution unfolded (see below). But, Aaron (1978) argued:

Social scientists, in emulation of physical scientists and mathematicians, seek simplicity and "elegance," though the question whether

the problems of social science *can* be solved elegantly remains unanswered. . . . In order [to reach these goals], problems are separated into
[distinct] components that can be managed and understood. Such
abstraction produces theory, apparently detached from reality, that
often provokes the layman's scorn [and undermines the legitimacy of
the enterprise].

(p. 156)

Rossi (1987) went so far as to introduce what he called the paradoxes of policy
and program evaluation. He offered two laws of the social science enterprise. The
first was an "iron law of evaluation" stating that the "expected value of any net
impact assessment of any large-scale social program is zero" (p. 4). The second—
or "stainless steel law of evaluation"—was that the "better designed the impact
assessment of a social program, the more likely is the resulting estimate of net
impact to be zero" (p. 4). Thus, the better the research design of the evaluation,
the less likely researchers would find positive program effects.

Still others argued that precisely because of the complexity and interdependency of social life that social scientists since the mid-19th century had given as
their rationale for authority, the idea of focusing on independent variables was a
fool's errand (Lindblom, 1977). Meanwhile, others joined Aaron (1978) in his
claim that "research and experimentation would detect the failures (of policies
and programs) but have no way to indicate the hypothetical potential success"
(pp. 156–157) (see more below).

Nevertheless, the growing dominance of statistical and econometric analyses
continued. This, not only because modeling improved understanding but also
because of the path dependency established by the corporate–social science nexus
of interests in America and their links to both government and business. It was
also supported by political rationality. President Nixon, in fact, saw program
evaluation as a way to *discredit* Great Society programs and to pave the way for
reducing or ending them. He promoted these methods, knowing how difficult
it would be to show success in the short term and the likelihood that conflicting
results would reduce the authority of experts.

A second adverse administrative result of the Great Society that cried out for
reform was the complex bureaucratic implementation structures it created in
amplifying earlier renditions of the compensatory state (Hjern & Porter, 1981).
For starters, a new component of the compensatory state was added in the hope
of advancing the SRP: the channeling of some money directly to community
action groups to get around state and local government resistance. Despite some
notable accomplishments, this effort bred political conflict and accountability
problems. Waste, fraud, and abuse charges mounted, as did critiques of program performance. More broadly, intergovernmental relations (IGR) programs
not only created greater administrative complexity but also amplified a vast

expansion of subsystem politics. These subsystems of actors both surrounded programs at the federal level and created "vertical" subsystems of interests that stretched from Washington to the states and, more frequently, to localities. This arrangement was dubbed "picket-fence federalism" (Sanford, 1967).

By the late 1970s, critics claimed that driving policymaking in these vertical subsystems was a professional–bureaucratic complex specific to each policy area (e.g., health, housing, and transportation), one that left elected officials and nonexperts out of the deliberative and allocative processes (Beer, 1978; Wright, 1990). The horizontal slats in the picket fence were elected officials at various levels of government who had difficulty coordinating grants across different policy areas and who felt excluded from the vertical professional–bureaucratic complex. Basically, bureaucratic and policy experts in various policy areas holding similar professional values developed rules and regulations and pushed grant money to their bureaucratic counterparts to support them in state and local agencies. Federal agencies had a perverse incentive to push the grant monies as fast, far, and strategically as they could to maintain or increase political support for their agencies. Meanwhile, state and local bureaucracies in the compensatory state were pushed both to pursue grants to address citizen needs and because grants were inaccurately viewed by many citizens as "free money" from the federal government.

Also expanding were the inflexibility and subnational costs of the rules and unfunded mandates placed on grant recipients (e.g., the need to create plans before receiving funds) (Robertson, 2012). Moreover, many states and localities began excoriating federal IGR programs as "unfunded mandates" when Congress pushed the costs of financing their programs to states and localities. These problems brought calls for consolidating grants during the Nixon, Gerald Ford (D-MI), and Jimmy Carter (D-GA) administrations, yet only a few were consolidated (e.g., the Community Development Block Grant). This, because of resistance from subsystem actors at all levels of government. Among other more laudable reasons, they feared a loss of access and influence if block grants were established. Meanwhile, cries of inequities in grant funding increased between larger and smaller cities and towns, further exacerbating historical urban–rural rifts. Small and more rural jurisdictions lacked the resources to hire skillful grant writers, thus giving larger urban areas greater ability to obtain grants (see, e.g., Pressman & Wildavsky, 1984; Radin & Posner, 2010; Robertson, 2012).

A third ramification of Great Society programs was the grist that academic researchers gave to conservative critics of activist government. During the 1970s, many qualitative researchers studying the implementation of these programs found large gaps between their promises and the results they produced (Hill & Hupe, 2014; O'Toole, 1986; see more on the implementation literature in Chapter 7).[8] They argued that federal grant programs erred by, in effect, treating states and localities as mere administrative extensions of the federal government

(Elmore, 1979–1980). Thus, the top-down and bureaucratically driven implementation regimes they imposed were compliance-based; deviations from federal procedures were called "failures" (Derthick, 1972; Elmore, 1978, 1979–1980; Rein & Rabinovitz, 1977).

This approach failed to consider how local circumstances differed and, thus, required procedural changes to make programs work. It also failed to acknowledge that if governments vigorously implemented every law on the books, they would easily go bankrupt. As such, state and local governments set priorities that varied by political party, and they made tradeoffs among programs. As one leading scholar put it, subnational governments engaged in "portfolio management," investing heavily in some programs but not in others depending on local circumstances and power structures (Elmore, 1985).

Nonetheless, what sociologists Paul DiMaggio and Walter Powell (1983) call "institutional isomorphism" or "institutional mimesis" also occurred in subnational governments in the compensatory state. Researchers found that federal administrative structures, processes, and approaches were replicated at the state and local levels without concern for effectiveness or success. Indeed, "bureaucratization and other forms of [organizational] homogenization emerge[d] . . . [as part of a] process . . . effected largely by *the state and the professions, which have become the great rationalizers of the second half of the twentieth century*" (p. 147, emphasis added). This happened partly to show that jurisdictions were applying "best practices" in their organizations and, thus, buttress perceptions of their legitimacy. It also was done so agencies at different levels of government would know who to contact at other levels and help interest groups identify where to concentrate their lobbying efforts. Replication also was done in reaction to grant regulations requiring, for example, the aforementioned creation of regional planning agencies to produce comprehensive plans (a major component of the IRP).

A final aspect of the questioning of Great Society programs was the travails of implementing their SRP-based legislative mandates for "maximum feasible participation" of citizens. Not only was this an ambiguous term, but many state and local implementers saw it as costly and a luxury to pursue. They merely went through the motions, exhibiting the pentimento effect. Participation was viewed as a "contextual" goal (Wilson, 1989) or "non-mission-based value" (Baehler, Liu, & Rosenbloom, 2014). Typically, such efforts also were largely underfunded. Even in cities where participatory efforts succeeded, they were usually "temporary," one-off initiatives rather than institutionalized in agency operations and cultures. They also often lacked a demographically representative group of participants (i.e., racially and socioeconomically).

Experts also took advantage of laypersons' lack of substantive and procedural knowledge by engaging in a "decide, announce, and defend" strategy void of meaningful citizen deliberation (Durant, 2007; Ingram & Smith, 1993; Kerwin et al., 2010; Lee, McQuarrie, & Walker, 2015; Musso, Weare, Bryer, & Cooper,

2011; Nabatchi, 2010; Soss, Hacker, & Mettler, 2007). Those who continued to have the most influence in agency deliberations were established subsystem members. Once again in American history, researchers found that businesses' "preferred place" in American politics was amplified in public agency decision making and administration (Hacker & Pierson, 2010; Lindblom, 1977, 1990; Phillips-Fein & Zelizer, 2012; Smith, 2000; Schlozman, Verba, & Brady, 2012).[9]

****

Although the aforementioned attacks on government activism and the federal bureaucracy from the Right marinated in the 1960s, attacks from the extreme Left also impugned public agencies—and the IRP more generally. With Johnson's decision in 1967 to impose a 6-percent surcharge on income and corporate taxes to help pay for the Vietnam War, popular disaffection with the conflict grew. And despite enactment of the Civil Rights Act of 1964 and the Voting Rights Act of 1965, so, too, did anger grow among inner-city minorities and proponents of activist government. Like earlier progressives, their hopes for the Great Society were dashed as war funding cut into domestic programs. And with deaths and casualties mounting (especially among working-class youths not attending college), antiwar demonstrations spiraled across the country. So, too, did riots by blacks in major US cities, as well as activism by both the nascent LGBTQ+ (e.g., the 1969 Stonewall riots) and women's movements. These were accompanied by political assassinations (Senator Robert F. Kennedy [D-NY] and Dr. Martin Luther King). After Johnson withdrew from the 1968 presidential race, these helped propel the more conservative Republican Richard Nixon to victory, running on a platform of "law and order" and a "secret plan" to end the Vietnam War.

More generally, however, young New Left activists railed against established authority structures generally, as well as social taboos (e.g., contraception—the pill—promised "copulation without population" (Kirk, 1993) and delay in child-bearing for women). Recall that, except for the Roaring 20s, earlier cultural shifts in America incorporated the tenets of faculty psychology. Their focus was on individual self-development (meaning the triumph of reason over emotions and passion) leading to the benefit of society's development. In part, the countercultural movement of the 1960s was no different. But, this time, the focus was centered on how the bureaucracy (public and private), technocracy, and scientism thwarted self-development and societal development. Thus, unlike cultural conservatives such as Russell Kirk (1993) who trusted in tradition rather than scientism to bring wisdom, the New Left attacked both.

A vocal mass of Americans believed that America's commercial republic had morphed into a plutocracy of elites who ran the world to the detriment of citizens of all nations. These elites had started immoral wars—namely, Vietnam—on false premises and for economic gains. Moreover, the United States had created bureaucracies of nameless, faceless bureaucrats guided by scientism. In the Pentagon, for example, Secretary of Defense Robert McNamara and his aides applied quantitative systems analyses to gain a power advantage over their more numeracy-challenged colleagues (see more below). They also used flawed measures of America's progress in the war (e.g., body counts) and issued rules and regulations that individually and cumulatively were mind-numbingly complex to average citizens. Administrative systems were difficult to navigate, geared toward marginalizing citizens, and insufficiently grounded in social equity. William McLoughlin (1978) encapsulates the discontent of the 1960s' countercultural movement as the turning point in challenging the IRP adopted by earlier progressives in their millenarian quest to escape history.

Although leaders of this countercultural movement saw power as the ultimate reality, they still embraced the Enlightenment's conceit regarding the linear perfectibility of humankind and nation as reason developed. In effect, they inaptly saw the human mind as a blank slate untethered to biological and evolutionary constraints and, thus, infinitely malleable (Pinker, 2002). Bourgeois societal conventions were the root of the problem. Some of the more extreme elements in the movement (e.g., the Weathermen) even embraced Richard Niebuhr's contention that "if a season of violence can establish a just social system and can create the possibilities of its preservation, there is no purely ethical ground upon which violence and revolution can be ruled out" (McLoughlin, 1978, p. 182).

For others in the countercultural movement, however, "aggressive nonviolence" was the road to personal and national growth. Their views were spelled out in the Port Huron Statement (PHS) of the Students for a Democratic Society in 1962 (revised in 1964).[10] Led, among others, by Tom Hayden and grounded in the Frankfurt School arguments of Theodor Adorno and Herbert Marcuse (see more below), the PHS identified the key issues of the times as apathy, the decline of hope in human and societal progress, racism, and oppressive bureaucracies and technocracies that supported existing authority structures. As Michael Kazin (2012) of the magazine *Dissent* writes in critiquing the internal inconsistency of the statement, the authors held, first, the "romantic desire for achieving an authentic self through crusading for individual rights and, second, the yearning for a democratic socialist order that would favor the collective good over freedom of the self" (p. 50). The latter, despite the reality that democracy and socialism are conceptually (and practically) incompatible, with the former grounded in individualism and the latter in bureaucratic collectivism (Hayek, 1944).

Basically, the PHS called for "participatory democracy" in SRP-informed ways. It was reminiscent of earlier calls by settlement women of the early 20th century and, later, Ordway Teed and David Lilienthal. It also helped inform the "New Public Administration" movement (see more below) and, more recently, the "argumentative turn" in the policy sciences (see Chapter 7). Participatory democracy was "based on listening to local people and taking action on behalf of their demands. Listening and speaking in clear vernacular English [rather than bureaucratise] was crucial" (Kazin, 2012). Moreover, participatory democracy—albeit unclearly defined—was envisioned in economic, community, and foreign policy, as was decentralization of policymaking and administration to communities and neighborhoods. Participatory democracy, in turn, would advance the psychic development of citizens, much as Woodrow Wilson had claimed in 1887 and that Jane Addams and the "efficient citizen" movement did in the early 20th century.

The PHS also called for cleansing conservative elements from the Democratic Party to make it one of the tools for social advancement in the United States, along with a revitalization of the union movement. Contending that unions were the "most liberal—and most frustrated—institution in mainstream America," the statement sought to renew unions' original idealism in fighting corporate America. It also encouraged unions to affiliate with blacks to advance racial justice (Kazin, 2012). Finally, the New Left saw universities as a "base for their assault upon the loci of power" (Kazin, 2012).

Arguing that the "civil rights and peace and student movements are too poor and socially slighted, and the labor movement too quiescent," the authors (much as earlier progressives such as Herbert Croly) saw universities as holding a "permanent position of social influence" (Kazin, 2012). They also were the "only mainstream institution that is open to participation by individuals of nearly any viewpoint." Most needed were "national efforts at university reform by an alliance of students and faculty" who "must wrest control of the educational process from the administrative bureaucracy." This alliance had to partner with external groups to integrate "major public issues into the curriculum" and to "make debate and controversy center on social ills." Such rhetoric, again, will be familiar to contemporary readers.

Public trust in government further waned during the 1970s, stimulated, first, by the forced resignation of President Nixon due to the Watergate scandal. Nor did the end of the gold standard, introduction of floating exchange rates, and use of the US dollar as the world's major reserve currency help by buttressing inflationary forces and prompting international backlash (Gilpin, 1987). Next came two Arab oil embargoes (1973 and 1979), the first during the Nixon presidency and the second during the Carter presidency (1977–1981). Both created gasoline shortages for automobiles, raised energy costs enormously, and helped produce double-digit inflation and unemployment that Keynesian economic theory said was impossible. Americans grew more dispirited when Iranian students stormed the US embassy and held dozens of Americans hostage for 444 days. As Chapter 7 will elaborate further, sown were the intellectual and emotional foundations for the next phase of American administrative reform in the 1980s under President Reagan.

****

Stimulated partially by arguments such as those put forward by the extreme Left and Right—as well as mounting social unrest—the 1960s and 1970s witnessed the development of the aforementioned Rights Revolution in America. Enacted were "goals" rather than "rules" statutes (Schoenbrod, 1983) that addressed such things as civil rights, physical and mental disabilities, gender biases, abortion, birth control, interracial marriage, environmental protection, labor rights, access to public housing, due process in criminal and administrative procedures, gay rights, and erosion of the doctrine of sovereign immunity (Epps, 1998).

As Orren and Skowronek (2017) argue, the US Constitution had originally been crafted as a "containment structure" to ensure limited government (see Chapter 4). But as the Rights Revolution proceeded, a needed—seemingly insatiable—demand for government to respond to problems amplified. In the process, this institutional framework became an "opportunity" structure for liberal and conservative policy entrepreneurs to pursue their policy ends legislatively, judicially, and administratively. But again, all this set the stage for a conservative backlash in the late 1970s and beyond against the courts and federal agencies (see, e.g., Glenn & Teles, 2009; Toobin, 2008; Zelizer, 2012).

Initially, the courts in the 1970s became the "most aggressive of the three branches in opening new pathways" for rights expression (Orren and Skowronek, 2017, p. 115). This, as a spiraling number of liberal activist groups formed and began petitioning Congress and the courts for protection of claimed individual rights when supportive legislative majorities could not be garnered (Berry, 1999). Similar dynamics soon ensued at the state and local government levels of the compensatory state.

Importantly, many of the rights the Supreme Court identified (e.g., the right to privacy) were not specifically enumerated in the Constitution's Bill of Rights (itself premised on the British Declaration of Rights of 1689). But they were inferred by the Supreme Court as necessary for realizing them in the modern era. Best illustrating this "living" or "organic" view of the Constitution was the Supreme Court's decision identifying a right to marital privacy regarding the use of contraceptives in *Griswold v. Connecticut* (1965). Writing for the majority, Justice William O. Douglas stated (in words ridiculed by conservatives for their abstractness) that "specific guarantees in the Bill of Rights have penumbras, formed by emanations from those guarantees that help give them life and substance. Various guarantees create zones of privacy" (Toobin, 2008, p. 64).[11] Judicial decisions like this sparked conservative outrage that endures to this day, especially when the Court used it to declare bans against abortion unconstitutional in *Roe v. Wade* (1973).[12] As conservative jurist Robert Bork put it, the right to privacy "does not come out of the Constitution but is forced into it. . . . This is not legal reasoning but fiat" (p. 65).

Part and parcel of the Rights Revolution was the "new social regulation" (Lilley & Miller, 1977) introduced in the 1960s and 1970s. The regulatory aims of early progressive reformers and their New Deal heirs was to regulate *and* promote the development of single industries within their legal purview. But the new social regulatory agencies (e.g., the Environmental Protection Agency, the Equal Employment Opportunity Commission, the Occupational Safety and Health Administration, and the Consumer Protection Bureau in the Federal Trade Commission) focused solely on the regulation of discrimination violations, environmental protection, health and safety, and consumer protection. Moreover, their regulatory purview cut across industries and all types of employees and customers, including the behavior of other public agencies (Durant, 1985; Konisky & Teodoro, 2016; Wilson & Rachal, 1977).

Forged was a new kind of iron triangle, this time comprised of agency experts, the press (often informed by social science research), and the courts. Some saw a "new partnership" emerging among liberal interest groups, activist agency officials, and congressional committee staff (Melnick, 1985). Staff purportedly put expansive government language into lengthy legislative reports that liberal activist judges would find to support their policy agendas when legislation was challenged.

Meanwhile, Supreme Court clerks graduating from Ivy League and other top law schools brought an activist liberal agenda to their role in helping judges to winnow through prospective rights appeals for review (i.e., for certiorari). Such rights-conscious justices as William Brennan and, later, Sandra Day O'Connor put it to their clerks as follows: "Find us some good cases!" (Toobin, 2008, p. 252). And find them they did, including cases that riled social conservatives even more. In the 1960s and 1970s, these included not only *Roe v. Wade* (1973) but also cases banning official state prayer in schools as violations of the establishment clause in *Engel v. Vitale* (1962); requiring that arrested persons be read their rights under the 5th Amendment in *Miranda v. Arizona* (1966); requiring due process before ending a welfare recipient's benefits in *Goldberg v. Kelly* (1970); and supporting affirmative action (while rejecting racial quotas and granting Bakke's admission) in *Regents of the University of California v. Bakke* (1978).

The Rights Revolution and the new social regulation were profound for public agencies. A shift of power occurred within agencies from program experts to legal experts, as well as a transfer of resources from some programs to others based on court consent degrees (O'Leary, 1993). This further judicialized administration and heightened risk aversion among agency personnel (Wilson, 1989). It also produced public law litigation in which public institutions (e.g., school districts) were placed under the administration of judges for violating persons' rights (Chayes, 1976; Wise & Christensen, 2005).

Agency rulemaking was also affected by the Rights Revolution and the new social regulation. As Richard Stewart (1988) argues, "faced with the necessity of regulating very large numbers of firms, agencies shifted from case-by-case adjudication to adoption of highly specific regulations of general application" (p. 107). In turn, the "large numbers of firms and industries affected, and the conflicts of interests among them, made negotiated solutions more difficult" (p. 107). Informal rulemaking also displaced "political decision-making mechanisms with bureaucratic and technocratic ones," thus further marginalizing unorganized interests (p. 108).

Perhaps most profoundly, however, legislatures and the courts amplified pressures on agencies in the compensatory state to become progressively more synoptic (i.e., rational–comprehensive) in their rulemaking in order to pass judicial scrutiny. They demanded wider "evidentiary and disciplinary bases" for rulemaking that involved consideration of a "broader range of social impacts" (Orren & Skowronek, 2017, p. 157). These demands were complemented by corporate business pressures on agencies to support their regulatory rulemaking with greater amounts of research and to have that research peer reviewed by independent researchers. Thus began the proliferation of outside expert advisory panels—including for both the natural sciences and the social sciences.

Almost immediately, gaming of the composition of advisory boards began and remains today. Quite quickly, progressives' conceit that the scientific method was objective and could resolve disputes without politics and emotions proved impractical (again) in practice. Debates often centered on what constitutes "good science." Agencies issuing regulations were expected to act expeditiously, often because of justiciable statutory deadlines for action. They thus looked for science that was "good enough" to support their actions. In contrast, advisory board members from the sciences were more cautious and tended to have more rigorous standards and broader bases of research. At times, this desire was prompted by tenets of good academic science; at others, it was induced by industry-linked advisors seeking to delay or stop agency regulations. But, more broadly, gaming consisted of getting members on these advisory boards whose research records supported the policy agendas of various interests. The same occurred as government "in-and-outers" (Heclo, 1977) from the social sciences became identified with particular policy positions (e.g., Keynesians versus monetarists and pro-regulatory versus deregulatory economists). Thus, it became relatively easy to identify advisory board candidates who would support various policy preferences.

****

Unquestionably, social scientists applying scientific methodology and involved (directly or indirectly) in the Rights Revolution during the 1960s and 1970s certainly benefited professionally from the ratcheting up of the IRP in agencies and in the courts. But some social science research called into question the validity of the IRP itself, as well as the early progressives' vision of objective, expertise-based administration. Nor was this surprising. Findings on the same topic often differ over time. Moreover, they use varying data and methodologies, are subject to rival interpretations of findings, and differ in controlling contextual and contingency factors (see, e.g., Walker & Andrews, 2015).

This chapter has already noted the later critiques of researchers such as Aaron, Rossi, and the first generation of implementation researchers. In addition, some researchers questioned the Great Society itself and often used scientific methodology to do so. By the late 1960s, such prominent sociologists as Daniel Bell and Nathan Glazer saw the New Deal as part of an important social contract but viewed the Great Society as a distortion of New Deal principles. They also questioned its merits for overstating the ability of government to bring about massive behavioral change among human beings. Although not supporting the views of the Austrian School, they saw the New Deal as focusing on equal opportunity, while claiming that the Great Society focused on equality of outcome (a charge also leveled by critics of the social equity movement, nationally and in public administration).

To encourage the application of social scientific methodology to the study of Great Society programs, Bell and Glazer joined Irving Kristol in founding the journal *The Public Interest*. Contributors to the journal typically found that Great Society programs had created "unintended consequences," "negative externalities," and "perverse incentives" to work and strive for self-development and advancement, as well as "nonmarket failures." They were joined by social democrats and Marxist scholars such as Francis Fox Piven and Richard Cloward (1993), who contended that the expert bureaucracies running these programs were more concerned about their own interests than their clients' needs. They also joined conservatives in claiming that these programs and agencies created a "culture of dependency" among clients.

Others in sociology (as well as in the arts, cultural studies, literature, and philosophy) pursued neo-Marxist perspectives in the post-Cold War era, especially critical theory derived from the Frankfurt School in Germany. Members of the Frankfurt School (e.g., Theodor Adorno, Jürgen Habermas, Martin Heidegger, Max Horkheimer, and Herbert Marcuse), albeit with differences in perspectives among them, tried to understand why Marxism did not become a rallying cry for the proletariat as Marx predicted. Marx, they concluded, had overlooked the power of culture to create a "false consciousness" among citizens in which they did not see the oppressive reality of their lives accurately. Moreover, they argued that the oppressive power of capitalism, the corporate-dominated media, and bureaucracy shaped citizens' false consciousness (see more in Chapter 7). The task of theory was to "emancipate" persons by stripping away what Marxist philosopher Antonio Gramsci earlier called the "hegemony" of cultural metanarratives supporting the status quo. These were framed by, and made citizens subservient to, market, bureaucratic, and patriarchal hierarchies.

Grounded sometimes in the epistemology of phenomenology founded by Edmund Husserl, the postmodern heirs of the Frankfurt School of this period were explicitly normative in their aims, challenging the fact–value dichotomy of the social sciences. They also argued that interdisciplinary research was necessary to understand social phenomena better, thus, for example, linking philosophy and history to the social sciences in ways anathema to the wishes and specialization of the social sciences. Most also revived earlier critiques of the scientific method for its atomism (independent variables made little sense in an interdependent world), its instrumentalism, and its images of a mathematically calculable social world. Nor, in terms of democracy, should instrumental rationality be the focus of the social sciences. Rather, an SRP-based "communicative rationality" should be the focus to determine how to ensure that all perspectives are heard. Moreover, most of these heirs of early critical theory saw globalization requiring a readjustment of institutions and of public spaces "to ensure self-consciously constructed publics of relevant stakeholders [can] act as 'mini-publics' that are empowered to deliberate and make decisions" in transnational settings (Bohman, 2016) (see more in Chapter 7).

Likewise, elite theory gained a stronghold on some social scientists' thinking as early as the 1950s and 1960s. According to sociologist C. Wright Mills (1956), and as Eisenhower and Lasswell had earlier predicted, a power elite existed that consisted of the military, corporations, and political elites (also see Bachrach & Baratz, 1962; Domhoff, 2018; Parenti, 2010). Although contested as empirically unverifiable by many pluralists in political science and as masking a true reality of plural elites, elite theory and critical theory also eventually found their way into public administration scholarship and often yielded important but critical perspectives regarding public agencies (e.g., see Adams & Balfour, 1998, as well as scholarship by members of the Public Administration Theory Network).

At the same time, the "social turn" in the natural and social sciences that had begun with the works of Michael Polanyi (1958) and, later, Thomas Kuhn (2012) questioned both the mechanical view of the scientific method and the objectivity of the scientific enterprise. Their aim was not to reject scientific methodology but to portray more accurately how it worked. They argued that a linear view of scientific development was empirically inaccurate. Science was a "socially based enterprise that [did] not rely on empiricism and reason alone, but on social communities, behavioral norms, and personal commitments" (Nye, 2011, p. xvi).

Meanwhile, political scientists studying bureaucratic discretion in the 1950s and 1960s concluded that "iron triangles," more so than objective expertise, were driving policymaking in agencies. This, although, as illustrated in previous chapters, these relationships had been present, worrisome, and sometimes corrupt since the nation's founding. As then Attorney General Richard Olney had understood in regard to the creation of the Interstate Commerce Commission in 1887, and Woodrow Wilson had originally predicted more broadly in 1912, they developed among regulatory agencies, interest groups, and the legislative committees overseeing them (e.g., Freeman, 1965; Lowi, 1969; Redford, 1969).

Beginning in the late 1970s, however, political science and public administration research support began waning for the iron triangle as a driver of the dynamics of public agencies in the compensatory state. Hugh Heclo (2013) described the iron triangle as "not so much wrong as disastrously incomplete" in explaining bureaucratic dynamics. More accurate was the image of "issue networks" of actors on various sides of policy issues who were more motivated by normative than material stakes than were members of iron triangles. This made compromise among actors more difficult and sometimes impossible. It also made it easier to create a perception of policy disagreement, uncertainty, and confusion among experts, thus further stymying consensus building and questioning government activism.

Heclo also argued that the legitimacy of the career bureaucracy in government suffered from these dynamics. The prior influence of midlevel public managers in closed subsystem politics was reduced significantly. *Policy* knowledge, rather than *administrative* skill, was now much more valued by elected officials. Moreover, public agencies no longer had a monopoly on that expertise because of the growing number of experts in policy think tanks and consultants. Importantly, that monopoly had been a major part of their legitimacy.

Heclo further argued that "technopols" now dominated the American political system. These were "policy politicians" and "entrepreneurs" working in universities and think tanks—plus the media, interest groups, congressional staffs, associations, and other nongovernmental organizations. Based on their shared knowledge, continuing policy agendas developed that were very difficult for elected officials to penetrate, redirect, or change. Also, because of their narrow expertise, technopols contributed to a "stovepiping" of perspectives on policies. This, in combination with the aforementioned picket-fence federalism, made it difficult to coordinate and manage across policy arenas. Moreover, technopols had negative implications for the SRP and democratic administration: the

> trouble is that only a small minority of citizens, even of those who are seriously attentive to public affairs, are likely to be mobilized in the various networks. . . [while the] sophisticated claims and counterclaims [of experts got] to the point that the non-specialist [became] inclined to concede everything and believe nothing that he hears.
> (Heclo, 2013, pp. 74–75)

Meanwhile, some researchers in public administration decided that progressives' focus on the pursuit of economy, efficiency, and effectiveness (the so-called "3 Es") was misguided and needed to be reformed. They saw the 3 Es as metanarratives that only advantaged society's elites. This New Public Administration movement was midwifed by Dwight Waldo at Syracuse University's Minnowbrook Conference in 1968 during the Vietnam War (Marini, 1971). The "Young Turks" in attendance expressed various views, but a dominant theme emerged: the link between democracy and bureaucracy was malfunctioning in government. Moreover, public managers and academics were enablers of this disconnect.

In the late 1940s, legendary academics—such as Paul Appleby, John Gaus, Norton Long, Herbert Simon, and Waldo (like Herring in the mid-1930s)—had already challenged the politics/policy–administration dichotomy of the early progressives (see Svara, 2001, for a more nuanced view of the dichotomy). Their experiences serving in government agencies during World War II convinced them that politics was integral to public administration. Moreover, policymaking was shifting to the executive branch, meaning that politics would flow to wherever bureaucratic discretion was exercised. As Long (1949) famously wrote, "power is the lifeblood of administration. Its acquisition, maintenance, increase, and dissipation [by agencies] is something that students and practitioners ignore at their peril" (p. 257). To survive and be effective in a Madisonian system where no central authority exists and presidential attention to their efforts is episodic, agencies have to build "horizontal power" bases with interest groups. Still, Long saw the competition among programs and agencies as real and a way to coordinate the bureaucracy (much as had earlier Jacksonians).

Due to the social conflicts of the 1960s, most participants in the Minnowbrook Conference went a step further by declaring that social equity—not efficiency—should be the central animating premise of public administrators. They not only joined Waldo in arguing that efficiency was a normative (rather than objective) term for guiding their actions, but they also noted that administrators who couched their arguments in efficiency often used it to avoid questions of social justice. As such, they were co-conspirators, in effect, against the disadvantaged in society and, thus, violated John Rawls' (1971) definition of social justice. Most also agreed that citizen participation in agency decision making was vital for democracy. And if agencies were constrained from offering citizens direct participation, administrators should become advocates for them within agencies. Not all in public administration agreed with this assessment, with Victor Thompson (1975) speaking for some in warning that public administrators' imposing a single value—or any values—lacking democratic–constitutional legitimation was an effort to foil popular sovereignty. Since then, a focus on social equity has been touted as one of the "three pillars" of public administration (along with economy and efficiency), especially in the 21st century (see, e.g., Svara & Brunet, 2005). However, that privileged status is still challenged by some on normative, conceptual ambiguity, and practical grounds (Durant & Rosenbloom, 2017; Rosenbloom, 2005).

Relatedly, another critique of the administrative reformers' IRP approach from within political science was offered by Vincent Ostrom (2008) in his classic, *The Intellectual Crisis in American Public Administration*. Ostrom not only critiqued the incongruity of the IRP approach with the Constitution but also alleged the vacuity of one-best-way administrative reforms. In this, he joined Herbert Simon's (1997) earlier charge that the principles of administration were no more than proverbs. Instead, the problems one sought to address determined the type of organizational structure needed (McGinnis & Ostrom, 2012). Contesting the centralization in Washington and government consolidation movements pushed by progressives in metropolitan areas in the compensatory state, Ostrom argued for what Catholicism calls *subsidiarity*. Responsibility for various social problems should be delegated to the lowest level of government capable of handling them. Moreover, jurisdictional boundaries should fit the scope of the problem and advance economies of scale, a structural nod to the IRP.

Ostrom also critiqued public administration reformers' resistance to overlap and duplication, as per the principles of administration. These principles violated practical necessity and the nation's democratic principles. In grounding his administrative reform prescriptions in the principles of subsidiarity, polycentrism, and public choice theory, Ostrom offered "democratic administration" as an alternative vision of administrative reform. However, because of his prescriptions' grounding in public choice theory (borrowed from economics), many of his intellectual heirs in that school inaccurately saw citizens only as rationally self-interested consumers of public services (McGinnis & Ostrom, 2012). Citizens shared no explicit role in making policy decisions. Their participation would come indirectly through the public service "packages" and levels they chose as "shoppers" using such tools as education vouchers. Moreover, and in contrast to much earlier public administration thinking, the public interest was grounded in the methodological individualism of the Austrian School—i.e., it could be discerned by adding up individual preferences and ignoring the direct roles of society and social evolution.

Meanwhile, as the economics profession became more influential in political science and in the public management subfield of public administration, such public choice economists as James Buchanan and Gordon Tullock (1965) portrayed government bureaucrats very negatively. They were self-aggrandizing, utility-maximizing, and risk-averse individuals (also see Chapter 7). They were this way because public agencies were monopoly providers of services and enjoyed the advantage of information asymmetry relative to legislators. Consequently, they could maximize their budgets and the size of their staffs to gain power, regardless of their agency location in the compensatory state. No incentives existed for them to rein in agency growth. Added economist Anthony Downs (1993), public agencies did have personnel who were "statesmen" concerned with doing the right thing. However, civil servants were mostly "conservers" and "climbers" more concerned with their own interests than those of their clients. What is more, conservers eventually took over public agencies as climbers moved to better opportunities, thus making innovation, responsiveness, and flexibility in government agencies extremely difficult to realize.

Finally, noting these trends, some scholars urged a return to the nondelegation doctrine of the courts in the 1930s that overturned New Deal legislation (see Chapter 5). Referring to his prescription for interest group capture of the federal bureaucracy as "juridical democracy," Theodore Lowi (1969) called on the courts to declare unconstitutional any vague, ambiguous, or contradictory statutes that enhanced bureaucratic discretion without giving clear principles for action. Critics charged that juridical democracy was an untenable and unworkable proposition. But Lowi insisted that key decisions made by unelected bureaucrats must be returned to the legislative arena to enhance accountability, a position later taken by strict constructionist and textualist judges.

Together, these social science critiques—plus the recognition that many policy problems were not constrained by political jurisdictions—flipped various tenets of progressivism and the IRP on their heads. Informed by these critiques, many proposed that the public interest was best served by *lowering* expectations about what government agencies should and could do, by cutting back on the number of agencies that had to cooperate to get something done, and by eliminating as much direct delivery of services by public agencies as possible. Government agencies were like greyhounds chasing a mechanical rabbit that they would never catch (Banfield, 1974). Nonetheless, the durability of the IRP—and the relative power over other alternatives of the corporate–social science nexus of technocratic and associationalist interests that embraced and encouraged it—again ensured its embrace by administrative reformers for any remaining downsized public agencies.

****

Faced with these critiques and perplexed by the situation these dynamics presented them, presidents, governors, and mayors in the compensatory state did not merely watch their power to influence bureaucracies wane. Sparked was yet another episode of a coevolution of executive and legislative institutions to regain influence through additional administrative reform predicated on the IRP (Durant, 2015). Much as was done by FDR and Truman before him, and as early 20th-century progressives had tried, President Johnson and his successors sought to centralize policymaking power in the White House to advance their policy agendas. Also like them, they turned to the latest innovations taking place in business. These were innovations that corporations and many social science-based think tanks believed in and were eager to share and profit from through consultancy fees (Rich, 2004; Sheingate, 2016; see more in Chapter 7). Although eroding trust and legitimacy with citizens were major challenges for agencies, reformers eschewed a focus on building legitimacy in favor of one emphasizing bureaucratic control. Once again, they assumed incorrectly that efficiency alone would build legitimacy.

Moreover, as in earlier administrative reform eras, reformers spoke as if political rationality would not affect their plans. They did so, again, while largely ignoring alternative means for influencing bureaucratic behavior offered by others in the social sciences (see below). Moreover, most relied on businesspersons to head reform commissions, and they marginalized public managers from the process. Consistently, as well, their recommendations were offered in an across-the-board fashion applied uniformly to all agencies, regardless of type or function. They were also grounded in the principles of administration that were now widely discredited as inappropriate for organizational environments requiring flexibility, discretion, and innovation—as did most public agencies.

As political scientist Peri Arnold (1998) calculated in 1998, 11 of 14 prior 20th-century presidents tried to reorganize the federal government according to the principles of administration. Although limited success occurred when Congress' approval was not necessary, members of Congress saw most presidential reorganization efforts as assaults on their political turf and fought against or defeated them. By failing to get congressional input (as both Hoover commissions had done in the 1940s and 1950s), reformers ignored a major political reality.[13] Specifically, efforts to reorganize the federal bureaucracy threaten the access and influence established by congressional oversight committees and program clientele. Thus, although chief executives at all levels of government in the compensatory state rationally try to put like functions and program goals together in one agency, legislators focus on the "parts" or programs relevant to their constituents and reelection. Administrative reformers also ignored the by then timeworn reality that reorganizations are disruptive and seldom produce economy and efficiency in the short term—points well appreciated by minimal statists who wanted to cripple agencies.

Reminiscent of FDR, for example, Johnson established two commissions in the 1960s to bring administrative rationality to his Great Society programs. The first recommended pulling together all environment and natural resources programs into a Department of Natural Resources. His second commission recommended creating a Department of Natural Resources and Development, a prescription that Congress similarly ignored. Also rejected were proposals to put related programs together in departments of economic affairs and social services. Undaunted, President Nixon created an Advisory Council on Executive Organization (the Ash Commission). Founded on the principles of administration, the commission unsuccessfully proposed a massive reorganization to combine seven departments (Agriculture, Commerce, Housing and Urban Development, Interior, Labor, Transportation, and Health, Education, and Welfare) into four reconstituted departments. Likewise, President Carter's plans for a massive reorganization were nixed by Congress. Moreover, he wound up *adding* two departments—Education and Energy—partly to satisfy elements of his electoral base and congressional allies.

Also marginalized in comprehensive administrative reform efforts were the SRP-related findings of the human relations school in business and public administration. Although corporations tried to apply this research in their own organizations, they curiously stuck to structural (reorganization and procedural) recommendations when prescribing administrative reforms for government. Since the Hawthorne experiments in the late 1920s and early 1930s, industrial psychologists understood that all organizations have "informal organizations" with profound influence on organizational dynamics (e.g., Roethlisberger & Dickenson, 1939). Regardless of formal structure, informal groups developed, and they could increase or decrease the nature, pace, and motivation to work. In addition, authority was not given to those in hierarchical positions but had to be *earned* from employees. Moreover, understanding the informal group offered ways to motivate employees and even to control them (as critics noted).

From the 1940s through the 1960s, such social scientists as psychologist Abraham Maslow (1943) also argued that top-down control efforts could not motivate organizational subordinates; only appeals to such higher-level needs as self-esteem, employee recognition, and self-actualization could do so. Others such as Douglas McGregor (1960) built on Maslow's work to condemn top-down styles of management (so-called Theory X styles) as counterproductive. They also embraced Maslow's higher-order needs (e.g., for recognition and self-actualization) as having more effect on motivation than structural concerns. Frederick Herzberg (1964) then offered a "two-factor theory" of employee motivation. As noted earlier, Herzberg found that even if organizations allowed employees to attain Maslow's lower-order needs, workers *expected* those needs to be met. Thus, they were not motivated by them to improve their performance. For motivation to occur, organizations had to facilitate employees' attainment of self-actualization (e.g., opportunities for training and increasing employee engagement with the organization).

These theories were subsequently refined by Paul Hersey and Ken Blanchard (1988) and others into "contingency" theories of leadership and motivation. Essentially, management styles had to differ according to various situational and employee characteristics. At the same time, a controversial but widely cited perspective undermining the IRP developed called the "new institutionalism." Its originators, James March and Johan Olsen (1989), argued that, in contrast to the administrative logic of rationality, a "logic of appropriateness" and a "logic of consequentialism" drove organizational arrangements and specified when different logics prevailed in institutional design.

Granted, individual organizational leaders in the compensatory state might—and did—apply these nonstructural administrative reforms within their organizations. However, they could do so only within the dominating and bureaupathology-inducing constraints of IRP-based structural, process, and procedural reforms. What IRP-based approaches such as reorganization did create, however, were images of power for the officials decreeing them (March & Olsen, 1983; Seidman, 1998). In contrast, human relations approaches conveyed an image incompatible with Americans' longstanding conception of leaders, especially business and military leaders. They evoked images of shared authority and, thus, could be stereotyped as effeminate. Real (i.e., "manly") leaders mounted heroic efforts to control organizations through personal charisma and adroit wielding of authority. In the process, the tenets of bureaucratic administration viewing public servants as instruments of political officials—rather than constitutive actors working with them—triumphed again.

****

During this period, structural reforms based on the IRP were accompanied by rationality-based procedural reforms.[14] As in prior efforts, they, too, were largely infused by political considerations and overwhelmed by political rationality. Consider some of the major procedural or process-based administrative reforms instituted by chief executives in the 1960s and 1970s. For example, the Kennedy administration introduced into the Department of Defense the systems-based Planning, Programming, and Budgeting System (PPBS) approach to financial management used in business (West, 2011). This application of PPBS had two aims. The first was to create an objective (i.e., rationally grounded) tool for ranking alternative weapons systems in terms of cost-effectiveness and to think of arms procurement in terms of five-year plans. The second, and more political side, was Secretary of Defense McNamara's desire to bring the Pentagon's weapons procurement system under his control. This system had previously been dominated by the individual military services and their congressional allies.

Although McNamara enjoyed success with the PPBS at the Department of Defense, it was largely inadequate when President Johnson tried to extend it to the social programs of the Great Society. Professionals in these agencies were not familiar with planning and evaluation techniques and were dealing with issues distinctly less well understood than weapons systems. They also were more geared professionally toward providing services to needy individuals, not making choices among them. As such, substantial resistance to the PPBS emerged in these agencies, as well as on Capitol Hill, most especially in the appropriations committees. The latter saw the PPBS as a threat to members' existing subsystem access and influence. They insisted that proposed budgets be sent to them in both the PPBS *and* traditional line-item and program formats. Nor did Congress feel that only the executive branch should set priorities and, thus, circumvent legislative–executive bargaining over them.

Similarly affected by political rationality was the Nixon administration's Management by Objectives (MBO) initiative. Borrowed again from the business sector, MBO required each level of an agency to show how its activities related to the goals of agency leadership. Resources were then allocated in an "objective" way to those activities best aligned with top-level agency goals. In response, and quite simply, program managers and employees rhetorically framed what they—and key actors in their subsystems—wanted done to align them with the already existing goals of the organization. Gaining traction in agencies thus, again, proved elusive for the IRP.

Likewise, zero-based budgeting (ZBB) was developed at Texas Instruments and brought to federal agencies by President Carter. Premised again on systemic IRP-based thinking, ZBB initially called for program managers to start their budget proposals from scratch rather than from existing program bases. They were then to consider what they could do with varying levels of funding. Agency leaders first had to identify decision units—that is, where the basic decisions on program budgets were made—and then identify a program manager to analyze each decision unit in terms of its cost-effectiveness and efficiency. Next, decision packages were ranked by higher-level agency administrators in terms of priority across all units. Those that became high-priority items were submitted for funding and the remaining decision packages discarded. Thus, not unlike PPBS and MBO, ZBB directly challenged the traditional politics of decision making and "incremental budgeting" in agencies at all levels of government in the compensatory state. Not surprisingly, its failure to incorporate political rationality resulted in underperformance.

But the IRP did not end there, as presidents mounted efforts to regain traction for their policy agendas through reform of the personnel process. Eisenhower became president after Democrats FDR and Truman had controlled personnel appointments and blanketed them into the civil service for two decades. To gain leverage for his policy agenda, he sought greater control (i.e., responsive competence) to advance his policy aims in federal agencies by creating Schedule C appointments (Lewis, 2008). Appointees were—and remain today—involved in confidential duties and/or policy advisory roles and include management positions just below the political-appointee level in agencies. Although nominally appointed by agency heads, presidents have regarded Schedule C employees as White House appointments, giving them leverage over the career bureaucracy.

More broadly, Eisenhower's successor (after Kennedy and Johnson)—Richard Nixon—also launched a series of administrative reforms to undermine the constitutive role of federal agencies and to "presidentialize" them. Designed to circumvent a Democratic Congress hostile to his agenda, this strategy became known as the administrative presidency (Aberbach & Rockman, 2000; Durant, 1992, 2009a, 2009b; Maranto, 1993; Nathan, 1983; Waterman, 1989; West, 2006, 2015). Nixon's strategy involved (1) centralizing policymaking authority from key agencies into the White House; (2) having political appointees use their personnel, budgeting, and reorganizational authorities to comport with his policy agenda; and (3) taking unilateral actions (e.g., EOs, presidential signing statements, national security directives, and agency guidance documents) to advance his agenda (e.g., Howell, 2003; Krause & Cohen, 2000; Mayer, 2001; Warber, 2006; Waterman, 2009). No longer content to shift policymaking from the legislature into the executive branch as early progressives were, now presidents wanted to shift major executive branch decisions into the White House.

Nixon also tried to presidentialize and control agency rulemaking by creating clearance processes for major regulations. These included the Quality of Life Review process, where each agency had to sign off on Environmental Protection Agency regulations, as well as review of major regulations after 1980 by the Office of Information and Regulatory Affairs in the Office of Management and Budget (OMB). President Carter next made cost–benefit analyses part of the review process of major rules. Requiring that benefits exceed costs, however, was not done until the Reagan administration (Durant, 1992, 2014c; Hult & Walcott, 2004; Moe, 1985).

Nixon's administrative presidency approach was cut short by his resignation after impeachment in 1974, but, to this day, each of his successors amplified its use because of the increase in legislative polarization (see more in Chapter 7). They have done so by typically couching their efforts as agency administrative reforms enhancing economy and efficiency. This, despite researchers finding that centralization of policymaking in the White House has become highly bureaucratized and laced with turf wars, information hoarding, and internecine conflicts (Burke, 2000; Warshaw, 2004). Nor does the administrative presidency exhibit the kinds of overall strategic guidance expected by proponents (Rudalevige, 2002; West, 2006, 2015).

But it was left to President Carter, based on the recommendations of leading public administration scholars, to persuade a Democratic Congress to fulfill partially FDR's and Nixon's goals to control personnel administration. Produced was the most important federal legislation affecting personnel management since the Civil Service Act of 1883: the Civil Service Reform Act (CSRA) of 1978. Partially reacting to personnel abuses condoned and then covered up by the Civil Service Commission (CSC) during the Watergate affair, the CSRA created the Merit Systems Protection Board to protect merit provisions of the original act and the Office of Personnel Management to take over all other CSC responsibilities.

The CSRA also tried to emulate aspects of the British civil service by creating the Senior Executive Service (SES) (Lewis, 2008; Maranto & Schultz, 1991; Resh & Durant, 2015). Its aim was to produce a team of skilled executives who would move from agency to agency, bringing needed managerial talent and broader perspectives on governance. The SES was comprised of up to 7,000 positions. Of these, up to 10 percent could be political appointees. Those joining the SES would, among other things, be evaluated on performance and receive monetary bonuses for outstanding work.

Performance measurement and pay for performance were again ideas borrowed from the private sector and brought a strong executive-centered, IRP-informed, control perspective to the federal government component of the compensatory state. Moreover, they were often tried first at the state and local government levels. These were particularly attractive at the federal level, because (under the CSRA) a greater number of political appointees could be placed deeper into the bureaucracy than ever before and were given greater flexibility to apply private-sector tools to enhance their control. As Chapter 7 will document, Carter's defeat in 1980 left most of the implementation of the CSRA to Reagan, a conservative president much more bent than Carter on downsizing, destabilizing, deskilling, and controlling the discretion of agency personnel to pursue his policy agenda (Aberbach & Rockman, 2000).

Nor did Congress stand by and watch these efforts at presidentializing the federal bureaucracy. Consonant with coevolution theory, for instance, it passed the Budget and Impoundment Control Act (BICA) of 1974 partly to counter top-down control efforts by presidents. BICA was also a direct congressional response to Nixon's refusal to spend money allocated by Congress for programs that he disliked. But it also aimed to counter mounting budget deficits.

The epitome of the IRP, BICA tried to centralize the budgeting process by creating a House Budget Committee and a Senate Committee on the Budget, imposing a timetable for steps in that process, and requiring projections of tax revenues and expenditures to inform budget decisions. It also created the Congressional Budget Office (CBO), in part to perform econometric modeling in the hopes that Congress would become less dependent on OMB's econometric modeling, assumptions, and multi-year projections regarding the US economy.

Again, however, political rationality overwhelmed instrumental rationality. "Dueling models"—one the president's and the other the CBO's—soon rendered executive budgets "dead on arrival." Challenged were the other branch's assumptions of such things as unemployment, inflation rates, generated tax revenues, projected expenditures, and, thus, whether (and in what amounts) deficits or surpluses would arise. Moreover, small miscalculations of, say, inflation or unemployment meant that budget predictions could be off by billions of dollars.

In addition, BICA created the two budget committees to relate projected revenues to projected spending and then to "reconcile" them (i.e., to put them in balance). But they could only send reconciliation figures back to existing appropriations committees in each house of Congress. The so-called cardinals—that is, chairpersons—of the appropriations committees were not ready to see their power of the purse shift to the House and Senate budget committees. They doggedly fought centralization—and continue to do so today (albeit now more centralization of the House and Senate leadership exists). Moreover, because the assumptions underlying budget projections are susceptible to challenge, the cardinals had ample grounds to challenge both committees. Consequently, timetables for action were—and continue today to be—routinely flouted. Between 1973 and 2012, for instance, the federal budget was balanced only four times. During that period, federal expenditures as a share of gross domestic product averaged 21 percent, while tax revenues averaged only 18 percent (Samuelson, 2013). Thus, by 2017, the national debt rose to above $19 trillion and, shortly, exceeded $21 trillion.

In sum, a familiar pattern arose: politics impeded any form of "rational" budgeting reform—or any other IRP-based administrative reform. The disappointments relative to the across-the-board claims of the business and social science promoters of the IRP helped foster citizen perceptions of governments' incompetence in the compensatory state. And, ultimately, reforms predicated on the IRP marginalized average citizens lacking the interest, time, expertise, and/or understanding to become involved. These, in turn, set the stage for the next round of American administrative reform and state building covered in Chapter 7: the diminution of bureaucratic rationality and the rise of market and quasi-market rationality as theories of administrative reform.

Notes

1. The terms "thou shalt not" and "thou shalt" statutes were coined by Theodore Lowi (1995).
2. For example, a number of justices (especially, Sandra Day O'Connor and Stephen Bryer) began seeing the death penalty as cruel and unusual punishment. They were influenced by European nations repealing the death penalty.
3. It should be noted that liberal judges and legal scholars can also hold originalist beliefs (e.g., US Supreme Court Justice Hugo Black).
4. This discussion of migration relies heavily on Barone (2013).
5. Under Keynesian economics, the government uses taxing and spending as a "countercyclical" device to smooth out the business cycle through the manipulation of consumer purchasing power.
6. The remainder of this discussion of migration patterns and legislation relies heavily on Tichenor (2002).
7. For example, he led a largely vibrant economy, creating the interstate highway system, establishing the National Aeronautics and Space Administration after the Soviet launch of Sputnik, and sending troops to support integration of a high school in Little Rock, Arkansas. Moreover, he ended the Korean War and preserved an internationalist perspective on foreign affairs against attacks by isolationists led by Senator Robert Taft.
8. The classic study is Pressman and Wildavsky (1984). Implementation research is prodigious and consists of three generations (case, comparative case, and large-N studies) (Goggin et al., 1990). For the most comprehensive summary of that literature, see Hill and Hupe (2014).

9. Not all agree with these perspectives and have refined our understanding of the business–government power relationship, typically taking a contingency perspective. See, for example, Berry (1999); Baumgartner and Leech (1998); Kamieniecki (2006); Vogel (2003).

10. www.google.com/search?q=port+huron+statement&oq=Port+Huron+s&aqs=chrome. 1.69i57j0l5. 6293j0j7&sourceid=chrome&ie=UTF-8.

11. The Supreme Court decision in *Griswold* declared prohibition of the sale of contraceptives as unconstitutional.

12. Blackmun's majority opinion in *Roe* was based on privacy but also focused on physicians' rights to provide adequate services to women. Later, in *Casey*, Justice Sandra Day O'Connor argued that abortion could be justified under the Equal Protection Clause of the US Constitution (see Toobin, 2008).

13. This discussion of presidential administrative reform efforts relies on Arnold (1998); Burke (2000); Durant (1992); Golden (2000); Hult and Walcott (1990, 2004); Nathan (1983); Neustadt (1990); Patterson (2008); Shapiro, Kumar, and Jacobs (2000—see, especially, ch. 7 [Thomas Preston], ch. 8 [Bert Rockman], ch. 9 [Kenneth Mayer & Thomas Weko], ch. 10 [Matthew Dickenson]); Zegart (1999).

14. For the most definitive examination of structural reforms at all levels of government prior to the mid-1940s, see Waldo (1984). Since then, see, for example, Arnold (1998); Burke (2000); Hult and Walcott (1990, 2004); Neustadt (1990); Patterson (2008); Shapiro et al. (2000); Zegart (1999).

Chapter 7

Neoliberalism, the Corporate–Social Science Nexus, and American Administrative Reform, Circa 1980–2016

As chronicled in Chapter 6, World War II and the first 35 years of the Cold War were momentous when it came to the evolution of American administrative reform and state building. This was especially true in their amplification of the compensatory state, subsystem politics, and the instrumental rationality project (IRP). Noteworthy, too, was how the IRP ran into political rationality during its implementation, thus again underperforming relative to proponents' claims. Also apparent, again, was how the corporate–social science nexus of interests pursuing greater legitimacy pushed for, helped shape, and initially benefited from the IRP—until challenges to its efficacy began growing in the late 1970s. To which were added critiques from both the Left and Right, members of academia, and interests marginalized from policymaking by the IRP.

Heard in the process were calls for the next round of administrative reform and state building in America, a response that Donald Kettl (1993) aptly calls the "competition prescription," the epitome of market rationality. For minimal-state proponents, this market-modeled version of administrative reforms was called the New Public Management (NPM) (Barzelay, 1992, 2001; Hood, 1991, 1998, 2005; Hood & Dickson, 2015; Lane, 2000; Peters, 2001). Its intellectual foundations were microeconomics, public choice theory, and transaction cost analysis. In an age of neoliberal economics prompting rule-based economic globalization in a new "information age," the NPM fit neatly into the political zeitgeist and informed the Reagan Revolution of the 1980s.[1] Moreover, it continued in various iterations into the Republican presidencies of George H. W. Bush (R-TX) (1989–1993) and, later, George W. Bush (R-TX) (2001–2009).

Proponents of the NPM—also referred to as the "new managerialism," "market-based administration," and "entrepreneurial government"[2]—believed that "there is something called 'management' which is generic [to all organizations], purely instrumental activity, embodying a set of principles that can be applied to a public business [sic], as well as in private business" (Painter, 1988, p. 1). NPM's primary aim was to realize "efficiency, effectiveness, and value for money" (Saint-Martin, 2000, p. 1; Enteman, 1993). In this sense, the NPM was hardly "new." It reiterated the generic organizational goals of the 18th century adapted from Europe, as well as the early progressives' politics/policy–administration dichotomy, the associationalism of Herbert Hoover in the 1920s, and the cross-sectoral elite perspective of the Harvard Graduate School of Business in the late 1920s and 1930s. The NPM also rhetorically noted the importance of citizens in public administration. This, again, was hardly novel. It was redolent earlier in the Populist movement in the late 19th century, of the efficient citizen and settlement women movements of the early 20th century, and in the Great Society programs of the 1960s.

But NPM reform proponents put a different ideological spin on these emphases. Although earlier progressives saw public administration as the solution to *market failures*, proponents of the NPM saw market competition as the solution to *government failures*. They aimed at creating a minimal federal administrative apparatus in the compensatory state by hiving off national government functions and programs to subnational governments, as well as to the private and nonprofit sectors.

Although this might seem like another extension of the compensatory state, the NPM's not-so-subtle rationale was shrinking the federal component of the compensatory state rather than enhancing its capacity. Those public agency components that remained would, as much as possible, become rationality-driven "business centers" with their budgets linked to performance. Also, in contrast to Woodrow Wilson and the progressives' arguments for shifting power from the legislative to the executive branch, NPM proponents argued that both institutions were no longer capable of effectively holding public agencies accountable. In a by now classic invoking of the historical–structural argument, problems and public bureaucracies were now so complex that elected officials could not hold administrators accountable for their actions by purely structural and process means.

NPM proponents argued that metrics—market competition, performance measurement, outcomes-based administration, and citizen satisfaction scores—should override bureaucratic procedures as accountability mechanisms. Thus, in contrast to the "maximum feasible participation" of Lyndon Johnson's War on Poverty, NPM proponents saw the rationality of markets and quasi-market administrative structures as the mechanism for citizen participation (but see Kroll, Neshkova, & Pandey, 2017, for a discussion of how performance management can sometimes lead to greater citizen participation). Competition, measurement, and "consumer sovereignty" were the new tools of accountability.

Meanwhile, for positive-state Democrats, a political antidote was necessary to the Reagan Revolution and its NPM, as well as to stymie a third-party movement led by corporate titan Ross Perot during the 1992 presidential election. Positive-state proponents such as presidents Bill Clinton (D-AR) (1993–2001) and Barack Obama (D-IL) (2009–2017) embraced a New Governance Model (NGM) of administrative reform. Like the NPM, the NGM applied the logic of business. But with its progressive roots, Clinton's Reinventing Government (REGO) initiative—led by Vice President Al Gore (D-TN)—stressed cross-sectoral partnerships, delayering of agencies by cutting managers, reengineering administrative processes, and customer service. Consistent with the Democratic Party's public-sector labor union support, public managers were not portrayed as the problem; the outdated structures, processes, and systems in which they operated were the problem and in need of reform (Kettl & DiIulio, 1995; Osborne & Gaebler, 1993; Osborne & Plastrik, 1997).[3] In addition, although REGO incorporated privatization, it stressed it much less than the NPM. Moreover, contracting's aim was to force managers to compete with private service providers in order to improve management rather than use it merely to shrink federal agencies, devolve federal responsibilities, and denationalize social program benefits.

Still, both initiatives shared commonalities. Both the NPM and REGO, for example, outsourced significant portions of the development and implementation of their reforms to private-sector management consulting firms. In addition, each criticized federal agencies, further marketized public administration, and, thus, amplified the compensatory state and the IRP within it. This, as the global ascendancy of neoliberal economics combined with the embrace of supranational and transnational institutions to add further downward pressure on the visible size of governments in a world transitioning to the information age. This downward pressure also offered administrative reforms geared toward reducing regulatory barriers to domestic and international trade. Yet, as in earlier periods of "creative destruction" (Schumpeter, 1942), these efforts also amplified income gaps between the rich and poor, further inflamed charges of ascriptive hierarchy, and aroused calls for government intervention and administrative reform.

Compounded atop earlier historical periods was the complexity of governance, as well as the power and influence of elements of the corporate–social science nexus, especially microeconomists. This, as the Austrian School's (Chapter 6) focus on methodological individualism regained the legitimacy it lost after World War I. The aims of the elements of the nexus, once again, were an expressive belief in the need for market rationality to trump political and conventional administrative rationality while also enhancing material and authority gains from such an enterprise.

Yet, this market-informed version of the IRP only again helped amplify citizen distrust and estrangement from government in vocal segments of the American population. This involved a crisis of faith of the extreme Left and Right in the American political system, generally, and in all bureaucratically structured institutions (international and national). This ended in populist revolts in both the Democratic and Republican parties, the "hostile takeover" of the Republican Party by those forces, and the 2016 election of political neophyte and businessman Donald Trump. Central to his agenda was what one Trump advisor called an anti-elite "deconstruction of the administrative state" apparatus in Washington and internationally (Rucker & Costa, 2017).

****

As in earlier historical eras, it is important to analyze American administrative reform during this period from cultural, demographic, social, religious, and political perspectives. Shifts in these factors amplified downward pressures on the visible size of government and, thus, on the administrative capacity of public agencies in the compensatory state. This, by initially setting the stage for a Right-leaning shift in the American political landscape (albeit one challenged later from the Left).

Analyzing survey data since the 1950s, Robert Putnam and David Campbell (2012) argue that three "shocks" in religious communities had occurred by the 2010s. These had negative political implications for progressive government activism and administrative capacity building in the public agency components of the compensatory state. The first shock they identified was evangelical (and charismatic) Protestantism expanding beyond its fundamentalist roots in the rural South (see Chapter 3). This, as "televangelists" and, later, "megachurch" preachers (see more below) took to the airwaves.[4] In the process, denominational splits among Catholics, Jews, and Protestants further splintered and bled into liberal versus conservative politics.

In response to the countercultural social revolution of the 1960s and early 1970s discussed in Chapter 6, conservatives in all religions joined with evangelicals to condemn the counterculture. They saw it as an assault on traditional values and authority structures, just as they had in the First and Second Great Awakenings, as well as in the aftermath of the Scopes Trial in the 1920s. A diversity of perspectives existed among traditional conservatives and evangelicals over the wisdom of using political parties to advance sectarian religious views. But most agreed with Richard John Neuhaus' thesis in *The Naked Public Square* (1986) that secular humanists were using the courts to exclude consideration of religious values in public debates. Thus, they were witnessing a judicialization of what "neoorthodox Christians" such as Reinhold Niebuhr (2013) and H. Richard Niebuhr saw as too much accommodation of liberal Protestantism with secular humanist values. Prevalent among many mainline Protestant churches (and later elements of Catholicism embracing liberation theology) since the earlier Social Gospel movement had linked them to activism in progressive causes, a marginalization of transcendent religious values had developed in the public square. This, much as the logical positivists of the earlier Vienna Circle of social scientists had done in marginalizing evaluative discourse.

The influence of the "Religious Right" (or "Christian Right") became a vocal and major part of the Republican Party's base in the 1980s and remains so today.[5] Most notable in this regard were such groups as the "Moral Majority" (founded by the Reverend Jerry Falwell) promoting a "pro-life," "pro-traditional family," "pro-moral," "pro-American," and federal bureaucracy- and judiciary-bashing agenda. In doing this, they replicated and amplified the "spiritual mobilization" efforts of the 1950s discussed in Chapter 6, including the mounting of a series of mass-media, mass-mailing, and pulpit-based campaigns. All this in the face of a reissue (albeit with fewer contributors and signatories of the stature of John Dewey in the original) of the 1933 *Humanist Manifesto* calling for a secular society, with the natural and social sciences the engines of that society (Neuhaus, 1986).

Reagan's presidential campaign then began aggressively courting evangelical votes. It did so partly to continue splitting off blue-collar and social-value conservatives from the old Democratic coalition and partly to redefine class in America. As the preceding chapters illustrate, class historically had been premised on one's economic status. Republicans were associated with the wealthy and the corporate world (so-called country club Republicans), while lower- and middle-class working families affiliated with the Democratic Party.

Beginning with Reagan, however, Republicans rhetorically reframed "class" to mean differences in *cultural* rather than economic status. The Religious Right spoke of bicoastal, highly educated, and secularly oriented "cultural elites" running the country: the media, academia, liberal judges, and experts in the federal bureaucracy. This elite was foisting a pro-choice, pro-LGBTQ⁺, anti-family, anti-American, globalist, and secular policy agenda on the country. In the end, the Moral Majority was credited with delivering two-thirds of the evangelical vote to Reagan.

The conservative religious movement and its political success relative to the Republican Party also had profound implications for the courts and its oversight of public agencies. As noted in Chapter 6, the judicial activism of justices during the Warren Court and, then, the Burger Court became a target for the Religious Right. This happened as administrative decisions over issues they cared deeply about were appealed to the courts and in the wake of subsequent Supreme Court decisions regarding, for instance, abortion, freedom of religious assembly, and school prayer.

Taking a page from liberal activists, conservatives and the Religious Right began using the courts to advance their agenda. Although court decisions limiting freedom of religious expression had been framed by them in the past as violations of the 1st Amendment, religious conservatives led by the American Center for Law and Justice successfully reframed this argument as one of free speech and assembly under the same amendment.[6] This happened in conjunction with groups such as Focus on the Family, as well as the National Right to Life movement on abortions and the National Rifle Association on gun control.

With survey data indicating that elite law schools at Yale and Harvard were dominated by liberals, conservatives and the Religious Right believed that the place to start a judicial revolution was by altering the faculty and student composition of law schools. To this end, the Federalist Society was begun in 1980 by three conservative Yale Law School graduates. The society was supported financially by such conservative organizations as the Scaife Family Foundation and John M. Olin Foundation, and established Federalist Society chapters of faculty and students at leading law schools.

The Reagan administration then actively sought members associated with these societies to staff agency positions and fill judicial appointments to federal courts (e.g., Robert Bork and Antonin Scalia, the latter self-described as a textualist and a "faint-hearted originalist"). These appointees then worked ostensibly to implement "originalist" interpretations of the Constitution, as well as "textualist" views of statutes. In reality, these judicial appointees had little respect for precedent (i.e., stare decisis) in overthrowing sometimes long-established legal precedents (e.g., finding an individual right to bear arms in the 2nd Amendment in *District of Columbia v. Heller* [2008] and *McDonald v. City of Chicago* [2010]).

By the end of the first decade of the 21st century, seven of nine justices on the Supreme Court had been appointed by Republican presidents. But a more "centrist" group comprised of Democratic nominee Stephen Breyer and Republican appointees Anthony Kennedy, Sandra Day O'Connor, and David Souter often limited the impact of originalists and textualists such as Scalia and Clarence Thomas. This only further infuriated the Religious Right and social conservatives and made the nomination of originalist justices a key promise of almost every Republican presidential campaign since. Particularly galling to the Religious Right was the Supreme Court's failure to overturn *Roe v. Wade* (1973) and ban all abortions in *Planned Parenthood v. Casey* (1992) and *Stenberg v. Carhart/ Gonzales v. Carhart* (2000, 2007), as well as its later embrace of gay marriage in *Obergefell v. Hodges* (2015).

In the interim, fierce battles over nominations to the federal courts became routine and involved marshalling support or opposition for nominees from outside groups. They also involved delaying tactics by both parties (e.g., slowing down the confirmation process), including unprecedented use of the filibuster to reject nominees.[7] Moreover, although the litmus test for traditional Republican nominees to the courts was identification as a corporate conservative, only conservative social and religious nominees were acceptable to a party dependent on the Religious Right for electoral success. In effect, the courts now reflected the polarization of the larger society (Toobin, 2008).

****

Putnam and Campbell (2012) also identified a second religious "shock" that occurred in the 1990s with similar implications for administrative reform and compensatory state building. This time, however, it involved a reaction to the *excesses* of the Religious Right. A sizable spike occurred in non-affiliation with traditional religions (from 7 to 35 percent), bringing with it the growth of nondenominational "megachurches" (Putnam & Campbell, 2012). These churches focused on such matters as personal development and its link to economic prosperity in ways consistent with the faculty psychology tradition in America, as well as with American exceptionalist values. This approach was especially appealing to many in the rising millennial and the aging baby boom generations.

Millennials (those born between 1982 and 2004) were generally just as anti-establishment as activist baby boomers (those born between 1946 and 1964) in their youth. They tended to be sympathetic to ethnic, racial, gender, and sexual identity diversity, and skeptical of corporations. They also tended to stress more quality-of-life issues (e.g., climate change), including better work/life balance. Many American millennials also were frustrated by bureaucratic administration, much as expressed in the earlier Port Huron and Sharon statements. They also sought more collaborative workplaces than those afforded by conventional government bureaucracies, were nonetheless committed to making a difference in the world, and expected to have multiple careers in different sectors. Although still tending to embrace public service, many saw themselves doing so in nonprofit organizations, not public agencies, in the compensatory state. After decades of the rationality project in government, they saw nonprofits as less bureaucratic, more mission-focused, and producing more immediate and tangible results than government (Light, 1999).

At the same time, a more secularly based movement begun by postmodern scholars of various perspectives (e.g., Jacques Derrida, Michel Foucault,

Jean-François Lyotard, and Richard Rorty) spread to the humanities and some social science faculties on many leading US college campuses. As had the historical economists of the Verein in the late 19th century, and as countered by the Austrian School of economics and associationalists, they (many of whom were neo-Marxists) spoke of the false and exploitive metanarratives of capitalism. But they also expanded their "oppressor-versus-oppressed" critique to institutions generally, government in particular, and bureaucracy specifically. Essentially, they denied the Burkean idea that these metanarratives were *not* arbitrary choices but, rather, the experientially derived wisdom of the ages about the constrained set of viable options for ordering and maintaining society.

Perhaps more devastatingly, and in the latest iteration of the ancient Greek Sophists and Rousseaunian romantics, they questioned the idea of objective truth itself. Extrapolating to what some called a "post-truth" era, postmodernists set the stage for arguments in the 2010s that institutions, including government and its bureaucracies, did not tell the truth and were involved in conspiracies to undermine democracy (e.g., the "Deep State" of national security agencies). As the authors of the Port Huron Statement had advocated in the 1960s, elements on campuses became levers for challenging existing authority structures and replacing them with what later conservatives attacked as a hostile bureaucratic "culture of nothingness" (e.g., Scruton, 2007).

All this put additional pressures on public agencies to defend their actions and motives, reform themselves and their management approaches to appeal to millennials, and handle intergenerational workplace tensions between millennials and baby boomers. Agencies found themselves competing with private employers for the talents of millennials. The latter were already creating such work environments, had state-of-the-art information technology (IT) and analytics software, and offered higher pay and benefits (see more below). In addition, and although just as susceptible to deconstructionist critiques, private companies offered more rapid opportunities for mobility than did government agencies—something that millennials desired.

****

A third major religious and cultural shock identified by Putnam and Campbell (2012) was a turn to spirituality in the 21st century as a substitute for organized religion. Once again, this shock was consistent in several ways with the focus of the humanists in the Renaissance, the Second Great Awakening of the early 19th century, the transcendentalists of the mid- to late 19th century (e.g., Ralph Waldo Emerson, Henry David Thoreau, and Walt Whitman), and aspects of the countercultural movement in the mid-20th century. Devotees sought nonsectarian approaches that stressed the universality of humankind, yet, at the same time, embraced personal spiritual growth. Unlike faculty psychology, however, spiritualism was more concerned with individual growth as an end in itself rather than for society. In millennials, this instantiated in a preference by many for self-actualization in the workplace and training designed to give them employability rather than guaranteed employment. But government agencies lagged well behind the private sector in affording such opportunities, making them less attractive to many millennials.

Meanwhile, baby boomers began to retire in increasing numbers, a trend that, in 2016, promised to continue for the next decade and a half. This left fewer workers to pay for retiree benefits (e.g., Medicare and Social Security). Relatedly, a graying government workforce offered threats and opportunities to public agencies (Durant, 2014c, esp. chs. 2, 3, & 7). If addressed strategically by aligning agency recruitment, training, succession planning, and outsourcing initiatives with evolving agency missions, retirements could improve agency operations. They also could bring needed IT and other skills to agencies that were superior to those of most baby boomers. However, they typically were not handled strategically. The downsizing demanded by elected officials and administrative reformers was done using either across-the-board cuts that punished agencies or employees doing a good job or they were employee-driven. Even when replacement of positions was allowed (in whole or in part), replacement skills were not always available to agencies, thus furthering reliance on the proxy components of the compensatory state.

Moreover, hiring continued to be complicated by a civil service system that was "unable to keep up with modern-day management practices and to plan for the future. It was, and remains, a system hamstrung by rigid federal employment directives, some of which, ironically, were aimed at freshening up the workforce" (Vinik, 2017). The classification system for federal workers, for instance, dated back to 1949, and

> despite progress in updating it, the rules still create[d] huge challenges for agencies by forcing them to fit workers into certain prescribed categories rather than giving them the flexibility to hire and pay workers as they see fit. There [was] no exact government-wide hiring policy. It [was] filled with exemptions and carve-outs, and thick with paperwork.
> (Vinik, 2017)

Thus, as in prior chapters, political rationality, both internally and from Congress, trumped other considerations. In the process, many public workforces grew older, unable to attract or retain talented younger workers in sufficient numbers. At the federal level—and in contrast to World War I, the New Deal, and, later, the Kennedy years—data from the Office of Personnel Management (OPM) between 1997 and 2017 indicated that the percentage of full-time federal workers younger than 45 years of age went down. This, while the percentage over the age of 55 grew by 83 percent. Relatedly, only 1.2 percent of workers in the federal government were under 24 years of age, compared to 13 percent in the private sector (Vinik, 2017).

The aging of America also put severe administrative and budget stress on pension liabilities and healthcare costs for maintaining the compensatory state. For example, the largest spending categories in the proposed fiscal year (FY) 2018 federal budget were defense, health, income security, and social security. Interest costs on the national debt had risen as the latter hit over $19 trillion by 2016. Nearly 70 percent of the federal budget did not go through the annual authorization and appropriation processes. This meant that discretionary spending for domestic agency budgets in the compensatory state during Republican congresses continued to decline.

These dynamics also spawned further downward pressures on the visible size of government at all levels of the compensatory state. The Congressional Budget Office (CBO) estimated that until a "grand bargain" could be reached on raising taxes and cutting entitlement spending, interest costs would continue to spiral.[8] Conservatives countered that if you gave tax increases without first cutting spending, elected officials would never get to those cuts and would only spend the additional revenue. Meanwhile, given an aging population, spending on healthcare alone was estimated to reach 19.6 percent of the nation's gross domestic product (GDP) by 2020. Without legislative adjustments, this would leave tax revenues in 2025 able to finance only interest payments, Medicaid, Medicare, and Social Security (Health-Spending Projections, 2012). Absent legislative changes, this meant that agency budgets in all other domestic policy areas would have to be cut, and it amplified America's historical propensity to undervalue capacity building in public agencies. Likewise, recognition of unfunded pension funds in the state and local government component of the compensatory state arose during this era, a major challenge that varied across states and localities (*Moody's*, 2013).

****

Were all this not challenging enough for public agencies and the compensatory state more broadly, public managers had to operate in a political environment that grew even more hostile toward government as the period progressed. Nor did it help that many elected officials ran campaigns impugning the merits of public agencies and career civil servants. The historically unprecedented turn to congressional careerism that occurred in this era allowed for further polarization among members (Orren & Skowronek, 2017). Prior to the 1970s and 1980s, congressmembers typically worked their way up through different home-state elected offices and maintained local ties that gave them room to buck congressional party leaders. But starting and finishing their political careers in Congress tended to sever these ties, making them more dependent on party leadership for perks that helped their reelection chances.

Similarly, polarization in Washington and, increasingly, in state capitals stemmed from a shift of conservative Democrats to the Republican Party and the defeat of moderate Democrats. It also led to the capture of election primaries by extreme wings of both parties, as well as the "sorting out" of Americans geographically into socioeconomic and political enclaves of like-minded persons. So polarized was the nation that three presidents of this era (Clinton, G. W. Bush, and Obama) were labeled "illegitimate" by vocal segments of the American population. A fourth, Donald Trump, would be similarly labeled after the 2016 election. Also produced were repeated partisan stalemates in Congress as legislators viewed compromise as risky, fearing that opponents from the extreme Left (Democrats) or Right (Republicans) would (and did) challenge them in party primaries.

In effect, by the 2000s, America had parliamentary parties endeavoring to operate in a Madisonian system (Mann & Ornstein, 2006). Passing major legislative items (e.g., the Affordable Care and Patient Protection Act) was only possible using straight-party voting premised on parliamentary procedures (e.g., budget reconciliation rules) where only 51 votes were needed in the US Senate (rather than 60 votes) to gain cloture on debates. The same was done, first, for the lower federal courts and, then, for US Supreme Court nominations, with Senate confirmation reduced to 51 votes. As Barbara Sinclair (2006, 2016) contends, various legislative gimmicks were also used to avoid regular order in the House and to try to enact legislation by unanimous consent in the Senate.

Yet, stalemate on many major and conflictual issues still occurred (e.g., on immigration reform), leaving House and Senate leaders to rely on partisan rather than bipartisan or co-partisan coalitions to pass legislation. With the expansion of primaries over the last 110 years—plus the enactment of the Legislative Reorganization Act in 1970, the Subcommittee Bill of Rights in 1973,[9] and the Rights Revolution—Senate and House members elected as entrepreneurs had their own personal electoral coalitions and only a passing acquaintance with control by the parties. This, until Speaker of the House Newt Gingrich (R-GA) effectively repealed the Subcommittee Bill of Rights in the 1990s by "enhanc[ing] the prerogatives of the Speaker, and . . . cut[ting] the minority [party] further out of the legislative process" (Orren & Skowronek, 2017, p. 145). But, in the interim, the Rights Revolution pursued by the influx of scores of reform-minded "Watergate babies" holding their first elected office set the foundation for more polarized politics in America. They did so by, among other things, decentralizing legislative power, enhancing the transparency of the legislative process (e.g., more recorded votes and allowing C-SPAN to cover Congress, making incumbents vulnerable to primary challenges and interest-group influence), and contributing to the rise of single-issue politics that sorely complicated compromise (Jacobs, King, & Milkis, 2019; Lawrence, 2018). Thus, trends noted by Hugh Heclo (2013) in the late 1970s were amplified during this period.

Even after Gingrich was removed from the speakership on ethics grounds by a rank-and-file revolt, "resentment of the power of the Speaker [and the party caucuses] . . . magnified the difficulties of maintaining order, testing at once the policy-making capacities of the House and its identity as the backbone of representative government" (Orren & Skowronek, 2017, p. 145). Meanwhile, although Senate majority leaders had greater power than the Speaker, "Senators assert[ed] their rights so as to cultivate their individual reputations as policy entrepreneurs, thus further polarizing the Senate" on controversial issues (Orren & Skowronek, 2017, p. 142).

****

Further inflaming polarization and placing downward pressures on the visible size of the federal bureaucracy and its administrative capacity were the rise of social media (with a concomitant contraction of traditional media) and the advent of 24-hour cable news. Produced were a nationalization of news, segmentation of news markets, acceleration of news cycles, and political commentary marginalizing news reporting. In effect, what late-20th century postmodernists such as French philosopher Jean Baudrillard called "hyperreality" in an electronic media age seemed verified. Viewers had difficulty differentiating fact from fiction, and they became what sociologist David Riesman called "other-directed" personalities. Concomitantly, technology-mediated "relationships" (e.g., "friends" on Facebook) eroded traditional face-to-face relationships among young and old, creating algorithmic-driven "communities" of like-minded persons in their wake. What the philosopher, Martin Buber, called I–Thou relationships of authenticity and mutual care seemed decidedly in jeopardy. This, as "clicks" became the new measure of self, business, or professional worth, thereby eroding traditional norms and standards of assessment.

In the 1960s, about a dozen media outlets and wire services dominated the news business and afforded a "common experience" for viewers (for good or ill).[10] But, by 2016, newspaper subscriptions fell nearly 40 percent, while newspapers lost 37 percent of their employees. National news media in New York and Washington fared better, with one in five jobs in the newspaper business located in these cities in 2016 (compared to one in eight jobs in 2004) (Musgrave & Nussbaum, 2018). In the process, a nationalization of news coverage and politics occurred, especially with the closure or downsizing of local newspapers. With this contraction of local news sources and concentration of reporting in major metropolitan markets, it was easier for citizens in so-called news deserts in nonmetropolitan areas to feel marginalized from news coverage and to become distrustful of the news generally. Amplifying traditional rural/urban political divides in American history, the demise of local newspapers also made it easier for conservative politicians to talk about "fake news," refer to "bicoastal elites" as out of touch with average Americans' concerns, and attack the traditional media as biased in coverage. Reinforcing these perceptions were studies showing that newspersons' campaign contributions went overwhelmingly to Democrats, the partisan imbalance on major cable networks of so-called expert panels, and the hiring by networks of partisans associated with past administrations and political campaigns.

But the development of social media was the main culprit—and financial beneficiary—of these trends. The growth in users was exponential, as was the algorithmic-driven advertising revenue for social media corporations. Via social media such as Facebook and Twitter, millions of users downloaded and shared articles from traditional news media, partisan media, and fake media. Moreover, both the posting of news and news sharing was done without the gatekeeper role played by traditional news outlets to ensure the accuracy of stories. Hate language also spread virally across social media, while mounting evidence existed of the Russian Federation's use of social media to inflame social tensions in the United States (and in Europe). The media vitriol of the day was, unfortunately, a throwback to the newspapers of the Founding Era in America and elements in the 1950s (Burns, 2006), but on a greater scale and faster pace.

So, too, did 24-hour news, plus hundreds of stations available to viewers surfing for entertainment, vastly accelerate traditional daily news cycles. In this competitive market environment, the need also grew to grab the attention of viewers. Networks turned to conflict among extreme partisans to grab the attention of listeners "surfing" stations on their television remotes. To the same end, running headers and footers (sometimes rife with opinions) were ever present on television screens proclaiming "Breaking News" or "News Alerts," regardless of how old or repetitive were the news stories. At the same time, most of the 24-hour cable news outlets spent significantly more time featuring newspersons interviewing other newspersons who "interpreted" for listeners what they just heard rather than putting it into a broader context. Meanwhile, average Americans' historical tendency to "look inward" was bolstered as stories from foreign bureaus declined significantly during this period; coverage of all three major TV networks combined was less than any single network covered in 1988 (Zakaria, 2019).

Also relevant to news ratings and their role in amplifying "negative partisanship" among Americans in the 2000s (Abramowitz, 2010; Abramowitz & Webster, 2016),[11] cable news networks began differentiating themselves by presenting different partisan or ideological slants on the news and by selectively choosing topics that would resonate with their respective audiences. This began with Fox News, created in 1996 by media mogul Rupert Murdoch and conservative Republican operative Roger Ailes as its founding CEO, with MSNBC (1996) later offered as a liberal counterpoint. Both focused more on ideological and incendiary commentary in the evenings rather than investigative reporting. Fox typically won the ratings war, offering an anti-government, anti-federal bureaucracy, anti-regulation, and free-market spin on news events. Diminished in the minds of many listeners was the legitimacy of both the media and trained experts, as uncertainty and conflict played into the hands of minimal-state conservative proponents (King & Stivers, 1998), as well as populist extremists on the Right and Left. But this *agitation–affirmation–addiction complex* of electronic and social media proved a highly profitable business model for them.

Nor did it help the social sciences when a perverse set of incentives linked to the media, scientific research conventions, journal practices, and university research rewards was exposed in some of the natural and social sciences (see Camerer et al., 2018; Head, Holman, Lanfear, Kahn, & Jennions, 2015; O'Connor, 2018). Ongoing for decades among a very small number of offenders, prominent instances of so-called data mining or p-hacking were widely publicized. Estimates are that scientific journals retracted approximately 1,400 published scientific papers per year (out of the two to three million published) (O'Connor, 2018). P-hacking, sometimes driven by university publication pressures, involved repeated analyses on large datasets and rounding down of p-values to tease out relationships that were statistically significant at a .05 level. In a perversion of the scientific method, offenders then generated hypotheses that made them attractive to journals and media outlets increasingly evaluated by journal impact scores and reader "clicks," respectively. Some journals began taking preventive measures (e.g., requiring the sharing of raw data for replicability purposes). These reactions, however, were not persuasive to those already skeptical about social science or seeking to delegitimize it outright. Indeed, Republican members of Congress in the 21st century tried to cut the National Science Foundation's budget, restrict what it could fund, eliminate political science research grant funding, and dispose of its Social, Behavioral, and Economic Sciences Directorate.

But, by the 2016 presidential campaign, perhaps the most underreported political development in the electronic media was the gain in market share of evangelical television stations such as the Christian Broadcasting Network, Daystar, and the Trinity Broadcasting Network (TBN) (Graham, 2018). These networks had limited their coverage historically to countercultural and religious developments. But, in the 2010s, they began devoting portions of their airtime to news reporting and commentary, including interviews with conservative elected officials in the United States and abroad. The number of their affiliates and viewers increased substantially. For example, TBN had more local affiliated stations in 2016 than Fox or the three major networks. In addition, the racial and ethnic diversity of these stations and viewers often exceeded that of cable news and the major networks. As Ruth Graham (2018) writes,

> Charismatic and Pentecostal preaching, and the related health-and-wealth "prosperity gospel," [were] strong traditions within the black

community. Popular black pastors including Creflo Dollar, Tony Evans, and TD Jakes . . . all preached regularly over the years on TBN, Daystar, and other Christian networks.

Paralleling these dynamics was the rise of the Tea Party within the Republican Party in the midst of America's Great Recession (circa 2007–2009; see more below). The Tea Party sprung from perceptions that the federal government bailed out the financial community despite their role creating the crash, while working- and middle-class victims lost jobs, homes, and retirement savings. Moreover, many blue-collar workers understood that their fate was directly attributable to a conscious strategy of "deindustrialization" and financial "deregulation" pursued by both political parties since the 1980s. Tea Party members also understood how to turn their policy agenda into "theatre" to capture media attention. They turned town hall meetings by congressmembers into boisterous shouting matches instantly shared through the electronic and social media.

But their policy agenda was even broader in that many members shared concerns of the Religious Right regarding abortion, gun control, and judicial originalism. Although a disparate collection of actors, one common theme Tea Party members shared was that private- and public-sector elites—especially President Obama and his "similarly credentialed experts" in the executive branch—were out of touch with, and uncaring about, average Americans (Toobin, 2012, p. 230). A revival of the "common men with common-sense" narrative of earlier eras occurred, as many believed they were just as—if not more—capable of understanding the nation's problems than these academically credentialed elites. And, legislatively, the election of Tea Party members to Congress created a conservative voting block (viz., the Freedom Caucus) averse to compromise.

****

Further compounding these downward pressures on the visible size, capacity, and legitimacy of the federal bureaucracy in the compensatory state was the ascent of economic globalism. The rise of the new global economy was akin to the economic globalization that took place in the late 19th and early 20th centuries, and it continued post-World War II efforts to institutionalize international economic ties. But, like those earlier periods, economic globalization—and visions of supranational and transnational governance bodies usurping national policies (Mathews, 1997)—did not happen by accident. Nor did it occur without opposition from the extreme Right and Left or absent a strong role for the corporate–social science nexus of interests in shaping and benefiting from further administrative reform of the compensatory state.

Late 20th and early 21st-century globalization was, as in earlier periods of administrative reform, technology-driven, only this time by IT, data analytics, and artificial intelligence (AI). IT, in turn, had severe consequences for the politics and administration of America's public finances, the power of financial institutions, and, thus, revenue for administrative capacity-building in government (Fountain, 2001). IT allowed the globalization of business product lines, because it enabled "real-time" monitoring of assembly lines and trade in services across the globe (Friedman, 1999). Relatedly, international corporations pursued "income shifting" to lessen their taxes. They claimed their expenses in countries with higher corporate tax rates and assigned their profits to nations with lower corporate tax rates (Greider, 1997). But just the threat to shift income put downward pressures on corporate tax rates and revenues in the United States and abroad. The same downward pressures took place as well among state and local governments as they competed against each other for business. Also driving the offshoring of production lines, jobs, and income-shifting was a US tax system that made companies pay twice for profits—once in foreign countries and again in the United States.

In addition, IT made it harder for the United States to control its money supply, a key tool of Keynesians and monetary policies. With IT, arbitragers could transfer money from nation to nation almost instantly to take advantage of differences in countries' interest rates or in the event of instability. Consequently, although Americans cast their preferences on election days, financial markets "voted" every day and could affect what governments did and how they did it. Thus, not unlike the grip they held over public finance during the Civil War, the Gilded Age, and the two world wars, the financial industry in the "information age" amplified their influence over American governance and its administrative capacity.

Along with economic globalization and less control over money supply came the ascendancy of neoliberal economics in the United States and abroad. Given theoretical heft by the "Chicago School" of economics and the revival of the Austrian School was a turn from the legitimacy of Keynesian economics toward a focus on monetary policy. Free-market monetarists such as Nobel Laureate Milton Friedman argued, difficulty aside, that controlling the size of the money supply, not taxing and spending policy (as per Keynesianism's focus), was critical to resolving a major problem in the United States in the late 1970s: stagflation. Friedman and his wife Rose then expanded his libertarian thinking to lay audiences in their ten-part public television series, *Free to Choose*.

According to the Keynesian model embraced by corporate liberals and others prior to the 1980s (see Chapter 6), high unemployment and high inflation (stagflation) could not happen at the same time. Moreover, fiscal policy (taxing and spending) as a countercyclical device was more important than the size of the money supply or nominal budget deficits. Yet the nation witnessed a combination of double-digit inflation and unemployment during this period. Conservatives seized on "supply-side economics" as the latest means for reviving the American economy and restoring American exceptionalism by limiting government activism. They argued, much as did many identifying with the Austrian School (e.g., von Mises), that Keynesians did not consider that higher marginal tax rates and regulatory costs imposed on businesses lowered the incentive to work and invest and, thus, lowered collected tax revenues.[12] And because the regulatory costs imposed by regulators on businesses were not reflected in measures of total government spending relative to gross national product (GNP), the influence and power of the compensatory state were masked. Essentially, ignoring the significant growth in the size of the Code of Federal Regulations spawned by the Great Society and the Rights Revolution masked the visible size, scope, and power of government in society. As such, one of the major tools for pursuing economic recovery was shrinking the domestic side of the public sector and its administrative capacity to issue regulations, thus constraining government intervention in markets and decreasing its influence over society.

Conservative business elites, plus many economists, also argued that standardizing technological, product-line, and environmental regulations across nations was necessary for regional and global markets to function effectively. Governments around the world began shifting responsibility for standards and trade regulations to such transnational bodies as the International Organization for Standardization and the World Trade Organization. These were comprised of representatives from business, government, and (less prominently) nongovernmental organizations (Koppell, 2010b).

By the 2010s, these combined actions—plus financial deregulation and the creation of complex and opaque forms of financial instruments such as derivatives (Gilpin, 1987)—caused significant political pushback in many nations, including the United States. Critics charged that the burden of these policies fell on the working class in the developed world (e.g., through the offshoring of jobs—see more below). Meanwhile, although neoliberal economics lifted billions of people out of abject poverty worldwide, benefits accrued overwhelmingly to the wealthy. They also claimed that these efforts—as intended by neoliberals fearing economic nationalism (Slobodian, 2018)—reduced national sovereignty and caused a "democratic deficit" (Durant, 1995).[13] This, as aspects of policymaking and trade migrated toward regional bureaucracies (e.g., the European Commission) and international bodies (Gilpin, 2001). Produced, in reaction, was a rising worldwide threat of illiberal nationalism (rather than liberal nationalism based on inclusivity and international engagement (Lepore, 2019), including (from the Right) a new "America First," anti-globalization, anti-immigration, anti-elite movement in America. This was precisely the opposite of what the neoliberals and the globalist heirs of the Enlightenment rationality project had predicted. Still, some foreign policy intellectuals predicted that nations would be obsolete and usurped by supranational institutions, coordinating bodies, and networks of experts and professional activists (Mathews, 1997). Yet, citizens feeling marginalized from decision making in this situation grew increasingly vulnerable to calls for the revival of nationalism.

****

Against this backdrop, the US neoliberal economic agenda began with President Reagan's election in 1980 and his focus on supply-side economics. This economic theory was the perfect political platform for Reagan in his effort to roll back the progressives' liberal nationalist agenda. He sought to shrink the size and ambitions of the domestic and regulatory federal bureaucracy in the compensatory state. Along with a stress on social issues (e.g., prayer in school and abortion), supply-side economics inclined many so-called blue-collar Democrats (later renamed "Reagan Democrats") to support his campaign. Reagan portrayed massive tax cuts and deregulation as also benefiting the working classes. Tax cuts and deregulation would spawn greater investments, thus reducing inflation and unemployment. Tax rate cuts also kept the wealthiest in Reagan's coalition satisfied. Moreover, he kept senior citizens and defense hawks in political tow by exempting Social Security and Medicare from spending cuts (after a failed attempt to cut the rate of growth in the former), gaining the largest tax cut in history, and providing the largest peacetime defense spending increase to that point (Mullins & Mikesell, 2010).[14] By 1984, the economy improved to near pre-stagflation levels, a development that Reagan attributed to supply-side economics and that resulted in his landslide reelection that year.

But as budget deficits continued mounting, Congress passed the Tax Reform Act of 1986. This act eliminated many tax subsidies, loan guarantees, deductions, and exemptions. Most, however, crept back into the tax code over time, rekindled by various organized interests (e.g., the real estate industry and fossil-fuel industries). In addition, as the rationality project of the 1974 Budget and Impoundment Control Act (BICA) unraveled under interest-group pressures and amplification of the institutional politics discussed in Chapter 6, Congress tried unsuccessfully to combat mounting deficits with versions of its own IRP project.

For example, it enacted the 1985 Balanced Budget and Emergency Deficit Control Act—more popularly known as the Gramm–Rudman–Hollings (GRH) Act. This bipartisan effort at administrative reform tried to use BICA's sequestration component to achieve a balanced budget by FY 1991. If Congress did not reduce $36 billion in deficit cuts annually, then across-the-board cuts would be made in the remaining discretionary portion of the budget (domestic and defense expenditures). Political rationality, however, again entered the picture to reduce the impact of GRH. The size of budget deficits triggering sequestration was set higher to lower the odds of sequestration happening (Rubin, 2016). The GRH also moved Social Security and Medicare "off budget" when it came to sequestration and other cost-cutting measures, while counting as "on budget" the annual surpluses of the Social Security Trust Fund.[15] Thus, spending cuts fell largely on programs and their administration in domestic agencies that were less well politically protected by subsystem politics.

Supply-side economics also increased the regressivity of the tax system by cutting income tax rates and increasing dependence on payroll taxes. This shifted the tax burden proportionally toward working- and middle-class earners and away from higher earners by exempting capital gains on investments. In the end, promised federal revenue gains shrunk as a percentage of GDP from 19.6 percent in FY 1981 to 17.3 percent in FY 1984, before rising to 18.4 percent by FY 1989. But expenditures remained at approximately 21 percent of GDP. This gap resulted in the national debt rising dramatically during Reagan's presidency from approximately $900 billion to $2.8 trillion (TreasuryDirect, 2013).

Alongside internal economic and social problems in the Soviet Union, plus Mikhail Gorbachev's miscalculations in trying to save socialism in the Russian Federation (see, e.g., Taubman, 2017), Reagan's historically large peacetime defense budgets contributed to the demise of the Soviet empire. But his budget cuts and defense expenditures also resulted in significant reductions in the size and administrative capacity of many social and regulatory agencies. Critics saw these cuts—and the national debt Reagan left behind—as deliberate efforts to "starve the beast" of activist government and hobble the capacity of regulators to function effectively (Rubin, 2016).

****

With political polarization growing, gridlock in Congress on major issues mounting, and the national debt spiraling, the attention of both mainstream conservatives and progressives shifted to calls for administrative reform for cost savings and to advance their policy agendas. Aside from the attempted rationalization of budget processes and tax-cutting efforts noted earlier, the most concerted administrative reform effort from conservatives in the 1980s was President Reagan's embrace of the aforementioned NPM. The NPM was the perfect administrative complement to Reagan's supply-side, neoliberal economics approach to reducing government activism and, again, brought elements of the then prevalent "logic of business" to the compensatory state.

Reagan's rhetoric successfully turned on its head the logic of earlier progressives and their New Deal and Great Society heirs. As noted, although progressives saw *government* as the solution to market failures, Reagan and NPM proponents argued that *markets* were the solution to *government's* bureaucratic failures. Market rationality and the competition it bred were the single best administrative means for bringing efficiency, effectiveness, and responsiveness to what was left of the federal government after his "starving the beast" strategy had its way. Markets—not government bureaucracies—were the best means to ensure voluntary coordination of individuals without limiting their freedom. Also, incorporating the thinking of public choice economists, NPM proponents worldwide claimed that public agencies were monopoly providers of services. They had no incentive to be efficient, responsive to citizens or their elected representatives, or effective. Nor did they have any incentive to be mission-focused, priority-driven, or customer-focused.

Upon these economic premises, and like many of their reform predecessors, proponents again turned to running government like a business and to the IRP to implement their administrative reform agenda. There was a major difference with them, however. This time, it was the presumed rationality of market and quasi-market competition, not principles of bureaucratic administration, that should drive administrative reform. Nor did NPM proponents turn to political science (as with the early progressives), public administration (as in the 1930s under FDR), or macroeconomics (as in the 1960s and 1970s) for reform ideas and intellectual legitimation. Rather, they turned to the microeconomic-based theory of the firm in economics, while operationally, they leaned heavily on national and international consulting firms for legitimation (see more below).

As noted in earlier chapters, the legitimacy and ascendancy of statistical analyses and econometric analyses over other social science methods were already well established through their affiliation with government efforts beginning with the early Progressive Era. Likewise, Keynesianism had propelled *macroeconomics* to new heights of legitimacy and centrality in the minds of post-World War II leaders. Now, with the NPM, the affiliation of *microeconomics* with government organizations and policy acquired greater legitimacy. Moreover, realizing this, political science and public administration programs began incorporating ever-more sophisticated levels of econometrics into their methodology courses and research agendas. Disciplinary mimesis was not the only force driving this turn of events; expressive values animated many. But threats to material and authority gains that a loss of legitimacy brings relative to other disciplines cannot be ignored as motives.

One of the major aspects of microeconomic theory introduced by the NPM was "principal–agent" theory.[16] It portrayed organizations as a series of contracts between principals (e.g., chief executives, legislators, and political appointees) and agents (e.g., public managers). NPM proponents argued that the career civil service enjoyed an information advantage over political appointees. The two most important problems facing political principals were (1) managers shirking duties or orders imposed on them by appointees and (2) avoiding the creation of moral hazard, meaning perverse incentives leading to bad behaviors. These limited the ability of technocratic rationality to prevail.

In addition, and despite its claims of devolving discretion to public managers, the NPM limited their discretion to determining the *means* for carrying out goals developed solely by political principals. Proponents also joined public choice theory and transaction cost analysis scholars in inaccurately portraying all organizations in Benthamite terms as rational utility maximizing entities. Grounded in the IRP and instrumental perspectives on the bureaucracy, their prescription for controlling public agency behavior for efficiency and effectiveness was to (1) determine core agency competencies and expertise; (2) hive off non-core tasks to subnational, private, and nonprofit actors; (3) aggressively downsize the agency remaining and cut the number of bureaucratic layers; (4) alter the decision calculus of public managers away from traditional procedural controls; (5) refocus managers on realizing goals by measuring agency and employee performance "outcomes" or "results" and citizen satisfaction; (6) link these performance metrics to budgets; (7) deskill agencies to minimalize existing expert opinion relative to political goals; and (8) substitute a vocabulary of metrics for the professional jargon boundaries of existing agency professionals, thus diminishing the power of the latter.

Importantly, although citizen satisfaction was viewed as critical to measuring agency performance, citizens mattered to NPM proponents solely as "customers." The only participation allotted to them in the United States were choices over services (through vouchers) or as participants in surveys of service quality. They had little role as participants in deliberative processes of governance (although a variety of participation mechanisms were afforded in other nations where versions of the NPM took hold). Nor did the NPM give any special credence to the idea of a "public interest." Proponents relied on markets and quasi-market competition to produce the closest approximation to a public interest that societies were capable of discerning. This, just as James Madison and early pluralists had erringly argued that competing interests would provide the closest approximation possible of a public interest, rather than rent-seeking.

Just as public choice theorists repeatedly found their original theory empirically undermined and had to modify their assumptions over the years, so too did those promoting principal–agent theory (critics include March & Olsen, 1984; Simon, 1997; Waterman & Meier, 1998). The NPM's portrayal of classical bureaucratic theory was not only a caricature. NPM proponents also perpetuated the familiar "rationality" mantra of American administrative reformers in the early 20th century that politics and policy should be separated from administration. They also assumed that administrative reforms under way in parliamentary governments (e.g., Australia, Great Britain, and New Zealand)—where authority is concentrated in the executive—could be applied to America's Madisonian system—where authority is deliberately dispersed. Lastly, although NPM proponents saw contracting (especially), partnerships, and networks as the solutions to government failures, they failed to realize that these had been central components of the compensatory state since the nation's founding *and* a major cause of its complexity rather than a solution to it.

Still, the NPM's durability rested on several factors. For starters, and unlike public administration, it had the advantage of economics' theoretical elegance and appeals to rationality. This, at a time of fiscal stress when public managers were desperate to show they were trying to address policy and management problems. The NPM also was consonant with the perpetually reigning image in America of public organizations as rational machines or brains to be fine-tuned. In addition, its market- and business-based reform agenda was highly consistent with American exceptionalism's emphasis on limited government, economic liberalism, and civic responsibility. Also advantageous was its resonance with the dominant neoliberal economic spirit of the times and the propensity of elected officials to want to control administrative behavior to advance their own agendas and institutional interests (i.e., instrumentalism).

****

As noted in Chapter 6, prior research in policy studies also gave some academic legitimacy to Reagan's minimalist domestic state goals. With some public and private foundation grant money now flowing toward the qualitative study of the policy implementation process during the 1970s, the "first generation" of implementation research had attributed the gap between the promise of federal programs and their results to self-interested "games" played by agency implementers at the state and local levels of the compensatory state (Bardach, 1977; Browne & Wildavsky, 1984; Derthick, 1972; Elmore, 1978; Hill & Hupe, 2014; Mazmanian & Sabatier, 1983; Pressman & Wildavsky, 1984; Rein & Rabinovitz, 1977). In true instrumentalist fashion, they prescribed limiting bureaucratic discretion and flexibility and cutting the number of bureaucratic "veto points" (i.e., persons or agencies who could fail to implement a program) (Pressman & Wildavsky, 1984). Researchers also recommended taking the "most direct" path in choosing agencies by using more market-based approaches (e.g., contracting and subsidies) (Bardach, 1977).

However, a "second generation" of implementation research by social scientists in the 1980s took a somewhat more constitutive perspective, arguing that program success required implementers to have *more* discretion and flexibility (e.g., Elmore, 1979–1980). Consistent with the federalism tenets of American exceptionalism, this "bottom-up" perspective did not see policy or administrative wisdom residing exclusively in Washington bureaucracies (e.g., Elmore, 1979–1980; Goggin, Bowman, Lester, & O'Toole, 1990; Hill & Hupe, 2014). Researchers also decried the tendency of federal agency experts to design one-size-fits-all policies, both out of systems thinking and collectivist tendencies in the social sciences, plus bureaucratic convenience. These understated the importance of allowing state and local officials and administrators to tailor and trade off among policies to fit local circumstances; thus, less discretion meant less policy and program success.

This second generation of implementation research favored a policy tool—"backward mapping"—premised on a need to reduce bureaucratic veto points and use nongovernmental actors (private and nonprofit), when appropriate, to effect change (Elmore, 1979–1980). Backward mapping thus counseled circumventing agencies, bureaucratic red tape, and mandates, while expanding the proxy component of the compensatory state (e.g., churches and their associations). Its successor, "reversible logic," combined forward and backward mapping. But it still operated on the premise of instrumental rationality rather than political rationality, underestimating, for example, the political difficulty of eliminating veto points (Elmore, 1985). When applied, reversible logic engendered strong political pushback from subsystem actors who wanted to remain part of implementation structures.

Not surprisingly given their intellectual history, most US public administration scholars were critical of the NPM. The most notable critique—the Blacksburg Manifesto—was grounded in the constitutive perspective on public management (Wamsley et al., 1990). The Manifesto directly responded to the "bureaucracy-bashing" rhetoric and actions of the Reagan administration. It condemned assaults by elected officials on the capacity of agencies and the failure to appreciate the centrality of public managers helping "to run a constitution" (also see Bertelli & Lynn, 2006; Newbold & Rosenbloom, 2017). The Manifesto also called for a "refounding" of public administration based on that role, as well as a more citizen-centric view of the enterprise (Wamsley & Wolfe, 1996).

One of the contributors' fundamental premises was consonant with the ideas of John Gaus, Pendleton Herring, Norton Long, and Dwight Waldo noted in the 1930s and 1940s. Specifically, the politics–administration dichotomy on which the NPM (and, historically, the field itself) was based was descriptively and normatively inappropriate. Public managers *shared* in governance with elected officials and the courts. Moreover, they *must* do so for governance to be effective. Therefore, an "agency theory" of public agencies should replace the dichotomy, with "agency" defined as produced by a "combination of expertise, experience, and commitment to the public interest" (Wamsley et al., 1990, esp. ch. 1). The Manifesto also insisted that a public interest existed that transcended the interest-group struggle or market competition and, thus, should be the true lodestar of governance. In addition, and premised on the substantive rationality project (SRP), civic participation in agency deliberative processes was essential for efficacy and legitimacy. Public managers were in reflexive relationships with citizens and were "sense makers" and bridge builders" for them amid the complexity, turbulence, and discontinuities of this time period.

To others, however, the Manifesto's version of agency theory violated the field's historical commitment to neutral competence and could be dangerous in a democratic republic. After all, the Manifesto saw the career bureaucracy acting as a "balance wheel" throwing its support, when necessary, among the policy preferences of the executive, legislative, or judicial branches. As happened to the earlier New Public Administration movement, critics argued that policy advocacy was for elected officials, not public managers who were subordinate to the former and lacked the constitutional legitimacy to do so. Public administration legend Herbert Kaufman summarized such feelings as follows: the "Manifesto treats bureaucrats as members of a separate branch of government coordinate with the elected branches. . . [and who] are entitled to pursue their own visions of the public interest" (Wamsley et al., 1990, p. 314).

Critics also questioned the Manifesto for idealizing the neutrality of public managers. Philip Cooper, for instance, argued that managers were part of subsystems that blinded them to broader public interests and that the Manifesto "overstated" public administration's constitutional grounding. For Cooper, agency theory had potentially "destructive" implications for the "structural foundations of the Republic" (Wamsley et al., 1990, p. 311). For others, the Manifesto was, and remains, a clarion call for needed reform. Still, the relative power of the Manifesto's arguments compared with the market-driven NPM suffered—like those of proponents of the New Public Administration discussed in Chapter 6. The Manifesto, with some notable accomplishments, was no match in the 1980s for the ascendancy of economic theory among the social sciences and the path dependency of the instrumental model in the minds of administrative reformers of the compensatory state.

****

Although corporate and social science proponents of the NPM movement were largely animated by minimal-state political aims (or "negative-state" or "night watchman-state" goals), more positive-state-oriented progressives in the 1990s in the Clinton administration presented the REGO alternative to NPM. In academia, REGO was generally deemed part of an NGM of administrative reform. As Hoover had done with associationalism in the 1920s, the REGO reform project was framed politically as a "third-way" alternative between unbridled government bureaucracy and rapacious markets and interest groups. But consonant with prior progressive efforts stressing economy and efficiency to gain political traction, as well as Americans' self-conception of limited government, REGO's mantra was neither to cut nor to expand bureaucracy. Rather, it was sold as creating a "government that works better and costs less."

In running to succeed H. W. Bush in 1992, Clinton faced a third-party independent challenge from businessman Ross Perot. The latter ultimately won 19 percent of the vote, running on a platform opposing NAFTA, because it would lose American jobs; reducing budget deficits; and making government work better by applying "common-sense" business techniques. Wanting to stifle another independent challenge in the 1996 presidential election, Clinton's REGO initiative, led by Vice President Al Gore, picked up on Perot's notion of running government agencies more like businesses.

As Governor of Arkansas and a "New Democrat," Clinton had joined with others at the state and local government levels in the compensatory state in applying the logic of business to the public sector (Durant, 2006). He also recognized the American exceptionalist political appeal of Reagan's arguments for debureaucratization and market-based reforms, especially with technological innovation and budget constraints facing him. Still, although emphasizing a "post-bureaucratic" model of administrative reform, Clinton played to his Democratic Party base (especially public-sector unions) by contesting conservatives' claim that public managers were the reason for public agencies' underperformance. Rather, they were "good people trapped in bad bureaucratic systems." By pursuing REGO, Clinton also avoided the argument about "the proper role of government in society," a philosophical and political argument he was likely to lose after the historic Republican takeover of Congress in the 1994 midterm elections. Instead, he rhetorically framed REGO as taking what governments already did and making it run better, much as Dwight Eisenhower had pledged after FDR and Truman's 20-year reign in the White House.

However, in some ways, REGO was really "NPM-lite." Like Reagan, Clinton stressed debureaucratization, decentralization of authority within agencies, giving states greater flexibility in administering programs, focusing on customer service, and partnering. He also embraced making agencies more entrepreneurial by letting programs opt into becoming "reinvention laboratories" to encourage innovation. But REGO also eschewed deep budget cuts to agencies and wholesale personnel cuts that could cripple agencies. Instead, and to increase flexibility, REGO focused on cutting the number of personnel in central overhead agencies such as the Office of Management and Budget (OMB) and (especially) OPM and partnered with federal unions to inform REGO's development and implementation.

REGO also targeted additional "administrative overhead" by focusing on midlevel agency managers (including contracting monitors) (Light, 1999). It made simplistic numerical comparisons with the private sector, arguing that the ratio of managers to subordinates should be reduced. Targeting midlevel managers was also premised on the misguided assumption that managers only passed information up and down the hierarchy and, thus, played no constitutive role in governance. Conceived inaccurately in this way, advancements in IT made many midlevel managers superfluous.

In theory, cutting midlevel managers—as well as the levels of hierarchy in agencies—would give more authority to frontline workers directly engaged in service delivery. This would improve communication flow (and, thus, "outcomes") in agencies by cutting down on hierarchical distortion. It would also make decision times and implementation quicker because of fewer layers in the bureaucracy. Moreover, those closest to citizens were more familiar with their needs and, thus, could be more responsive to them. But taking the politically easier approach of letting downsizing be employee-driven rather than strategic, what actually happened was that frontline service deliverers left in greater numbers than did middle managers.

As in all administrative reform efforts historically in America, bureaucratic realpolitik also informed REGO. Theoretically, when combined with performance management (see more below) and the CSRA provisions, delayering of agency hierarchies would give more direct control of the career civil service to political appointees. It also promised to weaken one major component of subsystem politics—midlevel managers—and, thus, afford Clinton more policy reform capability as a New Democrat. Meanwhile, in Congress, Republican Speaker of the House Gingrich was attacking another major leg of subsystem politics but, this time, for minimal-state purposes: committee and subcommittee chairs. He did so to enhance his power to define policy by placing term limits on them, enhancing the power of the House Rules Committee, and allowing the Republican caucus to vote on chairpersons (rather than continuing to use seniority; see more below) (Orren & Skowronek, 2017; Sinclair, 2016).

Finally, although contracting continued under the Clinton administration, it never occurred at the same pace or scope. Nor was it based on merely cutting the size of the federal government, as was the NPM. REGO focused instead on collaborative governance by stressing various combinations of partnerships with subnational governing agencies, private organizations, and nonprofit agencies. Partnerships were a practical response to budgetary stress, agency silos limiting information sharing, and domestic and international problems stretching across agency boundaries. But, again, realpolitik was involved for a president trying to circumvent traditional subsystems, build new sources of support for positive-state activities, and expand his party's electoral and financial support to include high-tech businesses. Combined with contracting, partnerships also afforded incentives for private and nonprofit organizations to push for greater program funding from legislatures, as they had since the nation's founding.

****

Lest one think that the rationality projects of this period were exclusively the design of public agencies in the compensatory state, it is important to appreciate that both the NPM and the NGM were heavily informed and implemented by private-sector, profit-driven consulting firms (Saint-Martin, 2000). These often had direct ties to business schools, an aim going back at least to the Harvard Circle in the 1930s as part of their quest for legitimacy. Moreover, consulting firms had huge marketing budgets to spread their respective versions of the IRP nationally and internationally. As such, an enormously powerful thumb was put on the scale favoring the IRP over alternative administrative reform approaches.

The rise of corporate management consulting firms actually began in the 1960s when traditional accounting firms began losing business worldwide and future growth looked problematic. In search of new markets, and seeking to reestablish their own legitimacy after scandals, many firms began setting up management consulting divisions for private, public, and nonprofit organizations. Early entries into this market included Arthur Young, Coopers & Lybrand, Peat Marwick, and Touche Ross. Then, as citizens increasingly saw governments negatively and fiscal stress mounted, public agencies came under increasing pressure to reengineer their operations, downsize, engage in strategic planning, develop Total Quality Management systems, and construct performance measurements.

Whether or not promised results occurred, adopting the "best practices" sold by private consulting firms became highly attractive for elected officials at all levels of government. But, in contrast to the legitimacy they enjoyed in the 1930s when invited to staff FDR's Committee on Administrative Management, public administration (and, later, public management) was seen as more theory-oriented than practice-oriented, unlike business schools and consulting firms. Because of the "ideological dominance of private-sector management," even central administrative units in public agencies put more value on analyses done by private-sector consultants than on those done by internal agency analysts (Saint-Martin, 2000, p. 4, fn. 1). The former gave external legitimacy to cutback management in agencies.

With calls mounting for further downsizing of federal, state, and local governments in the compensatory state, this highly profitable market blossomed and the number of private-sector consulting firms spiraled. Among the additional leaders in this now $71-billion market were corporate entities such as Avascent, Bain and Co., Booz Allen Hamilton, Boston Consulting Group, Cadmus Group, Deloitte, Ernst & Young, IBM, KPMG, Lazard, Maximus, McKinsey & Company, PwC, and Unisys. And, as IT demands skyrocketed, profits soared for consulting firms such as IBM, Unisys, and CSC, who sold and serviced these government accounts. Like their predecessors, these firms applied "lean" models of agency redesign (Denvir, 2012). These IRP-based models were guided by elaborate Fordist and scientific management systems designs, flow charts, and structural redesigns that paid little heed to the differences between public- and private-sector management challenges (for differences and similarities, see Rainey, 2014).

Aside from downplaying these sectoral differences, the most pernicious element of this development was the potential, once again, for corruption. Consulting firms sometimes got contracts to implement or oversee recommendations made by company consultants in other divisions. Moreover, with salaries much higher for management skills in consulting firms, government employees sometimes left current positions for jobs in those firms.

For public administration and public management, this situation dripped with irony. Recall that in the early 20th century, the field defined itself as management- (or business-) focused and marginalized law as its definitive anchor (see, e.g., Moe & Gilmour, 1995). A key differentiation from business management was thus lost. But, by the 1970s (see Chapter 6), policy expertise was already marginalizing administrative concerns in public agencies. Then, as public administration and public management sought to revive relative legitimacy in academia by moving toward more scientific methodologies in the 1980s and 1990s, these methodologies were already losing legitimacy among significant segments of citizens as authority structures. Meanwhile, policy schools attacked the legitimacy of public administration as a field of study (see more later). Next, because of its natural and historic ties to business and Keynesianism, economics (with microeconomics and econometrics now added) assumed a dominant place not only in policy schools but also in the social sciences more generally. As a consequence, business schools, consulting firms, and business graduates were seen by agencies as more grounded in administrative practice than political science and public administration graduates. Thus, the former became the go-to advisors for public-sector administrative reforms. And, in a major reversal of fortunes, governments now sought legitimacy by outsourcing administrative reform directly to business and private consulting firms, rather than vice versa. Meanwhile, the legitimacy of government among vocal segments of the citizenry increasingly expanded into SRP-based perceptions of legality, ethics, and justice.

****

Regardless of their origins, and amid this spate of administrative reform, efforts at budget reform to cope with spiraling deficits continued during the H. W. Bush and Clinton administrations (Rubin, 2016). This placed additional downward pressures on the visible size of federal agencies, and by extension, state and local programs. Bush inherited Reagan's deficit problems after his election as president in 1988. In the wake of unsuccessful efforts to reduce budget deficits (e.g., the GRH), Bush and Congress began a downward path in annual budget deficits by reducing the rate of spending growth and increasing marginal tax rates in the Omnibus Budget Reconciliation Act of 1990. The Budget Enforcement Act (BEA), included in the Omnibus Act, also mandated that trust funds, such as the Highway Trust Fund, could not be used as part of the unified budget. However, the BEA did allow for Medicare trust funds to be used in calculating the annual deficit. It also addressed budget deficits by including a pay-as-you-go (PAYGO) decision rule. PAYGO was designed to protect bipartisan tax increases and entitlement cuts from future changes.

Bush paid a high political price for his agreement to raise tax rates and cut government spending. Republican conservative populist opponents of the deal, led by Newt Gingrich and Patrick Buchanan (R-VA), alleged he had broken his earlier pledge not to raise taxes. This split Republican voters and helped cost Bush heavily in his 1992 reelection bid against Democrat Clinton (and Perot). The victorious Clinton administration then successfully enacted the Omnibus

Budget Reconciliation Act of 1993 (OBRA-93)—without any Republican support.

Among other things, OBRA-93 raised tax rates on the wealthy. This brought additional revenue to Washington, especially in combination with a revenue bonanza that occurred during the high-tech boom of the 1990s. The boom brought in hundreds of millions of unanticipated dollars from capital gains taxes on stocks and from higher salaries. But, like Bush, Clinton and his party also paid a heavy price in the 1994 midterm elections. As noted, Democrats lost control of the House of Representatives for the first time in 40 years. Many Democratic moderates also were defeated who had supported an unpopular House tax reform bill that was later changed in the Senate to become OBRA-93.

Still, the 1990s produced not only a balanced budget on paper from 1998 to 2001 but, also, the potential for a sizeable budget surplus going forward. In the 2000 presidential election, Clinton's vice president, Al Gore, adopted Clinton's proposal to use budget surpluses to pay down the national debt and improve the Social Security fund so they would not be used by Republicans for tax cuts. But Gore lost to G. W. Bush, an election controversially resolved by the US Supreme Court, leading sizeable and vocal segments of the populace to deem the Bush presidency illegitimate, just as the Clinton presidency had been labeled by his opponents. A return to growing budget deficits soon followed during the Bush presidency (2001–2009) in the post-September 11 era after terrorist attacks on US soil. This, as the United States fought two wars simultaneously (Afghanistan and Iraq), pursued a worldwide War on Terror, enacted three large tax cuts, and tried to reboot economically after the Great Recession of 2007–2009.

With two major wars still ongoing during his two terms as president and with a nearly $900 billion infusion of capital into the system to stimulate the economy after the Great Recession, Bush's successor—President Obama—incurred rising deficits and a soaring national debt after the financial system nearly collapsed and recovery was slow (about 1.5 percent GDP growth annually). He left office with the national debt nearly doubled (approximately $19 trillion) during his tenure. Continued congressional failure to produce a "grand bargain" followed, with Republicans continuing to oppose higher taxes and Democrats continuing to oppose cuts in spending rates in social programs, including entitlements.

Next, Congress—with Obama's endorsement—again turned for relief to BICA's sequestration process. Designed to be so draconian that neither party would risk it, sequestration nonetheless happened. The total federal workforce, including postal workers, fell by 20 percent to 2.7 million employees from its high of 3.4 million employees in 2010. Excluding postal workers, the federal workforce fell by over 9,000 employees, its lowest level since 2009 (Losey, 2013). This, as federal domestic and international agency responsibilities intensified. Combined with increased revenues from an improving economy and lower-than-expected increases in medical costs, sequestration nonetheless narrowed the expected short-term funding gaps predicted by the CBO only months earlier.

Still, in an era of spiraling political polarization, BICA continued to be routinely flouted by political games. Since BICA was enacted in 1974, Congress passed all 12 appropriations bills on time in only FYs 1977, 1989, 1995, and 1997 (DeSilver, 2018). Instead, it relied on continuing resolutions (CRs) as a series of stop-gap funding measures for agencies and programs. The Government Accountability Office reports that, since 1999, an average of five CRs occurred annually (with the highest being 21 CRs in one year) (White, 2017). Planning and managing risk under CRs, plus uncertainties in implementation funding, became very difficult for federal, state, and local managers in the compensatory state.

Compounding this problem, the start of each FY and the date a final spending bill became law grew from 56 days to 216 days between FY 1998 and FY 2017. Rather than passing individual spending bills, Congress relied on omnibus spending bills combining various appropriations bills (DeSilver, 2018). These were large in size and often delayed until the last minute, meaning that legislators and their staffs had little time to read, let alone understand, the bills on which they were voting. Nor did they have time to understand or care about the immense implementation responsibilities being heaped upon agencies amid budget uncertainties.

****

Economic globalization, neoliberal economics, and failures to enact a grand bargain on budgets during this period brought other significant problems to the US economy. Although downward pressures on the visible size of the public sector mounted, so too did countervailing pressures continue to rise to expand both domestic spending and defense. For starters, a rise in income inequality begun in the late 1980s grew more pronounced, with a temporary respite in the 1990s. So profound were these income gaps that some refer to the 2010s as a "New Gilded Age" (Bartels, 2008). Especially noteworthy were soaring income gains for the top 1 percent of earners in the nation. Minority families and families headed by single females were particularly hard hit by income inequality. The Bureau of Labor Statistics reported in 2011 that black and Hispanic families were significantly more likely to have an unemployed member (18.9 and 16.3 percent, respectively) than white and Asian families (10.4 and 10.9 percent, respectively). More than 70 percent of all mothers, and more than 60 percent of mothers with children under 3 years of age, were in the workforce. Two-thirds of these workers earned less than $30,000 a year and 90 percent made less than $50,000 a year (Durant, 2014c).

Economic globalization and neoliberal economics also produced a major contraction of the US labor movement and greater ethnic diversity as an accelerated influx of Mexican and Central American immigrants performing low-skilled jobs occurred. Provoked was a reduction in unions' influence on politics, public policies, and administrative reform, as New Left intellectuals such as Marcuse and Cornelius Castoriadis had predicted in the 1960s. The share of US union membership fell from nearly 30 percent of all workers in 1970 to approximately 7 percent in 2016 (Faux, 1999, p. 72; Hacker & Pierson, 2010). And although public-sector unionization became the most vibrant part of the labor movement (with a 30-percent share of the public workforce), it too was again under assault by conservative minimal-state actors using tactics from earlier eras. Moreover, with union campaign contributions and political clout declining, many Democrats turned to corporate contributions to make up the gap. This, in turn, increased the real or perceived influence of corporations on the Democratic Party. Meanwhile, despite their benefits to corporations, business in general, shareholders, and many workers, international trade deals such as NAFTA also helped facilitate this decline in particular industries (especially, US manufacturing jobs).

In terms of immigration, business—especially the agricultural, building, and high-tech industries in Silicon Valley—continued to put heavy pressure on the federal government to allow more foreign workers to enter the country during this period. They claimed that Americans were either unwilling (e.g., agriculture) or insufficiently credentialed (engineering and IT) to do these jobs. As noted, however, working-class Americans, who bore the financial hardships of the Great Recession and watched manufacturing jobs shipped overseas, had no real net increase in income or purchasing power for three decades. This, while profits and bonuses soared for corporations and the financial industry. Not surprisingly, citizen trust plummeted in government and the so-called establishment of experts associated with these treaties, deindustrialization policies, and financial deregulation initiatives (Kettl, 2017).

This, combined with terrorist acts throughout the post-September 11 era, also amplified economic, illiberal nationalist, and nativist fears in the United States (and in Europe). It also heightened pressures on immigration and other national security agencies. Sparked were humanitarian, national security, and immigration policy conflicts among Americans that produced political and administrative challenges for the nation. Most notably, questions arose regarding the ability of federal agencies to protect national borders, most especially the Mexican border, and whether the states might do a better job.[17]

Also prompted was a backlash against affirmative action (a key component of the social equity "pillar" of public administration referenced earlier) in many quarters of the compensatory state. This, despite evidence from public management scholars that increasing the representation of historically discriminated-against groups (passive representation) can produce policy outcomes more advantageous to those segments of society (active representation) (see, e.g., Andrews, Boyne, Meier, O'Toole, & Walker, 2005; Dolan, 2000;

Hindera, 1993a, 1993b; Hindera & Young, 1998; Lewis & Pitts, 2011; Meier, 1993; Meier & Nicholson-Crotty, 2006; Meier, Pennington, & Eller, 2005; Meier & Stewart, 1992; Wilkins & Keiser, 2006). Meanwhile, the Supreme Court seemed more willing to limit affirmative action in the workplace by allowing it only when it was the least repressive option for remedying a demonstrated historical bias against minorities (e.g., in *City of Richmond v. J. A. Croson Co.* in 1989 and *Adarand Constructors, Inc. v. Peña* in 1995). Despite mixed evidence that broader representation of minorities and women positively affected organizational decision making and policy outcomes, opponents continued to characterize diversity as part of a dysfunctional "identity politics" begun by progressives and dramatically expanded by the Rights Revolution that was tearing apart the nation's social fabric. Others argued that a focus on affirmative action by class rather than race was more appropriate.

****

Throughout this time period and in classic coevolutionary form, complexity-generating efforts to "presidentialize" and "congressionalize" the federal bureaucracy were consistently amplified. The same dynamics occurred in the state, local, and volunteer components of the compensatory state. This was done through repeated doses of the IRP to advance different policy and ideological agendas administratively. For example, informed by Richard Nixon's administrative presidency strategy (see Chapter 6), the Reaganites used Carter's Civil Service Reform Act (CSRA) of 1978 to impose contextual and unilateral tools on the career bureaucracy with an unprecedented intensity and scope (see Chapter 6).[18] Reagan appointees worked assiduously to use non-career Senior Executive Service (SES) positions to advance their policy goals and made even heavier use of Schedule C appointments at the GS 13–15 levels than had their predecessors.

Between 1980 and 1986, for example, the Reagan administration significantly increased the overall proportion of non-career SES members to maximum allowable limits (an increase from 8.4 percent to 9.8 percent of all SES positions). The administration also targeted specific agencies for installing disproportionate numbers and percentages of non-career SES members, depending on Reagan's policy predilections. Likewise targeted for disproportionate increases in non-career SES appointees were such central staff agencies as the OMB, the OPM, and the General Services Administration.

The Reagan administration also used threats of unattractive job transfers to coax careerists into accepting (or at least not overtly opposing) Reagan's agenda. It also "sorted out" career SES members in terms of the likelihood of their supporting the president's agenda. Those most likely to oppose Reagan's policies were placed in less influential agency positions, either by transfer or internal reorganization. By 1986, the number of SES members indicating that they had a "great deal" of influence over policy dropped to 20 percent from nearly 50 percent five years earlier, and a significant exodus from the SES ranks occurred. However, this exodus was also prompted by Congress, as it later reduced the percentage of SES members eligible for bonuses in any agency (from up to 50 percent to 20 percent) and cut the size of bonuses.

Data from 1986 to 2000 caused some to question politicization as an apt description overall of what had happened to the SES since the early Reagan years. The percentage of non-career appointees fell from 9.3 percent in 1986 to 8.7 percent in 1992, whereas the total number of SES positions filled by the Clinton administration in 1998 declined by 16 percent from 1991. These trends did not mean that the H. W. Bush and Clinton administrations failed to use SES appointments strategically to advance portions of their agendas. For example, the total number of SES appointees (i.e., positions filled) increased by nearly 22 percent (from 6,702 to 8,130) from 1986 to the end of the H. W. Bush administration in 1992.

SES appointments during both the H. W. Bush and the Clinton administrations were decidedly less ideological in tone and more concerned about patronage (H. W. Bush) or diversity (Clinton) than policy. They were also predicated more on promoting cooperative relationships with the career bureaucracy. Efforts to maximize the political responsiveness of the SES were then revived during the G. W. Bush administration as the percentage of non-career SES members increased to 9.97 percent of the total ranks. But then the ratio of non-career to careerists during the Obama administration fell to pre-G. W. Bush levels (8.6 percent in 2013). Moreover, to advance one goal of the President's Management Agenda (PMA) to promote strategic human capital management, the G. W. Bush administration launched a substantial reform of the SES that became part of the FY 2004 National Defense Authorization Act. Under the act and a subsequent executive order, agencies not certified by OMB as making real merit distinctions in rewarding SES members were given lower pay scales than certified agencies. These efforts were scaled back, however, after court suits.

****

Under the earlier Clinton administration, yet another major initiative began to decentralize personnel authority from OPM. This was hardly a new idea, as a cycle of centralization–decentralization had begun at the federal level since the Classification Act of 1949 (Ingraham & Rosenbloom, 1990). As public personnel expert Frederick "Fritz" Mosher (1982) put it earlier, human resource management systems "should be decentralized and delegated to bring them into more immediate relationship with the middle and lower managers they served" (p. 86). But Clinton's decentralization effort was also aimed at giving his political appointees the authority to use personnel policies to advance his policy agenda.

To these ends, the Clinton administration in 1996 created almost 700 "delegated examining units" in federal agencies. However, agencies lacked expertise in handling personnel issues, thus causing substantial backlogs in hiring and other types of personnel actions. Moreover, without a job-application procedure to cover all federal government hires during these years, applicants were faced with nearly 200 hiring authorities, each with its own hiring procedure (Henry, 2013, p. 318, fn. 78).

Later, during the Obama administration, all levels of government in the compensatory state tried administratively to reform recruitment systems by again using the private sector as a model. Actions replicated by or borrowed from states and localities included selecting from among a larger number of qualified applicants by using a "category-rating" approach rather than the traditional "rule-of-three" approach.[19] In addition, the administration's Hiring Reform Initiative overhauled the federal recruiting process, purportedly for greater simplicity and consistency. Among other things, OPM moved to a résumé-based system, eliminating the "KSA essays" (knowledge, skills, and abilities essays). Launched, too, was the Pathways Programs to recruit younger agency talent—especially minorities and veterans—by creating clear pathways to federal employment for students and recent graduates. Targeted were "mission-critical jobs and professional careers where there [were] skill gaps" (*Federal News Radio* Staff, 2012). While quite successful over time, significant technical glitches and embarrassments occurred in these reforms (Vinik, 2017).

Meanwhile, in the states, civil service coverage begun in the 1880s peaked in the 1980s, with three-quarters of the states and 60 percent of their employees in civil service systems. In localities, 88 percent of jurisdictions used merit systems. By the first decade of the 21st century, however, the most notable characteristic in the state and local components of the compensatory state was NPM-based administrative reform of the civil service. Not unlike the attempt during the G. W. Bush administration in the federal government components of the compensatory state, approximately 22 states had incorporated aspects of "at-will" employment (Bowman & West, 2006; Condrey & Battaglio, 2007; Hays & Sowa, 2006; Kellough & Selden, 2003). At-will employment meant that employees could be fired for cause at any time, subject to appeals. Under attack was the Progressive Era notion of lifetime employment in the civil service. Borrowed from the private sector, reformers' ideas of a performance-based, "just-in-time" workforce now took precedence. Additionally, of the 28 state governments reporting at-will policy expansion, 25 also reported some degree of decentralization of personnel systems to agencies where political appointees could better influence hiring.

Other efforts at using administrative reform to presidentialize the federal bureaucracy (with similar approaches by chief executives in state and local governments; see, e.g., Thompson & Gusmano, 2014) by means of the IRP involved White House coordination of agency rulemaking. These efforts were amplified, accelerated, and broadened over the years. Yet, they, too, met the same fate.

Recall that the Carter administration required executive branch agencies and OMB (especially the Office of Information and Regulatory Affairs [OIRA]) to *consider* the costs and benefits of major regulations, but benefits did not have to exceed costs and were much harder to estimate than costs. Next, however, the Reagan administration *required* that benefits exceed costs before rules could be issued. Then, the H. W. Bush administration revived Reagan's defunct Presidential Task Force on Regulatory Relief by creating a Council on Competitiveness led by Vice President Dan Quayle (R-IN). The council became a back door for interests to petition the White House directly for deregulation.

The Clinton administration next disbanded the council and returned its authority to OIRA. It did so, however, by issuing an executive order mandating the primacy of federal agencies in the regulatory process and, consistent with its vision of proactive government, by using "prompt letters" to prod agencies into issuing desired rules. The G. W. Bush administration then jacked up OIRA review. In contrast to the more activist Clinton administration, OIRA issued 23 "return" letters *opposing* proposed agency regulations during Bush's first six years in office (compared to nine during the Clinton years). The administration also initiated "prompt" letters telling agencies to *reconsider* existing regulations. It also created regulatory policy offices in agencies headed by political appointees and tried to make guidance documents to agencies reviewable by OMB.

But, as mentioned in Chapter 6, claims of centralization, integration of initiatives, and strategic coherence in the White House (and in governors' and mayors' offices) during this period were again exaggerated. One analysis found that only 11 percent of policy proposals originated exclusively in the White House or the EOP rather than in Congress or the bureaucracy (Rudalevige, 2002). Another scholar found that "little if any effort was made in the [OIRA] review process to think about the implementation of different programs in a comprehensive and comparative way" or "to reduce conflicts [and] to ensure consistent application of the regulatory analysis process" (West, 2006, p. 445). Rather, presidents tended to use regulatory reviews in ways similar to the "fire alarm" oversight of agencies by congressional committees (and subnational legislatures) (West, 2006, 2015). Moreover, when various administrative initiatives were viewed from the grassroots where they interact, little evidence existed that a cohesive strategy either existed or was even possible (Durant, 1992).

It is also important to note that although distrust of public managers was an impetus for these and other top-down administrative reform initiatives (and similar strategies in states and localities in the compensatory state), these efforts negatively affected the trust that *bureaucrats* had in political appointees. This, as the G. W. Bush administration's IRP-based PMA and politicization reduced information sharing between career executives and appointees and hurt agency performance (Resh, 2015). Subsequently, a 2011 survey of senior managers and career executives found that 40 percent of respondents gave President Obama's appointees Ds or Fs on "collaboration and communication with their [own] staffs" (Dumbacher, 2011).[20]

****

The remainder of the IRP envisioned by proponents of the NPM and the new governance faced similar operational and realpolitik challenges. Taking collaborative governance first, it proved neither as easy nor complexity-reducing as claimed by NPM and NGM administrative reformers (see Agranoff, 2007, for a summary of the variety of forms that collaboration took). In most collaborative formats, these initiatives actually (again) increased the complexity—especially the transaction costs—of administration by further expanding the proxy components of the compensatory state. Thus, public administration scholars spoke of a networked (O'Toole, 1997), "proxy" (Kettl, 1988), "hollow" (Milward & Provan, 1993), "post-bureaucratic" (Farrell & Morris, 2003), "dismantled" (Suleiman, 2003), or "neoadministrative" (Durant, 2000) state.

As subsequent research revealed, in most types of collaborative initiatives, administrative reform proponents understated the difficulties posed in bringing together different organizations with varying missions and disparate constituencies to work in a sustained way toward a common end (e.g., Agranoff, 2007; Durant, Fiorino, & O'Leary, 2017; Durant & Warber, 2001; Emerson & Nabatchi, 2015; Goldsmith & Eggers, 2004; O'Leary, 2015; O'Leary & Bingham, 2009). Among the worst of these challenges were those posed by organizations not used to working with each other, imbued with self-referential tendencies in pursuit of their own disparate interests, and/or lacking the same urgency in meeting collaborative goals (Salamon, 2001, p. 1631). These problems were magnified when cross-sectoral partnerships were involved—with the public, private, and nonprofit sectors having different motivational bases for their behaviors.

As noted, entering into partnerships was especially risky for organizations that did not expect to work together in the future. Partners sometimes were reluctant to be the first to commit resources, in case others in the partnership withheld their contributions or shifted their priorities. Also, should members leave the partnership, provide shoddy work, or otherwise fail to live up to their commitments, those remaining in the partnership would be held accountable for failure. These were lessons already made clear in the policy implementation literature noted earlier for NPM and NGM administrative reformers to see, but this did not diminish their enthusiasm. Presumably they thought switching from hierarchy to heterarchy (O'Leary, 2015) would be different this time, as purveyors of the IRP had thought since America's founding.

In addition, reformers seeking to emulate partnerships in the private sector were asking public agencies to do things less daunting to companies with an agreed-upon profit motive to guide their actions: "network in the shadow of hierarchy" (Sharpf, 1994) and in the "shadow of society" (Peters & Pierre, 2016).

The former meant that although discretion could be allocated to network actors, it could always be overridden by existing regulations or grant conditions in various components of the compensatory state. The latter meant that citizens tended to assign blame for network failure to government rather than third-party proxy actors in networks and successes to private and nonprofit actors (Mettler, 2011).

Collaborative successes certainly occurred, were well documented in public administration research, and, thus, should not be understated in importance or positive impact (see, e.g., Emerson & Nabatchi, 2015; O'Leary, 2015; O'Leary & Bingham, 2009). But this same literature also clearly indicated that building, maintaining, and sustaining successful networks were not jobs for the meek, impatient, politically unastute, or unaware of the pentimento effect. Network management was akin to conducting a permanent political campaign. Leaders had to identify needs, persuade those within and outside their agencies of the need and advantages of collaboration, and then constantly nurture networks in the face of a tendency for entropy within them. Thus, network management produced an ultimate irony: the alleged complexity of getting things done in a public agency *increased* rather than subsided in cross-sectoral networks.

At the same time, some researchers and progressive critics argued that the power and authority of the state (in a continental European sense) to act on behalf of citizens was being transferred to the private and nonprofit sectors (e.g., Suleiman, 2003). Also infuriating to some (ignoring American history) was the idea that governments had to negotiate—and perhaps lessen the stringency of—government rules and regulations to get partners to collaborate. In contrast, others worried that the state was becoming too involved in the private sector. They asked whether government was really getting "privatized" as many conservatives hoped or if the private sector was actually being "governmentalized" (Durant, 2000).

Concurrently, any promise of deliberative democracy was again largely foiled by proponents of either the NPM or the NGM. Proponents assumed that meaningful citizen engagement would arise from collaboration. But research offered mixed evidence of success and left many questions unanswered. As Lisa Bingham and Rosemary O'Leary (2006) summarized, "we do not know about how citizens connect with, participate in, and influence networks" (p. 164). Also, little research addressed whether increased engagement through collaboration trickled "out" to the general public or created new walls between the politically active and the community at large. Some found that the advantage of community collaborative approaches was that elected and agency officials shifted from irritation with community views to asking for input (Bryer, 2007; LeRoux, 2009; LeRoux & Feeney, 2015; Weber, 2009). Yet, even then, administrators still decided if they were going to be responsive to collaborators, broader populations, or both (Bryer, 2007).

Others concluded that local collaborations often excluded national and statewide advocacy groups (who represent broader citizen access), allowing for more influence by business interests (Leach, 2006; Neshkova & Guo, 2012). As Donald Moynihan and his colleagues (2011) argued and American history illustrates, networked governance could undermine democratic values when dominated by private-sector partners with different motives and fewer constraints than their public-sector counterparts. Also, when networks addressed complicated issues, they sometimes disenfranchised those who did not support network decisions (Bingham & O'Leary, 2006).

At the same time, professionalized nonprofits in collaborative networks used fewer volunteers and had less community representation on their boards. This amplified the disconnect between citizens, nonprofits, and governments (see more below) (Suárez, 2011). Additionally, although some collaborations stressing civic deliberation increased citizen perceptions of government legitimacy (Emerson, Nabatchi, & Balogh, 2012), in others, widespread citizen participation in agency decision making *weakened* the legitimacy of representative government (Jing & Savas, 2009). What was again clear was the contingent nature of American administrative reform—whether IRP- or SRP-based; it worked under certain conditions and less well under others (more broadly, see Walker & Andrews, 2015). One-size-fits-all claims were fatuous.

****

Equally vexing was the impact of contracting out. The traditional amount and scope of contracting out within the compensatory state was definitely amplified (Brown & Potoski, 2003; Brown, Potoski, & Van Slyke, 2006; Hodge, 2000; Johnston & Romzek, 2010). Not surprisingly based on history since the nation's founding, this amplification brought additional administrative and ethical problems in its wake. Curiously, at a time when corporate America was engaged in both vertical and horizontal integration to bring key parts of its supply chain into single companies, NPM reformers were recommending the opposite for the public-sector components of the compensatory state by stressing contracting out.

As noted, throughout the 19th century, contracting had been largely limited to specific projects. It then expanded over the decades to cover services performed by agencies. Thus, by 2007, 60 percent of federal procurement spending went to service contracts as opposed to the purchase of tangible goods (Barr, 2007). During the first two decades of the 21st century, contracting was amplified inappropriately to, once again, core government functions (e.g., national security). Combined, the "acquisition of goods and services from contractors consume[d] over one-fourth of discretionary spending government-wide and [was] a key function in many federal agencies" in the compensatory state (GAO, 2006, p. 1).

Although public resources allocated to contracting were significant, the results varied considerably and studies of contracting often were methodologically flawed. Proponents' analyses of contracting gains, as well as in-house analyses, often ignored transaction costs. When incorporated into analyses, cost savings tended, with exceptions, to disappear (Boyne, 1998; Brudney, Fernandez, Ryu, & Wright, 2005; Sclar, 2000). Evidence also existed of greater *inefficiencies* across a range of contracting tasks and at a cost to democratic values (Amirkhanyan & Lambright, 2018). Government employees also began to leave government and join the private sector. They were attracted by the opportunity to pursue policy ends that had been shortchanged within public agencies. Many were disheartened, forced into contract management monitoring the work they had previously done. Yet, agency contract-letting and oversight capacity continued to be woefully inadequate—and rapidly diminishing (Chen, 2009; GAO, 2006)—in the compensatory state, thus raising further SRP-based legitimacy concerns.

Contributing to this shortfall was the underfunding of contract management positions, as well as a lack of stature, mobility, and attractive career paths for contract managers in most agencies. Also culpable were perverse incentives encouraging "inefficient use of [public] monitoring and oversight" of contracts (Miller & Whitford, 2007, p. 213, 2016). Problems of "mixed workforces" also arose in agencies (e.g., public employees seeing coworkers in the private sector doing comparable work at higher wages and/or with better work schedules). Nor was the competition necessary to make market and quasi-market work always available. Competitors often did not exist, so agencies wound up trying to create competition (Johnston & Girth, 2012). Moreover, contracting sometimes did not provide "arms-length" relationships, inviting corruption and cost overruns. Both problems were even more acute at the state and local government levels of the compensatory state. Additionally, recipients of large contracts often made significant investments that drove out competitors when contracts were rebid. This made existing contractors monopoly providers of services—another ironic outcome, since contracting was touted as an alternative to public agency monopolies.

Contracting also meant that the aggregate building of in-house agency capacity suffered relative to existing and new responsibilities that legislation heaped upon agencies. Using constant 2013 dollars, John DiIulio (2014) reported that federal spending was four times larger than it was in 1960, yet the federal workforce was roughly the same size as in 1960. Granted, much of this spending growth came from entitlement programs such as Medicaid, Medicare, Social Security, and the Veterans Pension. But the gap was also attributable to downward pressures on the visible size of the federal government (and subnational governments) in the compensatory state.

For instance, in 2009, the Internal Revenue Service (IRS) had 27,000 fewer employees than it had ten years earlier servicing "hundreds of thousands more taxpayers" (Rucker, 2009, p. A1). Likewise, since the 1970s, Congress expanded the Environmental Protection Agency's (EPA's) responsibilities considerably but (with exceptions as in the Clinton years) reduced its full-time staffing levels from approximately 18,000 employees in 2001 to approximately 14,500 in mid-2015.

Nor had the perennial "skill mix" challenge been adequately addressed in such agencies as EPA, the Department of the Interior, and National Oceanic and Atmospheric Administration. Lacking in these agencies were leadership, management, technical, and scientific skills commensurate with the expanded responsibilities they had to assume since amendments to the Clean Air Act, the Food Quality Protection Act, the Safe Drinking Water Act, and, potentially, the Clean Power Plan (rejected later by the Trump administration).

President Obama tried to reduce contracting by converting some positions back into the civil service ("contracting in"). Especially targeted were those acquired with no-bid contracts. But the political economy surrounding contracting made reducing contracts a slow and arduous process politically; state and local jobs and economic benefits were frequently at stake. Moreover, because some skills required higher salaries than usual and involved seasonal fluctuations in need, contracting legitimately became a major feature of many agencies. In extreme cases such as in the Department of Energy, contractors made up nearly 90 percent of the workforce. Meanwhile, the same trends occurred in many subnational governments for social service delivery, prison operations, public school systems, and information systems.

****

Yet another component of the IRP promoted by and benefiting the corporate–social science nexus of interests was performance-based management (Lavertu & Moynihan, 2013; Moynihan, 2008; Moynihan & Beazley, 2006; Newcomer, 2015). This aspect of the logic of business took the form of performance-based management at the employee level and outcomes-based (or results-based) management at the organizational level. Cautionary tales quickly mounted, however, showing again the problem of applying business techniques across the board in public agencies without adapting them to the realpolitik of public agencies in the compensatory state.

As Moynihan (2015) argued compellingly regarding the results of outcomes-based management:

> Best-practice case stories can be found, and are repeated, but systematic studies of the impact of these approaches give little ground for optimism. For example, a meta-analysis of 49 empirical studies of performance reforms between 2000 and 2014 concluded that performance reforms generally have a small impact. A study of U.S. federal managers concluded that those exposed to Clinton and Bush-era performance reforms were no more likely to use performance data than managers who had not encountered these reforms. Historical case-based studies are similarly discouraging.
>
> (p. 3)

At the employee level, a major 2008 meta-analysis of pay-for-performance programs in both the public and private sectors from 1977 to 2008 showed that individual financial incentives alone were largely ineffective motivators in public agencies (Perry, Engbers, & Jun, 2013; see counterarguments in Durant & Durant, 2013). Again, context mattered. Success depended, among other things, on the type of public service involved, if it was used at lower organizational levels, if faithful and repetitive implementation occurred, and if rewards were perceived as fair and likely to be given. These all afforded much greater challenges in the public sector. Moreover, many politicians who pressed for performance-related pay also saw it as a way to control bureaucrats, punish them for noncompliance with their preferences, and make them conform to their policy agendas.

Relatedly, momentum generated by many in the public management scholarly and practitioner communities, as well as by elected officials, touted the use of evidence-based decision making and offered some empirical support for their position (e.g., Getha-Taylor, Holmes, & Moen, 2018; Isett, 2010). Borrowing once more from the hard and applied sciences (e.g., medicine and dentistry), elected officials and administrative reformers touted the usual across-the-board applications and made exorbitant claims about what could be done with evidence-based policy and management. Evidence-based policy purportedly provided a way to "avoid . . . ideological roadblocks," "revolutionize America's government," and even "change history" (Pasachoff, 2018; but see Stoker & Evans, 2016). Forgotten among this exuberance is what Kant called in the 18th century the necessity for integrated frameworks to make sense of facts (what contemporary public opinion scholars and psychologists call "confirmation bias").

As legal scholar Eloise Pasachoff (2018) illustrates, evidence-based decision making proved highly vulnerable to political rationality:

> "Evidence" is a word that garners bipartisan support because it sounds rational, serious, and limiting, but in many instances it does little to influence or restrain policymaking and implementation. Calls for evidence-based policymaking mask deep disagreements about what evidence is available and what it shows, as well as about value judgments for which research evidence has little to offer. This dynamic is especially true in social policy areas, where there is little shared consensus on what appropriate goals should be. Calls for evidence-based policymaking therefore allow policymakers to claim credit for their actions without taking any heat for specific contested policy choices.

Again, this is not to suggest that organizational and social learning informed by evidence-based decision making are always failures. It *is*, however, to stress their contingent nature and the need to turn down the decibel level of claims, as a raft of recent research demonstrates (e.g., Heikkila & Gerlak, 2013; Kroll & Moynihan, 2018).

****

Similar over-the-top pronouncements and disappointments were also associated with the IT, Big Data analytics, and AI machine-learning components of the IRP in public agencies. Recall that since the American Social Science Association in the mid-19th century, proponents had argued that social science experts could see patterns of interdependence that citizens could not. Indeed, they had in many ways (e.g., during the early Progressive reform movement and the two world wars). Now the argument was that computerized analyses of massive (related and unrelated) datasets would allow experts to see patterns *in the data* that had eluded them in the past. These would offer unprecedented insights into social problems facing Americans, allowing more rational policy decisions. In addition, social media would be a tool of the SRP by helping improve citizen input, participation, and even deliberative democracy. Meanwhile, "enterprise management"-based IT systems would also break down the stovepiping of agencies that plagued the complexity already produced by the rationality project. In effect, agencies and networks could become "brains" making rational decisions, as well as become more citizen-centered.

But the idea that these technological developments could advance rational–comprehensive analyses, economic rationality, and top-down instrumental control in the compensatory state was soon challenged by resource and organizational behavior-related variations in success, as well as social equity and privacy concerns. Consonant with America's historical reluctance to engage in administrative capacity building commensurate with its responsibilities, IT purchases were chronically underfunded in agencies relative to private-sector IT advances and procurements. Thus, most agencies operated with legacy systems that were generations behind private-sector systems. Moreover, the costs of fixing interoperability issues among fragmented databases and systems were large, challenging, and mounting.

The problematic implementation of the Federal Information Technology Acquisition Reform Act (FITARA) is illustrative. FITARA assigned a significant role to federal agency chief information officers (CIOs) in IT governance, management, and oversight processes. FITARA also directed the OMB to assist agencies in developing strategies, methods, and measures to improve IT investment performance. However, a 2015 survey found that only 22 percent of agencies had sufficient resources to implement the needed FITARA acquisition reforms (Gunter, 2016). Even when IT systems were upgraded at significant cost or contracted out, problems arose. Most notable were multibillion-dollar IT investment failures at the IRS, problems critics framed inaccurately as endemic to public agencies in the compensatory state.

Granted, the Obama administration allocated nearly $87 billion to IT acquisition in his FY2016 budget. But, despite the administration's strong rhetorical commitment to move agencies away from their multiple legacy systems and onto cloud-based systems, only 4 percent of that budget was allocated to cloud computing. Political rationality also typically trumped technical rationality. For example, the political process produced over 60 employment training programs located in different agencies. When the CBO and others urged presidents to consolidate or coordinate these using enterprise management IT systems, political subsystems often kicked in to complicate, if not stymie, success. For instance, when applying data analytic packages to human resource planning as done in private corporations, success required various agency management "leads"—namely, CIOs, chief financial officers, chief human capital officers, and chief acquisition officers—to collaborate with personnel security, privacy, and records management officers. Some agencies added specialized data management officers or "data stewards" to coordinate technical, privacy, and security issues. But, again, these efforts frequently encountered the usual data hoarding and coordination problems of bureaucracy.

Nor did the deliberative democracy benefits adduced by reformers fully materialize. Undeniably, the federal government, along with states and localities in the compensatory state, was heavily involved in ramping up social media, mobile apps on iPhones, and self-service iPhone applications. With few exceptions (e.g., Nabatchi & Amsler, 2014), however, research on e-government, IT, geospatial, and social media initiatives was discouraging (Cooper, 2011; Haque, 2001; Musso et al., 2011). As Jane Fountain (2001) observed, at best, the "outcomes of technology enactment are . . . multiple, unpredictable, and indeterminate. . . [because they] . . . result from technological, rational, and political logics" (p. 98).

Granted, the *Governing Institute*'s 2015 survey of local government officials indicated that approximately 40 percent of government respondents had a strong interest in using social media, mobile apps, and self-service sites for citizen participation. However, several obstacles constrained them. These included a lack of appropriate technology, the absence of external mandates requiring it, inadequate time and resources to engage citizens, and uncertainty over compiling the information gathered. Thus, the most common use of e-government by 2016 involved information sharing and service transactions rather than collaboration (also see Brainard & McNutt, 2010; Bryer & Zavattaro, 2011). Additionally, most IT applications focused on monitoring the status quo to make systems run more efficiently (a worthy goal) rather than affording meaningful citizen involvement in agency goal setting and implementation.

Others warned that IT systems not only were vulnerable to cybersecurity threats but also simplified real-world complexity and, thus, narrowed policymakers' focus to quantifiable problems where data were available. This could divert attention from issues and solutions deserving equal or more attention. Social media could also limit citizen input solely to those with network access, in the process marginalizing disadvantaged citizens and privileging better off and organized interests (Newland, 2003). The algorithms they used could also intentionally or unintentionally exclude particular points of views (e.g., conservative or liberal opinions).

A 2017 study of social media use in nonprofit organizations and county governments was also discouraging (Campbell, Lambright, & Wells, 2014). Social media use was modest, although nonprofit organizations were much more likely to use it than county government departments. Both also used social media primarily to market organizational activities, remain relevant to key constituencies, and raise community awareness. Also, most either had a narrow view of social media's potential value or lacked a long-term vision. Other barriers to use included institutional policies, concerns about the inappropriateness of social media for target audiences, and client confidentiality.

Normative concerns also arose about the ability of AI and machine learning to balance efficiency and social equity concerns. In 2017, the University of Pennsylvania's Optimizing Government Project (Schlabs, 2017) summarized the conundrum this way:

> Nowadays, government is armed with algorithms that can forecast domestic violence and employee effectiveness, allowing it to perform its duties more effectively and to achieve correct results more often. But these algorithms can encode hidden biases that disproportionately and adversely impact minorities. What, then, should government consider when implementing predictive algorithms? Where should it draw the line between effectiveness and equality?

Certainly, none of these problems were insurmountable and will no doubt be addressed by future IT advances. But they did point out the organizational, political, and equity concerns that private IT companies and IT consulting firms had played down or failed to mention or recognize when promoting them as part of the IRP.

****

As alluded to earlier, the logic of business, and its promotion by the corporate–social science nexus in a neoliberal era, also infiltrated the nonprofit components of the compensatory state. As the numbers of nonprofits spiraled in this period, as many grew larger, and as more sought grants, competition for funding increased. In response, so too did the professionalization of nonprofit staffing and operations for grant writing and accountability. Moreover, competition made appeals to niche markets and causes more attractive to these professionals, as opposed to building cross-class memberships.

Theda Skocpol (2003; also see Smith, 2012) summarizes this evolution and further illustrates the negative implications of the IRP in this key component of the compensatory state:

> In [traditional] huge membership federations, regional or state plus local chapters were widespread, full of intermediate leaders and members seeking to recruit others. Hundreds of thousands of local and supralocal leaders had to be elected and appointed every year. . . [meaning that] . . . all of the men and women who climbed the ladders of vast membership associations had to interact in the process with citizens of humble or middling means and prospects. Class membership federations built two-way bridges across classes . . . and between local and trans-local affairs. [But] in a civic America dominated by centralized, staff-driven advocacy associations, such bridges began eroding . . . incentives [shifted] to . . . specific "hot button" issues that appeal just to well-delineated constituencies, who are likely to be relatively sophisticated and already involved in public life.
>
> (p. 226)

Again, these dynamics were not inevitable. The funding policies of private foundations and political choices were involved. Between 1975 and 2000, the total number of private foundations doubled (from 21,877 to more than 50,000), while philanthropic foundation funding increased four-fold in inflation-adjusted dollars (Guthrie, 2010). Not only did this put pressures on private foundations for functional differentiation in their organizational structures, but these requirements were also passed on to nonprofit grant recipients.

Under these circumstances, Elisabeth Clemens and Doug Guthrie (2010) summarize how and why the logic of business came to dominate the nonprofit arena in the compensatory state:

> Funding from the philanthropic community . . . shifted in ways that . . . created new levels of accountability for nonprofit organizations. This pressure [came] from changes in the priorities of independent foundations, but it also [came] from the growth in funding from the corporate sector. As funders of nonprofit activities, independent foundations, corporate foundations, and corporations themselves all place[d] greater demands for an *accounting of practical and measurable outcomes* from the activities of nonprofit organizations, and these pressures . . . fundamentally

changed the ways that nonprofit organizations operate today. . . . They [were] also shaped by the increasing salience of firms and markets in many aspects of social life.

(p. 9; emphasis added)

As earlier chapters attest, this impact from the corporate, social science, and foundation worlds in constructing, driving, monitoring, and benefiting from the compensatory state was hardly novel. What *was* new were the effects of tax changes launched during the 1980s by the Reagan administration. Recall how FDR tried unsuccessfully to governmentalize nonprofits; in contrast, Reagan tried to assert greater corporate control by the private sector. Since the late 1980s, Reagan's efforts sparked a rapid and significant decline in federal grants for nonprofits and allowed corporations to seek and secure dominant influence in nonprofit operations. Some nonprofits refocused their missions on grant-funded areas. This caused worries about the "commercialization" of the nonprofit sector, interpreted as losing their charitable missions (Smith, 2012). In response, nonprofits turned to public and private capacity-building grants and services (Smith, 2012). Created was another big financial boon for private consulting firms.

Two other developments further increased the resource dependency of nonprofits on the corporate sector. First, recession (in the early 1990s and 2000s) and scandals (e.g., at United Way) reduced donation amounts to nonprofits, thus further increasing competition for grants. Second, a social enterprise movement created "mixed profit" hybrid social service organizations in the compensatory state (Weisbrod, 1997, 1998). Thus, social entrepreneurship married the civic republicanism principle of community service with the classic economic liberal embrace of individual entrepreneurialism, and business schools began offering degrees in it.

The overall competition among nonprofits for resources also prompted them—especially larger nonprofits—to amplify their contacts with legislators and agency grant administrators at all levels of government in the compensatory state. These efforts focused, among other things, on gaining or protecting their grant funding and influencing regulatory requirements on their operations. This spawned the creation of cross-organizational nonprofit alliances seeking further consulting services, as well as an expansion of the size of the nonprofit share of government spending (Smith, 2012). Moreover, just as subnational governments often mimic the organizational structures and procedures of federal agencies for ease of interaction, so, too, have many of the larger nonprofits.

****

The 20th century was the bloodiest in history and plagued by two failed totalitarian ideologies (communism and fascism). As such, the Enlightenment idea of the perfectibility of man as reason progressed and the "ordering" of society by means of the rationality project looked naïve, dangerous, and sometimes deadly. Meanwhile, the amplification and complexity of the compensatory state in America caused many to question the governability of the nation. Notwithstanding the shortcomings and uneven successes of neoliberal administrative reforms, some leading public administration scholars now saw in the compensatory state—typically called the "networked" state—an opportunity to (re)legitimize their field as a unique scientific discipline known as public management. Founded was the Public Management Research Association. Critics for decades had argued that public administration lacked an overarching identity and theory of its own. But some leading scholars now argued that the study of "governance" could supersede the study of "government" agencies as a new paradigm for scholarship and practice.

H. George Frederickson (1999) became a leading proponent of the governance paradigm. He argued that networks—what he called the "disarticulated state"—offered an unprecedented opportunity to build a unifying theory of public administration that was unique to the social science disciplines. In offering a normative "theory of administrative conjunction," Frederickson argued that the bond among political jurisdictions, public problems, and public management "disarticulates" amid spiraling policy and administrative complexity. Thus, public managers were uniquely positioned to become "bridge builders" fusing together bureaucracy and democracy—a common, yet unrealized theme in all earlier IRP administrative reforms. Left decidedly unclear, however, was why and how the pentimento effect (Adams, 1992), noted in Chapter 1 and that plagued earlier SRP projects, would result in anything different this time (Durant & Ali, 2013). Also left unacknowledged was that the disarticulated state was but the latest amplification of the proxy components of the compensatory state that had characterized American political development since the nation's founding.

Nonetheless, public management scholars argued that the field's legitimacy as a scientific discipline was not only important but also only possible by enhancing social science methods of theory development, empirical testing, and refinement. Based on this logic, the public management and the Herbert Simon-esque "scientific study of public administration" (Krause & Meier, 2005) movements presented themselves as substantive and methodological alternatives to what these scholars saw as the traditional study of public administration. Arising, again, was the allure of applying the ever more sophisticated methodology of the natural sciences to social and administrative problems to discern underlying dynamics and connections that laypersons and practitioners could not see.

In the process, however, the universe of questions asked in much of scholarship was dramatically narrowed. Focus largely shifted to what was measurable as new datasets came online or old ones were combined to produce larger datasets. The use of existing surveys designed with questions for other purposes also became common (e.g., the Federal Employee Viewpoint Survey). As in the 1960s and 1970s, these often produced "concept stretching" and "concept shrinking" due to data availability and were abstruse to laypersons (Sartori, 1970). Proxies for important values also were sometimes used, thus oversimplifying the multidimensionality of concepts.

Nonetheless, this approach produced an abundance of research and significant gains in understanding of topics where research energies were focused (e.g., on representative bureaucracy, network performance, public service motivation, and collaboration). But this development made other public administration scholars join critics in other disciplines who worried that the social sciences knew more and more about less and less (e.g., Schein, 2015). Relatedly, a disconnect between the research and practice communities that had started after the "high noon of orthodoxy" in the mid-1930s came to full fruition in some public administration subdisciplines, causing some scholars to argue that a hollowing of American public administration was underway (Durant & Rosenbloom, 2017; relatedly, see Milward et al., 2016; Peters & Pierre, 2017; Pollitt, 2017; but see, among others, Stazyk & Frederickson, 2018). Regardless, developing a science of public administration in America and linking it to practice (as early progressive reformers hoped) had proven difficult (Durant & Rosenbloom, 2017; Meier, 2015). Indeed, some research evidence showed that the two groups had drastically different perceptions of the importance of different substantive values and tradeoffs among them (e.g., responsiveness, representativeness, due process, respect for the rule of law, and transparency) (van der Wal, 2008). This, as scholars attributed a lack of relevancy to national security policy because of the social sciences' focus on statistically sophisticated basic versus applied research (e.g., Desch, 2019).

Disciplinary arguments soon arose regarding the need, and most useful methodologies (e.g., phenomenology), to increase the relevancy of public management research to practitioners. Some argued that the two must be linked, while others argued that no need for linkage existed at all and that the field should focus on basic rather than applied research (e.g., Head, 2010; Kieser & Leiner, 2009; but see Ospina & Dodge, 2005, advocating cooperative academic–practitioner research). This, at a time when research universities promised to recognize scholarship with real-world applications and "impact" and as political science and other social sciences were more open than at any time since the early 20th century to the study of history, context, contingency, and even social advocacy akin to the Verein model of scholarship (see Yanow & Schwartz-Shea, 2014).

****

Although embracing the Popperian notions of falsifiability and probability rather than the pursuit of unrevisable truths (as had most social scientists before postpositivism emerged in the mid-20th century), the embrace of the natural science model in public administration still continued apace. Ironically, this came at a time when salient segments of citizens, practitioners, and some major scholars were growing even more skeptical about its utility to practice or reform (Orren &

Skowronek, 2017). These more SRP-based critics did so for reasons not directly related to the concerns mounted in the 1970s by scholars such as Rossi and Aaron, but neither did they reject them.

Some in the policy field saw the focus on performance measurement as a challenge to democracy (Radin, 2006). Others, joining earlier critics (e.g., Marcuse, 1964; Polanyi, 1958), talked about the argumentative turn in policy analysis and argued that positivist methodologies promoted by the social sciences were inadequate for addressing most contemporary social problems (e.g., Fischer, 1993, 2009; Majone, 1992; Stone, 2011). They claimed that "solutions" were not so much objectively "right" or "wrong" but contingent and conditional. Their "meaning depend[ed] upon the setting in which they arise" and the values traded off (Wagenaar & Cook, 2003, p. 170).

Negatively linking this argument to the dominant methodology in contemporary social science journals and PhD training, Hendrick Wagenaar and Noam Cook (2003) wrote:

> Problem solving . . . is not manipulation of preconceived variables, but more the discovery of preferences, position, and identity; it is finding out where one stands in relation to the problem at hand. . . . Success is not measured in terms of the one best solution, that is, in terms of a position on a set of hard, preferably quantitative, criteria, but rather . . . in terms of transitions. Is it possible, we need to ask, given a particular social problem, to move to a different situation that, although perhaps not optimal, is perceived by the parties involved as a gain in value and/ or understanding, while the reverse does not hold?
>
> (p. 170)

To this, Dvora Yanow (2003) added:

> To understand the consequences of a policy [or administrative action or rules] for the broad range of people it will affect requires *local knowledge*— the very mundane, but still expert, understanding of and practical reasoning about local conditions derived from lived experience.
>
> (p. 236; also see Farmer, 1995)

Grounded in the tradition of American pragmatism, she argued that this "logic of localism" and the wisdom of citizens turns traditional policy analysis and administration on its head. Indeed, research by this time began taking note of the variety of coproduction approaches (e.g., Nabatchi et al., 2017), their relative increase (primarily at the state and local government levels of the compensatory state) (e.g., Andrews & Brewer, 2012), and the obstacles and facilitating factors to implementing coproduction strategies both within and outside public agencies (see, e.g., Loeffler & Bovaird, 2016). But, not coincidentally, it was at the local and state levels of the compensatory state that citizens had most trust in government (Kettl, 2017).

Finally, in one of the major ironies of the contemporary social science agenda and of administrative reform, the underlying power of what John Dewey (1916) called "like-mindedness" began unraveling in the 1970s and continues in vocal quarters today. So, too, did what Mary Parker Follett (1926) called in the early 20th century the "law of the situation." In the process, the legitimacy of the social sciences as what Walter Lippman (1961) called the "discipline of democracy" grew increasingly precarious among politically vocal and active segments of the citizenry.

Both like-mindedness and laws of the situation depend on discovery of an objective reality that breeds a general, accepted consensus among experts on basic issues. But, as during the Great Society of the 1960s, growth in the number of experts—and especially the growth of think tanks producing "advocacy" or "bent science" (McGarity & Wagner, 2008, esp. pp. 150–156) research that was not blind peer-reviewed—produced a crescendo of competing claims that challenged the legitimacy of the social sciences as an authority structure in many citizens' eyes who could not differentiate legitimate from bent science.

Fashioned was "think-tank competition" over policy initiatives and "ideologically charged expertise" (Orren & Skowronek, 2017, p. 183). These advocacy-based think tanks differed substantially from traditional think tanks and scholarly research committed to so-called public-interest objectives. Moreover, reflecting their funding sponsors (e.g., the conservative Scaife Family Foundation or the liberal TomKat Foundation), their research "findings" could often be predicted without reading them. As Karen Orren and Steven Skowronek (2017) provocatively put the state of this conundrum today on many important social and administrative problems, social "science has turned in on itself" (p. 159) (also see Feldman, 1989; Jasanoff, 1990). Stoked again in the evolution of American political and administrative reform among vocal segments of the population was distrust of experts and a politically impactful belief in "common men with common sense."

****

As in prior time periods, the downsides of and challenges to the NPM movement and the NGM set the stage for the next round of calls for administrative reform. The NPM that was promoted partially as a cure for bureaucratic fragmentation produced even greater fragmentation in cross-sectoral networks, partnerships, and contracting. NPM and NGM proponents' claims of begetting from them a "government that works better and costs less" were found wanting in studies assessing their impact (Hood & Dickson, 2015; Moynihan, 2013; Olsen, 2008; Peters & Pierre, 2017; Radnor & Osborne, 2013). Ironically, the

NPM had largely created greater transaction costs, increased bureaucracy and stovepiping, crowded out public service motivation, and offered less efficiency once the "low hanging fruits" of reengineering were harvested. Not surprisingly, the end of this era found leading experts in the academy and around the world seeing the necessity for many contracted services to be brought back into government agencies.

The chances for doing so on a significant scale seemed bleak, however. Public confidence in government at all levels of the American compensatory state fell significantly during this period, with only a brief respite after terrorist attacks on September 11. In the process, positive ratings for seven of 13 agencies covered in surveys between 1997 and 2007 fell significantly, including the Centers for Disease Control and Prevention, the Department of Education, the Food and Drug Administration, the National Aeronautics and Space Administration, and the Social Security Administration. Meanwhile, the percentages of respondents who held positive views of the impact of state government on their lives dropped from 62 percent in 1997 to 42 percent in 2007. Then, in 2016, Forrester Consulting found that citizens' evaluations of their experiences with 15 federal agencies were three times more likely to be poor or very poor than evaluations of private-sector businesses. Two-thirds of the organizations in the lowest 5 percent category of satisfaction were federal agencies (Kettl, 2017, p. 72).

Granted, many reasons for this level of distrust exist for the falling faith in government (King & Stivers, 1998). Events in the 1970s, for example, undermined government legitimacy. First came Nixon's impending impeachment and resignation in 1974 for abuses of power, including obstruction of justice. Then came the 1975 Senate hearings led by Senator Frank Church (D-ID), who identified a spate of illegal activities by the Federal Bureau of Investigation, the National Security Agency, and the IRS. Also revealed was the CIA's involvement in overthrowing governments in Chile, Guatemala, and Iran, plus multiple assassination attempts by the United States against Cuba's Fidel Castro. Unacceptable, too, were the CIA's dosing of hundreds of unsuspecting Americans with LSD (1953–1964), the Public Health Service's 40-year Tuskegee experiments in which black men were left untreated for syphilis, and radiation experiments on unknowing Americans. Equally powerful, no doubt, was the 2007–2009 Great Recession. The aforementioned infiltration of deconstructionist postmodernism might even be cited as an overarching contributor to the problem. This, by claiming the existence of "many truths," personalizing it (e.g., "speaking one's truth") absent criteria for weighing alternative truth claims, and rejecting existing "truths" as metanarratives by oppressors (i.e., "truth as dominance" or the "hermeneutics of suspicion" in literature). Concomitantly, Russia (and China) was using "sharp power" (i.e., cyberwarfare on social media) to amplify existing divisions in American society, discredit the idea of objective truth, and deny universal values (Diamond, 2019; Pillsbury, 2015).

But the recent decline in evaluations of public agencies generally, and of specific agencies, remains troubling. Events chronicled in this chapter—events arising from the IRP of American administrative reform pursued so consistently since the nation's founding—also contributed to it, as they had done so historically. Yet, amid these concerns, some European scholars speculated, variously, about an IRP-based return in governance to classical public bureaucracy (du Gay, 2005; Pollitt & Bouckaert, 2011) or an undefined post-NPM era (Olsen, 2006). Precisely how much the IRP has contributed relative to other factors has yet to be studied and, thus, remains ripe for future research. But, throughout American history, citizen perceptions of elitism engendered by IRP-inclined administrative reformers—including those in corporate America and the social sciences—cannot be ignored. For example, following in their midst was the rise of conservative populism in the 1970s through the 1990s (e.g., the failed George Wallace [D, I-AL] and Patrick Buchanan presidential campaigns) and in the 2016 populist-framed election of Donald Trump, plus the popularity of Democratic Socialist Bernie Sanders (VT) in an unsuccessful challenge to Hillary Clinton (NY) in the Democratic Party presidential primaries.

The Trump administration immediately began disengaging from international agreements, reviving economic nationalism, assembling a robust deregulatory agenda, and marshalling a contingent of White House advisors and political appointees with, ironically for a populist, strong corporate, Wall Street, and military backgrounds. They also took office with at least a rhetorical commitment to the rationality project and running government like a business but amid unusual operational and personnel chaos. In 2018, that commitment came partially true when OMB announced reorganization plans for various departments and solicited ideas from agencies for cutting regulations that were too burdensome to get their work done (as had the Reagan administration). Talk of "deconstructing the administrative state" flourished, pursued through the instrumental lens of budget cuts, reorganization, significant downsizing of agencies, contracting, leaving positions vacant, and devolution of responsibilities to the states. Moreover, external consultants from the corporate and consulting worlds were brought in to lead reforms. The more things changed, but in a familiar pattern of increasing intensity, the more they remained the same in the evolution of American administrative reform and its links to state building.

Notes

1. The political birth of the NPM is associated with Margaret Thatcher in Great Britain, followed by Reagan in the United States, and based on efforts in New Zealand and Australia. Reagan's was a reaction to earlier progressive reframing of American exceptionalist values.
2. For these terms, see, respectively, Hood (1991); Lan and Rosenbloom (1992); Osborne and Gaebler (1993).

3. The term "new governance," or variants of it (e.g., New Public Governance), has recently been applied to other movements. These share some commonalities but also *differ* in various ways from the New Governance Model offered by the Clinton administration in reinventing government. See, for example, Denhardt and Denhardt (2015); also see Chapter 8.

4. The Scopes decision in 1925 (*The State of Tennessee v. John Thomas Scopes*) made evangelicals feel mocked by, and alienated from, the larger secularizing culture. They largely left politics. It was the civil rights movement and cultural revolution of the 1960s that saw them reengage politically as the "New Right" or "Religious Right" in America.

5. This, at the same time that many churches were active in providing needed social services and counseling to the poor, and remain so today.

6. Key cases in this vein were protections of freedom of speech in *Board of Airport Commissioners of Los Angeles v. Jews for Jesus, Inc.*; *Westside Community Schools v. Mergens*; and *Lamb's Chapel v. Center Moriches Union Free School District*.

7. The most acerbic dynamics began with the nomination of strict constructionist Robert Bork to the US Supreme Court in the 1980s and, later, with the nomination of Clarence Thomas to the same court. Mounting outside campaigns to kill or delay nominations have since become standard practice.

8. Entitlement programs are said to be "untouchable" because of the political costs elected officials fear they will pay in cutting them (or their rate of spending).

9. The Subcommittee Bill of Rights was a reaction against the seniority system and the power of committee chairs in Congress. Among other things, it dramatically increased the number of subcommittees, thus increasing the number of subcommittee chairpersons, ranking minority members, and subcommittee staffs. This accelerated the legislative activities of subcommittees and created further opportunities for policy entrepreneurship.

10. These included the three major television networks (ABC, NBC, and CBS), the Associated Press, wire services such as the *New York Times* and *Washington Post*, news services that sent out their stories for publication in smaller local newspapers, and weekly magazines such as *Time* and *Newsweek*. Collectively, tens of millions of viewers and readers received the same news.

11. Negative partisanship means that citizens do not so much identify with either the Democratic or Republican party, as vote reflexively and ideologically against one of these parties.

12. Not all economists agreed with the neoliberal economic diagnosis and prescriptions of the Chicago School. Critics noted that persons work and invest for a variety of other reasons—regardless of marginal tax rates. Nor did many economists attribute the economic growth that occurred during the Reagan years to supply-side economics, arguing that rising deficits—as Keynesian economics expects—drove the recovery.

13. Basically, the concept of a democratic deficit refers to worldwide citizen perceptions that they have little influence compared with private interest groups in governing institutions.

14. Granted, working with the Congress, the administration did take some pressure off the Social Security Trust Fund by gradually increasing the retirement age for baby boomers. But costs for Medicare services continued to rise faster than inflation.

This discussion of budget reform relies on Mullins and Mikesell (2010) and Rubin (2016).

15. To avoid budgeting confusion and lower budget deficits, President Johnson created a "unified budget" in 1968 wherein Social Security and approximately 150 other trust funds were included in his budget presentation to Congress.

16. For an excellent summary and defense of the use of principal–agent theory in the study of bureaucracy, see Wood (2010). The same goes for a review of choice-theoretic approaches and contributions to the study of bureaucracy in Bendor and Hammond (2010).

17. This discussion of immigration history relies heavily on Tichenor (2002).

18. The Senior Executive Service data reported in this section rely on Resh and Durant (2015).

19. The former allows agencies to avoid having to select from only the three highest-scoring applicants.

20. www.govexec.com/magazine/features/2011/06/c-is-for-change/34161/.

Chapter 8

Seeing With New Eyes?

As Michael Howlett and Jeremy Rayner (2006) argue in discussing path-dependency theory, the

> sequence of events is not a strictly necessary one, predictable from the conditions of the starting point according to general laws. . . [but] there is nonetheless an explicable pattern which relates one point [event] to another, especially in the early part of the sequence [of events]. . . . [Produced is a] . . . contingent sequence [of events in which] each turning point renders the occurrence of the next point more likely until, finally, lock-in occurs and a general causal mechanism, such as increasing returns, takes over the work of explanation.
>
> (p. 5)

The preceding chapters show the explanatory power of these insights when applied to the intellectual history and evolution of American administrative reform and its role in state building in the United States. They also illustrate Francis Fukuyama's (2011) observation that nations

> are not trapped by their pasts. But in many cases, things that happened hundreds . . . of years ago continue to exert major influence on the nature of politics. If we are seeking to understand the functioning of contemporary institutions, it is necessary to look at their origins and the often accidental and contingent forces that brought them into being.
>
> (p. x)

Since America's founding, complex domestic and international problems have challenged the ability of the federal government to cope with them. This, partly because of America's rhetorical self-conception as a nation premised on, and largely sustained by, limited government, economic liberalism, and civic republicanism. And a major part of sustaining this self-conception is that elected officials have hid the visible size of government since the nation's founding as best they could—especially, the federal government. They have done so by working through and cogoverning with subnational governments, the private sector, and the nonprofit sector. In combination with federal agencies, these actors comprise a "compensatory state." That is, together, they compensate (with and without conflict) for the shortcomings of the others.

This does not mean that the visible size of the federal government did not grow, become more capacious in its reach, and acquire more power at various times in history as part of the compensatory state. By some measures, the overall size of the visible federal component grew immensely during most of the 20th century before leveling off after the 1970s. But, based on rulemaking in federal agencies, the activity of the federal component of the compensatory state has, with variations across presidential administrations, increased in regulatory scope and costs (as well as benefits). Moreover, the major growth in the visible size of the compensatory state took place in states and localities and among private and nonprofit contractors in both the domestic and defense domains of public policy and administration.

Nor does it mean that conflict between and among elements of the compensatory state has not occurred and relative power advantages shifted or differed across policy arenas (often with judicial involvement). In addition to continuous conflict over 10th Amendment states' rights issues and expansive interpretation of the 9th Amendment regarding unenumerated rights, the natural state of intergovernmental relations and networked governance was—and remains—bargaining among the actors and mutual adaptation. Moreover, although the federal government still maintains a monopoly on the use of US military power, domestic and international policy ("intermestic policy") are frequently entangled and require mutual accommodation.

It *does* mean, however, that by ignoring recent developments in history, cultural studies, intellectual history, legal studies, and epistemology and methodology in these and other cognate fields, public administration scholarship has understated the historical extent and overstated the weakness of the American state prior to the Progressive Era. It has done so by too narrowly defining it as including only federal agencies and administrators wielding state power rather than as federal agencies, subnational governments, and the private and nonprofit sectors wielding aspects of state authority collectively on behalf of society (abetted or constrained by the courts).

Recent acknowledgement of these dynamics since the late 1980s has led some in the field to see a new "governance paradigm" for public administration.

However, claims that all this is "new" are problematic when the nature of the state is examined from an infrastructural perspective. Since its founding, America has relied on a compensatory state, with federal agencies in Washington an important part of it and, occasionally, a dominant force within it. But the rest of the proxy components of the compensatory state—subnational and cross-sectoral administrators—have compensated for the historical, inefficiently path-dependent, and deliberately designed lack of visible federal administrative capacity driven by American exceptionalist values and the broader self-conception of Americans.

Prior chapters also show how administrative reform initiatives throughout US history were launched from similar arguments by reform proponents with different political, philosophical (e.g., activist versus minimal government), ontological, cultural, and administrative ideas on American state building. Most were couched explicitly or implicitly in arguments that their time period was uniquely complex and dangerous; that their reform prescriptions were not only necessary and inevitable but enhanced democracy; and that reforms could help revive American exceptionalism's millenarian vision that the nation could avoid the fate of earlier republics.

Prior chapters also illustrate why, despite other alternatives and repeated disaffection with the results produced, technocratic administrative reform prescriptions—one major component of the instrumental rationality project (IRP)—that eschew constitutive views of the bureaucracy have repeatedly prevailed historically. The dominant preference of administrative reformers and elected officials for the federal, state, and local agencies that comprised part of the compensatory state started earlier in time with the "logic of the military" and, later and shortly after, the "logic of business." In pursuit of this IRP, reformers persistently focused on building an expertise-driven set of bureaucratic executive agencies, concentrating power in the executive and away from the legislative branch, and trying to depoliticize policymaking and administration as much as possible. At times, they also sought instrumental rationality by invoking the rationality of markets and quasi-markets as tools of administrative reform. Even when substantive rationality approaches—that is, the substantive rationality project (SRP)—were pursued, a pentimento effect occurred, with the IRP diluting the SRP's staying power and effectiveness.

Whether administrative or market-based in nature, this theoretical quest for instrumental rationality ran into political rationality in practice, thus attenuating the promised effectiveness of the IRP. Moreover, a paradox developed that is consistent with institutional coevolution theory: the more agencies sought relative autonomy by building horizontal relationships, the more presidents and Congress—as well as governors, mayors, legislatures, and city councils—took steps to counter these efforts. Repeatedly, they used the IRP to "weaponize" reforms to advance their own agendas. The courts, in turn, were often called upon to adjudicate their differences over means or ends, hence, over time, increasing perceptions of judicial politicization.

Thus, although portrayed as objective and necessary responses to historical–structural mismatches, each of the competing administrative reform alternatives offered in any historical period was more fundamentally about state building and (re)defining the relationship between citizens and the state. This involved advancing preferred philosophical, political, and policy positions of reformers, including those to expand or contract state power. Not surprisingly, and regardless of proponents' aims, the competing philosophical approaches of actors played a major role in keeping federal agencies on the defensive. Virulent attacks from the political Right and Left throughout US history, as well as from well-meaning and more moderate reformers in all political parties, helped amplify Americans' historical skepticism about government into total cynicism at various points in time.

Nonetheless, elected officials' predilection for seeing the IRP as superior for administrative reform and state building to other alternatives prevailed and endured. This, despite being diametrically at odds with the realpolitik of the Madisonian system and being involved in significant business and macroeconomic failures. In doing so, technocratic and associationalist progressivism's model of public managers as instrumental "bridge builders" also prevailed in each era. Dwarfed were more constitutive views of the career civil service as minimalist-state opponents framed them as unconstitutional, threatening liberty, and perpetuating incompetence, immorality, and unaccountability.

Commenting on what the cumulative impact of these IRP-based dynamics was for civic deliberation in the United States, C. Wright Mills (1956) wrote that Americans know they are "liv[ing] in a time of big decisions; they [also] know that they are not making any" (p. 5). The perdurability of this situation in the United States and abroad led Colin Crouch (2004) more recently to comment that the United States is in a "post-democracy" era. Others referred to a "crisis of representative democracy" (Tormey, 2016) or "anomic democracy" (Crozier, Huntington, and Watanuki, 1975). In the process, public agencies' abilities "to support and develop responsible governance" (du Gay, 2005, p. 6) were acutely diminished.

As noted, other perspectives related to the SRP, such as citizen participation, surfaced occasionally in US history. But the staying power of these approaches has been limited. Participation at the local government level of the compensatory state showed some success stories. Still, many efforts since the nation's founding

> suffered from a lack of resources for their implementation, and administrators' logical response was to comply at the minimally required level so as not to drain resources otherwise allocated for the operation of their programs. . . [that is,] to do just enough to comply with the legal mandates but not enough to make them work well.
>
> (Cooper, 2011, p. 242)

Moreover, when SRP-related participatory successes occurred in any component of the compensatory state, they mostly involved individual projects (Berry, Portney, & Thompson, 1993; Thomas, 1986). Considerable evidence suggested that unsuccessful efforts resulted from "poor planning or execution" or because "administrative systems based upon expertise and professionalism [left] little room for participatory processes" (King, Feltey, & Susila, 1998; also see DeLeon, 1992; Forester, 1989). Yet another problem was that public managers often erroneously assumed they knew what information citizens wanted, how they wanted it presented, and what their preferred unit of analysis was. For instance, budgeting offices ostensibly committed to citizen responsiveness in recent years tended to collect performance information more to justify their agencies' actions than to determine citizens' preferences (Berman, 2012).

This is not to argue that meaningful and effective public participation schemes have not occurred. Truly deliberative involvement of citizens *has* occurred in recent decades and been rightly celebrated, but, in most cases, it has not been institutionalized. Fortunately, three relatively recent developments in public administration scholarship have picked up the baton from elements of the New Public Administration and Blacksburg Manifesto in trying to address this issue, primarily by refocusing reformers on a broader set of values than the IRP's focus on economy and efficiency. The first, the "public values governance" model (Bozeman, 2007)—also known as the "good governance" model (Aoki, 2015) or "new public governance" model (Osborne, 2010)—focuses on the value added to the public afforded by agencies in the compensatory state. It also offers dozens of values for agencies to consider and suggests this focus as a new paradigm for public administration research and practice. The second—the New Public Service model (Denhardt & Denhardt, 2015)—takes a similar view but offers deliberative democracy as a new paradigm for the field. The third perspective—the Constitutional School (Newbold & Rosenbloom, 2017—urges the field to reemphasize its constitutional and legal roots, roots that were lost in the early Progressive Era's focus on management. It is, thus, a direct descendent of the Blacksburg School and the "argumentative" and "interpretive" turns in the social and policy sciences.

Each of these emergent paradigms is valuable in raising the salience of a broader range of SRP-based values and participants in agency and network deliberative processes. Moreover, proponents can point to examples of how these perspectives have raised consciousness and produced positive results in practice (see, e.g., Bryson, Crosby, & Bloomberg, 2014; Denhardt & Denhardt, 2015; King & Stivers, 1998). Also, the heuristic devices these models offer for administrative reformers hold promise for moving their thinking beyond the IRP and toward both political rationality and the more legitimacy-provoking SRP. However, despite their impressive starts, each unsurprisingly requires additional conceptual development and clarification, awareness of contextual variation in success, explication of value tradeoffs, and (especially) integration of realpolitik in these processes (Bryson et al., 2014; Rhodes and Wanna, 2007). The same can be said of the New Public Administration's "pillar" of social equity research (Durant & Rosenbloom, 2017).

Relatedly, many public administration scholars have begun emphasizing "softer" administrative reform approaches that see efficiency and economy in a new light and that go beyond the aforementioned human relations approach. For example, Mary Guy, Meredith Newman, and Sharon Mastracci (2006) have helped bring the idea of emotional labor into public administration. They argue that person-to-person interaction and communication are critical to personal and agency success. In their research, a lack of these skills cuts down on agency effectiveness (e.g., loss of job satisfaction, absenteeism, and personal motivation). Meanwhile, led by James Perry and Lois Wise's (1990) seminal work, scholarship has boomed regarding the multidimensionality of employees' "public service motivation" (PSM) as a management tool for public managers, as well as on its impact on individual and agency-level performance (for overviews of this vast literature, see Crewson, 1997; Pandey & Stazyk, 2008; Perry, 1996; Stazyk, 2013). Yet, with over 50 journal articles appearing per year on PSM (Ritz, Brewer, & Neumann, 2016), researchers are just beginning to assess the value PSM adds to various types of performance, as well as whether and how it adds value to other well-known motivation techniques (Pinder, 2008).

In some ways, administrative reform alternatives such as these have shared the minority paradigmatic views in public administration expressed in the 1920s by settlement women. Some also shared the postmodernist premises of several of the Blacksburg scholars of the 1990s, the participative governance focus of the Great Society in the 1960s, and the epistemologies of critical theorists, social constructivists, and postmodernists in the late 20th and early 21st centuries (e.g., Hummel & Stivers, 2010; Miller & Fox, 2007; Denhardt & Denhardt, 2015). But, outside academia, they have thus far shared the same fate as their predecessors (e.g., the pentimento effect), although some research support exists for disparate successes: instrumentally grounded views of administrative reform trump other alternatives in the minds of most administrative reformers (elected and unelected) at all levels and sectors of the compensatory state.

Still, success in reestablishing the *legitimacy* of public agencies in the compensatory state is crucial—arguably the most crucial administrative challenge of our day. For many administrative reformers in American history, bureaucracy and markets—and the IRP more generally—would improve democracy and, thus, legitimacy. Most saw the two linked, much as capitalism had been linked to democracy in the nation's Founding Era as the commercial republic took root. Too often, however, the IRP has helped marginalize citizens from governance, making them less mobilizable politically in support for building administrative capacity commensurate with responsibilities placed on the public sector.

The IRP has also contributed periodically to perceptions of an elitist bureaucratic class impervious to the voices of large and vocal segments of the American citizenry. More fundamentally, the IRP's focus on efficiency implied a flawed causal theory: efficiency has been a hygiene factor rather than a motivating factor for citizen perceptions of government's value. An administrative reform focus on initiatives linked to the SRP at least offers administrative reformers a far-underutilized strategy for public agencies trying to build, retain, or regain legitimacy. Indeed, recent research suggests that focusing on fairness, employee engagement, citizen needs, and delivering "retail"-level services increases perceptions of legitimacy throughout the compensatory state (Kettl, 2017). But political rationality must still lie at the heart of such a strategy; the pentimento effect has typically marginalized efforts that have not considered agency and network realpolitik.

It is also critical to note how alternatives to the IRP such as these have been consistently marginalized throughout US history, a trend strongly abetted and shaped by the power of the corporate–social science nexus of interests. Working independently or jointly to pursue their perceived interests, the actors in this nexus have sought to enhance or restore legitimacy gains by associating themselves with government. This dynamic included the funding proclivities of private foundations that favored the scientific method over other methodological alternatives at various points in time. It also included the path dependency afforded to scientific methods by the amplification of sinewy subsystems of actors benefiting from compensatory state building and framing their efforts in American exceptionalist terms.

Moreover, given the importance of the economy to America's commercial republic, as well as the preference for business in market economies, business became the dominant partner in the nexus. And partly because of first-mover advantages, the nexus' links to market concerns afforded greater legitimacy—and, thus, greater voice—to the economics profession (first macroeconomics, then microeconomics) over the other social sciences (regardless of their level of legitimacy). Meanwhile, partially to improve their legitimacy as social sciences (including expressive, material, and authority gains), many public administration, public management, and policy scholars and programs shifted their emphases to econometric methodologies and economic theories. This, ofttimes at the cost of more substantive and values-based learning and research.

Also unrealized to the extent promised was the vast potential for using electronic media and social media to advance deliberative democracy. As earlier chapters illustrate, elements of the press throughout American history have not always had positive impacts on citizens' views of government agencies and public managers. But both the positive and negative effects of the media have been amplified by technology development. At the macropolitical level, 24-hour news, the segmentation of news outlets, and abuses perpetrated through social media have evolved to threaten democracy and its institutions, much as scholars such as Theodor Adorno, Martin Heidegger, and Herbert Marcuse contended they would. In addition, although many hoped social media might help build a coproduction, or even a cogovernance, service ethic in agencies, doing so has proven difficult. Preference for a "one-way" flow of information from agency experts to the public varied across levels of government but still largely prevailed by the end of the Obama administration. This, as most agencies continued using information technology (IT) and social media for information sharing and service transactions rather than for civic collaboration.

Evidence also exists that the repeated and amplifying ascendancy of the IRP throughout the history of American administrative reform and linked to state building helped create perceptions that a "bureaucratic class" detached from the attitudes and preferences of average citizens existed. For example, survey research by Jennifer Bachner and Benjamin Ginsberg (2016) finds that agency experts, White House and congressional staff, and policy think tanks tended *not* to value citizen opinions. Moreover, their attitudes and priorities differ considerably from ordinary citizens' priorities. They worked in an "echo chamber" in Washington within policy subsystems and issue networks, reinforcing each other's priorities and believing them best for the nation. Although additional research in this area is needed before definitive conclusions can be drawn, these findings lend credence to charges of a perceptual gap conflated into critiques of bureaucratic elitism in government.

Some might see these critiques as a positive development given the complexity of the age. Becoming authority structures in America can have positive effects and certainly reflects the vision held by large segments of the social science professions since at least the mid-19th century, as well as by the early progressives and the Harvard Graduate School of Business in the early 20th century. But this gulf in priorities can also be seen as a violation of the tenets of popular representation in a democratic republic and, thus, a threat to legitimacy. As Clinton Rossiter put it, despite their anti-majoritarian tendencies, the "framers of the Constitution seemed to endorse [the idea] . . . that the nation's rulers should possess a common interest and 'intimate sympathy' with the ruled" (Bachner & Ginsberg, 2016, p. 42). But, ironically, the IRP designed for expressive, material, and authority gains has helped diminish legitimacy in the eyes of a politically significant and aroused minority of Americans. Reinforced has been traditional citizen reluctance to give public agencies the resources they need to address the spiraling policy and administrative responsibilities heaped upon them by elected officials and the courts.

At the same time, the otherwise critical and beneficial Rights Revolution of the 1960s and 1970s placed tremendous administrative burdens on agencies for both good reasons (e.g., protecting due process and providing adequate legal support for agency decisions) and less noble ones (e.g., opponents of government activism promoting paralysis by analysis). Thus, like the APA of 1946 ever since, the implementation of the Rights movement's "goals statutes" further amplified a "procedural republic" that protects citizens and American values but ultimately politicizes the judicial nomination process. But the administrative complexity they have wrought also tended to favor well-healed business and interest groups engaged in rent-seeking at various stages of policy and administrative development (Kerwin et al., 2010).

Also challenged by recent events has been administrative reformers' vision of nonprofits as venues for citizen participation and civic education in the compensatory state. When nonprofits were "mass-based," participation and deliberative democracy occurred in confederated networks. But the otherwise beneficial professionalization of nonprofits, as well as the "logic of business" and the rise of "checkbook" participation within them, can pose a profound threat to this vision. These developments portended nonprofits untethered from local commitments, traditional agency missions, and mass political mobilization. Evidence exists that philanthropic funding to nonprofits can sometimes advance responsiveness to public values and has done so. Yet other evidence suggests that "philanthropic paternalism" can make nonprofits more responsive to donors' preferences than to clients (Salamon, 1996).

Thus, citizen estrangement based on the marginalization of average citizens through the best-intended applications of the IRP (both bureaucratic- and market-based reforms) should give observers and future administrative reformers pause. Otherwise, one has to dismiss the policy gap just noted between the views of bureaucratic experts and average citizens, the revolt against established US political parties that took place in recent years, and the role that the questioning of expert advice played in the 2016 election of Donald Trump. Likewise ignored or discounted must be research identifying the concepts of "policy feedback," interpretive effects," and "administrative burden" as a result of the IRP, with negative results for agency legitimacy in the compensatory state.

Policy feedback stems from such things as administrative structures, policies, and procedures. These can affect citizens' perceptions of themselves, their sense of political efficacy, and the value they give to public agencies and government, generally (Ingram, Schneider, & deLeon, 2007; Ingram & Smith, 1993; Schneider & Ingram, 2005; Soss & Schram, 2006). Erosion of direct service provision fostered by the proxy components of the compensatory state also creates "interpretive effects" that undermine citizens' perceptions of self-efficacy and political involvement (Campbell, 2003; Schneider & Ingram, 2005). Moreover, when these proxy elements are contracted to deliver public services, research indicates that citizens may not associate the benefits they *receive* from government *to* government. Rather, they tend to associate the benefits with the private or nonprofit provider of the service, while they attribute problems to government agencies. These negative perceptions reduce the propensity of citizens to pay attention to government, value what it does for them, participate in the political process, and be mobilizable for political action in support of agency capacity building.

The concept of administrative burden refers to the amount of various costs incurred by clients seeking to navigate the receipt of government benefits in public agencies (e.g., Moynihan & Soss, 2014). The IRP imposes such transaction costs on citizens as learning the system, the psychological stress incurred in navigating it, and the time invested in complying with rules and regulations. Each of these reactions compromises support for public agencies and lowers the prospects that citizens will see them as advancing the SRP in the United States.

The preceding chapters also show the impacts of ascriptive hierarchy on the evolution of American administrative reform and compensatory state building. Much needed legislative progress happened to combat de jure or state-sponsored discrimination in the mid- to late 20th century, progress building on earlier executive branch and judicial efforts (e.g., Truman's desegregation of the armed forces). But other forms of de facto or institutionalized discrimination still begged for reform, provoking the aforementioned Rights Revolution. Specifically, various forms of de jure and de facto racial, ethnic, and gender-based discrimination arose, much of which was developed and/or sustained by compensatory state actors. Moreover, a repetitive theme of opponents of activist government has been the painting of public employees as prostitutes and pimps during and after the Civil War, as "effeminate" during the Progressive period, as promiscuous and a threat to America during the Second Red Scare in the 1950s, and as conspiratorial and incompetent during the Populist movements on the Right of the late 20th and early 21st centuries.

****

The preceding chapters also challenge several of the "pictures" currently in our heads regarding the evolution of American administrative reform and state building. For starters, the analysis suggests potential rewards for public administration scholarship reconceptualizing the meaning of the "state" and "state power" in America to bring it more in line with contemporary research in history, American political development (APD) in political science, and other cognate fields. Better suited to America's Madisonian system is an "infrastructural" approach that reinterprets the still dominant image of the "peculiar stateless origins" of the nation. Validated is a governance paradigm, but one that is not "new."

Using an infrastructural approach leads to an understanding that the administrative state apparatus in Washington is only one part—albeit an important and sometimes dominant one—of a larger compensatory state. It also should temper tendencies to put the label "new" on each iteration of American administrative reform. What are usually portrayed as discontinuities are actually the amplification effects of IRP-based administrative reforms that have cascaded throughout US history to narrow the opportunities for alternative types of reform and state building. At certain points, a qualitative shift may occur regarding complexity, type, and scope in the nature of networks. But they are all grounded in amplifications of an IRP that has rendered more SRP- and constitutive-based approaches difficult to implement because of the pentimento effect.

Matching responsibilities to federal administrative capacity thus has persistently meant hiding the visible size of government by using third-party and cross-sectoral actors as proxies to help develop and deliver goods, services, and opportunities to Americans. Hiding the visible size of the federal government is hardly as new in American history as some reading public administration scholarship today might infer. Nor can the complexity of the policymaking and implementation structures involved in this growth be overstated—especially with the increasing judicialization of agencies and the activism of the federal courts (both liberal and conservative in orientation).

Also, given America's tendency to hide the visible size of the federal government in the 19th century, the proportion of what third parties did then compared to what the federal government *directly* delivers today in goods, services, and opportunities was no doubt higher during that century. Even during the Progressive Era, New Deal, and Great Society when federal agencies and programs spiraled in number, the proxy component of the compensatory state grew with them and amplified earlier trends. Relationships within, between, and among 20th-century and 21st-century networks vary significantly, and a greater variety of network types exist. But, like earlier partnerships and networks, they are often reciprocally resource dependent. Moreover, regardless of time period, partnering and networks often occurred with government encouragement, prodding, mandates, funding, and/or tax incentives (see, e.g., Mazzucato, 2015). Seen in this light, "America in the nineteenth century was no less fully governed than America in the twentieth" century (Orren & Skowronek, 2004, p. 23).

Thus, the "hollow state" (to the extent it is so), "publicness," and networked government have, by choice, been with Americans since the nation's founding and have been amplified over the nation's history. This reality has only been masked by the tendency for scholarship to measure the size, scope, and power of the state in continental European terms as the "organization of officialdom" in Washington and federal regions rather than the total "reach of public authority" (Novak, 2008, p. 762). As Sheldon Wolin (2004) argues, a "paradox of power" in the American state has always existed, because state "power is simultaneously concentrated and disaggregated" (p. xxi). Consequently, those proposing a focus on governance as a new paradigm for public administration are correct; where they go astray is in arguing that the concept of governance—meaning tracing the flow of state authority wherever it resides—is new to the American republic.

The second related need exposed when it comes to pictures in our heads is to grasp the importance of "initial conditions" (Pierson, 2004). Most important are the enduring effects of Americans' self-conception—in particular, its focus on American exceptionalist values, faculty psychology, and religion. For example, as Marc Allen Eisner (2000a) argues regarding World War I, "state capacity was expanded by appending the capacities of private-sector associations on to the state. . . . [N]ationalization [of industries] . . . was unavailable in the United States due to a combination of historical, institutional, ideological, [religious,] and political factors" (p. 12). Much the same occurred during World War II, the Cold War, and the post-Cold War era. But such an argument also characterizes the dynamics of compensatory state building since the nation's founding. Whether American exceptionalist values will prevail in the face of new waves of legal and undocumented immigrants and refugees from Mexico, Central America, war zones, and climate change disasters around the world is an empirical question for future study. However, earlier waves of immigration did not dent their impact (despite progressivism's challenges to them), although today's multiculturalism ideology differs from yesteryear and predicted majority–minority cities may change all this. Still, American exceptionalism's values and promises are often what motivate newcomers to seek entry to the United States in the first place.

Nor can the lasting impact of faculty psychology be exaggerated on the design of the Madisonian system, on attitudes toward limited government and markets, and on Americans' historical tendency to value the social wisdom of society over that of government to solve public problems. Repeatedly, the centrality of American exceptionalist values and traditions, faculty psychology, and the American millenarian focus on escaping the fate of earlier republics set administrative reform and its link to state building on a path. This path has advantaged the IRP, scientism, market- and quasi-market-based reforms, and volunteerism (including partnering and cross-sectoral cooperation) over other reform alternatives. This happened despite conflicts *within and across* administrative reform initiatives, the social sciences, and time periods, and they were resolved by power differentials among various reform proponents.

These initial philosophic predispositions—invoked and amplified by the corporate–social science nexus in pursuit of the IRP—consistently constrained the options available to American administrative reform in two ways. First, they made business, market-informed, community-based volunteerism, nonprofits, and state and local government-led initiatives easier "sells" to elected officials than the building of adequate federal (and subnational) administrative capacity to address the nation's challenges. Second, since the nation's founding, this predisposition persistently expanded the proxy component of private and nonprofit actors in the compensatory state. The logic of the IRP-based compensatory state sometimes succeeded but often produced paradoxical results. Although done in order to hide the visible size of the federal government, it has—along with the courts—produced greater levels of administrative complexity for the governance system as a whole. This, much to the chagrin of government activists. These proxy components also have persistently pushed for greater government activism, much to the chagrin of minimal statists embracing what Isaiah Berlin called negative rather than positive freedoms. This dynamic is also contrary to conservatives' expectations of shrinking government by downsizing, defunding, deskilling, delayering, or devolving its responsibilities to subnational and proxy components of the compensatory state.

In the process, the federal government (and state and local agencies) has become ever more dependent for resources—especially knowledge building, administrative capacity, and enforcement—on subnational governments and private and nonprofit actors (plus, sometimes, the courts). The only exceptions to building in-house federal capacity laggardly happened during the Great Depression and wartime (i.e., in both "hot" and "cold" wars). Yet, even then, some of the biggest expansions of the proxy components of the compensatory state and its amplifying and rent-seeking subsystems occurred. But, once wars ended, and while retrenchment was contested, a return to American self-conceptions embracing limited government, economic liberalism, and civic responsibility typically followed. The only exceptions were the Cold War following World War II and the War on Terror, as the urge for perpetual hot war preparation never really ended.

Prior chapters also indicate a need to reject imagery that the amplification of the IRP within the compensatory state occurred by chance, necessity, or lack of alternatives. The advocacy of the aforementioned corporate–social science nexus of interests striving to attain, maintain, or enhance their legitimacy repeatedly helped sell, shape, and often drive the consistent adoption of the IRP over competing reform alternatives. As noted, once ensconced as experts or proxies in agencies, markets, or networks, nexus members pushed for greater policy activism (liberal or conservative in nature). This produced greater policy, administrative, and/or market complexity and, thus, calls for new reforms informed by the IRP. And that complexity repeatedly amplified because of the competitive ratcheting up of otherwise needed accountability efforts by the three branches of government.

At the same time, although private and social science actors historically tried to gain legitimacy by affiliating themselves with government action, a new reciprocal relationship developed toward the late 20th and early 21st centuries. *Government agencies* tried to gain legitimacy by associating themselves with the best business practices (BBPs) and social science methodologies of the day. In the process, government agencies and the social sciences at all levels grew ever more dependent on corporate and private foundation funding. These were attractive as means to supplement existing agency and research resources in the compensatory state—that is, to address funding, personnel, and professional skill gaps.

The consequences and ironies of this resource dependency were multiple. For starters, by the 2000s, resource dependency and university–corporate ties (prevalent for decades and amplified in wartime) were extended to nearly all areas of public universities. This, as state legislatures cut back funding support for public universities. Not only did this mostly mean a large rise in tuition costs for families and student loan debt but also that universities became more dependent on military, foundation, and private-sector research funding. Not surprisingly, the logic of business also took hold in universities, as tenure-line positions were increasingly converted to adjunct positions to save money. Meanwhile, the number of administrative positions soared, partly to meet the responsibilities imposed on them by the Rights Revolution. In the same business spirit, online learning proliferated as universities sought additional revenues and cost savings.

Concerning in their own right individually, these dynamics collectively contributed to working-class sentiments that they were being ignored by an educated cultural elite. With a college education portrayed as imperative to success in the information age, many in this segment of the population felt that their children were left behind, because they could not afford college. These voters might not have known what they wanted in terms of reform, but they knew that they did not like what they saw. Large segments of Trump voters worried that both their future (a loss of economic security and traditional values) and their past (i.e., their loss of a national identity to a fragmented rather than nested identity politics) were in jeopardy.

Another consequence of this resource dependency was the difficulty of holding agencies and their collaborators accountable due to the compensatory state's growing complexity. Charles Merriam's early 20th-century complaint about the "hide-and-seek" nature of the Madisonian system seemed now on steroids. This, after decades of the IRP that, ironically, he and fellow progressives advocated. Amplified, again, was a disconnect in citizens' minds between their needs and what they perceived government was doing for them. At the same time, the quest for accountability of federal agencies through the IRP created the aforementioned administrative burdens for navigating the system.

Relatedly, with business typically enjoying a privileged position in American politics since the nation's founding, resource dependency meant that corporate dominance also existed *within* the corporate–social science nexus itself. For example, as Laurence Lynn argues, the "reactive nature of public administration [in America] create[d] a danger of ceaseless pursuit of the latest [business] fashions" (Moynihan, 2014, p. 60; also see Bertelli & Lynn, 2006). At the same time, and with the growing importance of macroeconomics and (later) microeconomics in the compensatory state, the economics profession typically (re)gained much more legitimacy—and, hence, power—than other social sciences *within* the nexus. Nor did it help that other social sciences lacked the theoretical elegance of neoclassical economics (although that elegance is now challenged by, among others, behavioral economics). Resource dependency, combined with inefficient path-dependency and legitimacy asymmetries, also meant that the "logic of business" and markets repeatedly triumphed in contests over administrative reform.

This, even in the wake of such mega-market failures as the Panic of 1893, the Great Depression of the 1930s, and the Great Recession of 2007–2009.

Preceding chapters also reveal a need to alter administrative reformers' images of agencies as "machines" to be reengineered or turned into markets or brains by statistical, econometric, IT, or artificial intelligence (AI) innovations. Since at least the mid-19th century, proponents of the IRP consistently stated or implied that politics and emotions could be marginalized in agency operations and decision making. But no silver bullets existed in the administrative reform arsenal for doing so, especially those that left out the human relations, legal, emotional, and organizational behavior pillars of organizational and network life. Moreover, "overselling" reforms with exaggerated claims—as administrative reformers have always done in American history—led to repeated disappointment, employee disenchantment, and citizen cynicism. These unrealized claims then sparked calls for the next round of American administrative reform and state building.

Although instrumental rationality is a worthy goal for all organizations, *political rationality* ultimately drives public organizations and networks in the compensatory state. As such, politics cannot be left out of the administrative reform equation. Nor, as Harvey C. Mansfield (2001) argues, can "facts" bring agreement. Both values and power are the lifeblood not just of administration but also of its reform. Moreover, as noted, economy and efficiency (and even effectiveness when delivered by proxy actors) are hygienic rather than motivational factors for enhancing legitimacy. They can be important, but not dispositive, factors in building, retaining, and increasing legitimacy. This, because they are simply expected by citizens and not substantively linked to the "higher order needs" of governance (e.g., respect for constitutional values, responsiveness, and representativeness). In addition, relativity confounds perceptions of administrative performance. Administrative improvements in economy, efficiency, and effectiveness are typically regarded (fairly or unfairly) in Americans' self-conception as lagging those of markets and society. Moreover, improvements in efficiency within a single agency may increase citizen satisfaction for that agency, but legitimacy is different from satisfaction. What is more, even individual agency increases in legitimacy do not necessarily improve perceptions of legitimacy for the public sector as a whole.

Also central to perpetuating the allure of a politically neutral, efficiency-focused IRP was the belief of much of the social sciences since the early 19th century that if organizations could only make their decisions data-based, then disagreements over purposes and goals would lessen or even disappear. But no matter how "big or small" the dataset in any historical period, nor how sophisticated the analyses employed, data have never spoken for themselves. Nor has the "evidence" offered by any actor or situation. They were—and always will be—interpreted, framed, and then reframed again by various "claims makers" inside and outside the compensatory state to advance their political, policy, and philosophical agendas. Accurate research-based evidence certainly leavens the debate, and arguing without it can lead to bad policy and administrative choices. But issue and alternative framing will never be eliminated in American governance—and should not be in a democratic republic.

To be sure, information-based decisions have made positive contributions throughout the nation's history (e.g., in identifying social problems during the Progressive Era and in targeting crime and health hotspots more recently). And, today, in many cities and towns, positive things are happening with Big Data, AI, and strategic-planning applications (e.g., Mergel, Rethemeyer, & Isett, 2016). AI also has brought important cost savings for routine operations. Yet, and aside from their data mining and p-hacking vulnerabilities noted earlier, the claims of administrative reformers touting these types of analyses throughout American history have consistently been overblown. This often stemmed from ignoring the reality that public agencies and the networks they work in cannot be reorganized, reengineered, or converted to a "brain" or "market" without something else happening: legislatures and the political subsystems that buttress their programs must agree and be simultaneously reorganized, reengineered, or transformed in the same fashion (see Raadschelders & Bemelmans-Videc, 2015, for a related argument). To say the least, this is a most unlikely development on the scale needed. Also unlikely is a return to the constitutional containment structures needed to help ameliorate, even partially, the governance and administrative complexity imposed by ever-mounting policy demands and IRP-based reforms.

The preceding chapters also illustrate how administrative reforms must be seen as *policies* in themselves (Barzelay, 2001), and they are often weaponized in practice (Durant, 2008). Both opponents and proponents of activist government since the nation's founding have embraced the IRP, with occasional adoptions of SRP initiatives. They did so, however, in drastically different ways. Opponents of activist government tried to enfeeble public agencies—especially regulatory agencies—in the name of instrumental rationality. But their real aim was to "de-rationalize" them. They did so by creating crazy-quilt organizational structures, imposing procedural and legal chaos, and creating paralysis by analysis—all in the name of reform. In the process, they tried to "starve the beast"—at least the domestic and regulatory beasts—by reducing their budgets. They then blamed those agencies alone when performance came up short, shortcomings spread by the media without context or acknowledgement of other operational successes or tradeoffs (Goodsell, 2014).

But proponents of government activism are culpable as well. They used an "intelligent design" approach to the rationality project to administer their well-intentioned but Sisyphean policy agendas. In effect, they consistently argued that "right now, these agencies or networks aren't operating like a machine or smoothly functioning network, so we'll fix them by turning them into more rational machines, markets, or brains; that is, into learning organizations." But, as noted, public agencies—and the networks where parts of them work—have never been *machines* with rational means–ends goals that can be fine-tuned or *brains* that function based on mathematical algorithms alone. Nor are they animated by market rationality. They are *polities* with multiple goals, varying and sometimes contradictory missions and priorities, differing legal requirements, and competing constituencies. Their decisions are fraught with politics, precarious causal theories, and unintended consequences. Thus they are often reluctant to change or modify their behaviors; they fear disrupting the delicate political and legal balances they have worked out over time (within and outside organizations) (Wamsley & Zald, 1973). These protect them from uncertainty, buffer their core competencies, preserve order, and guard mission essences. This may or may not be a good thing, but it *is* the realpolitik of the evolution of American administrative reform and state building that IRP proponents have propounded throughout history.

As such, and although typically ignored or downplayed in practice by IRP-informed administrative reformers, across-the-board, one-size-fits-all efforts at large-scale administrative reform cannot ignore context—political or otherwise (Fernandez & Rainey, 2006). Some reforms work better in some types of agencies than in others (e.g., the Planning, Programming, and Budgeting System); for different types of tasks; and under various contingencies. Much as Oliver Wendell Holmes said about the law, the life of organizations is not based on logic but on experiences and, thus, on the logic of appropriateness and consequences (March & Olsen, 1984). This does not mean selecting one element of reform context as a driver of administrative reform, as some scholarship has done. Reform opportunity structures—in agencies, private and nonprofit organizations, and networks—are complex, dynamic, and replete with interacting contextual factors (including the law) and relative power differentials among actors. Thus, the real research question is not "which factor is dominant?" but, rather, "why now and not earlier or later, and interacting with what factors?"

Finally, the preceding chapters also highlight a need to rethink metaphors that currently dominate public administration's view of the evolution of American administrative reform. This evolution should be seen less as one of tides, cycles, or tectonics and more in terms of a "spiral" or "pulse model" of reform (McFarland, 2004). Recall from Chapter 1 that in a pure cyclical model, the "arrows" of the fundamentals of reform travel "through some pattern but eventually go back to point A, or perhaps just swing back and forth between points A and B" after excesses in any one direction occur (p. 79). In a pulse model, however, the deep structures of initial reform adoption—in this case, reliance on the IRP by the best military and BBPs of the day—reinforce and amplify each other over time as a secular, slow-moving, hardly visible phenomenon. This, regardless of prior disappointments premised on the promises of reformers.

****

The approach taken in this book also yielded an empirically grounded legitimacy theory of the evolution of American administrative reform informed by this pulse model. Recall from Chapter 1 that this theory posits that the ascendancy of the IRP over alternative reform prescriptions in each historical period has been shaped, propelled, and compounded over time by an evolving nexus of business (including private and nonprofit foundations) and social science interests both inside and outside the compensatory state. Propelling this nexus of actors is the interaction of three motives designed to gain, retain, or regain their legitimacy: (1) a sincere belief that the IRP offers greater collective benefits for society than other administrative reform alternatives (an expressive motive); (2) the financial gains they will acquire to implement their expressive goals (a material motive); and (3) a desire to gain, enhance, or regain status as an authority structure in society (an authority motive).

Premised on these motives, legitimacy theory affords a model-like narrative describing how and why the IRP has repeatedly triumphed and the compensatory state expanded as a function of structured agency and inefficient path dependency:

1. Calls for administrative reform arise from elected officials and administrative reformers arguing that (a) existing institutions are not able to deal effectively with current or emerging threats to the nation (i.e., a historical–structural mismatch exists), and (b) Americans' exceptionalist values and millenarian vision cannot escape the fate of other republics and are threatened unless reform occurs.

2. Various sets of reformers with different perspectives and political/philosophical goals (e.g., government activists and minimalists) take advantage of this window of opportunity to pursue expressive, material, and authority benefits and to link their arguments to American exceptionalist values (especially limited government, economic liberalism, and civic republicanism) in pursuit of (re)legitimacy gains. In the process, the original political coalition supporting the last round of reform (typically the IRP) must contend with alternative visions of administrative reform. In this battle, the combatants pursue their aims in whatever forums—public (including the courts), private, or nonprofit—hold potential in the compensatory state to advance their visions and legitimacy.

3. The IRP repeatedly trumps other reform alternatives (often based on substantive rationality; i.e., the SRP) because of the relative power of elements in the corporate–social science nexus of actors promoting and

benefiting from it from within and outside public agencies. Elected proponents of activist government turn to the IRP to either bring "order" to its operations or maintain influence when the executive branch is in the hands of political opponents. Elected opponents of activist government turn to the IRP to add complexity to its operations when the executive branch is controlled by proponents of activist government. Cumulatively, both camps add complexity to governance by amplifying the compensatory state in order to hide the government's visible size. This also happens because of the scramble by coevolving branches of government to rachet up "responsive competence" by means of the IRP.

4. The IRP, coevolution, and the amplifying of the compensatory state not only diminish citizen support for improving the administrative capacity of public agencies by tending to marginalize citizens from government but also disappoint operationally and in terms of the SRP because of the exaggerated claims of proponents. As such, they contribute to citizen confusion, estrangement, and distrust of government. The IRP also reinforces the idea of a government of elite experts out of touch with average Americans and, thus, paradoxically helps undermine government legitimacy. Hence, the initial advantage of adopting the IRP that has been amplified over the centuries produces collective irrationality in its negative effects on legitimacy.

5. All this leads to calls for the next round of administrative reform based on claims of a historical–structural mismatch. But triumphant again for the reasons noted is the IRP over other alternatives, especially those designed to advance substantive rationality. And even when initiatives related to the SRP are taken, the IRP tends to "seep through the canvas" of these initiatives to dominate agency and network operations.

This legitimacy theory, as well as other arguments made in this book, are offered in the belief articulated by Marcel Proust that the "real voyage of discovery consists not in seeking new landscapes but in having new eyes." Hopefully, the "new eyes" offered in this theory place American administrative reform and state building in a broader contextual arc than typically offered today in public administration. Ideally, the book will also encourage new pictures in our heads of the evolution of American administrative reform, revive studies on this topic and other "big questions" in public administration, and prompt a revisiting of canonical thinking in public administration and among administrative reformers.

Bibliography

Aaron, H. J. (1978). *Politics and the professors: The Great Society in perspective.* Washington, DC: Brookings Institution Press.

Aberbach, J. D., & Rockman, B. A. (2000). *In the web of politics: Three decades of the US federal executive.* Washington, DC: Brookings Institution Press.

Abramowitz, A. I. (2010). *The disappearing center: Engaged citizens, polarization, and American democracy.* New Haven, CT: Yale University Press.

Abramowitz, A. I., & Webster, S. (2016). The rise of negative partisanship and the nationalization of U.S. elections in the 21st century. *Electoral Studies, 41,* 12–22.

Adams, G. B. (1992). Enthralled with modernity: The historical context of knowledge and theory development in public administration. *Public Administration Review, 52*(4), 363–373.

Adams, G. B., & Balfour, D. (1998). *Unmasking administrative evil.* Armonk, NY: M. E. Sharpe.

Adams, H. B. (1918). *The education of Henry Adams: An autobiography.* Boston, MA: Houghton Mifflin.

Agranoff, R. (2007). *Managing within networks: Adding value to public organizations.* Washington, DC: Georgetown University Press.

Alchon, G. (1985). *The invisible hand of planning: Capitalism, social science, and the state in the 1920s.* Princeton, NJ: Princeton University Press.

Allen, F. L. (1931). *Only yesterday: An informal history of the 1920s.* New York, NY: HarperCollins.

Amirkhanyan, A. A., & Lambright, K. T. (2018). *Citizen participation in the age of contracting: When service delivery trumps democracy.* New York, NY: Routledge.

Andrews, R., Boyne, G. A., Meier, K. J., O'Toole, L. J., Jr., & Walker, R. M. (2005). Representative bureaucracy, organizational strategy, and public service performance: An empirical analysis of English local government. *Journal of Public Administration Research and Theory, 15*(4), 489–504.

Andrews, R., & Brewer, G. A. (2012). Social capital, management capacity and public service performance: Evidence from the US states. *Public Management Review, 15*(1), 1–24.

Aoki, N. (2015). Let's get public administration right, but in what sequence? Lessons from Japan and Singapore. *Public Administration and Development, 35*(3), 206–218.

Appleby, J. (2001). *Inheriting the revolution: The first generation of Americans.* Cambridge, MA: Belknap Press.

Arnold, P. E. (1972). Herbert Hoover and the continuity of American public policy. *Public Policy, 20,* 525–544.

Arnold, P. E. (1998). *Making the managerial presidency: Comprehensive reorganization planning, 1905–1996* (2nd ed., rev.). Lawrence, KS: University Press of Kansas.

Arnold, P. E. (2007). The Brownlow committee, regulation, and the presidency: Seventy years later. *Public Administration Review, 67*(6), 1030–1040.

Arnold, P. E. (2009). *Remaking the presidency: Roosevelt, Taft, and Wilson, 1901–1916.* Lawrence, KS: University Press of Kansas.

Aron, R. (1955). *The opium of the intellectuals.* Paris, FR: Calmann-Lévy.

Aronson, S. H. (1964). *Status and kinship in the higher civil service.* Cambridge, MA: Harvard University Press.

Bachner, J., & Ginsberg, B. (2016). *What Washington gets wrong: The UNELECTED officials who actually run the government and their misconceptions about the American people.* Amherst, NY: Prometheus Books.

Bachrach, P., & Baratz, M. S. (1962). Two faces of power. *American Political Science Review, 56*(4), 947–952.

Backgrounder on the Pendleton Act. (1883). *U.S. statutes at large,* 22, 403. Retrieved from http://usa.usembassy.de/etexts/democrac/28.htm.

Baehler, K., Liu, A. C., & Rosenbloom, D. H. (2014). Mission-extrinsic public values as an extension of regime values: Examples from the United States and China. *Administration & Soc*iety, *46*(2), 199–219.

Bailyn, B. (1992). *The ideological origins of the American revolution* (enlg. ed.). Cambridge, MA: Belknap Press.

Baldwin, P. (2005). Beyond weak and strong: Rethinking the state in comparative policy history. *Journal of Policy History, 17*(1), 12–33.

Balogh, B. (1991). *Chain reaction: Expert debate and public participation in American commercial nuclear power, 1945–1975.* Cambridge, UK: Cambridge University Press.

Balogh, B. (2009). *A government out of sight: The mystery of national authority in nineteenth-century America.* New York, NY: Cambridge University Press.

Banfield, E. C. (1974). *The unheavenly city revisited: A revision of the unheavenly city* (2nd ed.). Glenville, IL: Scott, Foresman.

Bardach, E. (1977). *The implementation game: What happens after a bill becomes a law.* Cambridge, MA: MIT Press.

Barone, M. (2013). *Shaping our nation: How surges of migration transformed America and its politics* New York, NY: Crown Forum.

Barr, S. (2007, July 18). Making agencies better customers. *Washington Post,* p. D04.

Barrett, F. J. (2015). Social constructionist challenge to representational knowledge. In G. R. Bushe & R. J. Marshak (Eds.), *Dialogic organization development: The theory and practice of transformational change* (pp. 59–76). Oakland, CA: Berrett-Koehler Publishers.

Barry, J. M. (1997). *Rising tide: The great Mississippi flood of 1927 and how it changed America.* New York, NY: Simon & Schuster.

Bartels, L. M. (2008). *Unequal democracy: The political economy of the new gilded age.* Princeton, NJ: Princeton University Press.

Barzelay, M. (1992). *Breaking through bureaucracy: A new vision for managing government.* Berkeley, CA: University of California Press.

Barzelay, M. (2001). *The new public management: Improving research and dialogue.* Berkeley, CA: University of California Press.

Baumgartner, F. R., & Leech, B. L. (1998). *Basic interests: The importance of groups in politics and in political science.* Princeton, NJ: Princeton University Press.

Beard, C. A. (1918). *An economic interpretation of the constitution of the United States.* New York, NY: Macmillan Company.

Beard, C. A., & Beard, M. R. (1933). *The rise of American civilization* (2 vols.). New York, NY: Macmillan Company.

Beard, C. A., & Beard, M. R. (1944). *A basic history of the United States.* New York, NY: Doubleday, Doran, & Company.

Beatty, J. (2008). *Age of betrayal: The triumph of money in America, 1865–1900.* New York, NY: Vintage Books.

Becker, W. H. (1982). *The dynamics of business–government relations: Industry and exports, 1893–1921.* Chicago, IL: The University of Chicago Press.

Beer, S. H. (1978). Federalism, nationalism, and democracy in America. *American Political Science Review, 72*(1), 9–21.

Bellamy, E. (1888). *Looking backward: 2000–1887.* Boston, MA: Ticknor & Co.

Bendor, J., & Hammond, T. H. (2010). Choice-theoretic approaches to bureaucratic structure. In R. F. Durant (Ed.), *The Oxford handbook of American bureaucracy* (pp. 638–665). Oxford, UK: Oxford University Press.

Bensel, R. F. (1990). *Yankee Leviathan: The origins of central state authority in America, 1859–1877.* New York, NY: Cambridge University Press.

Bensel, R. F. (2000). *The political economy of American industrialization, 1877–1900.* Cambridge, UK: Cambridge University Press.

Bentley, A. F. (1908). *The process of government: A study of social pressures.* Chicago, IL: University of Chicago Press.

Berle, A. A., & Means, G. C. (1933). *The modern corporation and private property.* New York, NY: Macmillan Company.

Berlin, I. (1992). *The crooked timber of humanity: Chapters in the history of ideas.* New York, NY: Vintage Books.

Berman, B. J. C. (2012). *When governments listen: Moving toward publicly engaged governing.* New York, NY: National Center for Civic Innovation.

Berry, J. M. (1999). *The new liberalism: The rising power of citizen groups.* Washington, DC: Brookings Institution Press.

Berry, J. M., Portney, K. E., & Thompson, K. (1993). *The rebirth of urban democracy.* Washington, DC: Brookings Institution Press.

Bertelli, A. M., & Lynn, L. E., Jr. (2006). *Madison's managers: Public administration and the Constitution.* Baltimore, MD: Johns Hopkins University Press.

Bingham, L. B., & O'Leary, R. (2006, December). Conclusion: Parallel play, not collaboration: Missing questions, missing connections. *Public Administration Review, 66*(s1), s161–s167.

Bohman, J. (2016, Fall). Critical theory. In E. N. Zalta (Ed.), *The Stanford encyclopedia of philosophy.* Retrieved from https://plato.stanford.edu/archives/fall2016/entries/critical-theory.

Boorstin, D. J. (1953). *The genius of American politics.* Chicago, IL: The University of Chicago Press.

Bourne, R. (1917, October 2). Twilight of idols. *The Seven Arts*, 688–702.

Bowers, C. (1922). *Party battles of the Jackson period.* New York, NY: Houghton Mifflin Company.

Bowman, J. S., & West, J. P. (2006). Ending civil service protections in Florida government: Experiences in state agencies. *Review of Public Personnel Administration, 26*(2), 139–157.

Box, R. C. (2018). *Essential history for public administration.* Irvine, CA: Melvin & Leigh.

Boyne, G. A. (1998). Bureaucratic theory meets reality: Public choice and service contracting in U.S. local government. *Public Administration Review, 58*(6), 474–484.

Bozeman, B. (1987). *All organizations are public: Bridging public and private organizational theories.* San Francisco, CA: Jossey-Bass.

Bozeman, B. (1993). A theory of government red tape. *Journal of Public Administration Research and Theory, 3,* 273–303.

Bozeman, B. (2004). *All organizations are public: Bridging public and private organizational theories* (2nd ed.). San Francisco, CA: Jossey-Bass.

Bozeman, B. (2007). *Public values and public interest: Counterbalancing economic individualism.* Washington, DC: Georgetown University Press.

Brainard, L. A., & McNutt, J. G. (2010). Virtual government—citizen relations: Informational, transactional, or collaborative? *Administration & Society, 42*(7), 836–858.

Brands, H. W. (2010). *Corporate colossus: The triumph of capitalism, 1865–1900.* New York, NY: Doubleday.

Brinkley, A. (1995). *The end of reform: New Deal liberalism in recession and war.* New York, NY: Alfred A. Knopf.

Brown, T. L., & Potoski, M. (2003). Managing contract performance: A transaction cost approach. *Journal of Policy Analysis and Management, 22*(2), 275–297.

Brown, T. L., Potoski, M., & Van Slyke, D. M. (2006). Managing public service contracts: Aligning values, institutions, and markets. *Public Administration Review, 66*(3), 323–331.

Browne, A., & Wildavsky, A. (1984). Implementation as mutual adaptation. In J. L. Pressman & A. Wildavsky (Eds.), *Implementation: How great expectations in Washington are dashed in Oakland* (3rd ed., pp. 206–231). Berkeley, CA: University of California Press.

Brudney, J. L., Fernandez, S., Ryu, J. E., & Wright, D. S. (2005). Exploring and explaining contracting out: Patterns among the American states. *Journal of Public Administration Research and Theory, 15*(3), 393–419.

Burner, D. (1968). 1919: Prelude to normalcy. In J. Braeman, R. H. Bremner, & D. Brody (Eds.), *Change and continuity in twentieth century America: The 1920s* (pp. 3–32). Columbus, OH: Ohio State University Press.

Burner, D. (1979). *Herbert Hoover: A public life.* New York, NY: Alfred A. Knopf.

Bryer, T. A. (2007). Toward a relevant agenda for a responsive public administration. *Journal of Public Administration Research and Theory, 17*(3), 479–500.

Bryer, T. A., & Zavattaro, S. (Eds.). (2011). Symposium on social media and public administration. *Administrative Theory & Praxis, 33*(3), 325–432.

Bryson, J. M., Crosby, B. C., & Bloomberg, L. (2014). Public value governance: Beyond traditional public administration and the new public management. *Public Administration Review, 74*(4), 445–456.

Buchanan, J. M., & Tullock, G. (1965). *The politics of bureaucracy.* New York, NY: Public Affairs Press.

Burke, J. P. (2000). *The institutional presidency: Organizing and managing the white house from FDR to Clinton.* Baltimore, MD: Johns Hopkins University Press.

Burnham, J. (1941). *The managerial revolution: What is happening in the world*. Cambridge, MA: Belknap Press.

Burns, E. (2006). *Infamous scribblers: The founding fathers and the rowdy beginnings of American journalism*. New York, NY: Public Affairs.

Caldwell, L. K. (1988). *The administrative theories of Hamilton and Jefferson: Their contribution to thought on public administration* (2nd ed.). New York, NY: Holmes & Meier. Org. pub. 1944.

Califano, J. A., Jr. (1991). *The triumph and tragedy of Lyndon Johnson: The white house years*. New York, NY: Touchstone.

Camerer, C. F., Dreber, A., Holzmeister, F., et al. (2018). Evaluating the replicability of social science experiments in *Nature* and *Science* between 2010 and 2015. *Nature Human Behavior, 2,* 637–644.

Campbell, A. L. (2003). *How policies make citizens: Senior political activism and the welfare state*. Princeton, NJ: Princeton University Press.

Campbell, D. A., Lambright, K. T., & Wells, C. J. (2014). Looking for friends, fans, and followers? Social media use in public and nonprofit human services. *Public Administration Review, 74*(5), 655–663.

Caro, R. A. (2012). *The years of Lyndon Johnson: The passage of power*. New York, NY: Alfred A. Knopf.

Carpenter, D. (2001). *The forging of bureaucratic autonomy: Reputations, networks, and policy innovation in executive agencies, 1862–1928*. Princeton, NJ: Princeton University Press.

Carpenter, D. (2010). *Reputation and power: Organizational image and pharmaceutical regulation at the FDA*. Princeton, NJ: Princeton University Press.

Chace, J. (2004). *1912: Wilson, Roosevelt, Taft and Debs: The election that changed the country*. New York, NY: Simon & Schuster.

Chandler, A. D., Jr. (1993). *The visible hand: The managerial revolution in American business*. Cambridge, MA: Belknap Press. Org. pub. 1977.

Chayes, A. (1976). The role of the judge in public law litigation. *Harvard Law Review, 89*(7), 1281–1316.

Chen, C-A. (2009). Antecedents of contracting-back-in: A view beyond the academic paradigm. *Administration & Society, 41*(1), 101–126.

Cheng, Y. D. (2018, July 20). Exploring the role of nonprofits in public service provision: Moving from coproduction to cogovernance. *Public Administration Review*. Retrieved from https://doi.org/10.1111/puar.12970.

Churchman. (1894, July 7). *The churchman: The faith once delivered to the saints*, vol. 70.

Clarke, J., & Newman, J. (1997). *The managerial: Power, politics and ideology in the remaking of social welfare*. Thousand Oaks, CA: Sage Publications.

Clemens, E. S. (2010). In the shadow of the new deal: Reconfiguring the roles of government and charity, 1928–1940. In E. S. Clemens & D. Guthrie (Eds.), *Politics +partnerships: The role of voluntary associations in America's political past and present* (pp. 79–119). Chicago, IL: University of Chicago Press.

Clemens, E. S., & Guthrie, D. (Eds.). (2010). *Politics + partnerships: The role of voluntary associations in America's political past and present*. Chicago, IL: University of Chicago Press.

Clements, K. A. (1999). *Woodrow Wilson: World statesman*. Chicago, IL: Ivan R. Dee.

Clements, K. A. (2000). *Hoover, conservation, and consumerism: Engineering the good life.* Lawrence, KS: University Press of Kansas.

Clements, K. A. (2010). *The life of Herbert Hoover: Imperfect visionary, 1918–1928.* New York, NY: Macmillan Company.

Cohen, P. K. (1999). *A calculating people: The spread of numeracy in early America.* New York, NY: Routledge.

Condrey, S. E., & Battaglio, R. P. (2007). A return to spoils? Revisiting radical civil service reform in the United States. *Public Administration Review, 67*(3), 425–436.

Conlan, T. J., Posner, P. L., & Beam, D. R. (2014). *Pathways of power: The dynamics of national policymaking.* Washington, DC: Georgetown University Press.

Cook, B. J. (2014). *Bureaucracy and self-government: Reconsidering the role of public administration in American politics* (2nd ed.). Baltimore, MD: Johns Hopkins University Press.

Cooper, T. L. (2011). Citizen-driven administration: Civic engagement in the United States. In D. C. Menzel & H. L. White (Eds.), *The state of public administration: Issues, challenges, and opportunities* (pp. 238–256). Armonk, NY: M. E. Sharpe.

Corwin, E. S. (Ed.). (1952). *The constitution of the United States of America: Analysis and interpretation.* Retrieved from www.ispionline.it/sites/default/files/pubblicazioni/analysis_229_2013.pdf and www.gutenberg.org/files/18637/18637-h/18637-h.htm.

Crenson, M. (1975). *The federal machine: Beginning of bureaucracy in Jacksonian America.* Baltimore, MD: Johns Hopkins University Press.

Crewson, P. E. (1997). Public-service motivation: Building empirical evidence of incidence and effect. *Journal of Public Administration Research and Theory, 7*(4), 499–518.

Croly, H. (1909). *The promise of American life.* New York, NY: Macmillan Company.

Croly, H. (1914). *Progressive democracy.* New York, NY: Macmillan Company.

Crouch, C. (2004). *Post-democracy.* Cambridge, UK: Polity Press.

Crowley, J. E., & Skocpol, T. (2001). The rush to organize: Explaining associational formation in the United States, 1860s–1920s. *American Journal of Political Science, 45*(4), 813–829.

Crozier, M., Huntington, S. P., & Watanuki, J. (1975). *The crisis of democracy.* New York, NY: New York University Press.

Cuff, R. D. (1969). Bernard Baruch: Symbol and myth in industrial mobilization. *Business History Review, 43*(2), 115–133.

Davis, K. C. (1960). *Administrative law and government.* St. Paul, MN: West Publishing.

Davis, R. C. (1928). *Industrial organization and management.* New York, NY: Harper & Row, Publishers.

Deegan, M. J. (1988). *Jane Addams and the men of the Chicago School, 1892–1980.* New Brunswick, NJ: Transaction Publishers.

Dehart-Davis, L. (2008). Green tape: A theory of effective organizational rules. *Journal of Public Administration Research and Theory, 19*, 361–384.

deLeon, P. (1992). The democratization of the policy sciences. *Public Administration Review, 52*(2), 125–129.

Denhardt, J. V., & Denhardt, R. B. (2015). *The new public service: Serving, not steering* (4th ed.). New York, NY: Routledge.

Denvir, D. (2012, October 23). As local governments shrink, private consultants reap rewards. *CityLab.* Retrieved from www.citylab.com/equity/2012/10/local-governments-shrink-private-consultants-reap-rewards/3648/.

Derthick, M. (1972). *New towns in-town*. Washington, DC: The Urban Institute.

Derthick, M. (2010). Compensatory federalism. In B. G. Rabe (Ed.), *Greenhouse governance: Addressing climate change in America* (pp. 58–72). Washington, DC: Brookings Institution Press.

Desch, M. (2019). *Cult of the irrelevant: The waning influence of social science on national security*. Princeton, NJ: Princeton University Press.

DeSilver, D. (2018, January 16). Congress has long struggled to pass spending bills on time. *Pew Research Center*. Retrieved from www.pewresearch.org/fact-tank/2018/01/16/congress-has-long-struggled-to-pass-spending-bills-on-time/.

de Tocqueville, A. (2012). *Democracy in America*. Chicago, IL: University of Chicago Press. Org. pub. 1835.

Dewey, J. (1916). *Democracy and education*. New York, NY: Macmillan Company.

Dewey, J. (1935). *Liberalism and social action*. New York, NY: G. P. Putnam.

Diamond, L. (2019, July/August). Democracy demotion. *Foreign Affairs, 98*(4), 17–25.

Dickinson, M. J. (1767–1768). Letters from a farmer in Pennsylvania to the inhabitants of the British colonies. They appeared as a dozen articles in *The Pennsylvania Chronicle* between December 2, 1767 and February 15, 1768.

Dickinson, M. J. (1996). *Bitter harvest: FDR, presidential power, and the growth of the presidential branch*. Cambridge, UK: Cambridge University Press.

DiIulio, J. J., Jr. (2014). *Bring back the bureaucrats: Why more federal workers will lead to better (and smaller!) government*. West Conshohocken, PA: Templeton Press.

DiMaggio, P. J., & Powell, W. W. (1983). The iron cage revisited: Institutional isomorphism and collective rationality in organizational fields. *American Sociological Review, 48*(2), 147–160.

Dimock, M. E. (1980). *Law and dynamic administration*. New York, NY: Praeger.

Dolan, J. (2000). The senior executive service: Gender, attitudes, and representative bureaucracy. *Journal of Public Administration Research and Theory, 10*(3), 513–530.

Domhoff, G. W. (2018). *WhoRulesAmerica.net: Power, politics, & social change*. Retrieved from https://whorulesamerica.ucsc.edu/.

Downs, A. (1993). *Inside bureaucracy*. Long Grove, IL: Waveland Press. Org. pub. 1967.

du Gay, P. (2005). Introduction. In P. du Gay (Ed.), *The values of bureaucracy* (pp. 1–13). New York, NY: Oxford University Press.

Dumbacher, E. D. (2011, June 15). "C" is for change. *Government Executive*. Retrieved from www.govexec.com/magazine/features/2011/06/c-is-for-change/34161/.

Durant, R. F. (1985). *When government regulates itself: EPA, TVA, and pollution control in the 1970s*. Knoxville, TN: University of Tennessee Press.

Durant, R. F. (1992). *The administrative presidency revisited: Public lands, the BLM, and the Reagan revolution*. Albany, NY: State University of New York Press.

Durant, R. F. (1995). The democratic deficit in America. *Political Science Quarterly, 110*(1), 25–47.

Durant, R. F. (2000). Whither the neoadministrative state: Toward a polity-centered theory of administrative reform. *Journal of Public Administration Research and Theory, 10*(1), 79–109.

Durant, R. F. (2006). A "new covenant" kept: Core values, presidential communications, and the paradox of the Clinton presidency. *Presidential Studies Quarterly, 36*(3), 345–372.

Durant, R. F. (2007). *The greening of the U.S. military: Environmental policy, national security, and organization change.* Washington, DC: Georgetown University Press.

Durant, R. F. (2008). Sharpening a knife cleverly: Organizational change, policy paradox, and the "weaponizing" of administrative reform. *Public Administration Review, 66*(2), 282–294.

Durant, R. F. (2009a). Back to the future? Toward revitalizing the study of the administrative presidency. *Presidential Studies Quarterly, 39*(1), 89–110.

Durant, R. F. (2009b). Getting dirty minded: Implementing presidential policy agendas administratively. *Public Administration Review, 69*(4), 569–585.

Durant, R. F. (2014a). Progressivism, capitalism, and the social sciences: Confronting the paradox of federal administrative reform in America. *Administration & Society, 46*(6), 599–631.

Durant, R. F. (2014b). Taking time seriously: Progressivism, the business-social science nexus, and the paradox of American administrative reform. *PS: Perspectives on Political Science, 47*(1), 8–18.

Durant, R. F. (2014c). *Why public service matters: Public managers, public policy, and democracy.* New York, NY: Macmillan Company.

Durant, R. F. (2015). Whither power in public administration? Attainment, dissipation, and loss. *Public Administration Review, 75*(2), 206–218.

Durant, R. F., & Ali, S. B. (2013). Repositioning public administration? The new governance, civic society, and the disarticulated state. *Public Administration Review, 73*(2), 278–289.

Durant, R. F., & Durant, J. R. S. (Eds.). (2013). *Debating public administration: Management challenges, choices, and opportunities.* Boca Raton, FL: CRC Press.

Durant, R. F., Fiorino, D. J., & O'Leary, R. (Eds.). (2017). *Environmental governance reconsidered: Challenges, choices, and opportunities* (2nd ed.). Cambridge, MA: MIT Press.

Durant, R. F., Girth, A., & Johnston, J. (2009). American exceptionalism, human resource management, and the contract state. *Review of Public Personnel Administration, 29*(3), 207–229.

Durant, R. F., & Resh, W. G. (2009). Presidential agendas, administrative strategies, and the bureaucracy. In G. C. Edwards & W. G. Powell (Eds.), *The Oxford handbook of the American presidency* (pp. 577–600). Oxford, UK: Oxford University Press.

Durant, R. F., & Rosenbloom, D. H. (2017). The hollowing of public administration. *American Review of Public Administration, 47*(7), 719–736.

Durant, R. F., & Warber, A. (2001). Networking in the shadow of hierarchy: Public policy, the administrative presidency, and the neoadministrative state. *Presidential Studies Quarterly, 31*(2), 221–244.

Eatwell, R. (1995). *Fascism: A history.* New York, NY: Penguin Books.

Edling, M. M. (2003). *A revolution in favor of government: Origins of the U.S. Constitution and the making of the American state.* New York, NY: Oxford University Press.

Edling, M. M. (2009). Review of B. Balogh. *A government out of sight. Journal of Policy History, 21*(4), 462–468.

Eisenach, E. J. (1994). *The lost promise of progressivism.* Lawrence, KS: University Press of Kansas.

Eisenhower, D. D. (1961, January 21). *Farewell radio and television address to the American people.* Washington, DC: Public Papers of the Presidents.

Eisner, M. A. (2000a). *From warfare state to welfare state: World War I, compensatory state building, and the limits of the modern order*. University Park, PA: Pennsylvania State University.

Eisner, M. A. (2000b). *Regulatory politics in transition* (2nd ed.). Baltimore, MD: Johns Hopkins University Press.

Elkin, S. L. (2006). *Reconstructing the commercial republic: Constitutional design after Madison*. Chicago, IL: University of Chicago Press.

Elmore, R. F. (1978). Organizational models of social program implementation. *Public Policy, 26*(2), 185–228.

Elmore, R. F. (1979–1980). Backward mapping: Implementation research and policy decisions. *Political Science Quarterly, 94*(4), 601–616.

Elmore, R. F. (1985). Forward and backward mapping: Reversible logic in the analysis of public policy. In K. Hanf & T. A. J. Toonen (Eds.), *Policy implementation in federal and unitary systems: Questions of analysis and design* (pp. 33–70). Dordrecht, The Netherlands: Martinus Nijhoff Publishers.

Ely, R. (1886). Report of the organization of the American economic association. *Publications of the American Economic Association, 1*(1), 6–8.

Emerson, K., & Nabatchi, T. (2015). *Collaborative governance regimes*. Washington, DC: Georgetown University Press.

Emerson, K., Nabatchi, T., & Balogh, S. (2012). An integrative framework for collaborative governance. *Journal of Public Administration Research and Theory, 22*(1), 1–29.

Enteman, W. F. (1993). *Managerialism: The emergence of a new ideology*. Madison, WI: University of Wisconsin Press.

Epps, C. R. (1998). *The Rights Revolution: Lawyers, activists, and supreme courts in comparative perspective*. Chicago, IL: University of Chicago Press.

Evans, J. A. (2010). Nonprofit research institutes: From companies without products to universities without students. In E. S. Clemens & E. Guthrie (Eds.), *Politics + partnerships: The role of voluntary associations in America's political past and present* (pp. 151–182). Chicago, IL: University of Chicago Press.

Farmer, D. (1995). *The language of public administration: Bureaucracy, modernity, and post modernity*. Tuscaloosa, AL: University of Alabama Press.

Farrell, C., & Morris, J. (2003). The "neo-bureaucratic" state: Professionals, managers and professional managers in schools, general practices and social work. *Organization, 10*(1), 129–156.

Faulkner, W. (2011). *Requiem for a nun*. New York, NY: Vintage. Orig. pub. 1951.

Faust, D. G. (2008). *This republic of suffering: Death and the American Civil War*. New York, NY: Alfred A. Knopf.

Faux, J. (1999, Spring). Lost on the third way. *Dissent*, 67–76.

Fayol, H. (1930). *Industrial and general administration*. London, UK: Sir Isaac Pitman & Sons. Orig. pub. 1916.

Federal News Radio Staff. (2012, September 13). Top 10 agency initiatives: Office of Personnel Management. *Federal News Radio*. Retrieved from www.federalnewsradio. com/1011/3035948/Top-10-Agency-Initiatives-Office-of-Personnel-Management.

Feldman, M. S. (1989). *Order without design: Information production and policy making*. Stanford, CA: Stanford University Press.

Fernandez. S., & Rainey, H. G. (2006). Managing successful organization change in the public sector. *Public Administration Review, 66*(2), 168–176.

Ferrell, R. H. (1994). *Harry S. Truman: A life*. Columbia, MO: University of Missouri Press.

Finer, H. (1941). Administrative responsibility in democratic government. *Public Administration Review, 1*(4), 335–350.

Fischer, F. (1993). *The argumentative turn in policy analysis and planning*. Durham, NC: Duke University Press.

Fischer, F. (2009). *Democracy and expertise: Reorienting policy inquiry*. Oxford, UK: Oxford University Press.

Fitzhugh, G. (1854). *Sociology for the South, or the failure of free society*. Richmond, VA: A. Morris.

Fleming, T. (2001). *The New Dealers' war: F.D.R. and the war within World War II*. New York, NY: Basic Books.

Follett, M. P. (1918). *The new state: Group organization the solution of popular government*. New York, NY: Longsmans, Green and Co.

Follett, M. P. (1926). The giving of orders. In H. C. Metcalf & H. A. Overstreet (Eds.), *Scientific foundations of business administration* (pp. 29–37). Baltimore, MD: The Williams & Wilkins Company.

Foner, E. (1995). *Free soil, free labor, free men: The ideology of the Republican Party before the Civil War*. New York, NY: Oxford University Press.

Foner, E. (2005). *Forever free: The story of emancipation & reconstruction*. New York, NY: Vintage Books.

Foner, E. (2015). *A short history of reconstruction* (paperback ed.). New York, NY: Harper Perennial.

Ford, H. J. (1920, February). Present tendencies in American politics. *American Political Science Review, 14*(1), 1–13.

Forester, J. (1989). *Planning in the face of power*. Berkeley, CA: University of California Press.

Foster, C. I. (1960). *An errand of mercy: The Evangelical United Front, 1790–1837*. Chapel Hill, NC: University of North Carolina Press.

Fountain, J. E. (2001). *Building the virtual state: Information technology and institutional change*. Washington, DC: Brookings Institution Press.

Frederickson, H. G. (1999). The repositioning of American public administration. *PS: Political Science & Politics, 32*(4), 701–712.

Frederickson, H. G., Smith, K. B., Larimer, C. W., & Licari, M. J. (2012). *The public administration theory primer* (2nd ed.). Boulder, CO: Westview Press.

Freeman, J. L. (1965). *The political process: Executive bureau-legislative committee relations* (rev. ed.). New York, NY: Random House.

Friedberg, A. L. (2000). *In the shadow of the garrison state: America's anti-statism and its Cold War grand strategy*. Princeton, NJ: Princeton University Press.

Friedberg, A. L. (2002). American antistatism and the founding of the Cold War state. In I. Katznelson & M. Shefter (Eds.), *Shaped by war and trade: International influences on American political development* (pp. 239–266). Princeton, NJ: Princeton University Press.

Friedman, T. L. (1999). *The Lexus and the olive tree*. New York, NY: Farrar, Straus & Giroux.

Friedrich, C. J. (1940). Public policy and the nature of administrative responsibility. *Public Policy, 1*, 3–24.

Fukuyama, F. (2011). *The origins of political order: From prehuman times to the French Revolution*. New York, NY: Farrar, Straus and Giroux.

Fussell, P. (2000). *The great war and modern memory*. New York, NY: Oxford University Press.

Gaddis, V. (2005). *Herbert Hoover, unemployment, and the public sphere: A conceptual history, 1919–1933*. Lanham, MD: University Press of America.

Galambos, L. (1970). The emerging organizational synthesis in modern American history. *Business History Review, 44*(3), 279–290.

Gaus, J. M. (1947). *Reflections on public administration*. Tuscaloosa, AL: University of Alabama Press.

Getha-Taylor, H., Holmes, M. H., & Moen, J. (2018, March 22). Evidence-based interventions for cultural competency development. *Administration & Society*. Retrieved from https://doi-org.proxyau.wrlc.org/10.1177/0095399718764332.

Gibbon, E. (1776–1789). *The history of the decline and fall of the Roman Empire* (vols. 1–6). London, UK: Strahan & Cadell.

Gilpin, R. (1987). *The political economy of international relations*. Princeton, NJ: Princeton University Press.

Gilpin, R. (2001). *Global political economy: Understanding the international economic order*. Princeton, NJ: Princeton University Press.

Glenn, B. J., & Teles, S. M. (Eds.). (2009). *Conservatism and American political development*. Oxford, UK: Oxford University Press.

Goggin, M. L., Bowman, A., Lester, J., & O'Toole, L. J., Jr., (1990). *Implementation theory and practice: Toward a third generation*. Glenville, IL: Scott, Foresman.

Goldberg, D. T. (2002). *The racial state*. Malden, MA: Blackwell Publishers.

Goldberg, J. (2018). *Suicide of the West: How the rebirth of tribalism, populism, nationalism, and identity politics is destroying American democracy*. New York, NY: Crown Forum.

Golden, M. M. (2000). *What motivates bureaucrats? Politics and administration during the Reagan years*. New York, NY: Columbia University Press.

Goldsmith, S., & Eggers, W. D. (2004). *Governing by network: The new shape of the public sector*. Washington, DC: Brookings Institution Press.

Goodnow, F. J. (1916). *The American conception of liberty and government*. Providence, RI: Standard Printing Company.

Goodsell, C. T. (2014). *The new case for bureaucracy*. Washington, DC: Congressional Quarterly Press.

Gordon, J. S. (2004). *An empire of wealth: The epic history of American economic power*. New York, NY: HarperCollins.

Government Accountability Office (GAO). (2006, October). *Highlights of a U.S. GAO Forum: Federal Acquisition Challenges and Opportunities in the 21st Century*. Washington, DC: U.S. GAO-07-45SP.

Graham, R. (2018, May–June). Church of the Donald. *Politico Magazine*. Retrieved from www.politico.com/magazine/story/2018/04/22/trump-christian-evangelical-conservatives-television-tbn-cbn-218008.

Greenstone, J. D. (1993). *The Lincoln persuasion: Remaking American liberalism*. Princeton, NJ: Princeton University Press.

Greider, W. (1997). *One world, ready or not: The manic logic of global capitalism*. New York, NY: Simon & Schuster.

Grisinger, J. (2014). *The unwieldy American state: Administrative politics since the New Deal*. Cambridge, UK: Cambridge University Press.

Gulick, L., & Urwick, L. (Eds.) (1937). *Papers on the science of administration.* London, UK: Routledge.

Gunter, C. (2016, December 6). Agencies still aren't acing FITARA. *FCW: The Business of Federal Technology.* Retrieved from https://fcw.com/articles/2016/12/06/fitara-hurd-hearing.aspx.

Guthrie, D. (2010). Corporate philanthropy in the United States: What causes do corporations back? In E. S. Clemens & E. Guthrie (Eds.), *Politics + partnerships: The role of voluntary associations in America's political past and present* (pp. 183–207). Chicago, IL: University of Chicago Press.

Guy, M. E., Newman, M. A., & Mastracci, S. H. (2006). *Emotional labor: Putting the service in public service.* Armonk, NY: M. E. Sharpe.

Hacker, J. S. (2002). *The divided welfare state: The battle over public and private social benefits in the United States.* Cambridge, UK: Cambridge University Press.

Hacker, J. S., & Pierson, P. (2010). *Winner-take-all politics: How Washington made the rich richer—and turned its back on the middle class.* New York, NY: Simon & Schuster.

Hacker, J. S., & Pierson, P. (2012). Presidents and the political economy: The coalitional foundations of presidential power. *Presidential Studies Quarterly, 42*(1), 101–131.

Haidt, J. (2012). *The righteous mind: Why good people are divided by politics and religion.* New York, NY: Pantheon Books.

Haque, A. (2001). GIS, public service, and the issue of democratic governance. *Public Administration Review, 61*(3), 259–265.

Hart, D. M. (1994). *Herbert Hoover's last laugh: The enduring significance of the "associative state" in the United States.* Presented at the Society for the History of Technology meeting, Lowell, MA, and the Northeastern Political Science Association meeting, Providence, RI, October/November.

Hartz, L. (1955). *The liberal tradition in America: An interpretation of American political thought since the Revolution.* New York, NY: Harcourt.

Haskell, T. L. (2000). *The emergence of professional social science: The American Social Science Association and the nineteenth-century crisis of authority.* Baltimore, MD: Johns Hopkins University Press.

Hattam, V., & Lowndes, J. (2007). The ground beneath our feet: Language, culture, and political change. In S. Skowronek & M. Glassman (Eds.), *Formative acts: American politics in the making* (pp. 199–219). Philadelphia, PA: University of Pennsylvania Press.

Hawley, E. W. (1966). *The New Deal and the problem of monopoly.* Princeton, NJ: Princeton University Press.

Hawley, E. W. (1974). Herbert Hoover, the commerce secretariat, and the vision of an "associative state," 1921–1928. *Journal of American History, 61*(1), 116–140.

Hawley, E. W. (Ed.). (1981). *Herbert Hoover as Secretary of Commerce: Studies in new era thought and practice.* Iowa City, IA: University of Iowa Press.

Hawley, E. W. (1997). *The great war and the search for a modern order: A history of the American people and their institutions, 1917–1933* (2nd ed.). Long Grove, IL: Waveland Press.

Hayek, F. A. (1944). *The road to serfdom.* New York, NY: Routledge.

Hayek, F. A. (1988). *The fatal conceit: The errors of socialism.* W. W. Brantley, III (Ed.). Chicago, IL: University of Chicago Press.

Hays, S. P. (1972). The new organizational society. In J. Israel (Ed.), *Building the organizational society: Essays on associational activities in modern America* (pp. 1–15). New York, NY: Free Press.

Hays, S. P. (1980). *American political history as social analysis.* Knoxville, TN: University of Tennessee Press.

Hays, S. P. (1995). *The response to industrialism, 1885–1914* (2nd ed.). Chicago, IL: University of Chicago Press.

Hays, S. W., & Sowa, J. E. (2006). A broader look at the "accountability" movement: Some grim realities in state civil service systems. *Review of Public Personnel Administration, 26*(2), 102–117.

Head, B. W. (2010). Public management research: Towards relevance. *Public Management Review, 12*(5), 571–585.

Head, M. L., Holman, L., Lanfear, R., Kahn, A., & Jennions, M. D. (2015, March 13). The extent and consequences of p-hacking in science. *PLOS: Biology.* Retrieved from https://journals.plos.org/plosbiology/article?id=10.1371/journal.pbio.1002106.

Health-Spending Projections. (2012, June 16). Up, up and away. *The Economist.* Retrieved July 1, 2012, from www.economist.com/node/21556931.

Heclo, H. (1974). *Modern social politics in Britain and Sweden: From relief to income maintenance.* New Haven, CT: Yale University Press.

Heclo, H. (1977). *A government of strangers: Executive politics in Washington.* Washington, DC: Brookings Institution Press.

Heclo, H. (2013). Issue networks and the executive establishment. In S. Z. Theodoulou & M. A. Kahn (Eds.), *Public policy: The essential readings* (2nd ed.) (ch. 9). Boston, MA: Pearson.

Heikkila, T., & Gerlak, A. (2013). Building a conceptual approach to collective learning: Lessons for public policy scholars. *Policy Studies Journal, 41*, 484–512.

Heilbroner, R., & Singer, A. (1999). *The economic transformation of America, 1600 to the present* (4th ed.). New York, NY: Wadsworth.

Hendrickson, M. (2010). Steering the state: Government, nonprofits, and the making of labor knowledge in the new era. In E. S. Clemens & E. Guthrie (Eds.), *Politics + partnerships: The role of voluntary associations in America's political past and present* (pp. 54–78). Chicago, IL: University of Chicago Press.

Henry, N. (2013). *Public administration and public affairs* (12th ed.). Boston, MA: Pearson.

Herring, E. P. (1936). *Public administration and the public interest.* New York, NY: McGraw Hill.

Herring, G. C. (2008). *From colony to superpower: U.S. Foreign relations since 1776.* Oxford, UK: Oxford University Press.

Hersey, P., & Blanchard, K. H. (1988). *Management of organizational behavior: Utilizing human resources* (5th ed.). Englewood Cliffs, NJ: Prentice-Hall.

Herzberg, F. (1964). The motivation-hygiene concept and problems of man-power. *Personnel Administration, 27*, 3–7.

Hill, M., & Hupe, P. (2014). *Implementing public policy* (3rd ed.). Los Angeles, CA: SAGE Publications.

Hindera, J. J. (1993a). Representative bureaucracy: Imprimis evidence of active representation in the EEOC district offices. *Social Science Quarterly, 74*(1), 95–108.

Hindera, J. J. (1993b). Representative bureaucracy: Further evidence of active representation in the EEOC district offices. *Journal of Public Administration Research and Theory, 3*(4), 415–429.

Hindera, J. J., & Young, C. D. (1998). Representative bureaucracy: The theoretical implications of statistical interaction. *Political Research Quarterly, 51*(3), 655–671.

Hjern, B., & Porter, D. O. (1981). Implementation structures: A new unit of administrative analysis. *Organization Studies, 2*(3), 211–227.

Hodge, G. A. (2000). *Privatization: An international review of performance.* Boulder, CO: Westview Press.

Hoffer, P. C. (2013). *For ourselves and our posterity: The preamble to the federal constitution in American history.* New York, NY: Oxford University Press.

Hoffer, W. H. (2007). *To enlarge the machinery of government: Congressional debates and the growth of the American state.* Baltimore, MD: Johns Hopkins University Press.

Hofstadter, R. (1955). *The age of reform.* New York, NY: Vintage Books.

Hofstadter, R. (1989). *The American political tradition and the men who made it.* New York, NY: Vintage Books.

Holden, M. (1966). 'Imperialism' in bureaucracy. *American Political Science Review, 60*(4), 943–951.

Hood, C. (1991). A public management for all seasons. *Public Administration, 69*(1), 3–19.

Hood, C. (1998). *The art of the state: Culture, rhetoric, and public management.* Oxford, UK: Clarendon Press.

Hood, C. (2005). Public management: The word, the movement, the science. In E. Ferlie, L. E. Lynn, Jr., & C. Pollitt (Eds.), *The Oxford handbook of public management* (pp. 7–26). Oxford, UK: Oxford University Press.

Hood, C., & Dickson, R. (2015). *A government that worked better and cost less? Evaluating three decades of reform and change in UK central government.* Oxford, UK: Oxford University Press.

Hoover, H. (1922). *American individualism.* New York, NY: Doubleday, Page & Company.

Hoover, H. (1934). *The challenge to liberty.* New York, NY: Charles Scribner's Sons.

Hopkins, J. (1999). *Harry Hopkins: Sudden hero, brash reformer.* New York, NY: St. Martin's Press.

Howe, D. W. (1979). *The political culture of the American Whigs.* Chicago, IL: University of Chicago Press.

Howe, D. W. (2007). *What hath God wrought: The transformation of America, 1815–1858.* New York, NY: Oxford University Press.

Howe, D. W. (2009). *Making the American self: Jonathan Edwards to Abraham Lincoln.* Oxford, UK: Oxford University Press.

Howell, W. G. (2003). *Power without persuasion: The politics of direct presidential action.* Princeton, NJ: Princeton University Press.

Howlett, M., & Rayner, J. (2006). Understanding the historical turn in the policy sciences: A critique of stochastic, narrative, path dependency and process-sequencing models of policy-making over time. *Policy Sciences, 39*(1), 1–18.

Hult, K. M., & Walcott, C. E. (1990). *Governing public organizations: Politics, structures, and organizational design.* Pacific Grove, CA: Brooks/Cole.

Hult, K. M., & Walcott, C. E. (2004). *Empowering the White House: Nixon, Ford, and Carter.* Lawrence, KS: University Press of Kansas.

Hummel, R. P., & Stivers, C. (2010). Postmodernism, bureaucracy, and democracy. In R. F. Durant (Ed.), *The Oxford handbook of American bureaucracy* (pp. 324–348). Oxford, UK: Oxford University Press.

Huntington, S. P. (1968). *Political order in changing societies.* New Haven, CT: Yale University Press.

Ingraham, P., & Rosenbloom, D. H. (1990, June). *The state of merit in the federal government.* Occasional Paper, National Commission on the Public Service, Washington, DC.

Ingram, H. (1977). Policy implementation through bargaining: The case of federal grants in aid. *Public Policy, 25*(4), 499–526.

Ingram, H., Schneider, A. L., & DeLeón, P. (2007). Social construction and policy design. In P. A. Sabatier (Ed.), *Theories of the policy process* (2nd ed.) (pp. 93–126). Boulder, CO: Westview Press.

Ingram, H., & Smith, S. R. (1993). *Public policy for democracy.* Washington, DC: Brookings Institution Press.

Isett, K. R. (2010). . . . *And the pendulum swings: A call for evidence-based public organizations.* In R. O'Leary, D. M. Van Slyke, and S. Kim (Eds.), *The future of public administration, public management, and public service across the world: A Minnowbrook perspective* (pp. 59–66). Washington, DC: Georgetown University Press.

Jackson, A. (1829, December 8). *First annual message to congress.* Washington, DC.

Jacobs, N. F., King, D., & Milkis, S. (2019). Building a conservative state: Partisan polarization and the redeployment of administrative power. *Perspectives on Politics, 17*(2), 453–469.

James, W. (1907). *Pragmatism: A new name for some old ways of thinking.* New York, NY: Longmans, Green, and Co.

Jaques, E. (1990). In praise of hierarchy. *Harvard Business Review, 68*(1), 127–133.

Jasanoff, S. (1990). *The fifth branch: Science advisers as policy makers.* Cambridge, MA: Harvard University Press.

Jensen, L. (2003). *Patriots, settlers, and the origins of American social policy.* Cambridge, UK: Cambridge University Press.

Jessop, B. (1993). Towards a Schumpeterian workfare state? Preliminary remarks on post-Fordist political economy. *Studies in Political Economy, 40*(1), 7–39.

Jing, Y., & Savas, E. S. (2009). Managing collaborative service delivery: Comparing China and the United States. *Public Administration Review, 69*(s1): s101–s107.

John, R. R. (1995). *Spreading the news: The American postal system from Franklin to Morse.* Cambridge, MA: Harvard University Press.

John, R. R. (Ed.) (2006). *Ruling passions: Political economy in nineteenth-century America.* University Park, PA: Pennsylvania State University Press.

Johnson, K. (2007). *Governing the American state: Congress and the new federalism, 1877–1929.* Princeton, NJ: Princeton University Press.

Johnson, K. (2010). *Reforming Jim Crow: Southern politics and state in the age before Brown.* Oxford, UK: Oxford University Press.

Johnston, J. M., & Girth, A. M. (2012). Government contracts and "managing the market": The implications of strategic management responses to weak vendor competition. *Administration & Society, 44*(1), 3–29.

Johnston, J. M., & Romzek, B. S. (2010). The promise, performance, and pitfalls of government contracting. In R. F. Durant (Ed.), *The Oxford handbook of American bureaucracy* (pp. 396–420). Oxford, UK: Oxford University Press.

Jones, T. (2012). *More powerful than dynamite: Radicals, plutocrats, progressives, and New York's year of anarchy.* New York, NY: Bloomsbury Publishing.

Kagan, R. A. (2003). *Adversarial legalism: The American way of law.* Cambridge, MA: Harvard University Press.

Kagan, R. (2006). *Dangerous nation: America's foreign policy from its earliest days to the dawn of the twentieth century.* New York, NY: Vintage Books.

Kamieniecki, S. (2006). *Corporate America and environmental policy: How often does business get its way?* Stanford, CA: Stanford University Press.

Kanigel, R. (1997). *The one best way: Frederick Winslow Taylor and the enigma of efficiency.* New York, NY: Penguin Books.

Karl, B. D. (1983). *The uneasy state: The United States from 1915 to 1945.* Chicago, IL: The University of Chicago Press.

Katz, M. B. (1986). *In the shadow of the poorhouse: A social history of welfare in America.* New York, NY: Basic Books.

Katznelson, I. (2002). Rewriting the epic of America. In I. Katznelson & M. Shefter (Eds.), *Shaped by war and trade: International influences on American political development* (pp. 3–23). Princeton, NJ: Princeton University Press.

Katznelson, I. (2013). *Fear itself: The new deal and the origins of our times.* New York, NY: Liveright Publishing Corporation.

Kaufman, H. (1981). Fear of bureaucracy: A raging pandemic. *Public Administration Review, 41*(1), 1–9.

Kazin, M. (2012, Spring). The Port Huron statement at 50. *Dissent.* Retrieved from www.dissentmagazine.org/article/the-port-huron-statement-at-fifty.

Keller, M. (1977). *Affairs of state: Public life in late nineteenth century America.* Cambridge, MA: Harvard University Press.

Kellough, J. E., & Selden, S. C. (2003). The reinvention of public personnel administration: An analysis of the diffusion of personnel reforms in the states. *Public Administration Review, 63*(2), 165–176.

Kennedy, D. M. (2005). *Freedom from fear: The American people in depression and war, 1929–1945.* New York, NY: Oxford University Press.

Kerwin, C. M., & Furlong, S. R. (2010). *Rulemaking: How government agencies write law and make policy* (4th ed.). Washington, DC: Congressional Quarterly Press.

Kerwin, C. M., Furlong, S. R., & West, W. F. (2010). Interest groups, rulemaking, and American bureaucracy. In R. F. Durant (Ed.), *The Oxford handbook of American bureaucracy* (pp. 590–611). Oxford, UK: Oxford University Press.

Kettl, D. F. (1988). *Government by proxy: (Mis?)managing federal programs.* Washington, DC: Congressional Quarterly Press.

Kettl, D. F. (1993). *Sharing power: Public governance and private markets.* Washington, DC: Brookings Institution Press.

Kettl, D. F. (2002). *The transformation of governance: Public administration for twenty-first century America.* Baltimore, MD: Johns Hopkins University Press.

Kettl, D. F. (2009). *The next government of the United States: Why our institutions fail us and how to fix them.* New York, NY: W. W. Norton & Company.

Kettl, D. F. (2017). *Can governments earn our trust?* Cambridge, UK: Polity Press.

Kettl, D. F., & DiIulio, J. J., Jr. (Eds.). (1995). *Inside the reinvention machine: Appraising governmental reform.* Washington, DC: Brookings Institution Press.

Kieser, A., & Leiner, L. (2009). Why the rigour–relevance gap in management research is unbridgeable. *Journal of Management Studies, 46*(3), 516–533.

King, C. S., Feltey, K. M., & Susila, B. O. (1998). The question of participation: Toward authentic public participation in public administration. *Public Administration Review, 58*(4), 317–326.

King, C. S., & Stivers, C. M. (Eds.). (1998). *Government is US: Strategies for an anti-government era.* Thousand Oaks, CA: Sage Publications.

King, D., & Lieberman, R. C. (2009). Ironies of state building: A comparative perspective on the American state. *World Politics, 61*(3), 547–588.

Kingdon, J. W. (1999). *America the unusual.* New York, NY: Wadsworth.

Kirby, J. B. (1980). *Black Americans in the Roosevelt era: Liberalism and race.* Knoxville, TN: University of Tennessee Press.

Kirk, R. (1986). *The conservative mind: From Burke to Eliot.* New York, NY: Regnery.

Kirk, R. (1993). *The politics of prudence.* Wilmington, DE: ISI Books.

Kirk, R. (2002). *The American cause.* Wilmington, DE: The Intercollegiate Institute.

Kirk, R. (2003). *The roots of American order.* Wilmington, DE: The Intercollegiate Institute. Orig. pub. 1974.

Kirkland, E. C. (1956). *Dream and thought in the business community, 1860–1900.* Ithaca, NY: Cornell University Press.

Knight, L. W. (2010). *Jane Addams: Spirit in action.* New York, NY: W. W. Norton & Company.

Kolko, G. (1977). *The triumph of conservativism: A reinterpretation of American history, 1900–1916* (paperback ed.). New York, NY: Free Press.

Konisky, D. M., & Teodoro, M. P. (2016). When governments regulate governments. *American Journal of Political Science, 60*(3), 559–574.

Koppell, J. G. S. (2010a). Metaphors and the development of American bureaucracy. In R. F. Durant (Ed.), *The Oxford handbook of American bureaucracy* (pp. 128–150). Oxford, UK: Oxford University Press.

Koppell, J. G. S. (2010b). *World rule: Accountability, legitimacy, and the design of global governance.* Chicago, IL: University of Chicago Press.

Kramer, J. (2015). *The new freedom and the radicals: Woodrow Wilson, progressive views of radicalism, and the origins of repressive tolerance.* Philadelphia, PA: Temple University Press.

Krause, G. A. (1999). *A two-way street: The institutional dynamics of the modern administrative state.* Pittsburgh, PA: University of Pittsburgh Press.

Krause, G. A., & Cohen, J. E. (2000). Opportunity, constraints, and the development of the institutional presidency: The issuance of executive orders, 1939–96. *Journal of Politics, 62*(1), 88–114.

Krause, G. A., & Meier, K. J. (Eds.). (2005). *Politics, policy, and organizations: Frontiers in the scientific study of bureaucracy.* Ann Arbor, MI: University of Michigan Press.

Krislov, S. (1957). *The Negro in federal employment: The quest for equal opportunity.* Minneapolis, MN: University of Minneapolis Press.

Kroll, A., & Moynihan, D. P. (2018). The design and practice of integrating evidence: Connecting performance management with program evaluation. *Public Administration Review, 78*(2), 183–194.

Kroll, A., Neshkova, M., & Pandey, S. (2017, January 11). Spill-over effects from customer to citizen orientation. *Administration & Society.* Retrieved from https://doi-org.proxyau.wrlc.org/10.1177%2F0095399716687341.

Kuhn, T. S. (2012). *The structure of scientific revolutions* (4th ed.). Chicago, IL: University of Chicago Press.

Lan, Z., & Rosenbloom, D. R. (1992). Editorial: Public administration in transition? *Public Administration Review, 52*(6), 535–537.

Lane, J. E. (2000). *New public management: An introduction.* New York, NY: Routledge.

Lepore, J. (2019, March/April). A new Americanism: Why a nation needs a national story. *Foreign Affairs, 98*(2), 10–19.

Lasswell, H. D. (1941). The garrison state. *American Journal of Sociology, 46*(4), 455–468.

Lavertu, S., & Moynihan, D. P. (2013). Agency political ideology and reform implementation: Performance management in the Bush administration. *Journal of Public Administration Research and Theory, 23*(3), 521–549.

Lawrence, J. A. (2018). *The class of '74: Congress after Watergate and the roots of partisanship.* Baltimore, MD: Johns Hopkins University Press.

Leach, W. (1980). *True love and perfect unions: The feminist reform of sex and society.* New York, NY: Basic Books.

Leach, W. D. (2006). Collaborative public management and democracy: Evidence from western watershed partnerships. *Public Administration Review, 66*(Special Issue), 100–110.

Lears, J. (2009). *Rebirth of a nation: The making of modern America, 1877–1920.* New York, NY: HarperCollins.

Lee, C. W., McQuarrie, M., & Walker, E. T. (Eds.). (2015). *Democratizing inequalities: Dilemmas of the new public participation.* New York, NY: New York University Press.

Lee, M. (2008). *Bureaus of efficiency: Reforming local government in the progressive era.* Milwaukee, WI: Marquette University Press.

Lee, M. (2013). Glimpsing an alternate construction of American public administration: The later life of William Allen, cofounder of the New York bureau of municipal research. *Administration & Society, 45*(5), 522–562.

Lee, M. (2016). *A presidential civil service: FDR's Liaison office for personnel management.* Tuscaloosa, AL: University of Alabama Press.

Leffler, M. P. (1981). Herbert Hoover, the "new era," and American foreign policy, 1921–1929. In E. W. Hawley (Ed.), *Herbert Hoover as secretary of commerce: Studies in new era thought and practice* (pp. 148–182). Iowa City, IA: University of Iowa Press.

LeRoux, K. (2009). Paternalistic or participatory governance? Examining opportunities for client participation in nonprofit social service organizations. *Public Administration Review, 69*(3), 504–517.

LeRoux, K., & Feeney, M. K. (2015). *Nonprofit organizations and civil society in America.* New York, NY: Routledge.

Leuchtenburg, W. E. (1964). The new deal and the analogue of war. In J. Braeman, R. Hamlett, & E. Walters (Eds.), *Change and continuity in twentieth century America.* Columbus, OH: Ohio State University Press.

Leuchtenburg, W. E. (2009). *Herbert Hoover.* New York, NY: Times Books.

Lewis, D. E. (2008). *The politics of presidential appointments: Political control and bureaucratic performance.* Princeton, NJ: Princeton University Press.

Lewis, G. B., & Pitts, D. W. (2011). Representation of lesbians and gay men in federal, state, and local bureaucracies. *Journal of Public Administration Research & Theory, 21*(1), 159–180.

Lieberman, R. C. (2002). Weak state, strong policy: Paradoxes of race policy in the United States, Great Britain, and France. *Studies in American Political Development*, *16*(2), 138–161.

Light, P. C. (1997). *The tides of reform: Making government work, 1945–1995*. New Haven, CT: Yale University Press.

Light, P. C. (1999). *The new public service*. Washington, DC: Brookings Institution Press.

Light, P. D. (2019). *The government–industrial complex: The true size of the federal government, 1984–2018*. New York, NY: Oxford University Press.

Lilley, W., III, & Miller, J. C., III. (1977). The new "social regulation." *Public Interest*, *19*(2), 49–61.

Lindblom, C. A. (1977). *Politics and markets: The world's political-economic systems*. New York, NY: Basic Books.

Lindblom, C. A. (1990). *Inquiry and change: The troubled attempt to understand & shape society*. New Haven, CT: Yale University Press.

Lippmann, W. (1922). *Public opinion*. New York, NY: Macmillan Company.

Lippmann, W. (1961). *Drift and mastery: An attempt to diagnose the current unrest*. Englewood Cliffs, NJ: Prentice-Hall. Org. pub. 1914.

Lipset, S. M. (1996). *American exceptionalism: A double-edged sword*. New York, NY: W. W. Norton & Company.

Lipset, S. M., & Marks, G. (2000). *It didn't happen here: Why socialism failed in the United States*. New York, NY: W. W. Norton & Company.

Loeffler, E., & Bovaird, T. (2016). User and community co-production of public services: What does the evidence tell us? *International Journal of Public Administration*, *39*(13), 1006–1019.

Long, N. (1949). Power and administration. *Public Administration Review*, *9*(4), 257–264.

Losey, S. (2013, June 10). Federal workforce dips 20 percent since May 2010 peak. *Federal Times*. Retrieved from www.federaltimes.com/article/20130610/PERSONNEL/306100007/Federal-workforce-dips-20-percent-since-May-2010-peak.

Lowi, T. J. (1969). *The end of liberalism: The second republic of the United States*. New York, NY: W. W. Norton & Company.

Lowi, T. J. (1985). *The personal president: Power invested, promise unfulfilled*. Ithaca, NY: Cornell University Press.

Lowi, T. J. (1995). *The end of the republican era*. Norman, OK: University of Oklahoma Press.

Lubove, R. (1986). *The struggle for social security, 1900–1935* (2nd ed.). Pittsburgh, PA: University of Pittsburgh Press.

Lynn, L. E., Jr. (2006). *Public management old and new*. New York, NY: Routledge.

MacMillan, M. (2002). *Paris 1919: Six months that changed the world*. New York, NY: Random House.

Mahoney, J., & Thelen, K. (2010). *Explaining institutional change: Ambiguity, agency, and power*. New York, NY: Cambridge University Press.

Majone, G. (1992). *Evidence, argument, and persuasion in the policy process*. New Haven, CT: Yale University Press.

Mann, M. (1986). The autonomous power of the state: Its origins, mechanisms, and results. In J. A. Hall (Ed.), *States in history* (pp. 109–136). Oxford, UK: Oxford University Press.

Mann, T. E., & Ornstein, N. J. (2006). *The broken branch: How congress is failing America and how to get it back on track*. New York, NY: Oxford University Press.

Mannheim, K. (1929). *Ideology and Utopia: An introduction to the sociology of knowledge.* London, UK: Routledge.

Mansfield, H. C. (2001). *A student's guide to political philosophy.* Wilmington, DE: ISI Books.

Maranto, R. (1993). *Politics and bureaucracy in the modern presidency: Careerists and appointees in the Reagan administration.* New York, NY: Praeger.

Maranto, R., & Schultz, D. A. (1991). *A short history of civil service reform.* Lanham, MD: University Press of America.

March, J. G., & Olsen, J. P. (1983). Organizing political life: What administrative reorganization tells us about government. *American Political Science Review, 77,* 281–297.

March, J. G., & Olsen, J. P. (1984). The new institutionalism: Organizational factors in political life. *American Political Science Review, 78*(3), 734–749.

March, J. G., & Olsen, J. P. (1989). *Rediscovering institutions: The organizational basis of politics.* New York, NY: Basic Books.

Marcuse, H. (1964). *One-dimensional man.* Boston, MA: Beacon Press.

Marini, F. (Ed.). (1971). *Toward a new public administration: The Minnowbrook perspective.* Scranton, PA: Chandler Publishing.

Mashaw, J. L. (2006). Recovering American administrative law: Federalist foundations, 1787–1801. *Yale Law Journal, 115*(6), 1256–1344.

Maslow, A. H. (1943). A theory of human motivation. *Psychological Review, 50*(4), 370–396.

Mathews, J. (1997). Power shift. *Foreign Affairs, 76*(1), 50–66.

Mayer, K. R. (2001). *With a stroke of the pen: Executive orders and presidential power.* Princeton, NJ: Princeton University Press.

Mayo, E. (1945). *The social problems of an industrial civilization* (4th printing). Andover, MA: Andover Press.

Mazmanian, D. A., & Sabatier, P. A. (1983). *Implementation and public policy.* Lanham, MD: University Press of America. Glenview, IL: Scott, Foresman.

Mazzucato, M. (2015). *The entrepreneurial state: Debunking private & public sector myths.* New York, NY: PublicAffairs Books.

McCluskey, A. T., & Smith, E. M. (Eds.). (1999). *Mary McLeod Bethune: Building a better world.* Bloomington, IN: Indiana University Press.

McCormick, R. P. (1966). *The second American party system: Party formation in the Jacksonian era.* New York, NY: W. W. Norton & Company.

McFarland, A. S. (2004). *Neopluralism: The evolution of political process theory.* Lawrence, KS: University Press of Kansas.

McFaul, M. (2018). *From cold war to hot peace: An American ambassador in Putin's Russia.* New York, NY: Haughton Mifflin Harcourt.

McGarity, T. O., & Wagner, W. E. (2008). *Bending science: How special interests corrupt public health research.* Cambridge, MA: Harvard University Press.

McGerr, M. (2003). *A fierce discontent: The rise and fall of the progressive movement in America, 1870–1920.* New York, NY: Free Press.

McGinnis, M. D., & Ostrom, E. (2012). Reflections on Vincent Ostrom, public administration, and polycentricity. *Public Administration Review, 72*(1), 15–25.

McGregor, D. M. (1960). *The human side of enterprise.* New York, NY: McGraw Hill.

McGuire, M., & Agranoff, R. (2010). Networking in the shadow of bureaucracy. In R. F. Durant (Ed.), *The Oxford handbook of American bureaucracy* (pp. 372–396). Oxford, UK: Oxford University Press.

McLoughlin, W. G. (1978). *Revivals, awakenings, and reform.* Chicago, IL: University of Chicago Press.

McPherson, J. M. (2007). *This mighty scourge: Perspectives on the civil war.* New York, NY: Oxford University Press.

Meier, K. J. (1993). Latinos and representative bureaucracy: Testing the Thompson and Henderson hypotheses. *Journal of Public Administration Research and Theory, 3*(4), 393–414.

Meier, K. (2015). Proverbs and the evolution of public administration. *Public Administration Review, 75*(1), 15–24.

Meier, K. J., & Hill, G. C. (2005). Bureaucracy in the 21st century. In E. Ferlie, L. E. Lynn, Jr., & C. Pollitt (Eds.), *The Oxford handbook of public management* (pp. 51–71). Oxford, UK: Oxford University Press.

Meier, K. J., & Nicholson-Crotty, J. (2006). Gender, representative bureaucracy, and law enforcement: The case of sexual assault. *Public Administration Review, 66*(6), 850–860.

Meier, K. J., & O'Toole, L. J., Jr., (2006). *Bureaucracy in a democratic state: A governance perspective.* Baltimore, MD: Johns Hopkins University Press.

Meier, K. J., Pennington, M. S., & Eller, W. S. (2005). Race, sex, and Clarence Thomas: Representation change in the EEOC. *Public Administration Review, 65*(2), 171–179.

Meier, K. J., & Stewart, J., Jr. (1992). The impact of representative bureaucracies: Educational systems and public policies. *American Review of Public Administration, 22*(3), 157–171.

Melnick, R. S. (1985). The politics of partnership. *Public Administration Review, 45*(Special Issue), 653–660.

Menand, L. (2001). *The metaphysical club: A story of ideas in America.* New York, NY: Farrar, Straus and Giroux.

Mergel, I., Rethemeyer, R. K., & Isett, K. (2016). Big data in public affairs. *Public Administration Review, 76*(6), 928–937.

Merriam, C. E. (1920). *American political ideas, 1865–1907.* New York, NY: Macmillan Company.

Metcalf, H. C., & Urwick, L. (1968). *Dynamic administration: The collected papers of Mary Parker Follett.* Printed in the United States of America (no publisher cited).

Mettler, S. (1998). *Dividing citizens: Gender and federalism in new deal public policy.* Ithaca, NY: Cornell University Press.

Mettler, S. (2011). *The submerged state: How invisible government policies undermine American democracy.* Chicago, IL: University of Chicago Press.

Meyers, M. (1957). *The Jacksonian persuasion: Politics and belief.* Stanford, CA: Stanford University Press.

Mikesell, J. L. (2018, May). Often wrong, never uncertain: Lessons from 40 years of state revenue forecasting. *Public Administration Review.* Retrieved from https://doi.org/10.1111/puar.12954.

Milkis, S. M., & Nelson, M. (1999). *The American presidency: Origins and development, 1776–1998.* Washington, DC: Congressional Quarterly Press.

Miller, G. J., & Whitford, A. B. (2007). The principal's moral hazard: Constraints on the use of incentives in hierarchy. *Journal of Public Administration Research and Theory, 17*(2), 213–233.

Miller, G. J., & Whitford, A. B. (2016). *Above politics: Bureaucratic discretion and credible commitment.* New York, NY: Cambridge University Press.

Miller, H. T., & Fox, C. J. (2007). *Postmodern public administration* (rev. ed.). Armonk, NY: M. E. Sharpe.

Mills, C. W. (1956). *The power elite.* Oxford, UK: Oxford University Press.

Milward, H. B., Jensen, L., Roberts, A., Dussauge-Launa, M. I., Junjan, V., Torenvlied, R., . . . Durant, R. F. (2016). Symposium: Is public management neglecting the state? *Governance, 29*(3), 311–334.

Milward, H. B., & Provan, K. G. (1993). The hollow state: Private provision of public services. In H. M. Ingram & S. R. Smith (Eds.), *Public policy for democracy* (pp. 222–237). Washington, DC: Brookings Institution Press.

Milward, H. B., & Provan, K. G. (1998). Principles for controlling agents: The political economy of network structures. *Journal of Public Administration Research and Theory, 8*(2), 203–222.

Milward, H. B., & Provan, K. G. (2000). Governing the hollow state. *Journal of Public Administration Research and Theory, 10*(2), 359–380.

Mitchell, W. C. (1999). *The backward art of spending money.* New Brunswick, NJ: Transaction Publishers. Org. pub. 1937.

Moe, R. C., & Gilmour, R. S. (1995). Rediscovering principles of administration: The neglected foundation of public law. *Public Administration Review, 55*(2), 135–146.

Moe, T. (1985). The politicized presidency. In J. E. Chubb & P. E. Peterson (Eds.), *The new direction in American politics.* Washington, DC: Brookings Institution Press.

Moller, J. (2019). The ecclesiastical roots of representation and consent. *Perspectives on Politics, 16*(4), 1075–1085.

Moody's. (2013, June 27). New state adjusted pension liabilities show wide range of obligations: Effect of new discount rates highlighted. *Moody's.* Retrieved from www.moodys.com/research/Moodys-New-state-adjusted-pension-liabilities-show-wide-range-of-PR_276663.

Mooney, J. D., & Reiley, A. C. (1931). *Onward industry! The principles of organization and their significant to modern industry.* New York, NY: Harper & Brothers.

Morone, J. A. (1998). *The democratic wish: Popular participation and the limits of American government* (rev. ed.). New Haven, CT: Yale University Press.

Mosher, F. C. (1982). *Democracy and the public service* (2nd ed.). New York, NY: Oxford University Press. Org. pub. 1968.

Mosher, W. E. (1939). The making of a public servant. *National Municipal Review, 28*(6), 416–437.

Moynihan, D. P. (2008). *The dynamics of performance management: Constructing information and reform.* Washington, DC: Georgetown University Press.

Moynihan, D. P. (2013). Advancing the empirical study of performance management. *The American Review of Public Administration, 43*, 499–517.

Moynihan, D. P. (2014). History as a source of values for new public governance. In D. F. Morgan & B. J. Cook (Eds.), *New public governance: A regime-centered perspective* (pp. 55–76). Armonk, NY: M. E. Sharpe.

Moynihan, D. P. (2015). *Using evidence to make decisions: The experience of US performance management initiatives.* Commissioned article prepared for the Committee on the Use of Economic Evidence to Inform Investments in Children, Youth, and Families. The National Academies of Sciences, Engineering and Medicine. Retrieved from http://sites.nationalacademies.org/cs/groups/dbassesite/documents/webpage/dbasse_171855.pdf.

Moynihan, D. P., & Beazley, I. (2006). *Toward next-generation performance budgeting: Reflections on the experiences of seven reforming countries.* Washington, DC: World Bank.

Moynihan, D. P., Fernandez, S., Kim, S., LeRoux, K. M., Piotrowski, S. J., Wright, B. E., & Yang, K. (2011). Performance regimes amidst governance complexity. *Journal of Public Administration Research and Theory, 21*(s1), i141–i155.

Moynihan, D. P., & Soss, J. (2014). Policy feedback and the politics of administration. *Public Administration Review, 74*(3), 320–332.

Mullins, D. R., & Mikesell, J. L. (2010). Innovations in budgeting and financial management. In R. F. Durant (Ed.), *The Oxford handbook of American bureaucracy* (pp. 738–765). Oxford, UK: Oxford University Press.

Musgrave, S., & Nussbaum, M. (2018, April 8). Trump thrives in areas that lack traditional news outlets. *Politico: Special Report.* Retrieved from www.politico.com/story/2018/04/08/news-subscriptions-decline-donald-trump-voters-505605.

Musso, J., Weare, C., Bryer, T., & Cooper, T. L. (2011). Toward "strong democracy" in global cities? Social capital building, theory-driven reform, and the Los Angeles neighborhood council experience. *Public Administration Review, 71*(1), 102–111.

Nabatchi, T. (2010). Addressing the citizenship and democratic deficits: The potential of deliberative democracy for public administration. *American Review of Public Administration, 40*(4), 376–399.

Nabatchi, T., & Amsler, L. B. (2014). Direct public engagement in local government. *American Review of Public Administration, 44*(s4), s63–s88.

Nabatchi, T., Sancino, A., & Sicilia, M. (2017). Varieties of participation in public services: The who, when, and what of coproduction. *Public Administration Review, 77,* 766–776.

Nash, G. H. (1988). *The life of Herbert Hoover: The humanitarian, 1914–1917.* New York, NY: W. W. Norton & Company.

Nash, G. H. (1996). *The life of Herbert Hoover: Master of emergencies, 1917–1918.* New York, NY: W. W. Norton & Company.

Nathan, R. P. (1983). *The administrative presidency.* New York, NY: John Wiley & Sons.

Nelson, W. E. (1982). *The roots of American bureaucracy, 1830–1900.* Cambridge, MA: Harvard University Press. Esp. chapter 1. Reprinted by Beard Books, Washington, DC, in 2006.

Neshkova, M. I., & Guo, H. (D). (2012). Public participation and organizational performance: Evidence from state agencies. *Journal of Public Administration Research and Theory, 22*(2), 267–288.

Neuhaus, R. J. (1986). *The naked public square: Religion and democracy in America.* Grand Rapids, MI: William B. Eerdmans Publishing Company.

Neustadt, R. E. (1990). *Presidential power and the modern presidents.* New York, NY: Free Press.

Newbold, S. P., & Rosenbloom, D. H. (Eds.). (2007). Symposium on the 70th anniversary of the president's committee on administrative management. *Public Administration Review, 67*(6).

Newbold, S. P., & Rosenbloom, D. H. (Eds.). (2017). *The constitutional school of American public administration.* New York, NY: Routledge.

Newcomer, K. E. (2015). From outputs to outcomes. In M. E. Guy & M. M. Rubin (Eds.), *Public administration evolving: From foundations to the future* (pp. 124–156). New York, NY: Routledge.

Newland, C. A. (2003). The facilitative state, political executive aggrandizement, and public service challenges. *Administration & Society, 35*(4), 379–407.

Niebuhr, R. (2013). *Moral man and immoral society: A study in ethics and politics*. Louisville, KY: Westminster John Knox Press.

Novak, W. J. (2001). The American law of association: The legal—political construction of civil society. *Studies in American Political Development, 15*(2), 163–188.

Novak, W. J. (2008). The myth of the "weak" American state. *American Historical Review, 113*(3), 752–772.

Noyer, G. K. (2015). *Voltaire's revolution: Writings from his campaign to free laws from religion*. New York, NY: Prometheus Books.

Nye, J. S., Jr. (2017). Will the liberal order survive? The history of an idea. *Foreign Affairs, 96*(1), 10–16.

Nye, M. J. (2011). *Michael Polanyi and his generation: Origins of the social construction of science*. Chicago, IL: University of Chicago Press.

Oakeshott, M. (1962). *Rationalism in politics*. New York, NY: Basic Books.

O'Connor, A. (2010). Bringing the market back in: Philanthropic activism and conservative reform. In E. S. Clemens & D. Guthrie (Eds.), *Politics +partnerships: The role of voluntary associations in America's political past and present* (pp. 121–150). Chicago, IL: University of Chicago Press.

O'Connor, A. (2018, September 29). More evidence that nutrition studies don't add up. *New York Times*. Retrieved from www.nytimes.com/2018/09/29/sunday-review/cornell-food-scientist-wansink-misconduct.html.

O'Connor, M. (2014). *A commercial republic: America's enduring debate over democratic capitalism*. Lawrence, KS: University Press of Kansas.

O'Leary, R. (1993). *Environmental change: Federal courts and the EPA*. Philadelphia, PA: Temple University Press.

O'Leary, R. (2015). From silos to networks: Hierarchy to heterarchy. In M. E. Guy & M. M. Rubin (Eds.), *Public administration evolving: From foundations to the future* (pp. 84–102). New York, NY: Routledge.

O'Leary, R., & Bingham, L. B. (Eds.). (2009). *The collaborative public manager: New ideas for the twenty-first century*. Washington, DC: Georgetown University Press.

Olsen, J. P. (2006). Maybe it is time to rediscover bureaucracy? *Journal of Public Administration, 16*(1), 1–24.

Olsen, J. P. (2008). The ups and downs of bureaucratic organization. *Annual Review of Political Science, 11*, 13–37.

Orren, K., & Skowronek, S. (2004). *The search for American political development*. Cambridge, UK: Cambridge University Press.

Orren, K., & Skowronek, S. (2017). *The policy state: An American predicament*. Cambridge, MA: Harvard University Press.

Osborne, D., & Gaebler, T. (1993). *Reinventing government: How the entrepreneurial spirit is transforming the public sector*. New York, NY: Plume.

Osborne, D., & Plastrik, P. (1997). *Banishing bureaucracy: The five strategies for reinventing government*. New York, NY: Plume.

Osborne, S. P. (Ed.). (2010). *The new public governance? Emerging perspectives on the theory and practice of public governance*. New York, NY: Routledge.

Ospina, S., & Dodge, J. (2005). Narrative inquiry and the search for connectedness: Practitioners and academics developing public administration scholarship. *Public Administration Review, 65*(4), 409–423.

Ostrom, V. (2008). *The intellectual crisis in American public administration* (3rd ed.). Tuscaloosa, AL: University of Alabama Press. Org. pub. 1980.

O'Toole, L. J., Jr. (1986). Policy recommendations for multi-actor implementation: An assessment of the field. *Journal of Public Policy, 6*(2), 181–210.

O'Toole, L. J., Jr. (1997). Treating networks seriously: Practical and research-based agendas in public administration. *Public Administration Review, 57*(1), 45–52.

Paine, P. (1995). *Common sense.* New York, NY: Barnes & Noble Books. Org. pub. 1776.

Painter, M. (1988). Public management: Fad or fallacy. *Australian Journal of Public Administration, 47,* 1–3.

Pandey, S. K., & Stazyk, E. C. (2008). Antecedents and correlates of public service motivation. In J. L. Perry & A. Hondeghem (Eds.), *Motivation in public management: The call of public service* (pp. 101–117). New York, NY: Oxford University Press.

Parenti, M. (2010). *Democracy for the few* (9th ed.). Boston, MA: Cengage Learning.

Parrett, G. (2000). *Eisenhower.* New York, NY: Random House.

Pasachoff, E. (2018, March 13). The curious bipartisan push for evidence-based policymaking. *The Regulatory Review.* Retrieved from www.theregreview.org/2018/03/13/pasachoff-curious-push-evidence/.

Patterson, B. H. (2008). *To serve the president: Continuity and innovation in the white house staff.* Washington, DC: Brookings Institution Press.

Perrow, C. (1979). *Complex organizations: A critical essay.* Brattleboro, VT: Echo Point Books & Media.

Perry, J. L. (1996). Measuring public service motivation: An assessment of construct reliability and validity. *Journal of Public Administration Research and Theory, 6*(1), 5–22.

Perry, J. L., Engbers, T. A., & Jun, S. Y. (2013). Back to the future? Performance-related pay, empirical research, and the perils of persistence. In R. F. Durant & J. R. S. Durant (Eds.), *Debating public administration: Management challenges, choices, and opportunities* (pp. 27–40). Boca Raton, FL: CRC Press.

Perry, J. L., & Wise, L. R. (1990). The motivational bases of public service. *Public Administration Review, 50*(3), 367–373.

Pestritto, R. J., & Atto, W. J. (Eds.). (2008). *American progressivism: A reader.* Lanham, MD: Lexington Books.

Peters, B. G. (2001). *The future of governing* (2nd ed.). Lawrence, KS: University Press of Kansas.

Peters, B. G., & Pierre, J. (2016). *Comparative governance: Rediscovering the functional dimension of governance.* Cambridge, UK: Cambridge University Press.

Peters, B. G., & Pierre, J. (2017). Two roads to nowhere: 30 years of public administration research. *Governance, 30*(1), 11–16.

Pfiffner, J. M. (1940). *Research methods in public administration.* New York, NY: Ronald Press.

Philbrick, N. (2016). *George Washington, Benedict Arnold, and the fate of the American revolution.* New York, NY: Penguin Books.

Phillips-Fein, K. (2009). *Invisible hands: The making of the conservative movement from the new deal to Reagan.* New York, NY: W. W. Norton & Company.

Phillips-Fein, K., & Zelizer, J. E. (Eds.). (2012). *What's good for business: Business and American politics since world war II.* Oxford, UK: Oxford University Press.

Pierson, P. (2004). *Politics in time: History, institutions, and social analysis.* Princeton, NJ: Princeton University Press.

Pietrusza, D. (2007). *1920: The year of the six presidents*. New York, NY: Basic Books.

Pillsbury, M. (2015). *The hundred-year marathon: China's secret strategy to replace America as the global superpower*. New York, NY: St. Martin's Griffin.

Pinder, C. C. (2008). *Work motivation in organizational behavior* (2nd ed.). New York, NY: Psychology Press.

Pinker, S. (2002). *Blank slate: The modern denial of human nature*. New York, NY: Penguin Books.

Piven, F. F., & Cloward, R. (1993). *Regulating the poor: The functions of public welfare*. New York, NY: Vintage Books. Org. pub. 1971.

Polanyi, K. (1944). *The great transformation: The political and economic origins of our time*. Boston, MA: Beacon Press.

Polanyi, M. (1958). *Personal knowledge: Towards a post-critical philosophy*. Chicago, IL: University of Chicago Press.

Pollard, E. A. (1866). *The lost cause: A new Southern history of the war of the confederates*. New York, NY: E. B. Treat and Company.

Pollitt, C. (2017). Public administration research since 1980: Slipping away from the real world? *International Journal of Public Sector Management, 30*(6–7), 555–565.

Pollitt, C., & Bouckaert, G. (2011). *Public management reform: A comparative analysis—new public management, governance, and the neo-Weberian state* (3rd ed.). Oxford, UK: Oxford University Press.

Posner, P. L. (2010). The politics of vertical diffusion: The states and climate change. In B. G. Rabe (Ed.), *Greenhouse governance: Addressing climate change in America* (pp. 73–100). Washington, DC: Brookings Institution Press.

Postman, N. (1985). *Amusing ourselves to death: Public discourse in the age of show business*. New York, NY: Penguin Books.

Postman, N. (1999). *Building a bridge to the 18th century: How the past can improve our future*. New York, NY: Vintage Books.

President's Committee on Administrative Management (PCAM). (1937). *Reorganization of the executive departments*. Washington, DC: Government Printing Office.

President's Research Committee on Social Trends. (1933). *Recent social trends in the United States*. New York, NY: McGraw-Hill Book Company.

Pressman, J. L., & Wildavsky, A. (1984). *Implementation: How great expectations in Washington are dashed in Oakland* (3rd ed.). Berkeley, CA: University of California Press.

Prior, K. S. (2018). *On reading well: Finding the good life through great books*. Ada, MI: Brazos Press.

Putnam, R. D., & Campbell, D. E. (2012). *Amazing grace: How religion divides and unites us*. New York, NY: Simon & Schuster.

Raadschelders, J. C. N. (2008). The early years of the administrative state: Was there a "second state"? *Public Administration Review, 68*(5), 945–948.

Raadschelders, J. C. N. (2017). *Handbook of administrative history*. New York, NY: Routledge. Org. pub. 1998.

Raadschelders, J. C. N., & Bemelmans-Videc, M-L. (2015). Political (system) reform: Can administrative reform succeed without? In F. van der Meer, J. C. N. Raadschelders, & T. A. J. Toonen (Eds.), *Comparative civil service systems in the 21st century*. New York, NY: Macmillan Company.

Radin, B. A. (2006). *Challenging the performance movement: Accountability, complexity, and democratic values*. Washington, DC: Georgetown University Press.

Radin, B. A. (2013). *Beyond Machiavelli: Policy analysis reached mid-life* (2nd ed.). Washington, DC: Georgetown University Press.

Radin, B. A., & Posner, P. (2010). Policy tools, mandates, and intergovernmental relations. In R. F. Durant (Ed.), *The Oxford handbook of American bureaucracy* (pp. 447–471). Oxford, UK: Oxford University Press.

Radnor, Z., & Osborne, S. P. (2013). Lean: A failed theory for public services? *Public Management Review, 15*, 265–287.

Rainey, H. G. (2014). *Understanding and managing public organizations* (5th ed.). San Francisco, CA: Jossey-Bass.

Rawls, J. (1971). *A theory of justice.* Cambridge, MA: Harvard University Press.

Redford, E. S. (1969). *Democracy in the administrative state.* New York, NY: Oxford University Press.

Rehnquist, W. H. (2004). *The supreme court.* New York, NY: Alfred A. Knopf.

Reiman, R. A. (1992). *The new deal & American youth: Ideas and ideals in a depression decade.* Athens, GA: University of Georgia Press.

Rein, M., & Rabinovitz, F. F. (1977). *Implementation: A theoretical perspective.* Cambridge, MA: MIT Press.

Remini, R. V. (2008). *A short history of the United States.* New York, NY: HarperCollins.

Resh, W. G. (2015). *Rethinking the administrative presidency.* Baltimore, MD: Johns Hopkins University Press.

Resh, W. G., & Durant, R. F. (2015). The senior executive service. In D. A. Bearfield & M. J. Dubnick (Eds.), *The encyclopedia of public administration and public policy* (3rd ed.). Boca Raton, FL: CRC Press.

Rhodes, R. A. W., & Wanna, J. (2007). The limits to public value, or rescuing responsible government from the platonic guardians. *Australian Journal of Public Administration, 66*(4), 406–421.

Riccards, M. P. (1997). *The ferocious engine of democracy: A history of the American presidency* (vol. 1). Lanham, MD: Madison Books.

Riccucci, N. M. (2010). *Public administration: Traditions of inquiry and philosophies of knowledge.* Washington, DC: Georgetown University Press.

Rich, A. (2004). *Think tanks, public policy, and the politics of expertise.* New York, NY: Cambridge University Press.

Ritz, A., Brewer, G. A., & Neumann, O. (2016). Public service motivation: A systematic literature review and outlook. *Public Administration Review, 76*(3), 414–426.

Roberts, A. (1994). Demonstrating neutrality: The Rockefeller philanthropies and the evolution of public administration, 1927–1936. *Public Administration Review, 54*(3), 221–227.

Roberts, A. (2012). *America's first great depression: Economic crisis and political disorder after the panic of 1837.* Ithaca, NY: Cornell University Press.

Roberts, A. (2013). *Large forces: What's missing in public administration.* CreateSpace Independent Publishing Platform.

Robertson, D. B. (2012). *Federalism and the making of America.* New York, NY: Routledge.

Robertson, D. B., & Judd, D. R. (1989). *The development of American public policy: The structure of policy restraint.* Glenville, IL: Scott, Foresman.

Roche, J. P. (1961). The founding fathers: A reform caucus in action. *American Political Science Review, 55*(4), 799–816.

Rodgers, D. T. (1998). *Atlantic crossings: Social politics in a progressive age.* Cambridge, MA: Belknap Press.

Roethlisberger, F. J., & Dickenson, W. (1939). *Management and the worker.* New York, NY: Taylor & Francis.

Rohr, J. A. (1986). *To run a constitution: The legitimacy of the administrative state.* Lawrence, KS: University Press of Kansas.

Rosenbloom, D. H. (1977). *Federal equal employment opportunity: Politics and public personnel administration.* New York, NY: Praeger.

Rosenbloom, D. H. (1983). Public administration theory and the separation of powers. *Public Administration Review, 43*(3), 219–227.

Rosenbloom, D. H. (2000). *Building a legislative-centered public administration: Congress and the administrative state, 1946–1999.* Birmingham, AL: University of Alabama Press.

Rosenbloom, D. H. (2005). Taking social equity seriously in MPA education. *Journal of Public Affairs Education, 11*(3), 247–252.

Rosenbloom, D. H. (2007). Reinventing administrative prescriptions: The case for democratic-constitutional impact statements and scorecards. *Public Administration Review, 67*(1), 28–39.

Rosenbloom, D. H. (2008). The politics—administration dichotomy in US historical context. *Public Administration Review, 68*(1), 57–60.

Rosenbloom, D. H. (2013). Reflections on "public administration and the separation of powers." *American Review of Public Administration, 43*(4), 381–396.

Rosenbloom, D. H. (2014). *Federal service and the constitution: The development of the public employment relationship* (2nd ed.). Washington, DC: Georgetown University Press.

Rosenbloom, D. H., & McCurdy, H. E. (Eds.). (2006). *Revisiting Waldo's administrative state: Constancy and change in public administration.* Washington, DC: Georgetown University Press.

Rosenbloom, D. H., & Ross, B. H. (1994). Administrative theory, political power, and government reform. In P. Ingraham & B. Romzek (Eds.), *New paradigms for government: Issues for the changing public service.* San Francisco, CA: Jossey-Bass.

Ross, D. (1991). *The origins of American social science.* Cambridge, UK: Cambridge University Press.

Rossi, P. H. (1987). The iron law of evaluation and other metallic rules. *Research in Social Problems and Public Policy, 4,* 3–20.

Rothbard, M. N. (1974). *Society without a state.* Presented at a meeting of the American Society for Political and Legal Philosophy, Washington, DC, December 28.

Rubin, I. (2016). *The politics of public budgeting: Getting and spending, borrowing and balancing* (8th ed.). Washington, DC: Congressional Quarterly Press.

Rucker, P. (2009, March 3). Many hires needed for budget goals. *Washington Post,* p. A1.

Rucker, P., & Costa, R. (2017, February 23). Bannon vows a daily fight for "deconstruction of the administrative state." *Washington Post.* Retrieved from www.washingtonpost.com/politics/top-wh-strategist-vows-a-daily-fight-for-deconstruction-of-the-administrative-state/2017/02/23/03f6b8da-f9ea-11e6-bf01-d47f8cf9b643_story.html?utm_term=.ac7775fce49d.

Rudalevige, A. (2002). *Managing the president's program: Presidential leadership and legislative policy formulation.* Princeton, NJ: Princeton University Press.

Saint-Martin, D. (2000). *Building the new managerialist state: Consultants and the politics of public sector reform in comparative perspective.* Oxford, UK: Oxford University Press.

Salamon, L. M. (1989). The changing tools of government action: An overview. In L. M. Salamon (Ed.), *Beyond privatization: The tools of government action* (chapter 1). Washington, DC: Urban Institute.

Salamon, L. M. (1996). The crisis of the nonprofit sector and the challenge of renewal. *National Civic Review, 85*(4), 3–16.

Salamon, L. M. (2001). The new governance and the tools of public action: An introduction. *Fordham Urban Law Journal, 28*(5), 1611–1674.

Samuelson, R. J. (2013, December 15). The luxury of muddling through. *Washington Post.* Retrieved December 18, 2013, from www.washingtonpost.com/opinions/robert-samuelson-the-luxury-of-muddling-through/2013/12/15/9de8f1e8-641e-11e3-a373-0f9f2d1c2b61_story.html.

Sandel, M. J. (1984). The procedural republic and the unencumbered self. *Political Theory, 12*(1), 81–96.

Sandel, M. J. (1998). *Democracy's discontent: America in search of a public philosophy.* Cambridge, MA: Belknap Press.

Sanders, E. (1999). *Roots of reform: Farmers, workers, and the American state, 1877–1917.* Chicago, IL: University of Chicago Press.

Sanford, T. (1967). *Storm over the states.* New York, NY: McGraw-Hill.

Sartori, G. (1970). Concept misinformation in comparative politics. *American Political Science Review, 64*(4), 1033–1053.

Schachter, H. L. (2010). A gendered legacy: The progressive reform era revisited. In R. F. Durant (Ed.), *The Oxford handbook of American bureaucracy* (pp. 77–100). Oxford, UK: Oxford University Press.

Schattschneider, E. E. (1960). *The semisovereign people.* Hinsdale, IL: Dryden Press.

Schein, E. H. (2015). Organizational psychology then and now: Some observations. *Annual Review of Organizational Psychology and Organizational Behavior, 2,* 1–19.

Schlabs, E. (2017, October 3). Machine learning's implications for fairness and justice. *The Regulatory Review.* Retrieved from www.theregreview.org/2017/10/03/schlabs-machine-learning-fairness-justice/.

Schlesinger, A. M., Jr. (1945). *The age of Jackson.* Boston, MA: Little, Brown, & Company.

Schlesinger, A. M., Jr. (1949). The causes of the civil war: A note on historical sentimentalism. *Partisan Review, xvi,* 968–981.

Schlesinger, A. M., Sr. (1949). *Paths to the present.* New York, NY: Macmillan Company.

Schlozman, K. L., & Tierney, J. T. (1986). *Organized interests and American democracy.* New York, NY: Random House.

Schlozman, K. L., Verba, S., & Brady, H. E. (2012). *The unheavenly chorus: Unequal political voice and the broken promise of American democracy.* Princeton, NJ: Princeton University Press.

Schneider, A. L., & Ingram, H. M. (Eds.). (2005). *Deserving and entitled: Social constructions and public policy.* Albany, NY: State University of New York Press.

Schocket, A. M. (2007). *Founding corporate power in early national Philadelphia.* DeKalb, IL: Northern Illinois Press.

Schoenbrod, D. (1983, April). Goals statutes or rules statutes: The case of the clean air act. *UCLA Law Review, 30,* 740–828.

Schuck, P. H. (2014). *Why government fails so often and how it can do better*. Princeton, NJ: Princeton University Press.

Schuck, P. H., & Wilson, J. Q. (Eds.). (2008). *Understanding America: The anatomy of an exceptional nation*. New York, NY: Public Affairs.

Schumpeter, J. A. (1942). *Capitalism, socialism, and democracy*. New York, NY: Harper & Brothers.

Schurz, C. (1871, January 27). Speech of Hon. Carl Schurz, of Missouri, in the United States Senate. *U.S. Senate Journal*, 41st Cong., 3rd sess.

Sclar, E. D. (2000). *You don't always get what you pay for: The economics of privatization*. Ithaca, NY: Cornell University Press.

Scott, W. G. (1992). *Chester I. Barnard and the guardians of the managerial state*. Lawrence, KS: University Press of Kansas.

Scruton, R. (2007). *Culture counts: Faith and feeling in a world besieged*. New York, NY: Encounter Books.

Seidman, H. (1998). *Politics, position, and power: The dynamics of federal organization* (5th ed.). New York, NY: Oxford University Press.

Shafer, B. E. (Ed.). (1991). *Is America different? A new look at American exceptionalism*. Oxford, UK: Clarendon Press.

Shapiro, R. Y., Kumar, M. J., & Jacobs, L. R. (Eds.). (2000). *Presidential power: Forging the presidency for the twenty-first century*. New York, NY: Columbia University Press.

Sharpf, F. W. (1994). Games real actors could play: Positive and negative coordination in embedded negotiations. *Journal of Theoretical Politics*, *6*(1), 27–53.

Shefter, M. (2002). War, trade, and U.S. party politics. In I. Katznelson & M. Shefter (Eds.), *Shaped by war and trade: International influences on American political development* (pp. 113–133). Princeton, NJ: Princeton University Press.

Sheingate, A. D. (2003). Political entrepreneurship, institutional change, and American political development. *Studies in American Political Development*, *17*(2), 185–203.

Sheingate, A. D. (2007). The terrain of the political entrepreneur. In S. Skowronek & M. Glassman (Eds.), *Formative acts: American politics in the making* (pp. 13–31). Philadelphia, PA: University of Pennsylvania Press.

Sheingate, A. (2016). *Building a business of politics: The rise of political consulting and the transformation of American democracy*. New York, NY: Oxford University Press.

Sherman, J. (1896). *Recollections of 40 years in the house, senate, and cabinet: An autobiography*. Chicago, IL: The Werner Company. Retrieved from https://archive.org/stream/johnshermansreco00sher#page/n11/mode/2up.

Shlaes, A. (2007). *The forgotten man: A new history of the great depression*. New York, NY: HarperCollins.

Simon, H. A. (1997). *Administrative behavior: A study of decision-making processes in administrative organizations* (4th ed.). New York, NY: Free Press. Org. pub. 1945.

Sinclair, B. (2006). *Party wars: Polarization and the politics of national policy making*. Norman, OK: University of Oklahoma Press.

Sinclair, B. (2016). *Unorthodox lawmaking: New legislative processes in the U.S. congress* (5th ed.). Washington, DC: Congressional Quarterly Press, 2016.

Sitkoff, H. (1978). *A new deal for blacks: The emergence of civil rights as a national issue: The depression decade*. Oxford, UK: Oxford University Press.

Sklar, M. (1988). *The corporate reconstruction of American capitalism, 1890–1916*. Cambridge, UK: Cambridge University Press.

Skocpol, T. (1992). *Protecting soldiers and mothers: The political origins of social policy in the United States*. Cambridge, MA: Harvard University Press.

Skocpol, T. (2003). *Diminished democracy: From membership to management in American civic life*. Norman, OK: University of Oklahoma Press.

Skocpol, T., Ganz, M., & Munson, Z. (2000). A nation of organizers: The institutional origins of civic volunteerism. *American Political Science Review, 94*(3), 536–537.

Skocpol, T., Munson, Z., Karch, A., & Camp, B. (2002). Patriotic partnerships: Why great wars nourished American civic voluntarism. In I. Katznelson & M. Shefter (Eds.), *Shaped by war and trade: International influences on American political development* (pp. 134–180). Princeton, NJ: Princeton University Press.

Skowronek, S. (1982). *Building a new American state: The expansion of national administrative capacities, 1877–1920*. Cambridge, UK: Cambridge University Press.

Slobodian, Q. (2018). *Globalists: The end of empire and the birth of neoliberalism*. Cambridge, MA: Harvard University Press.

Smith, A. (1776). *The wealth of nations*. London, UK: William Strayan & Thomas Cadell.

Smith, J. S. (2006). *Building new deal liberalism: The political economy of public works, 1933–1956*. Cambridge, UK: Cambridge University Press.

Smith, M. A. (2000). *American business and political power: Public opinion, elections, and democracy* Chicago, IL: University of Chicago Press.

Smith, R. M. (1993). Beyond Tocqueville, Myrdal, and Hartz: The multiple traditions in America. *American Political Science Review, 87*(3), 549–566.

Smith, S. R. (2012). Social services. In L. M. Salamon (Ed.), *The state of nonprofit America* (2nd ed., pp. 192–228). Washington, DC: Brookings Institution Press.

Smith, S. R., & Lipsky, M. (1993). *Nonprofits for hire: The welfare state in the age of contracting*. Cambridge, MA: Harvard University Press.

Sombart, W. (1930). Capitalism. In *Encyclopaedia of the social sciences* (Vol. 3, pp. 195–208). New York, NY: Macmillan Company.

Soss, J., Hacker, J. S., & Mettler, S. (Eds.). (2007). *Remaking America: Democracy and public policy in an age of inequality*. New York, NY: Russell Sage Foundation.

Soss, J., & Schram, S. F. (2006). Welfare reform as a failed political strategy: Evidence and explanations for the stability of public opinion. *Focus, 24*(3), 17–23.

Sowell, T. (2007). *A conflict of visions: Ideological origins of political struggles* (rev. ed.). New York, NY: Basic Books.

Sparrow, B. H. (1996). *From the outside in: World war II and the American state*. Princeton, NJ: Princeton University Press.

Stanford Encyclopedia of Philosophy. (2014, June 20). Jane Addams. Retrieved from http://plato.stanford.edu/entries/addams-jane/#StaEpi.

Stazyk, E. C. (2013). Crowding out public service motivation? Comparing theoretical expectations with empirical findings on the influence of performance-related pay. *Review of Public Personnel Administration, 33*(3), 252–274.

Stazyk, E. C., & Frederickson, H. G. (Eds.). (2018). *Handbook of American public administration*. Northampton, MA: Edward Elgar Publishing.

Steffens, L. (1969). *The shame of the cities*. New York, NY: Hill and Wang. Org. pub. 1904.

Steinmo, S. (2010). *The evolution of modern states: Sweden, Japan, and the United States*. Cambridge, UK: Cambridge University Press.

Stewart, R. B. (1988). Regulation and the crisis of legalization in the United States. In T. Daintith (Ed.), *Law as an instrument of economic policy: Comparative and critical approaches* (pp. 97–133). New York, NY: Walter de Gruyter.

Stillman, R. J., II. (1990). The peculiar "stateless" origins of American public administration and the consequences for government today. *Public Administration Review, 50*(2), 156–167.

Stillman, R. J., II. (1998). *Creating the American state: The moral reformers and the modern administrative world they made.* Tuscaloosa, AL: University of Alabama Press.

Stillman, R. J., II. (2017). *Preface to public administration: Its study, scope, and substance* (3rd ed.). Irvine, CA: Melvin & Leigh.

Stinchcombe, A. (1968). *Constructing social theories.* New York, NY: Harcourt, Brace and World.

Stivers, C. (2000). *Bureau men, settlement women: Constructing public administration in the progressive era.* Lawrence, KS: University of Kansas Press.

Stivers, C. (2019). Forging new tools for new administrative houses: Comments on the symposium. *Journal of Public Affairs Education, 25*(2), 122–124.

Stoker, G., & Evans, M. (Eds.). (2016). *Evidence-based policy making in the social sciences: Methods that matter.* Bristol, GB: Policy Press.

Stone, D. (2011). *The policy paradox: The art of political decision making* (3rd ed.). New York, NY: W. W. Norton & Company.

Storing, H. J. (1981). *What the anti-federalists were for: The political thought of the opponents of the constitution.* Chicago, IL: University of Chicago Press.

Storrs, L. R. Y. (2013). *The second red scare and the unmaking of the new deal left.* Princeton, NJ: Princeton University Press.

Strauss, L. (1953). *Natural right and history.* Chicago, IL: University of Chicago Press.

Suárez, D. F. (2011). Collaboration and professionalization: The contours of public sector funding for nonprofit organizations. *Journal of Public Administration Research and Theory, 21*(2), 307–326.

Suchman, M. C. (1995). Managing legitimacy: Strategic and institutional approaches. *The Academy of Management Review, 20*(3), 571–610.

Suleiman, E. (2003). *Dismantling democratic states.* Princeton, NJ: Princeton University Press.

Svara, J. H. (2001). The myth of the dichotomy: Complementarity of politics and administration in the past and future of public administration. *Public Administration Review, 61*(2), 176–183.

Svara, J. H., & Brunet, J. R. (2005). Social equity is a pillar of public administration. *Journal of Public Administration Education, 11*, 253–258.

Sylla, R., Legler, J. B., & Wallis, J. J. (1987). Banks and state public finance in the new republic: The United States, 1790–1860. *Journal of Economic History, 47*(2), 391–403.

Tarnas, R. (1991). *The passion of the Western mind: Understanding the ideas that have shaped our world view.* New York, NY: Ballantine Books.

Taubman, W. (2017). *Gorbachev: His life and times.* New York, NY: W. W. Norton & Company.

Tead, O. (1933). *Human nature and management: The applications of psychology to executive leadership.* New York, NY: McGraw-Hill.

Teles, S. M. (2008). *The rise of the conservative legal movement: The battle for control of the law.* Princeton, NJ: Princeton University Press.

Thomas, J. C. (1986). *Between citizen and city: Neighborhood organizations and urban politics in Cincinnati.* Lawrence: University Press of Kansas.

Thompson, F. J., & Gusmano, M. K. (2014). The administrative presidency and fractious federalism: The case of Obamacare. *Publius, 44*(3), 426–450.

Thompson, P., & Alvesson, M. (2005). Bureaucracy at work: Misunderstandings and mixed blessings. In P. du Gay (Ed.), *The values of bureaucracy* (pp. 89–114). New York, NY: Oxford University Press.

Thompson, V. A. (1975). *Without sympathy or enthusiasm: The problem of administrative compassion.* Tuscaloosa, AL: University of Alabama Press.

Thrall, A. T., & Friedman, B. H. (2016). *U.S. grand strategy in the 21st century: The case for restraint.* New York, NY: Routledge.

Tichenor, D. J. (2002). *Dividing lines: The politics of immigration control in America.* Princeton, NJ: Princeton University Press.

Tichenor, D. J., & Harris, R. A. (2002–2003). Organized interests and American political development. *Political Science Quarterly, 117*(4), 587–612.

Toobin, J. (2008). *The nine: Inside the secret world of the supreme court.* New York, NY: Random Books.

Toobin, J. (2012). *The oath: The Obama white house and the supreme court.* New York, NY: Anchor Books.

Torfing, J., Sorensen, E., & Roiseland, A. (2016, November 28). Transforming the public sector into an arena for co-creation: Barriers, drivers, benefits, and ways forward. *Administration & Society.* Retrieved from https://doi-org.proxyau.wrlc.org/10.1177%2F0095399716680057.

Tormey, S. (2016). The contemporary crisis of representative democracy. *Papers on Parliament No. 66.* Australia: Parliament of Australia. Retrieved from www.aph.gov.au/About_Parliament/Senate/Powers_practice_n_procedures/pops/Papers_on_Parliament_66/The_Contemporary_Crisis_of_Representative_Democracy.

Trachtenberg, A. (2007). *The incorporation of America: Culture and society in the gilded age.* New York, NY: Hill and Wang.

TreasuryDirect. (2013, May 5). *Historical debt outstanding—annual 1950–1999.* Retrieved from www.treasurydirect.gov/govt/reports/pd/histdebt/histdebt_histo4.htm.

Turner, F. J. (1893). *The significance of the frontier in American history.* Presented at a meeting of the American Historical Association, Chicago, IL, July 12.

Turner, F. J. (1920). *The frontier in American history.* New York, NY: Henry Holt & Company.

van der Wal, Z. (2008). *Value solidity* (Doctoral dissertation), Vrije University, Amsterdam, Netherlands.

van Riper, P. (1958). *History of the United States civil service.* Evanston, IL: Row, Peterson.

Vinik, D. (2017, September 27). America's government is getting old. *Politico.* Retrieved from www.politico.com/agenda/story/2017/09/27/aging-government-workforce-analysis-000525.

Vogel, D. (2003). *Fluctuating fortunes: The political power of business in America.* Washington, DC: Beard Books. Org. pub. 1989.

von Mises, L. (1949). *Human action: A treatise on economics.* New Haven, CT: Yale University Press.

Wagenaar, H., & Cook, D. N. (2003). Understanding policy practices: Action, dialectic and deliberation in policy analysis. In M. A. Hajer & H. Wagenaar (Eds.), *Deliberative policy analysis: Understanding governance in the network society* (pp. 139–171). Cambridge, UK: Cambridge University Press.

Wakelyn, J. L. (2006). *America's founding charters: Primary documents of colonial and revolutionary era governance* (vol. 1). Westport, CT: Greenwood Press.

Waldo, D. (1952). Development of a theory of democratic administration. *American Political Science Review, 46*(1), 81–103.

Waldo, D. (1984). *The administrative state: A study of the political theory of American public administration.* New York, NY: Ronald Press. Org. pub. 1948.

Walker, R. M., & Andrews, R. (2015). Local government management and performance: A review of the evidence. *Journal of Public Administration Research and Theory, 25*(1), 101–133.

Wamsley, G. L., Bacher, R. N., Goodsell, C. T., Kronenberg, P. S., Rohr, J. A., Stivers, C. M., . . . Wolf, J. F. (1990). *Refounding public administration.* Newbury Park, CA: Sage Publications.

Wamsley, G. L., & Wolfe, J. R. (Eds.). (1996). *Refounding democratic public administration: Modern paradoxes, postmodern challenges.* Thousand Oaks, CA: Sage Publications.

Wamsley, G. L., & Zald, M. N. (1973). *The political economy of public organizations: A critique and approach to the study of public administration.* Lexington, MA: D. C. Heath and Company.

Warber, A. (2006). *Executive orders and the modern presidency: Legislating from the oval office.* Boulder, CO: Lynne Rienner Publishers.

Warshaw, S. A. (2004). *The keys to power: Managing the presidency* (2nd ed.). New York, NY: Routledge.

Waterman, R. (1989). *Presidential influence in the administrative state.* Knoxville, TN: University of Tennessee Press.

Waterman, R. W. (2009). Assessing the unilateral presidency. In G. C. Edwards & W. G. Powell (Eds.), *The Oxford handbook of the American presidency* (pp. 477–498). Oxford, UK: Oxford University Press.

Waterman, R. W., & Meier, K. J. (1998). Principal—agent models: An expansion? *Journal of Public Administration Research and Theory, 8*(2), 173–202.

Watkins, T. H. (1993). *The great depression: America in the 1930s.* Boston, MA: Back Bay Books.

Watkins, T. H. (1999). *The hungry years: A narrative history of the great depression in America.* New York, NY: Henry Holt.

Wayland, F. (1837). *The elements of political economy.* New York, NY: Leavitt, Lord.

Weber, E. P. (2009). Explaining institutional change in tough cases of collaboration: "Ideas" in the blackfoot watershed. *Public Administration Review, 69*(2), 314–327.

Weiner, G. (2012). *Madison's metronome: The Constitution, majority rule, and the tempo of American politics.* Lawrence, KS: University Press of Kansas.

Weinstein, J. (1968). *The corporate ideal in the liberal state, 1900–1918.* Boston, MA: Beacon Press.

Weisbrod, B. A. (1997). The future of the nonprofit sector: Its entwining with private enterprise and government. *Journal of Policy Analysis and Management, 16*(4), 541–555.

Weisbrod, B. A. (Ed.). (1998). *To profit or not to profit: The commercial transformation of the nonprofit sector*. Cambridge, UK: Cambridge University Press.

Weiss, C. H., & Bucuvalas, M. J. (1980). *Social science research and decision-making*. New York, NY: Columbia University Press.

West, W. F. (2006). Presidential leadership and coordination: Examining the theory of a unified executive. *Presidential Studies Quarterly, 36*, 433–456.

West, W. F. (2011). *Program budgeting and the performance movement: The elusive quest for efficiency in government*. Washington, DC: Georgetown University Press.

West, W. F. (2015). The administrative presidency as reactive oversight: Implications for administrative positive and normative theory. *Public Administration Review, 75*, 523–533.

White, E. (2017, September 22). Continuing resolutions have become the norm. *Federal News Radio*. Retrieved from https://federalnewsradio.com/federal-newscast/2017/09/continuing-resolutions-have-become-the-norm/.

White, L. D. (1948). *The Federalists: A study in administrative history, 1789–1801*. New York, NY: Macmillan Company.

White, L. D. (1951). *The Jeffersonians: A study in administrative history, 1801–1829*. New York, NY: Macmillan Company.

White, L. D. (1954). *The Jacksonians: A study in administrative history, 1829–1861*. New York, NY: Free Press.

White, L. D. (1958). *The republican era: A study of administrative history, 1869–1901*. New York, NY: Free Press.

Wiebe, R. H. (1967). *The search for order: 1877–1920*. New York, NY: Hill and Wang. Org. pub. 1917.

Wildavsky, A. (2007). *Speaking truth to power: The art and craft of policy analysis*. New York, NY: Transaction Press. Org. pub. 1979.

Wilentz, S. (1984). *Chants democratic: New York city and the rise of the American working class, 1788–1850*. New York, NY: Oxford University Press.

Wilentz, S. (2005). *The rise of American democracy: Jefferson to Lincoln*. New York, NY: W. W. Norton & Company.

Wilkins, V. M., & Keiser, L. R. (2006). Linking passive and active representation by gender: The case of child support agencies. *Journal of Public Administration Research and Theory, 16*(1), 87–102.

Will, G. F. (2019). *The conservative sensibility*. New York, NY: Hatchette Books.

Wills, G. (1999). *A necessary evil: A history of American distrust of government*. New York, NY: Simon & Schuster.

Wilson, J. H. (1975). *Herbert Hoover: Forgotten progressive*. New York, NY: HarperCollins.

Wilson, J. Q. (1989). *Bureaucracy: What government agencies do and why they do it*. New York, NY: Basic Books.

Wilson, J. Q., & Rachal, P. (1977, Winter). Can the government regulate itself? *The Public Interest, 46*, 3–14.

Wilson, W. (1887). The study of administration. *Political Science Quarterly, 2*(2), 197–222.

Wilson, W. (1908). *Constitutional government in the United States*. New York, NY: Columbia University Press.

Wilson, W. (1913). *The new freedom: A call for the emancipation of the generous energies of a people*. New York, NY: Doubleday, Page & Company.

Wilson, W. (1981). *Congressional government: A study in American politics*. Piscataway, NJ: Transaction Publishers. Org. pub. 1885.

Wise, C. R., & Christensen, R. K. (2005). A full and fair capacity: Federal courts managing state programs. *Administration & Society, 37*(5), 576–610.

Wolin, S. (2004). *Politics and vision: Continuity and innovation in Western political thought* (exp. ed.). Princeton, NJ: Princeton University Press.

Wood, B. D. (2010). Agency theory and the bureaucracy. In R. F. Durant (Ed.), *The Oxford handbook of American bureaucracy* (pp. 181–206). Oxford, UK: Oxford University Press.

Wood, B. D., & Waterman, R. W. (1994). *Bureaucratic dynamics: The role of bureaucracy in a democracy.* New York, NY: Routledge.

Wood, G. S. (2002). *The American revolution: A history.* New York, NY: Random House.

Wood, G. S. (2006). *Revolutionary characters: What made the founders different.* New York, NY: Penguin Press.

Wood, G. S. (2009a). *The purpose of the past: Reflections on the uses of history.* New York, NY: Penguin Press.

Wood, G. S. (2009b). *Empire of liberty: A history of the early republic, 1789–1815.* New York, NY: Oxford University Press.

Wood, J. (2019, September 12). Overruling Chevron could make congress great again. *The Regulatory Review.* Retrieved from www.theregreview.org/2018/09/12/wood-overruling-chevron-make-congress-great-again/.

Woodard, C. (2011). *American nations: A History of the eleven rival regional cultures of North America.* New York, NY: Penguin Books.

Wright, D. S. (1990). Federalism, intergovernmental relations, and intergovernmental management: Historical reflections and conceptual comparisons. *Public Administration Review, 50*(2), 168–178.

Wright, G. (2003). The role of nationhood in the economic development of the USA. In A. Teichova & H. Matis (Eds.), *Nation, state, and the economy in history* (pp. 387–403). Cambridge, UK: Cambridge University Press.

Yackee, J. W., & Yackee, S. W. (2006). A bias towards business? Assessing interest group influence on the US bureaucracy. *Journal of Politics, 68*(1), 128–139.

Yanow, D. (2003). Accessing local knowledge. In M. A. Hajer & H. Wagenaar (Eds.), *Deliberative policy analysis: Understanding governance in the network society* (pp. 228–246). Cambridge, UK: Cambridge University Press.

Yanow, D., & Schwartz-Shea, P. (Eds.). (2014). *Interpretation and method: Empirical research methods and the interpretive turn.* Armonk, NY: M. E. Sharpe.

Zakaria, F. (2019, July/August). The self-destruction of American power. *Foreign Affairs.* Retrieved from https://www.foreignaffairs.com/articles/2019-06-11/self-destruction-american-power.

Zegart, A. B. (1999). *Flawed by design: The evolution of the CIA, JCS, and the NSC.* Stanford, CA: Stanford University Press.

Zelizer, J. E. (2012). *Governing America: The revival of political history.* Princeton, NJ: Princeton University Press.

Ziegler, R. H. (1981). Herbert Hoover, the wage earner, and the "new economic system." In E. W. Hawley (Ed.), *Herbert Hoover as secretary of commerce: Studies in new era thought and practice* (pp. 80–114). Iowa City, IA: University of Iowa Press.

Ziparo, J. (2017). *This grand experiment: When women entered the federal workforce in civil-war era Washington, D.C.* Chapel Hill, NC: University of North Carolina Press.

Index

For Product Safety Concerns and Information please contact our EU
representative GPSR@taylorandfrancis.com
Taylor & Francis Verlag GmbH, Kaufingerstraße 24, 80331 München, Germany

www.ingramcontent.com/pod-product-compliance
Lightning Source LLC
Chambersburg PA
CBHW070546270326
41926CB00013B/2214